WILD WEST SHOWS

AND THE IMAGES OF AMERICAN INDIANS, 1883-1933

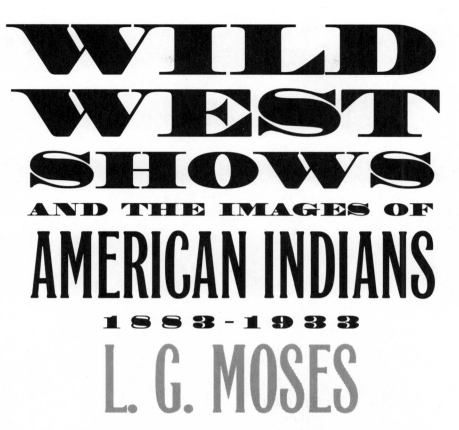

WILD WEST SHOWS

AND THE IMAGES OF

AMERICAN INDIANS

1883 - 1933

L. G. MOSES

University of New Mexico Press   Albuquerque

First paperbound printing, 1999

Moses, L. G. (Lester George), 1948–

Wild West shows and the images of

American Indians, 1883–1933 /

L. G. Moses. — 1st ed.

p.   cm.

Includes bibliographical references

and index.

ISBN 0-8263-1685-9

ISBN 0-8263-2089-9 (paper)

1. Wild west shows—History.

2. Dakota Indians—Public opinion.

3. Public opinion—United States.

4. Stereotypes (Psychology)—

United States. 5. Ethnic

attitudes—United States.

6. Indians, Treatment of—United

States. 7. United States—Ethnic

relations.

I. Title.

GV1833.M67   1996

791.8'4—dc20   95-32450

CIP

To Richard N. Ellis and Ferenc M. Szasz

Under the look of fatigue,

the attack of migraine and the sigh

There is always another story,

there is more than meets the eye.

—W. H. Auden

Contents

Illustrations, *ix*

Preface, *xi*

Acknowledgments, *xv*

Introduction, *1*

1 Before the Wild West Show, *10*

2 The First Years of Cody's Wild West, *21*

3 The Wild West of London, *42*

4 Reformers and the Image of the Show Indian, *60*

5 Indians Abroad, 1889–1890, *80*

6 Ghost Dancers of London, 1891–1892, *106*

7 Indians on the Midway:

      Fairs and Expositions, 1893–1903, *129*

8 Show-Indian Students in St. Louis, 1904, *150*

9 The Wild West Show in Its Prime, 1900–1917, *168*

10 Federal Policies and Alternate Images, 1900–1917, *195*

11 Filming the Wild West, 1896–1913, *223*

12 Decline of the Wild West Shows, 1917–1933, *252*

      Epilogue, *274*

      Abbreviations, *281*

      Notes, *283*

      Bibliography, *341*

      Index, *351*

Illustrations

1   Buffalo Bill leading the Show Indian troupe, *2*
2   First year of Cody's Wild West, *24*
3   "Buffalo Bill Indians", *26*
4   Sitting Bull and Buffalo Bill, *29*
5   Buffalo Bill's Wild West in Brooklyn, *35*
6   Sergeant G. H. Bates, *36*
7   "The Noble Red Shirt", *45*
8   Red Shirt and tipi, *47*
9   John Y. Nelson and his family, *51*
10 Nate Salsbury, Buffalo Bill, John Burke, and others, *52*
11 Rose Nelson, or *Wakachasha*, *56*
12 "Immigrant Act", *65*
13 Samuel Lone Bear, *72*
14 Buffalo Bill at his tent at an encampment, *83*
15 Buffalo Bill and cast members, *86*
16 Show Indians at Naples, *90*
17 Show Indians at the Doge's Palace, *92*
18 Show Indians and Buffalo Bill at St. Mark's Cathedral, *93*
19 Eagle Horn, *96*
20 No Neck, *99*
21 Black Heart, *102*
22 Bill Cody's Show Indians, 1890, *108*
23 Buffalo Bill, American Horse, and Indian police, *110*
24 Nineteen Sioux prisoners at Fort Sheridan, *112*
25 Kicking Bear, one of the leaders of the Ghost Dance, *113*
26 Mary Clementine Collins, *114*
27 Anne Oakley in "Indian costume", *120*
28 Kicking Bear and Short Bull, *122*
29 Has No Horses, *123*
30 Show Indians at the Columbian Exposition, 1893, *136*
31 Residential encampment near the arena, *138*
32 Bureau of American Ethnology exhibit, 1897, *143*
33 Cody's Wild West in Brooklyn, 1907, *148*
34 Samuel M. McCowan, *153*
35 Model Indian school at the Louisiana Purchase Exposition, *155*
36 Buffalo Bill's Wild West in Rome, 1906, *170*

37 Luther Standing Bear, *172*

38 Zack, Joe, and George Miller, *177*

39 101 Ranch Roundup, *178*

40 Walter Battice with the 101 Ranch Real Wild West, *181*

41 Walter Battice at the Hampton Institute, *184*

42 Bill Arthur and a group of Oglala Show Indians, *187*

43 Buffalo Bill and some Show Indians on Ocean Beach, 1907, *191*

44 Buffalo Bill at Pawnee Bill Lillie's ranch, *192*

45 Agricultural exhibit from the Fort Sill School, *211*

46 Red Shirt in later life, *214*

47 Zuni Indians at the Panama-California Exposition, *216*

48 A colonial pageant at Seger School, *217*

49 The final scene at the Seger School pageant, *219*

50 The colonial procession at the Seger School, *220*

51 The Virginia Reel at part of the pageant, *221*

52 Filming *The Indian Wars*, *230*

53 Agent John Brennan and Buffalo Bill at Pine Ridge, *233*

54 From the filming of *The Indian Wars*, *234*

55 Photograph of the Wounded Knee Battle scene, *235*

56 Close up of a scene from the Wounded Knee Battle, *236*

57 *Wovoka*, "The Indian Messiah," from *The Indian Wars*, *238*

58 Close up of a scene about the Indian Messiah, *239*

59 Chauncey Yellow Robe, *240*

60 *Wovoka*, or Jack Wilson, "The Indian Messiah", *247*

61 Indians from the film *The Covered Wagon* in London, *249*

62 *The Covered Wagon* party making camp in New York City, *250*

63 Indians dancing at Pine Ridge, *254*

64 Composite of Show Indians, *262*

65 Buffalo hunt by Sioux Indians, 101 Ranch Real Wild West, *266*

66 Oglala Show Indians dancing at the General Electric Plant, *267*

67 Navajo village at the Pacific Southwest Exposition, 1928, *268*

68 Goes in Lodge shaking hands at the International Boy Scout Convention in London, *273*

69 Charlie Bell and family at the International Boy Scout Convention in London, *276*

70 Buffalo Bill at Ocean Beach, San Francisco, *278*

PREFACE

When I returned to college in 1971 (after a number of misadventures during the previous decade), I encountered for the first time George Hyde's writing on the Sioux. One should attribute my discovery to serendipity rather than perspicacity. Undergraduate history majors at Sonoma State College during those notoriously permissive years had to complete two research seminars for the baccalaureate. In my first seminar that fall, I decided to examine the Ghost Dance religion as a challenge to late nineteenth-century federal Indian policy. That seminar paper set me on a path that eventually led to a master's degree, a doctorate, one book, a number of articles, and the sneaking suspicion that I haven't had an original thought since those "scuffling days" almost a quarter century ago. It also inspired the present work.

Before reading James Mooney, David Humphreys Miller, or Robert Utley, I started with George Hyde. *A Sioux Chronicle* (1956) piqued my curiosity. Hyde wrote that at the end of the "Sioux Rebellion" early in 1891, Short Bull, the Sicangu (Brule) ghost dance leader, his lieutenant, Mash the Kettle, and a few compatriots were the only ghost dancers ever punished by the government. General Nelson A. Miles, commander of the military campaign against the Lakota, sent them to Europe with Buffalo Bill! It seemed so implausible. Ghost dancers sent to Europe with Buffalo Bill? And were it true, how was it punishment? An attempt to answer that question, led me to many others about the American Indian participants in the Wild West shows, and eventually to write this book.

Whether legend or fact, much more is known about Buffalo Bill Cody and the Wild West shows he spawned, than about the Indian participants. Without them there would have been no Wild West. Although their role in creating the shows and the legends is often acknowledged, the Indians, largely nameless except for Sitting Bull, are nevertheless passed over by historians as marginalized human beings. According to a prevailing view, they lived on reservations with their primitive economies and on the borderlands of white society. Some Indians escaped them by joining shows. They became *extras*, to adopt a term from motion pictures that eventually replaced the Wild West shows as engines of popular culture. They acted out roles, again and again, of a defeated though colorful people who surrendered a continent to a hardier race. They created stereotypes that persist to this day. There is, however, much more to the story than

Wild West show Indians in full costume marking the end of the trail. It is the purpose of this book to tell the story, frequently using the words of the participants, of American Indians in the shows.

Although the book proceeds chronologically, the final four chapters are organized topically with occasionally overlapping time periods. The introduction examines certain legends of the American experience, chief among them the idea of savagery and civilization, and of the Indian as either noble or ignoble savage. The imagery created by Wild West shows is also examined. Historians have generally been critical of that imagery, in many instances repeating the criticisms of late nineteenth-century Indian-policy reformers. Chapter 1 briefly surveys a history of exhibitions, but devotes considerable attention to George Catlin. His career as artist and showman prefigures the Wild West show. Chapter 2 describes the origins of Buffalo Bill Cody's Wild West, his early employment of Pawnees, and, with the employment of Sitting Bull in the summer of 1885, the shift of Indian employment to the Sioux.

From the very first, Indian participation in Wild West shows was criticized by members of the Indian service and Indian policy reformers. The controversy between the shows on one side, and the Indian service and their reformer allies on the other, marked a struggle over whose image of Indians would prevail in the public mind. In addition to telling simply the story of Indian participants in the Wild West show, that battle of imagery is the central theme of the book.

Chapter 3 tells about Cody's first trip with the Wild West show to England in 1887. English newspapers reported the lives of American Indians with considerably more detail and in generally positive terms when compared to press coverage in the United States. Cody's first trans-Atlantic tour also marks the beginning of a more optimistic portrayal of Indians. Chapter 4, an interlude, then examines the attitudes of Indian policy reformers to the shows, and also discusses federal policies as they developed in the 1880s, culminating with the Dawes Act. Chapter 5 picks up the story again in 1889 with Cody's extended tour of Europe and the controversy back in the United States over his supposed mistreatment of his Indian employees. Chapter 6, continuing a discussion of Indian policy, explores the consequences of the Ghost Dance of 1890 on the Wild West shows, and the uproar in reformers' circles on Buffalo Bill's employment of the imprisoned ghost dancers from Fort Sheridan.

Chapters 7 and 8 analyze the competition of images that played out at the world's fairs between the government's version of Show Indians and the Wild West shows'. Chapter 9, on the heyday of the Wild West shows, introduces the Miller Brothers 101 Ranch Real Wild West to the discussion. Their organization is compared to Buffalo Bill's. The chapter ends with Cody's death early in 1917.

Chapter 10, like chapters 7 and 8, returns to a discussion of imagery. It goes back to the beginning of the twentieth century to assess changes in Indian policy and the attitudes of Indian commissioners about the shows down to World War I. It also describes the growth of Indian fairs and their promotion by the Indian service as an antidote to the Indian imagery created in Wild West shows.

Chapter 11 focusses on the development of western films. It also examines Indian themes depicted in the films of D. W. Griffith and Thomas Ince, and the attempt by Buffalo Bill in 1913 to recoup his fortune by filming his exploits once so rewardingly celebrated in the Wild West show arena. Chapter 12 chronicles the decline of the Wild West shows at the very time that Indian policy grew less hostile to Show Indian employment. Finally, a brief epilogue examines the collapse of the last traveling Wild West show, and the legacy of Show Indian employment.

I use the term *Show Indians* throughout the text. It first appeared in the correspondence of the Indian service during the 1890s. In this work it refers to those American Indians who found employment in the various Wild West shows. I also employ it within a larger setting of American Indian performance. It implies no condescension, but rather recognizes a professional status.

My use of the words *civilized* and *civilization* should be understood within the historical context, especially, of late nineteenth-century Indian-policy reform. Those words and the ideas they expressed burdened the language well into the twentieth century. In the current paleo-conservative climate, they still retain a certain cachet. In no way should it suggest my acceptance or endorsement of an arbitrary definition of culture, which, as reasonable people know, should never be defined in the singular. Surrounding the words with quotation marks, however, can be tedious and, indeed, condescending to the reader.

Sioux appears regularly and prominently in the records of Indian participation in Wild West shows. It was applied most often in reference to the *Titonwan,* or Teton Lakota, whose seven members include the Oglala, Minneconjou, Oohenumpa (Two Kettles), Hunkpapa, Sicangu (Brules), Sihasapa (Black Feet), and Itazipco (Sans Arcs) tribes. I also use *Sioux* in its popular context. The largest group of Show Indians were, nevertheless, Oglalas.

As any number of authors have done, I also acknowledge the misnomer *Indian*. Nevertheless, most Indians with whom it has been my privilege to work and learn, prefer the term *Indian* to the more cumbersome *Native American*. Indeed one of the things that Show Indians helped to create was a genuine "Indian" identity that went well beyond ethnic or national affiliation.

Although a number of oral-history sources have been consulted, and research has been conducted among the families of Show Indian veterans, knowledge gleaned from these has mostly provided background information and contributed to an appreciation for—if not always understanding of—cultural context. Such understanding comes only through immersion in a culture, often over a lifetime. Given the holes in the historical record regarding Show Indians, it is difficult to present much in their own words or from their perspective. I have tried nevertheless to use the exact words of the Show Indians wherever possible, knowing that sometimes, with translation, errors or muddled diction have marred the record. I have preferred direct quotation—of words preserved in some instances at the moment they were spoken—taken from correspondence, transcripts of hearings, newspaper accounts, and manuscript materials from a variety of repositories.

Acknowledgments

When an author composes the acknowledgments, it is usually a joyful occasion. It not only marks the completion of a project, but also provides an opportunity to repay, if only with a printed name, the debt one owes or the gratitude one feels for colleagues and friends whose generosity favored a work. Although both emotions are present, I feel also a certain wistfulness about the passage of time. It has been twenty years since I first thought about the possibility of doing the book; eleven years since a sabbatical from Northern Arizona University allowed me the time and resources to begin the research. In the intervening years, people at various institutions have changed jobs just as I have. A few people—friends, colleagues, and family members—will never hear or read my words of gratitude. Thus the passage of time, and the absence of certain friends, "wraps me in a most humorous sadness."

Librarians, curators, and archivists at the following institutions (in the order that they were visited, 1984–86) are owed a special debt of gratitude: University of Arizona Library, Special Collections, Tucson; the Southwest Collection, Texas Tech University, Lubbock; The Panhandle Plains Historical Museum, Canyon, Texas; the Indian Archives Division, Oklahoma Historical Society, Oklahoma City; the Cowboy Hall of Fame; the University of Oklahoma Library, Western History Collections, Norman; The Gilcrease Institute of American History and Art, Tulsa; the Federal Archives and Records Center, Kansas City, Missouri; the Iowa State Historical Department, Division of Historical Museum and Archives, Des Moines; the Nebraska State Historical Society, Lincoln; the Kansas State Historical Society, Topeka; Fort Hays State University Library, Hays, Kansas; South Dakota State Historical Society, Pierre; the incomparable Buffalo Bill Historical Center, Cody, Wyoming; Fremont County Pioneers Museum, Lander, Wyoming; the American Heritage Center, University of Wyoming, Laramie; Wyoming State Archives, Museums, and Historical Department, Cheyenne; the State Historical Society of Colorado, Denver; Federal Archives and Records Center, Denver; the Denver Public Library, Western History Department; Buffalo Bill's Memorial Museum, Golden, Colorado; University of New Mexico, Special Collections Library, Albuquerque; the Center for Western Studies, Augustana College, Sioux Falls, South Dakota; Minnesota Historical Society, Minneapolis; the Circus World Museum, Baraboo, Wisconsin; Chicago Historical Society; the

Field Museum of Natural History, Chicago; the New York State Archives and Records Service, Albany; the Museum of the American Indian, New York; National Archives and Records Service, Washington, D.C.; the Library of Congress, Manuscripts Division, Washington, D.C.; the Department of the Interior Library, Washington, D.C.; and Oklahoma State University Library, Special Collections, Stillwater.

Henry O. Hooper, graduate dean and associate vice-president for academic affairs at Northern Arizona University, Flagstaff, secured generous grants during two summers to carry out research. At Oklahoma State University (OSU), Dean Smith Holt awarded an incentive grant so that I could spend a summer free from teaching. Roger Biles, former chair of the history department at OSU, whose scholarship inspired his colleagues, released me from teaching duties one semester to finish the manuscript. He also read portions of the manuscript and provided valuable suggestions for revision. Special thanks are also due Peter Iverson who took precious time away from his own work to read the entire manuscript and to offer his usual insightful comments.

I am indebted to colleagues around the country who offered advice and encouragement, corrected some of my mistakes, and otherwise improved the manuscript in significant ways. Particular recognition is accorded Ron McCoy, Paul Fees, Margaret Connell Szasz, Richard White, Nancy Tystad Koupal, Rich Clow, Michael Lawson, Lillian Turner, Leonard Bruguier, Jim Ronda, and Bob Kvasnicka. Ray and Sharon Wilson always welcomed me and, over the life of this venture, provided countless acts of friendship. Ray on more than one occasion gathered a group of students and colleagues at Fort Hays State University to listen to and comment upon my research.

Edd and Leslie Cochran of Cushing, Oklahoma, helped to ease the transition of an erstwhile northern Californian making the reverse migration to Green Country. Edd's family and business interests took him to New Zealand in the fall of 1994. A postcard he sent, of Buffalo Bill and Sitting Bull which he purchased in the Out West Gallery, Nelson, New Zealand, reminded me at a critical time of how widespread the imagery of Show Indians had become. Leslie's friendship, and gentle prodding, during the last few months of writing helped in ways that can never be recompensed by a simple thank you.

My students showed great patience, even after passing their comprehensive examinations when it did them no earthly good. They allowed me, except for posted hours, to hide largely undisturbed in my office. They never complained—at least not so that I would find out—when I mislaid some of their work on what once could have been described accurately as a desk. Recognition for forbearance is due Kelly Robison, Cliff Coppersmith, Malcolm Brown, Pam Koenig, Bill Fournet, Greg Maphet, David Scott, Chris Lehman, and Trina Medley.

I am grateful to the editors of *South Dakota History* and the University of Oklahoma Press for allowing me to use some of my previously published material, two articles and a chapter in an anthology, throughout the present work. At UNM Press, David V. Holtby provided encouragement and wise counsel over the years. I have been fortunate indeed to work with such a talented editor.

I also owe my family special thanks. Ian and Bronwyn, who never tire of seeing their names in print, introduced Patrick and Julie, who joined the family since the last book was published, to my most treasured excuses. Although I've proved to be a slow learner, the children have nevertheless taught me that matters other than "the manuscript" take precedence at home. Finally, to Margaret, who approaches life with such joy and a seemingly endless supply of wonder, I offer my love and gratitude. She's made moving to Oklahoma a grand adventure.

INTRODUCTION

In the late afternoon of May 17, 1883, William Frederick Cody, better known as Buffalo Bill, led on horseback a group of Pawnees and locally recruited cowboys into the arena at the Omaha fairgrounds to receive the applause of the crowd. Although "The Wild West, Rocky Mountain and Prairie Exhibition" had been awkwardly staged and poorly performed, the crowd nonetheless enjoyed it. Reporters surveying the spectators found that many described it as a circus; but it was much more than that. As a poster proclaimed, "No Tinsel, No Gilding, No Humbug! No Side Show or Freaks."[1] Instead, as the Hartford *Courant* reported in Connecticut, later in that first season of the exhibition's tour, spectators marveled at the performers' skills of riding, roping, and shooting. They also witnessed the re-creation of events from the recent past that, to their urban tastes, seemed bizarre and menacing. The show began "with a pony bare-back riding race between Indians and went on to a climax with a grand realistic battle scene depicting the capture, torture and death of a scout by savages; the revenge, recapture of the dead body and a victory of the government scouts." The performance ended with a "startling, soul-stirring" attack by Indians on the Deadwood Stagecoach, which was repulsed by Buffalo Bill and his partner, Dr. William Frank Carver, sometime dentist and more recently heralded as "Champion Shot of the World."[2] Indian attacks became set pieces in all Wild West shows. Without them the shows would have remained raucous, but hardly wild.

North American Indians, principally those from the Great Plains of the United States, provided the Wild West shows with their enduring imagery. Real Indians, as the public came to believe, lived in tribes, slept in tipis, wore feather bonnets, rode painted ponies, hunted the buffalo, skirmished with the U.S. Cavalry, and spoke in signs. Eventually motion pictures, and later still television, perpetuated the imagery of Indians created by Wild West shows. Historians of American thought and culture have challenged the legends and the mythmakers; but in their assaults on Indian stereotypes, many have created their own legends about the shows. References to Buffalo Bill, his rivals, and Wild West show Indians have often been made with opprobrium. It is the "wildness" of the Wild West that appears either suspect or offensive.

Images of American Indians have long been subjects of historical inquiry. As generations of historians have demonstrated, when Europeans

1 : Buffalo Bill leading the Show Indian troupe into the arena at the conclusion of the performance of the Wild West, date unknown. (Buffalo Bill Historical Center, Cody, Wyoming)

arrived in the "New World," or another "Old World," during the sixteenth and seventeenth centuries, they were not bereft of ideas about the inhabitants of the Americas. Europeans grouped them all together as Indians, despite the diversity of languages and cultures. The Indians who lived in regions claimed by the English and French seemed to these alien observers to live in a state of nature when compared to the cultures of Mesoamerica. The Europeans referred to them as savages. At first the term indicated the manner of their lives; eventually it symbolized the condition of their souls.[3] To many of the English colonists who arrived in ever greater numbers in the seventeenth century, the Indians were often regarded as children of the devil.[4]

American savages, according to their European observers, could be either noble or ignoble—the two basic, though contradictory, images that persisted primarily in imaginative literature well into the nineteenth century. The noble savage lived a sylvan idyll free from the encumbrances of civilization. He offered European social philosophers a vision of a simpler time, a golden age, when humans lived in harmony with nature. The ignoble savage, on the other hand, had progressed but very little since the Fall; his primitivism suffered in comparison with the presumed civility of the colonists.[5] The noble savage welcomed the European colonists and treated them with generosity and courtesy; the ignoble savage contested the occupation and treated the interlopers with treachery and cruelty. The noble savage appeared handsome in features, dignified in manner, and brave in battle; his ignoble brother in life and demeanor more closely resembled the brute beasts with which he shared the howling wilderness. The threads of these conceptions intertwined in strange patterns, and observers drew on them as suited the occasion. The notions of otherness, dependency, and inferiority of the Indians persisted. Savagism contrasted with civility; natural life in the wilds was opposed to disciplined life in civil society.[6]

In the nineteenth century the dual image recurred and was modified, perhaps, by more pressing concerns. The continent had appeared so vast to Thomas Jefferson's generation at the beginning of the century that it might require three hundred years or more to fill with productive citizens. In the closing years of the century, however, people began to speak about the passing of the frontier and of land as a finite resource. As the century progressed, Indians became less a military threat and more an administrative problem. What was to be done with them?

In the decades before the American Civil War, removal of Indians to a permanent Indian frontier in the West had been, at best, only a temporary solution. It had been assumed by the molders of national policy for the Indians that the natives could be gradually raised to "civilization." In the decades after the Civil War, as Euroamerican settlement of the West accelerated, the government abandoned gradualism in favor of comprehensive programs for assimilation. The savage, noble or ignoble, was judged capable of civilization. Those who embraced it would be welcomed into mainstream society. Those who balked would nevertheless be compelled to behave. In a short time, no more than a generation, the old ways would die out. The savage would disappear with the passing of the frontier.[7] To the leaders of the Bureau of Indian Affairs and their allies among largely Christian humanitarian groups, the impediments to Indian advancement—their degraded cultures—would be removed. In a sense the noble savage, with his innate capacity for good, would prosper in the new environment of education, hard work, and Christianity. If the ignoble savage, willful and recalcitrant as ever, could not be broken through force-feeding programs of "civilization," then he and his stiff-necked compatriots would be cared for until they died. Less-compassionate reformers suggested that if they could not adapt to the present, then they should be allowed to fail on their own. "Ignoble savages," or rather those persons who clung tenaciously to their cultures, became the true vanishing Americans to the policymakers.

By the 1880s and the advent of Wild West shows, the last of the "hostile" western tribes, the Apaches of Arizona and New Mexico territories, had been subdued. It appeared to many Americans, and mostly to those who lived in the East, that the West and its native inhabitants, however wild they once may have been, were passing from existence.

The West, the centuries-old term for the Anglo-American frontier, was a place beyond the horizon that could ignite the imaginations of vicarious explorers. Instead of a geographical expression, the West became, in the imaginations of Americans stranded in the cities and towns of the late nineteenth century, a wild region inhabited by even wilder humans, some white and brown, but most red.[8]

By the 1880s most Americans encountered Indians, if at all, as carved statues that adorned shop entrances or as heads in profile impressed on coins that jingled in their pockets or purses. In their thoughts about the West and its original inhabitants, Americans variously imagined an Indian to be a noble savage, a rapacious killer, a reservation idler, the vanishing American, or a war-bonneted equestrian raider of the plains. The last image proved to be the most persuasive and, given Indian portrayals in motion pictures and television series during this century, the most persistent.

Many people who dreamed about the West and longed after excitement and diversion from mundaneness had few places to look except to the printed page—until, that is, the appearance of Wild West shows. Playing upon such signal events as the Fetterman Fight[9] and Custer's battle with the Lakota at the Little Bighorn, as well as countless skirmishes between Indians and other "settlers" on the western frontier, first writers and then Wild West shows created and thereafter maintained the image of Plains Indians—and mainly "Sioux"—as the distinctive American Indian. Among the shows themselves Buffalo Bill's ranked first. His employed the greatest number of Indians and enjoyed the most success.

Between 1883 and 1933, hundreds of North American Indians performed in Wild West shows. They toured the nation and the world. Most returned to their homes and reservations none the worse, and indeed a little richer, for their experiences. Yet it is also true, as the Indian Rights Association (IRA) and other protectionist groups continually asserted during these same years, that a number of Indians died in the adventure. Almost from the beginning of Indian participation in Wild West shows, reformers alleged mistreatment and exploitation. Secretaries of the interior and commissioners of Indian affairs became concerned about the shows' effects on assimilationist programs and on the image of the Indian in the popular mind. Although mistreatment and exploitation never approached the extremes claimed first by Indian-policy reformers and then later by historians, still their view of Wild West shows has prevailed.

Whereas the Indians' physical welfare remained a paramount concern of the humanitarians in the fifty years covered by this study, the major conflict between Wild West shows and Indian-policy reformers became largely a struggle to determine whose image of the Indians would prevail. According to reformers, the shows portrayed Indians as savages from a wild land, who were inimical to civilization. The shows celebrated the martial spirit of the natives, or those skills that made them worthy adversaries. Reformers, on the other hand, wished to foster the ideal of Indians as tamed humans in a tamed land, who were embracing civilization through land allotment, education, and industry. Once rescued from the impediments of savage life, the Indians would progress to a level approximating civilization. Wild West shows themselves, meanwhile, had found paying audiences to support their views of the Indians.

Like the Indian-policy reformers of an earlier generation, historians in the twentieth century generally have been critical of Wild West shows for the stereotypes of Indians they perpetuated. The impression persists, reinforced by a few spectacular examples of abuse, that Wild West shows did more than demean American Indians. Wild West shows, when compared with other forms of mass entertainment, have proved to be easy targets for the historian since they re-created, if only in pantomime, the theme of the "Winning of the West" with its attendant winners and losers. That theme included such ancillary representations as the near-annihilation of the American bison and the military victory over the Indians, both accomplished with plenty of shooting. Buffalo Bill and his many imitators became metaphors as agents of a ravaged wilderness, the exploiters cast as heroes. The Show Indians became symbols of debauched humanity. Finally, the warfare between Indians and non-Indians exposed the hypocrisy of the heroic ideal.[10]

In its worst manifestation, as in the ravings of Arthur Kopit, history itself is contrived in an attempt to deconstruct the fabricated hero. In debunking the buckskin-clad performers and their faithful Indian adversaries of the Wild West shows, or their successors in western movies, a number of historians seem to echo the question once posed by Chauncey Yellow Robe, a Sioux (Brule) reformer and member of the Society of American Indians, in 1913: "What benefit has the Indian derived from these Wild West Shows?" Yellow Robe's answer also has been often repeated: "None but what are degrading, demoralizing, and degenerating." [11] According to certain historians and critics, the shows accomplished nothing more than to reinforce "the classic cliches about Native Americans." [12]

Raymond Stedman, in *Shadows of the Indians*, finds a progression of Indian stereotypes coincident with the westward movement of the Euroamerican frontier. That progression repeated itself in the changes that transformed popular entertainment. He observes:

> As the frontier of Indian tales changed from colonial bowmen on foot or in canoe, to distant West, with its rifle-carrying warriors on horseback; as the theatrical milieu changed from proscenium stage to Wild West show, then flickering screen; as romantic poets abandoned the Noble Savage and the publication milieu changed from gentlemanly publishing house to mass-market industry, so did the American Indian's reputation decline, hastened down the path by brutal wars in the West. [13]

Stedman reads the history of Indian images as decline, holding Indians themselves partially accountable for their own degradation. "Indians whose ancestors did not wear the familiar plains attire," he comments, "should think twice about disregarding traditional dress patterns and selling out to the Wild West crowd." [14] Real Indians, in his view, should eschew the nontraditional, whether it is in dress or in employment. Passing muster under the discerning eye of the ethnologist, however, is hardly the criterion for establishing genuine Indianness.

Others hold Buffalo Bill Cody almost personally responsible for the denigration of Indian images. In Cody's Wild West show career that spanned nearly thirty-four years (1883–1917), two historians have written, "the Indians were firmly established as figures of entertainment like the stage Irishman and the comic Jew." [15] And as entertainers, another critic has written, Indians became "the first clear-cut victims of media bias." [16] Once Hollywood absorbed whatever was usable in the Indian stereotype from the Wild West shows, history, according to Donald Kaufman, dismissed the Indians as a "shaping force in American experience.

White paternalism, in league with the new media of the twentieth century, became the red man's burden."[17] The commercialization of Wild West show imagery by the new medium of motion pictures began, in the words of Ralph and Natasha Friar, "the filmic cultural genocide" of American Indians.[18]

In much the same vein, film historian Jon Tuska expresses the hope that "we may once and for all put to rest that killing 'mythical' Indians is only so much 'newspeak' for enjoying genocide and that the western film as it has been made deserves the strongest censure which can be brought to bear for the lies it has told."[19] In his opinion, it is critically irresponsible to exalt a racial stereotype to the level of mythology. "To put it bluntly," Tuska writes, "what apologists really mean by a 'mythic' dimension in a western film is that part of it which they know to be a lie but which, for whatever reason, they still wish to embrace."[20] What the filmmakers embraced was the Wild West show version of American Indians.

Because Wild West shows created stereotypes about Indians that have persisted for much of the twentieth century, the Show Indians have been treated as artless victims, dismissed as irrelevant, or worse, simply ignored. With only a few conspicuous exceptions, nothing is known about their experiences. They have remained merely caricatures, as wooden and artificial as supposedly were the images they created.[21]

Indian-policy reformers and their allies in the Indian service, so often themselves the targets of historical criticism, have largely prevailed thus far in the attitudes of historians toward Show Indians. Although the tipi-and-war-bonnet image of Indians persists in the public mind, in the polite company of historians and media critics the Show Indians are generally reviled or condescendingly excused for not having had the good sense to realize that they were being exploited. Had the Show Indians remained on their reservations and become ethnologists' informants, telling stories about how life used to be before the white man crossed west to Eden, then perhaps they would have fared better in the record. Instead, their experiences have remained unexamined, and their few recorded words discounted.

Indians who performed in Wild West shows beginning in the 1880s had known life before the reservation experience profoundly altered their cultures. They were members of a transitional generation, one that encountered for the first time the full weight of comprehensive government programs to eradicate native life. That they re-created portions of that life for public consumption caused great distress among Indian Bureau personnel and members of the protectionist associations. Yet try as they might, neither the reformers nor the members of the Indian service could compel the Indians to remain at home and lead more "productive" lives. Incapable on occasion of regulating the Show Indians' lives, the Bureau of Indian Affairs instead opted for regulating their employment—a decision for which it was criticized by the Indian-policy reformers. In 1889, for example, when the Bureau began to supervise more closely the contracting of Indians, the commissioner stipulated that Indians were to be paid "fair and reasonable" wages for their time and service, with salaries ranging from about twenty-five to ninety dollars a month (the higher amount, extended over twelve months, represented about two-thirds of the average salary of an Indian agent).[22] Few Indians who took out allotments and farmed the land or ran livestock could boast of comparable incomes. Commissioners of Indian affairs, however, never abandoned their advocacy of assimilation. Many came to believe that the Wild West show Indians, despite the evidence of self-sufficiency (a hallmark of acculturation), were incapable of civilization.

In the fifty years covered by this study, Indians traveled throughout the world, providing audiences with glimpses into a recent American past. They gave the Wild West show its most distinctive features. Although Indians played supportive roles in the victory tableau of pioneer virtue triumphing over savagery, they themselves had nevertheless survived the contest. They may have been defeated; but they were never destroyed. Instead, they were portrayed as worthy adversaries, for how else could the showmen-entrepreneurs like Cody validate their prowess in battle? As Cody's manager, "Arizona John" Burke, once explained to the commissioner of Indian affairs, it was Buffalo Bill's "honorable ambition to instruct and educate the Eastern public to respect the denizens of the West by giving them a true, untinselled representation of a page of Frontier history that is fast passing away."[23] Burke's statement, though self-serving, contains some truth. Wild West show promoters frequently claimed that they "educated" the public; but Cody insisted that Indians he employed were to be admired and understood. And if they were ever to be pitied, it was because the government had cowed them into submission. Let the people, instead, pity the poor Indian who was left to languish on the reservation with only his memories and a stingy government to sustain him. But Wild West shows never offered an alternative to forced assimilation. They were, after all, only entertainment. Nevertheless, Buffalo Bill saw the employment of Indians in the shows as a method to ease the transition of a proud and capable people to the cultural demands of the majority.

Indians never vanished. Some of them would earn a living between the era of the Dawes Act and the Indian New Deal as Show Indians. Unlike the wooden Indians that adorned shop entrances, or the Indians who appeared as silent, supportive characters in the histories of the period, the Show Indians left behind a few records, including sometimes their own words, that tell of their experiences.

1
BEFORE THE WILD WEST SHOW

*"Nature has nowhere presented
more beautiful and lovely scenes."*

Public exhibitions of American Indians did not originate
with Buffalo Bill. They are as old as the Europeans' first encounters with
the Americas. When Columbus returned to Spain from his first voyage,
he carried with him nine Indians as living proof of his arrival in the Indies.
Later voyagers conveyed natives to Europe, some to act as guides for
future expeditions, and others to serve as hostages. Some Indians were
taken abroad for the sole purpose of enriching their conductors.[1] Enter-

prising men quickly learned that Indians could work "Old World" crowds with as much facility as they could work "New World" mines.

In the three centuries after Columbus, European scientists studied Indians; artists painted their portraits; royalty received them as fellow sovereigns and bestowed gifts on them appropriate to their station; philosophers pondered their origins and behavior; poets, novelists, and essayists wrestled with metaphors that would capture the essence of natural humans and their world; and clerics anguished over the condition of their souls. The strange and exotic creatures of the Americas, among them Indians, commanded interest for generations of Europeans.

In North America as in Europe, unfamiliarity heightened curiosity. As Euroamerican settlements displaced the aboriginal occupants of the continent, and "civilization" after a fashion pushed back the "wilderness," Indians came to reside as much in the imaginations of Americans living east of the Mississippi River as they did in reality in the western regions of the United States. By the middle of the nineteenth century, Indians had become object lessons for the inexorable triumph of civilization over savagery. Their challenge to westward migration had become central to the most persistent legend of the American experience. Their defeat enlarged the victory of civilization; their heroism certified that of their adversaries; and, to some, their tragedy inspired compassion, or at least a willingness to raise those survivors of the contest to a level approximating that of other Americans. Finally, by the 1890s, civilization supposedly had tamed the wilderness and its denizens. Those Indians who were left breathing after the struggle bore witness to a process, centuries old, on the verge of completion—or so many Americans believed.

Among national myths, Richard Slotkin writes, the longest lived and most tenacious has been the Myth of the Frontier. All that is meaningful in American history is embodied in the story of expansion westward into the wilderness.[2] The myth itself, that special symbolic purpose that infuses people, events, and themes with meaning, was the province of writers and intellectuals long before 1893, when Frederick Jackson Turner brought together the various impressions and inchoate principles and provided for later generations of historians a topic of seemingly endless argument.[3] The heart of the thesis is contained in Turner's statement that the "existence of an area of free land, its continuous recession, and the advance of American settlement westward, explain American development."[4] Westward expansion stimulated economic growth and provoked disagreements that led to civil war; but also, especially after the American Civil War, it stimulated nationalism. Most important of all, it sustained the growth and development of political democracy and eased class conflicts.[5] In the process of taming the wilderness, a unique American character emerged, recognizable by its individualism, pragmatism, and egalitarianism.[6]

To some Americans, Turner principally among them, the disappearance of the frontier represented a loss so great that they anticipated the future with dread. With the safety valve of free western land closed, pressures would build up in the cities. In time, there would be an explosion of class conflict that would threaten democratic institutions. For most Americans, however, the passing of the frontier marked only another stage of progress. Even in the uncertain spring and summer of 1893, when the worst industrial depression created economic hardship for countless citizens, Americans saw little reason to abandon hope. If economic problems beset the present, certainly the future offered encouragement. The American character was yet intact. Recent history was not read as decline. The mass of *people*, to renovate Thoreau's phrase, may indeed have led lives of quiet desperation; but was it a despair born of routine, of the sameness in their lives? Or was it, instead, the nostalgia they felt at the disappearance of wild places, a longing after a lost Eden? It was a wistfulness born of the realization that they would never experience the adventure.

By the early 1880s, when Buffalo Bill Cody created the Wild West show, the generation that had fought the Civil War had bid farewell to its youth. The Union had been preserved and slavery eradicated. The middle-aged veterans, Northern and Southern, protected the traditions of noble sacrifice; but when their organizations shared the battlefields in annual convocations, they exchanged handshakes along with their memories. Americans, once again, looked to the West for truly national myths and legends. Younger Americans perceived the heroic in the lives of the pioneers and soldiers who went west in the years after the Civil War and survived. A newer generation of heroes, and a few heroines, acquired their fame on the high plains. Although some won renown as lawmen, gunfighters, pathfinders, scouts, soldiers, or hunters, most—whether civilians or soldiers—achieved their celebrity by fighting Indians. A few of the Indians they fought also attained notoriety. How better to substantiate the victory than to display the vanquished? In melodramas and Wild West shows, the Indians who performed in them became living trophies of the progress of civilization. But it also signaled, as Richard Slotkin writes, the integration of the Indian into national life as "Former Foe—Present Friend."[7]

Indians figured prominently as subjects in the self-conscious quest to create a truly American literature and art in the years between the War of 1812 and the Civil War. Cultural nationalism and romanticism sustained the quest. In their search for American themes, writers and artists declared their independence from Europe. They found in the eastern forests and their inhabitants sources for an American literature and art. Romanticism, in overthrowing the neoclassicism of the Enlightenment, extolled indigenous traditions and folk customs, and glorified the national past. Romantic writers and artists replaced rationalism with sentiment and feeling. The eastern woodlands represented immensity and wildness on such a scale as to dwarf anything European. Part of the wildness of the forest came from its very sublimity, the nature of its inhabitants, and the terrors of warfare between Native Americans and Euroamericans. Ambushes, torture, escape, ritual cannibalism, and reprisal aroused emotions of the most romantic kind. The noble and ignoble savages made ideal subjects for American high culture.[8]

A belief that they were the vanishing Americans doomed to extinction by the march of civilization became the most romantic of all impressions associated with Indians. The image of a doomed and dying race produced in the romantic mind melancholy and pity. Romantics enshrined the ephemeral. The last member of his tribe inspired poems by Philip Freneau in the 1780s and novels by James Fenimore Cooper in the 1820s and 1830s. Cooper's *The Last of the Mohicans* (1826) introduced to a world audience what became a staple of American literature.[9]

The transitory nature of Indian societies also influenced rationalists. Thomas Jefferson, the epitome of the Enlightenment in America, could regret the destruction of Indians. In his *Notes on the State of Virginia,* he remarked that it was "to be lamented . . . that we have suffered so many of the Indian tribes to [be] extinguish[ed]."[10] Jefferson, of course, stressed the practical value of knowledge about American Indians as a means to promote their eventual absorption into mainstream society. Reliable information about Indians would also promote peace on the frontier and the orderly extinguishment of Indian land titles. As president, therefore, Jefferson directed Lewis and Clark to record ethnographic data about the tribes they encountered along their route to the Pacific. "It will be useful to acquire what knowledge you can," he advised the explorers in a memorandum, "of the state of morality, religion and information among them, as it may better enable those who endeavor to civilize and instruct them, to adopt their measures to the existing nations and practices of those on whom they are to operate."[11] Reliable information, gathered scientifically, Jefferson believed, would serve the republic.[12]

George Catlin bridged science and art, rationalism and romanticism. In 1832, the lawyer-turned-artist ascended the Missouri River on a personal mission to paint the portraits of western Indians and to record their ways of life. Catlin regarded the tribes of the prairies and plains as the last Indians untainted by American civilization.[13] He thought the American public woefully ignorant about the natives. His portraits and sketches of daily life, he hoped, would change all that. To substantiate his claims that his paintings were accurate, he sought the endorsements of such luminaries as Secretary of War Joel R. Poinsett, Commissioner of Indian Affairs Carey Allen Harris (1836–38), and former governor and Indian superintendent William Clark.[14] Catlin's devotion to detail and his quest for accuracy did not, however, dampen his romanticism. He, as much as Cooper, helped to popularize the idea of the Indians' nobility before civilization had corrupted them. Catlin observed:

> Nature has nowhere presented more beautiful and lovely scenes, those of the vast prairies of the West and of *man* and *beast* no nobler specimens than those who inhabit them—the *Indian* and the *buffalo*—joint and original tenants of the soil, and fugitives together from the approach of civilized man; they have fled to the great plains of the West, and there under an equal doom, they have taken up their last abode, where their race will expire and their bones will bleach together.[15]

The statement is not so much epitaph as challenge. Destruction of the last Indian and buffalo, Catlin believed, could be avoided. He dedicated his art to their preservation.

Catlin believed that the government should gradually introduce "civilization" and Christianity among the Indians. Until this could be accomplished, perhaps only after generations of patient care, the government must protect the natives. "Long and cruel experience," he wrote, "has well proved that it is impossible for enlightened Governments or money-making individuals to deal with these credulous and unsophisticated people, without the sin of injustice."[16] The greatest injustice occurred when the races met on the frontier. In the vanguard of the westward movement came the traders, often of the most venal and mercenary sort. They brought liquor, which destroyed the harmony of Indian lives. Traders invited Indians to slaughter the buffalos and exchange their hides for whiskey. Catlin bemoaned the fact that the Indians, who once had harvested the buffalo for food and raiment, were now destroying their greatest resource for a few hours of inebriation. Such a practice assaulted the environment. Traders brought in guns so that Indians could war against other tribes to protect their exploitation of the buffalo. Worst of all, traders introduced diseases that decimated Indian populations. To prevent the destruction of Indians and the environment, Catlin wanted the government to restrict contact between the races and to create a vast national park. Civilized humans would be excluded. Indians would continue to live in a state of nature. Only such benefits as literacy and Christianity would be introduced slowly.[17]

Catlin was neither the first nor the only American to call for government protection of Indians. Almost from the birth of the republic the national government had tried to eliminate the plundering of Indians by traders and land jobbers. Trade and intercourse acts introduced a system of licensing traders. Methods used to transfer land title from the tribes were restricted to agents of the federal government. In this way, frontier conflicts would be eliminated. Even Indian removal, authorized by Congress two years before Catlin visited the Mandan villages, was justified as a humanitarian policy designed to protect natives from debauchery. By the time Euroamericans met Native Americans somewhere near the Hundredth Meridian, they could shake hands as near-equals. The Indians, protected from the nastiness of Euroamerican civilization for a few generations, would prosper under the tutelage of Christian missionaries and government agents.[18] Although Catlin's voice was only one among many raised on behalf of Indians, what distinguished the artist from other contemporaries was his willingness to take his message to the public.

Catlin believed that just as Indians should be educated over time in the ways of civilization, so also should American citizens be instructed in the ways of nature and nature's noblemen. Of all the artists and writers who explored the Far West in the years between Andrew Jackson's inauguration and the American Civil War, George Catlin sought to promote public awareness about Indians. In the enterprise, he combined the seemingly incompatible motives of artist, scientist, and showman.[19]

In 1837, the artist opened his exhibition at Clinton Hall in New York City. Catlin's Indian gallery displayed not only his nearly six hundred paintings and drawings completed since his first trip up the Missouri, but also a large collection of Indian artifacts and implements. Cabinets containing painted robes, fringed scalp shirts, headdresses, shields, bows and arrows, and Comanche lances stood beneath the paintings lining the walls. A twenty-five-foot-high Crow tipi, made from the hides of twenty buffalos, occupied the center of the room. Catlin erected a platform in the exhibition room from which he, his nephew Brice, or his assistant named David Kavenaugh could deliver evening lectures. Customers, once they had paid a fifty-cent admission, toured the gallery in the company of the artist or one of his assistants.[20] Catlin advertised his gallery in the New York *Morning Herald*, declaring that

> in order to render the exhibition more instructive than it could otherwise be, the paintings will be exhibited one at a time, and such explanation of [the Indians'] dress customs, traditions, [will be] given by Mr. Catlin as will enable the public to form a just idea of the customs, numbers, and conditions of the savages yet in a state of nature in North America.[21]

Catlin would occasionally dress himself in Indian attire to heighten the sense of immediacy with the subject. Better still, when Indian delegations passed through New York on their way to visit the Great Father in Washington, he invited them to visit his gallery. On such occasions, the Indians would verify the accuracy of his paintings and lectures, and entertain the patrons by talking to them through interpreters.[22] Thus was born, in the words of one biographer, "the first *Wild West* show, and an authentic one."[23]

Over the next two years, Catlin took his *Gallery unique* to Washington, Baltimore, Philadelphia, and Boston. In 1839, he reopened in New York, suggesting in his advertisements that it would be the last time he displayed the gallery in the United States. His lectures troubled certain people. In his desire to educate his audiences about the plight of American Indians, he often spoke passionately. He denounced the demoralizing influences of the fur trade and the methods used by the government to acquire Indian lands. He had hoped both to influence federal policy and to persuade Congress to purchase his collection. Because he had alienated certain expansionist congressmen by his criticisms of Indian policy, a bill to purchase his gallery remained in committee. His own countrymen, he believed, failed to appreciate his collection. He decided to take his show to England.[24]

Catlin's exhibition opened in London on February 1, 1840. He had leased space in Egyptian Hall. He enlivened his lectures with what he called *Tableaux vivants*, the reenactment of stirring scenes from Indian life. At first, he hired Cockney actors, twenty men and boys, to play the parts. He alternated two programs, which he continued to supplement with his lectures. The first program consisted of eleven scenes re-creating Indian warfare, which proved to be the most popular. The second performance featured scenes from domestic life, including a medicine man's cure of a patient.[25]

Despite critical success, Catlin never acquired the riches about which he dreamed. He lived comfortably, but his income rarely exceeded his expenses. After four years in London, the artist took his show to seventeen cities in Ireland, England, and Scotland. When he returned to London for an exhibition that he claimed would be "positively the last in the Kingdom, previous to embarking for New York," he received a letter from an Arthur Rankin that would change the nature of his show.[26]

Rankin, an officer in the British army during the War of 1812, had remained in Canada following the cessation of hostilities. He had involved himself in a number of worthy projects, among them helping runaway slaves escape to Canada. Rankin informed Catlin that he was on his way to Manchester with nine Ojibwas (Anishinaabeg) from the northern shore of Lake Huron. He wanted to lease the Indians to Catlin for one hundred pounds a month. The artist instead proposed that the Indians be shown as part of his *Tableaux vivants*, and that he and Rankin share expenses and profits.[27]

The Indians proved to be a sensation, so much so that Rankin soon ended his partnership with Catlin and organized his own show. Catlin's tableaus were rescued, however, by the arrival of fourteen Iowas in the care of George H. C. Melody, whom Catlin had met before in the United States. Melody shared more in common with Catlin's views toward Indians. With a new partnership, the artist changed his mind about returning to the United States. Instead, he and Melody took the exhibition to Paris. When the Iowas decided to return home after three members of the troupe had died from disease, Catlin contracted eleven Ojibwas and took his show to Belgium. Disasters, personal and financial, dogged him. As in England, his expenses often exceeded his income. His wife and son died in Paris; some of the Ojibwas died on tour. In time, circumstances forced him to flee his creditors by embarking for Venezuela under an assumed name.[28]

In Catlin's career as showman, art and extravaganza had not mixed well. As one of Catlin's biographers has observed, his *Tableaux vivants* raised troublesome doubts about his intellectual integrity and his instincts as an entertainer. He never devised a successful method to use the Wild West show to illustrate his ideas. Display of his paintings and artifacts may have prevented him from developing a Wild West show as large or as colorful as was perhaps needed to entertain the paying public. His indoor gallery restricted the kind of performances that could be given. Dances, lectures, and tableaus were all that could be presented in crowded lecture halls. He was an artist by talent and temperament; but a showman by accident.[29]

In his art and showmanship, Catlin had placed much emphasis on the mounted plains Indian, his true American hero. He had begun his western sojourn as another American image maker was finishing his. Catlin's had been a journey of the senses; James Fenimore Cooper's had been one of the imagination. In 1832, Cooper took his Leatherstocking hero out to the plains. Settlement surged westward into a region of little wood and less rain. The great prairies of the West appeared to Cooper as the final gathering place of American Indians. It was also the place where Leatherstocking would die. Catlin had gone beyond the prairies to the high plains. His art and writing marked the beginning of the movement away from the image of the American Indian as an inhabitant of the eastern woodlands.

Catlin died in 1872, the year that Buffalo Bill Cody, a plainsman dressed in buckskin, began his stage career. Stories and novels of Prentiss Ingraham and "Ned Buntline" (Edward Z. C. Judson) transformed William Frederick Cody, onetime army scout and railroad contract hunter, into Buffalo Bill. Before Cody launched his own version of western legend in the Wild West show, he appeared in melodramas based on these dime novels, re-creating his real and imaginary frontier exploits.[30] The pulp-novel reading public idolized the frontier scout as it would the cowboy in the twentieth century. The theater was a natural next step for many of the more flamboyant scouts who wore their hair long, dressed in eccentric attire, and adopted colorful nicknames as if they were titles of honor.[31]

Between 1872 and 1876, Cody divided his time between his employment as scout and guide on the plains, and his acting in a series of melodramas in the East. He formed his own "Buffalo Bill Combination," which at one time included Wild Bill Hickok. Although the melodramas were frivolous and the acting uninspired, Cody had discovered that the public embraced characters who, if not actors, were nevertheless genuine frontiersmen.[32] George Catlin had discovered that audiences were willing to pay money to witness re-creations of scenes of Indian life from western America, especially if those scenes included warfare; but Catlin hoped to educate while he entertained and his *Tableaux vivants* were always staged as if they were ethnological exhibits come to life. Buffalo Bill Cody succeeded in his entertainments where Catlin failed, perhaps because he retained some of the rapine and torture but introduced a hero with whom audiences could identify. To add authenticity to his melodramas, Cody hired a few Indians to perform with his combination. It would be just a simple step to take his combination out of the theater and into the arena; and when he finally entered the arena in 1883 he took with him his Show Indians.

As the careers of Catlin and others attest, there was nothing extraordinary in the employment of Indians to lend an air of authenticity to enterprises ranging from gallery exhibitions to melodramas. Indeed, Indians had been appearing regularly in circuses, carnivals, medicine shows, and plays since the 1840s.[33] As Buffalo Bill and other pitchmen discovered during the 1870s, businesses could exploit to their advantage eastern fascination with western lore. During the Jacksonian period, George Catlin had found that his criticisms of Indian policy angered many Americans. In response, he chose to take his gallery to Europe in search of more appreciative, and presumably less hostile, audiences. By the 1870s, however, a new generation had come of age in the United States and Indians were enough of a novelty to excite interest.

As Dr. N. T. Oliver, known professionally as Nevada Ned and the leading hawker for the Kickapoo Medicine Company (1881) claimed, audiences regarded Indians as romantic characters in ratio to the distance separating them from the frontier. Whereas westerners generally reviled Indians, easterners saw them as noble savages.[34] What is more, a new generation of reformers arose after the Civil War. For many, slavery had been the national apostasy. Once eliminated, other social issues called forth their best efforts and intentions. For a quarter-century after the Civil War, the "Indian Problem" appeared to many reformers to be the most vexing. With the abandonment of the treaty system in 1871, Congress transformed Indians (if only symbolically) from members of domestic-dependent, though sovereign, nations to a dependent minority—and one destined to be absorbed by the dominant culture.[35] That some tribes on the plains still possessed the means and the will to resist only added to the urgency with which reformers approached their task.

The horrors of Indian warfare, as John C. Ewers writes, became very real as emigrants, prospectors, stage, telegraph, and railroad lines pushed across the plains after the Civil War.[36] Sioux, Cheyennes, Arapahos, Kiowas, and Comanches resisted the invasion of their homeland and buffalo range. Newspaper and magazine reporters followed the military campaigns. Dime novelists found lurid themes with which to entertain readers. George Armstrong Custer, the "boy general" of the Civil War and a shameless self-promoter, published serially, in *Galaxy*, "My Life on the Plains," in which he expressed his admiration for "the fearless hunter, matchless horseman and warrior of the Plains."[37] Many army officers who had fought against these Indians expressed similar sentiments in widely read books about their experiences, some of which were illustrated with reproductions of drawings made from photographs. Whether one was a reformer or not, warfare on the plains heightened one's interest in Indians.

As Buffalo Bill discovered, audiences were willing to pay to see events from the American West re-created on stage or in arenas. Indian actors, playing themselves, would provide an aura of immediacy otherwise missing from proscenium or printed page.[38]

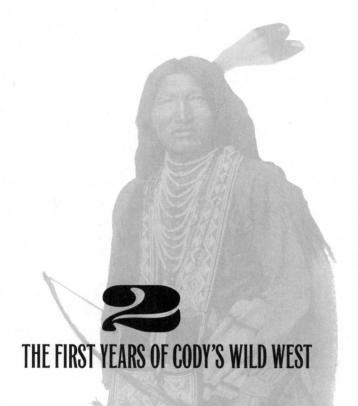

2
THE FIRST YEARS OF CODY'S WILD WEST

"To give public exhibitions of American frontier life."

By the time Buffalo Bill and partners opened the first Wild West show in 1883, Indians in small numbers had appeared in ethnological exhibits, medicine shows, circuses, and melodramas. Their presence gave the exhibits a patina of authenticity if not respectability.[1] Buffalo Bill, however, changed the nature of Indian employment and ushered in the heyday of the Show Indians.

There are a number of stories about the origin of Buffalo Bill's Wild West. Various partners claim responsibility for its inspiration. What facts that can be teased out of the legends are these: Sometime early in 1882, William Cody, while in New York performing in his latest celebratory melodrama, met for lunch with Nate Salsbury, a young actor and manager, who described a new kind of show, made up of American cowboys, Indians, Mexican *vaqueros*, bucking horses, and buffalos. The performances would be staged outdoors. The show would travel to cities in the United States and Europe.[2] Following the conversation with Salsbury, Cody returned to his home in North Platte, Nebraska. Town boosters had been making plans for an ambitious Fourth-of-July celebration. Planners appointed him grand marshal for an "Old Glory blowout." Cody added his own ideas to the celebration. He made up a lot of contests, arranged for prizes, and, with the success of the venture, determined to take this new combination to the eastern United States. The "Old Glory blowout" became the prototype for both the modern rodeo and the Wild West show.[3] Cody formed a partnership with the accomplished marksman William Frank "Doc" Carver and hired "Arizona" John Burke as his business manager. Burke, in turn, acquired a staff, planned a route, and prepared programs and posters of what was dubbed after considerable wrangling the "Hon. W. F. Cody and Dr. W. F. Carver's Wild West, Rocky Mountain and Prairie Exhibition."[4]

Salsbury, believing that Doc Carver knew nothing of the West and even less about show business, refused to join Cody's show for the 1883 tour.[5] Carver, who also billed himself as the "Evil Spirit of the Plains"—the spectral sobriquet he attributed to Spotted Tail of the Brule Sioux—put up twenty-seven thousand dollars and signed an additional note for two thousand dollars (Cody may have been a cosigner) on the First National Bank of Omaha to become Cody's sole partner.[6] The Cody and Carver show opened in Omaha on May 17, 1883, moved on to Council Bluffs, Iowa, and Springfield, Illinois, then eastward where it enjoyed some success in New York City and Boston.[7]

The program for the first season of the Wild West show included:

1. Grand Introductory March
2. Bareback Pony Race
3. Pony Express
4. Attack on the Deadwood Mail Coach
5. 100 Yard Race between an Indian on foot and
      an Indian on horseback
6. Capt. A. H. Bogardus [shooting exhibition]
7. Cody and Carver—shooting exhibition
8. Race between Cowboys

9. Cowboy's Fun
10. Riding Wild Texas Steers
11. Roping and Riding Wild Bison
12. Grand Hunt—including a battle with the Indians[8]

Counting the opening parade, Indians performed in six of the twelve events. The show that first season employed thirty-six Pawnees from Indian Territory. According to one story, the Pawnees had shown themselves to be such enthusiastic participants in the attack on the Deadwood Stage during dress rehearsals at Colville, Nebraska, that Major Frank North, who had at one time commanded four companies of Pawnee scouts, suggested to Cody that he might consider substituting older, more docile Indians. "Bill, if you want to make this d[amned] show go," North remarked, "you do not need me or my Indians." Instead, Buffalo Bill should hire about twenty old men. "Fix them up with all the paint and feathers on the market. Use some old hack horses and a hack driver. To make it go you want a show of illusion not realism."[9] Cody opted for realism. The ardent Pawnees remained for the tour.

Cody and Carver's Wild West played to ever larger crowds as it toured the East that first season; but due to poor management, the show barely broke even. The partnership dissolved, hampered by dissension and jealousy between the principals. Carver parted company and toured with the remainder of the troupe throughout the winter, adding Captain Jack Crawford, the cowboy poet, as partner. In 1889, Carver teamed with Fred C. Whitney of Detroit.[10] In the coming years, the Carver and Whitney circus often competed successfully with Buffalo Bill's.

Cody, exorcized of the evil spirit, joined with Nate Salsbury to perform the Wild West in the spring of 1884. Although plagued by rain during their first year as partners, the Cody and Salsbury show enjoyed considerable financial success. Audiences thrilled to the Indians' attack on the Deadwood Stage. So entertaining was the Wild West show inspired by Buffalo Bill that within two years of its first appearance in Omaha, nearly fifty circuses, medicine shows, and rival Wild West shows had incorporated, and in some instances copied, many of its features.[11]

During the 1884 and 1885 seasons, Cody's show continued to employ Pawnees from the Indian Territory. It was probably Cody's employment of Sitting Bull, the Hunkpapa leader, in 1885 that focused his attention on the Sioux. In the early years, Buffalo Bill himself visited the Sioux agencies looking for performers.[12] These "sign-up" days, according to an eyewitness (though the numbers are inflated), became events in themselves:

2 : The first year of Cody's Wild West, 1884. He and Doc Carver had dissolved their partnership the previous fall. Nate Salsbury appears to Cody's right. Standing behind them is Johnny Baker. To Cody's left is Captain A. H. Bogardus, champion pigeon shot, and his son. John Nelson and his family appear in the center foreground. Aside from the Nelsons, most of the Show Indians are Pawnees. Behind Johnny Baker is six-foot-five Buck Taylor, the first "king of the cowboys." Gordon Lillie, interpreter for the Pawnees, is the fourth person on Taylor's right. Major Frank North, commander of the Pawnee Scouts, appears to the right of Nate Salsbury. This photograph may have been taken after North returned to the show following a severe injury in July. The cinch on his saddle broke and he was trampled by his galloping horse. He never fully recovered from his injury and died in March, 1885. (South Dakota State Historical Society, Pierre)

The ceremony of selecting the Indians for the show became an annual spring affair, and when he could Cody selected the lucky individuals himself. The Indians, five or six hundred of them, would come to Rushville (a Nebraska town near the South Dakota border) where the selections were made, and they came in their finest buckskins, feathers, and beads. They were quite a sight in their gaudy finery. Only a small part of that number could be used, and the ones not chosen felt pretty bad about it. The government [eventually] required the Colonel, or his representative, to post bonds that the Indians would be well fed while away and that they would be returned to the reservation in good health and a new suit of clothes.[13]

Most of the performers in Cody's Wild West were enrolled at Pine Ridge agency (later, reservation). Rushville, to the south, was the nearest railroad town. These scenes at Rushville *and* Pine Ridge agency would be repeated each spring and fall as Lakota performers joined and later returned from the shows.[14]

From the 1860s on, dime novels and western-theme melodramas exploited the American fascination with the Indians' prowess as warriors. The Sioux, Cheyennes, Arapahos, Kiowas, and Comanches resisted the Euroamerican invasion of their buffalo hunting grounds. Newspaper and magazine reporters recorded the encounters. The exploits of Sioux leaders during the war on the Powder River in the late 1860s, up to the death of Custer in 1876, became legendary.[15] Sitting Bull (*Tatanka Iyotake*) was the last of the great Sioux leaders to surrender to the government. He and his remnant band returned to the United States in 1881, after a four-year exile in Canada.

A number of enterprising show people, hoping to capitalize on Sitting Bull's notoriety, wanted him to join their carnivals or dime museums upon his return from Canada. This proved to be impossible as long as the Hunkpapa holy man remained a federal prisoner at Fort Randall, Dakota Territory. Following his release in May 1883, the Bureau of Indian Affairs assigned Sitting Bull to the Standing Rock agency presided over by Major James McLaughlin. Requests continued to pour in. McLaughlin usually explained that the Indians in his charge were just beginning to show progress in adopting the trappings of a sedentary life, and that to remove one of their leaders would confuse them about what was truly important.[16] This is how McLaughlin rebuffed Buffalo Bill's first request to employ Sitting Bull.

Sitting Bull did tour cities in the East briefly in the late summer and early fall of 1884. Father Joseph A. Stephan, head of the Bureau of Catholic Indian Missions in Washington, D.C., and formerly the missionary at Jamestown, Dakota Territory, had received permission from the secretary of the interior to put Sitting Bull on exhibit, should the headman consent. McLaughlin thought Father Stephan incapable of handling Sitting Bull. To thwart the priest's plans, McLaughlin encouraged a friend, Alvaren Allen of St. Paul, Minnesota, to take the Hunkpapa leader on tour.

3 : *"Buffalo Bill Indians," on their way to join the show, gather at Pine Ridge agency. (Brennan Family Papers, South Dakota State Historical Society, Pierre)*

"The Sitting Bull Combination," as the group of eight Indians and two interpreters was known, appeared in twenty-five cities between September 2 and October 25 without much success, financial or critical. Having allowed Sitting Bull off the reservation once, McLaughlin proved more amenable the next time Cody made his request.[17]

On April 29, 1885, Cody wired the secretary of the interior that Sitting Bull had expressed a desire to join the Wild West. McLaughlin, the showman explained, approved the idea. Cody offered endorsements from Generals Philip Sheridan, Nelson A. Miles, George Crook, and Alfred Terry to strengthen his application. "Please answer," he closed the telegram, "as bull [*sic*] is anxious to come at once." Secretary of the Interior Lamar found the proposition unacceptable. He wrote on the telegram

"Make a *very* emphatic *No*" (underlining the word three times).[18] Commissioner John D. C. Atkins told Cody of both his and the secretary's opposition. Indians should be engaged in civilized pursuits and not in "roving through the country exhibiting themselves and visiting places where they would naturally come in contact with evil associates and degrading immoralities."[19] Rebuffed again, Cody forwarded endorsements from General William T. Sherman and Colonel Eugene A. Carr (commander, Sixth Cavalry) who expressed their confidence in the showman. In his own letter to the commissioner, Cody emphasized his long experience in "the management and care of Indians." He guaranteed that, once employed with the show, Sitting Bull would "receive the kindest treatment."[20] Secretary Lamar relented and, on May 18, wired Agent McLaughlin that Sitting Bull and a few of his followers and family would be permitted to appear in Cody's Wild West show.[21]

Sitting Bull and the Hunkpapa Sioux joined the show in Buffalo, New York, on June 12. The 1885 season confirmed the success of Cody's Wild West both financially and artistically. Cody and company toured more than forty cities in the United States and Canada.[22] A part of the show's success is explained by the presence of Sitting Bull.

When performing, he wore his buckskin, paint, and feathers. In the parade of performers at the opening of the show, he wore a red tunic. When not in the arena, his usual dress included a plush brocade waistcoat, black flowered pants, a scarlet tie, a printed shirt with its tails hanging down outside his trousers, and beaded, rubber-soled moccasins. He adorned himself with jewelry and sometimes wore a crucifix, mostly because he liked its design.[23] Introduced to the audiences simply as Sitting Bull, the famous Hunkpapa chief, he endured the taunts and boos of the crowd who associated him with Custer's death at the Little Bighorn. From all reports, he bore the insults impassively—or with greater dignity than those who screamed their insults. He made considerable money selling his photographs, perhaps gaining some measure of revenge upon the unfriendly crowds.[24]

The sheer numbers of Euroamericans and the size of their cities impressed him. According to Annie Oakley, much of the money he earned he gave to the ragged children he encountered in the cities. Their presence had corroborated what he already suspected. Euroamericans would not do much for Indians when they let their own people go hungry. "The white man knows how to make everything," Stanley Vestal has quoted him as saying, "but he does not know how to distribute it."[25] In press releases given out by the show, Sitting Bull remembered the time that Custer and the Seventh Cavalry menaced the Sioux encampment by the Greasy Grass (the Little Bighorn). "Nobody knew who killed Custer; everybody fired at him. Custer was a brave warrior but [he] made a mistake. The Indians honored him and did not scalp him. I fought for my people. My people said I was right. I will answer to my people. I will answer for the dead of my people. Let the palefaces do the same on their side."[26] On another occasion in Philadelphia, representatives of the Indian Rights Association visited Sitting Bull's tent. As Nate Salsbury, who witnessed the proceedings, explained, they had come to beseech the great leader "to flee from the wrath to come." Sitting Bull reportedly sat through the interview, the picture of resignation, answering such questions as he could understand—through an interpreter—but largely dismissing their entreaties with contempt. Finally one of the reformers said to the interpreter: "Ask Sitting Bull if he ever had any regret for his share in the Custer massacre." Like an enraged lion, Salsbury wrote, "the old fellow sprang to his feet, and thrusting his long lean fingers into his questioner's face he shouted, 'Tell this fool that I did not murder Custer; it was a fight in open day. He would have killed me if he could. I have answered to my people for the dead on my side. Let Custer's friends answer to his people for the dead on his side.'" With a gesture of disdain, Sitting Bull exited the tent, leaving "these worthy cranks" flabbergasted, as Salsbury described them.[27]

When taken to Washington, D.C., Sitting Bull studied the impressive buildings and marveled at the crowds in the streets. "I wish I had known this when I was a boy," he is supposed to have remarked. "The white people are so many that if every Indian in the West killed one every step they took the dead would not be missed among you."[28] It is little wonder, then, that he appeared phlegmatic to those who saw him enter the arena to the jeers of the American crowds. But in Canada, by contrast, crowds treated him warmly. Members of the Canadian Parliament and mayors who visited the performances hailed him as "the illustrious Indian general and statesman, . . . the beau ideal of a straight-forward and honest Indian."[29]

---

4 : Sitting Bull and Buffalo Bill, 1885. One in a series of cabinet photographs made by William Notman during the visit of Cody's Wild West to Montreal. The more famous pose from this series—at least the one that is most frequently reproduced—has Buffalo Bill pointing to an imaginary horizon with his right hand. Both he and Sitting Bull rest their left hands on the Hunkpapa holy man's Model 1873 Winchester. (Buffalo Bill Historical Center, Cody, Wyoming)

From Mercaldo Collection

Returning to the United States, the show played in Detroit and Saginaw, Michigan, and Columbus, Ohio, before finishing the season at St. Louis. After the final performance on October 11, newspaper reporters asked Sitting Bull, through an interpreter, what he thought about his travels and whether he would join the show the following year. He told them that his lodge was a better place to live. He had grown weary of the houses, and the noise and bustle of cities in which other Americans lived.[30] When he left the show, he took with him a trained gray circus horse and a size-eight white sombrero, both gifts from Buffalo Bill.[31]

Sitting Bull became the first great Show Indian. A headliner himself, he attracted perhaps as much attention as Buffalo Bill. Although he toured just one season, his employment established a course for all subsequent shows. Few of the Show Indians possessed the stature or notoriety of Sitting Bull; but his association with the Lakota victory over Custer at the Little Bighorn secured his exemplary status. His employment, along with eight others from his band, represented the shift of Show Indian employment to the northern plains. The Sioux became the most prized Show Indians. Their reputations as warriors confirmed the image of Indians in the minds of Americans and eventually Europeans who saw their performances. In newspaper advertisements for the 1885 season, Sitting Bull's name appears only slightly smaller than the caption "Buffalo Bill's Wild West" (in stylized print). The copy describes Sitting Bull as "the renowned Sioux Chief." With him were appearing "several of the celebrated warriors lately among the hostiles."[32] As if in afterthought to fill out the bill, "52 Pawnee and Wichita braves" would also perform. Cody, Burke, and Salsbury named only the Sioux members of the Indian contingent.[33]

Cody's Wild West, according to one assessment, had played to a million people during the summer of 1885. The show profited more than 100,000 dollars, which wiped out the remaining debts that had lingered from previous rain-soaked seasons.[34] Buffalo Bill performed during the winter in a melodrama. It was the last time he did so. Thereafter, he concentrated exclusively on his Wild West. He returned to St. Louis in the spring to reorganize the show. About this time, he began to refer to his show as the only true Wild West. His success, and Doc Carver's rival show, had inspired others to add features of the Wild West formula to their circuses.

The year 1886, as one historian of popular culture suggests, represents a dividing point between Cody's earlier efforts as a stage performer and Wild West show entrepreneur and his subsequent emphasis on ever larger productions. Buffalo Bill's Wild West made the transition from a small outdoor touring show to one of the "greatest amusement enterprises ever known."[35] Sarah Blackstone attributes three significant ideas to Cody and his partners: playing the Wild West in long engagements on permanent grounds; playing the show as a spectacle in Madison Square Garden during the winter; and taking the show to Europe the following spring and summer. At Madison Square Garden, Show Indians were not only featured in the more spectacular acts, but in the interludes as well.[36]

John Burke applied to the secretary of the interior in mid-February for permission to visit various Indian agencies for the purpose of selecting about sixty Show Indians. He visited the Sioux in early April. Cody had again wanted to employ Sitting Bull, but McLaughlin refused. The agent complained to Burke that Sitting Bull had spent the money he earned with Buffalo Bill in trying to secure his position in the tribe. McLaughlin, ever hostile to Sitting Bull, described scenes of profligacy. He wrote that Sitting Bull "is such a consummate liar and too vain and obstinate to be benefitted by what he sees." He made no "good use of the money he thus earns, but on the contrary spends it extravagantly among the Indians in trying to perpetuate baneful influences which the ignorant and non-progressive element are too ready to listen to and follow." He spent his money in feasting the Indians. Of the money he had brought back to the reservation the previous fall, not a dollar remained. "I had a great deal of trouble with him," the agent explained, "and through him with other Indians caused by his own bad behavior and arrogance."[37] A less-hostile observer might have understood that Sitting Bull's gift-giving was nothing more than the altruism expected of a Lakota leader by his people.

McLaughlin told Burke that Cody would need an order from the secretary of the interior before he allowed Sitting Bull to join the show.[38] Opposed by the agent, Cody gave up on his desire to travel with Sitting Bull. Instead, Burke contracted twenty-nine men from the Pine Ridge agency to perform with the show during the summer season. Wives and children who accompanied them did not appear on the affidavit.[39]

It was the first formal agreement (not counting the separate contract with Sitting Bull) between Cody and the Show Indians. The correspondence and negotiations in the hiring of Sitting Bull had introduced a more formal relationship between the Wild West show, on the one hand, and the Indian Bureau and Indian employees, on the other. In his desire to placate the secretary of the interior, Cody had affirmed his willingness to abide by any restrictions or suggestions which the department might impose. Cody and Salsbury used the same technique in the contracts for the 1886 season.

Despite its legal language of obligation, the descriptive portions detailing the showmen's duties are informal; indeed, compared to later contracts, its language appears artless. The Indians, paid twenty-five dollars a month, were "to give public exhibitions of American frontier life." In performing their roles as inhabitants of the frontier, the showmen agreed to follow their employer's orders until they proved inconsistent with "the laws of morality and the ordinary rules of propriety."[40] Questions did eventually arise concerning the morality and propriety of employing Indians to play themselves.

Indians playing Indians did on occasion offend good taste—if not the public's, then at least those people who set standards by which morality and propriety were judged. Indian-policy reformers and their allies in the Indian service probably would have been offended anyway by all the riding, shooting, and shouting in the Wild West shows' re-creations of frontier life; but they would have preferred that Indians remain at home. There was never a chance of banning the shows; but Indian employment in them might be prohibited. Failing that, Indian employment could at least be restricted. No sooner had Indians begun performing in Wild West shows than protests began to reach the Indian office asking that the practice cease. These were not the kinds of criticisms anticipated by Cody, Salsbury, and Burke. Buffalo Bill and his partners had hoped to divert any criticisms that they were leading their Indian employees along paths of wickedness. They could not have anticipated that wickedness to some people might be the very Indian performances in the shows.

Certain Americans entertained all sorts of anxieties about actors and performers. Show business offered enticements that might lead the unsophisticated or unwary into wickedness. If performers could not always avoid the near occasion of sin, they needed to be fortified in anticipation of the encounter. To quiet the concerns of officials in the Indian office, the first Cody contract stipulated that the organization agreed

> to protect [Indians] from all immoral influences and surroundings. . . . And . . . further agree that in selecting Indians for exhibition . . . they will, as far as possible select married men who shall be accompanied on the exhibition tour by their wives, and all such women shall be fed and clothed and cared for, and returned to their respective homes . . . [;] that they will select for their said Exhibition, Indians all of whom shall be of the same religious faith, and furthermore, the parties of the first part agree to pay a monthly salary of One Hundred dollars and expenses to a representative of the religious denomination to which the parties of the second part belong, who shall be selected by some religious church or society, or other religious organization, with a view to accompanying

the Exhibition on its tour through the country, and looking after their moral welfare.[41]

There were a few complaints during the summer of 1886 from missionaries attached to the Sioux agencies. In response, Buffalo Bill wrote to the secretary of the interior notifying him that the showmen had returned safely to the reservation and on schedule. He explained further that he had "thought to give [the Indians] a little recreation" that summer. All had profited from the tour. If the secretary had no objection, he planned to bring them east after a few weeks of rest at home.[42]

Authority was granted on October 26 for Buffalo Bill to employ Indians under the contracted provisions of the previous spring. The Department of the Interior retained the ten-thousand-dollar bond posted by Cody in March.[43] The show opened in St. Louis and then traveled east through Terre Haute, Dayton, Wheeling, and on to Washington, D.C. It then moved to New York City, whose officials scheduled a parade on June 27. Cowboys and Indians marched off the Twenty-third Street ferry to Eighth Avenue, where the Cowboy Band played "Oh Susannah" and paraded up to Forty-second Street, across to Fifth Avenue, and then down Fifth Avenue to Broadway and the Battery. Huge crowds turned out in greeting and to view the spectacle. All summer the show played at Erastina, a summer resort operated by Erastus Wiman, on Staten Island. General William Tecumseh Sherman attended opening day. Mark Twain witnessed the show two days in succession and proclaimed it genuine, free of sham and insincerity. An aged P. T. Barnum said, perhaps wryly, that Cody did not need spangles to make it a real show. Elizabeth Custer found it to be a faithful representation of western life that had ceased to be, what with advancing civilization.[44]

And what did the Show Indians think? A journalist asked American Horse the younger, who had replaced Sitting Bull as the Indian headliner for the 1886–87 seasons, what he thought of the East. American Horse replied: "I see so much that is wonderful and strange that I feel a wish sometimes to go out in the forest and cover my head with a blanket, so that I can see no more and have a chance to think over what I have seen."[45] Two other showmen remarked to John Burke that the travel, the tumult of cities, and going rapidly from place to place had disoriented them. They felt bewitched at times. They had to tie handkerchiefs around their eyes to block out the strangeness around them. Only then could they restore calm and order to their worlds.[46]

American Horse and the other Sioux arrived back at their agencies on

September 30. Most of them returned to the show by early November. Other Sioux and Northern Cheyennes joined them in December;[47] but for the winter season, Cody's Wild West had come indoors.

Profits earned from the show's extended summer run at Erastina encouraged Cody and Salsbury to rent Madison Square Garden for a winter engagement. Rental of the building alone cost eighteen thousand dollars per month. Cody and Salsbury invested almost ten thousand dollars in scenery, canvas backdrops, and machinery. The partners engaged the services of Steele Mackaye, a popular dramatic author, Matt Morgan, an artist, and Nelse Waldron, an expert with machinery, to create a grand spectacle called "The Drama of Civilization."[48]

The show opened on Thanksgiving eve, November 24. As one reporter commented, it seemed that the Wild West show, just as the West itself, had been tamed.[49] Steele Mackaye had resurrected George Catlin's *Tableaus vivants*. Mackaye divided civilization into four epochs, with interludes following the first, second, and third acts. The first epoch, "The Primeval Forest," featured wild animals leased from Adam Forepaugh's circus (with the occasional anomaly representing the fauna of North America) and Cody's Show Indians. Indians became a part of the natural environment. This act ended with a fight among Indian tribes. The first interlude included Indian dances and the sharpshooting of Miss Lillian Smith, a teenager recruited by Cody in California in 1886.[50]

"The Prairie" became the setting for the second epoch. It included a buffalo hunt by the Indians and the passage of an emigrant train through a hostile land. This act ended with a prairie fire and a stampede. Cowboys entertained the crowd in the second interlude with exhibitions of trick riding, roping, and "bronc busting," the "cowboy fun" of earlier shows.[51]

Cody starred in the third epoch, entitled "Cattle Ranch." The action centered on "The Attack on the Settler's Cabin," which had been borrowed as a set piece from the arena show. Gunfire and screaming Indians provided the danger, Cody's timely rescue the drama. The masterful shooting of Buffalo Bill and Annie Oakley followed the third act.[52]

"The Drama of Civilization" ended in the "Mining Camp." Nelse Waldron's machinery provided the stirring finale, a cyclone. Mackaye had divided the epoch into three scenes. The first featured the re-creation of the Pony Express, specialty acts of cowboys, and a classic shoot-out in the street of a western town. The second scene, again borrowing from the arena show, but with a subtle shift of nemesis, showed the crowds an attack on the Deadwood Stage by road agents. Finally, a cyclone devastated the mining camp.[53] Waldron accomplished this last scene by using a two-

5 : Buffalo Bill's Wild West in Brooklyn, 1907. "War Dance." The canvas backdrop depicting the landscape of the American West had been in use since the performances at Madison Square Garden. (American Heritage Center, University of Wyoming, Laramie)

hundred-horsepower steam engine that drove two large fans. The wind blew with enough force to unseat riders, topple their horses, and throw passengers off the Deadwood Stage.[54]

Later, Cody added a fifth epoch: "Custer's Last Stand," complete with a painted cyclorama of the valley of the Little Bighorn River. Buck Taylor, the six-feet-five-inches tall "King of the Cowboys" in the show, played Lieutenant Colonel Custer. The Show Indians fought the soldiers until Buck Taylor lay down. After a pause so the audience could ruminate upon the tableau made deafening by the silence, Cody would gallop into the arena at the head of his cowboy command, react to the carnage he beheld upon the battlefield, and sweep his hat from his head in respect for the fallen soldiers. As the garden's lights dimmed, a spotlight trained on Cody. The words *Too Late* were projected on the cyclorama behind him.[55] Buffalo Bill, scouting for the Fifth Cavalry on June 25, 1876, was actually hundreds of miles away from the valley of the Little Bighorn. In the

Sergt. G. H. BATES

And the Flag carried by him through the late Confederate States and through England, and around which he has rallied over 12,000,000 people for the promotion of Patriotic Citizenship and National Unity.

arena, however, he shamelessly created the impression that, with better timing, he could have saved the day.

"The Drama of Civilization" played into February, when Cody and Salsbury made preparations to take the Wild West to Europe. The successful winter run of the show augured even greater success the following summer.

Not much information is available in the records about the thoughts and feelings of the Show Indians during the 1886–87 season. An occasional quotation appears from the pen of journalists. Much of the time, however, the reports about Indians are derogatory. What correspondence exists is so warped by stereotypes as to be almost useless. For example, one of Cody's employees took twenty Sioux to hear Henry Ward Beecher preach at the Plymouth Church in Brooklyn. As reported to the commissioner of Indian affairs, the size of the "great medicine teepees" impressed them. One visitor is supposed to have remarked after viewing the congregation, "Heap much good white man and white woman who talk and sing to 'Great Spirit.'"[56] Already whites had condemned Indians to speak a largely imaginary version of English.

On another occasion, G. H. Bates, from the show's cowboy contingent, sporting a large cut over his left eye received in the performance of the Custer rally, took a group of thirty Indians to visit a public school in New York City early in January. Bates, a Civil War veteran, had distinguished himself before joining Cody by tramping around the country carrying an American flag and giving patriotic speeches. He carried the flag in the opening of the show. His tent at the Wild West show encampment served as the rendezvous for veterans of the Grand Army of the Republic. The Sioux who accompanied Bates that day sang for the children, but refused to perform a "war dance" requested by the principal of P.S. 40. The

---

6 : Sergeant G. H. Bates joined Cody's show in 1886. Richard J. Walsh, in The Making of Buffalo Bill (257–58), wrote that he had made such a nuisance of himself tramping about the country—particularly the former Confederate States of America—carrying an American flag and giving patriotic lectures that Cody received praise for getting him off the public roads. A recipient of the Medal of Honor, Bates became the standard bearer for the show. Given his patriotic strivings, he became the perfect chaperon for the Show Indians on their excursions into late nineteenth-century Euroamerican urban culture. (Buffalo Bill Historical Center, Cody, Wyoming)

showmen listened politely to recitations from Emerson, Spencer, and Sir Walter Scott. A journalist recording the event was amused to think that Scott's Waverley novels "do not adorn the centre tables of the teepees of the rampant West."[57] In fairness, however, it was just as likely that a copy of Lone Dog's winter count did not embellish the occasional tables of Euroamerican reporters.

One can imagine, however, some pride taken by the Show Indians in, say, the re-creation of "Custer's Last Fight" (sometimes rendered as "Custer's Last Stand" or "Custer's Last Charge") that winter in Madison Square Garden. They had convincingly repelled—if only for a short while, as it turned out—the Euroamerican invaders just ten years before. One can also imagine that, like American Horse, many of the performers felt cut off from familiar surroundings in the more crowded East. They must have felt, on occasion, as alienated and alone as did Custer by the banks of the Greasy Grass. Still, given the alternative of staying home on the reservation, where their cultures increasingly came under attack from government officials and religious groups determined to reform them, Indians continued to join Wild West shows and to travel about in relative freedom.

Easterners, such as General Sherman, Elizabeth Custer, P. T. Barnum, and even Mark Twain (though a Missourian) who had sojourned in the West endorsed the Cody and Salsbury show as the genuine article. The Show Indians had made it so.

There were, however, a few critics. Republican Congressman Darwin Rush James from Brooklyn offered a resolution in the House of Representatives on January 10, 1887. It directed the secretary of the interior to explain to Congress why certain "Wild Indians" were absent from their reservations. By whose authority, James wanted to know, were the Indians engaged in "presenting before the public scenes representing their lowest savage characteristics, and . . . to what extent the exhibitions are under the auspices of the Government of the United States." James denounced the show as "the Drama of Savagery."[58]

When asked by reporters after the evening performance for his response to the congressman's resolution, Buffalo Bill expressed his surprise. "I certainly have no objection," he said, "to the Secretary . . . furnishing Congress with all the information regarding the employment by me of these Indians." He wished to remind the congressman, however, that the government in no way directed the show. "It is purely a private enterprise of my own." He offered in his defense what would become the official position of his company when met with criticism:

I claim that these Indians, as Americans, have a perfect right to hire their services where they please. They earn a good salary here and send their money home for the support of their wives and children. The "savage" sports are simply their every day form of amusement and sport in their own country. All their associations here are elevating morally. They visit places of interest and instruction; they have attended worship at Dr. Talmage's and Mr. Beecher's churches and they have also visited the office of *The World.* Not one of them out of seventy-five or eighty has ever been known to be drunk since they came to New York.[59]

Others in Cody's entourage picked up the beat and hammered the secretary of the interior with testimonials as to the educational, moral, and cultural value of Indians touring with Buffalo Bill.

James himself had his critics, mostly New York Democratic colleagues from the House. Representative Timothy Campbell observed that if "Madison Square Garden was situated in Brooklyn you would never hear anything from him." It would then have been a "glorious move" on the part of the Interior Department to take the remaining Indians away from all reservations and "scatter them around large cities."[60] Retired Congressman Samuel S. Cox, whom Campbell replaced through a special election, stated that he was in favor of taking Indians away from the wilds of Dakota and other territories in the Far West and bringing them East "to let them see the utter fallacy of their again becoming hostiles."[61] Congressman Truman Merriman wired his constituents in New York that at the time of James's resolution,

I indignantly protested against it . . . in the name of the people of the United States; that the Wild West is a grand entertainment, free from anything of a vulgar or pernicious nature; that it is instructive and entertaining, and is calculated to do a great amount of good, not only to the Indians themselves, but the people who witness it.[62]

The most humorous denunciation of James came from excongressman and former Confederate officer Tom Ochiltree of Texas, who had retired to New York City. "It was a blank blank shame for a blank blank obscure hayseed Congressman" to attack a national hero like Buffalo Bill. Ochiltree warned that he was ready to take a dozen cowboys down to Washington to teach "this blank blank fool" a lesson he would not soon forget. Having been a congressman for a number of years, this was the first time in his recollection that such an August body had been fooled by "such puerile blank blank nonsense."[63] Still, it was wise of Cody to seek support from influential persons in and out of government. James's resolution threatened more than forfeiture of his bond. There would be no Wild West without the Show Indians. For its part, the Bureau of Indian Affairs would in the coming months seek to insulate itself from criticism, especially as the chorus of disapproval mounted from Indian-policy reformers concerning the employment of Indians.

Nothing came of James's resolution. Cody retained his bond and again received permission to employ Indians, this time for his show in England. Others, however, were not as well connected as Buffalo Bill. When Gordon Lillie, who had traveled for two seasons with Buffalo Bill as interpreter for the Pawnees, applied to the secretary of the interior in April to hire thirteen members of the tribe to perform in his Wild West Museum and Encampment with the Sells Brothers's Circus, he was rebuffed. "It is not considered advisable," the acting secretary of the interior informed Lillie, "for [the] interest of Indians or the public service to grant your request."[64] Arguments against the employment of Indians in Wild West shows would grow more elaborate in the next few years. The Indian Office developed an orthodoxy to rival Cody's. Wild West shows, according to the Bureau, set back civilizing the savage.

Cody had confirmed his plans, late in the summer of 1886, to take the show to London. As his hometown newspaper, the North Platte *Tribune*, reported on September 11, 1886:

> Under the management of an English Syndicate he is to go to London next season with his Wild West show to give two performances daily for six months, receiving one-third of the gross receipts, the company paying the expenses. Mr. Cody considers this the biggest deal he has ever made and something of its magnitude may be imagined when it is confidentially expected . . . that the receipts will run away above $600,000. Mr. Cody has made money this season but he will make barrels next year.[65]

A Yorkshire businessman, John Robinson Whitley, had envisioned a vast exposition of American "Arts, Industries, Manufactures, Products and Resources"—the first such exhibition outside the United States—to coincide with the celebration of Queen Victoria's Golden Jubilee.[66] The scheme stalled until he found a suitable drawing card, Buffalo Bill's Wild West. Nate Salsbury as business manager was somehow able to include the show under the semiofficial sponsorship of the trade fair.[67]

In April, Buffalo Bill and his troupe arrived at Earl's Court outside

London. The Indian invasion of Europe had begun. The English and, in time, other Europeans showed themselves to be as interested in the "Red Indians" as they were in the other residents of wild America. There would be just as many gaping onlookers in Europe as in the United States who thought of the Indians as curiosities. Newspapers often commented in stereotypic fashion about their gaudy savagery;[68] but because of their novelty, Indians were often described in English and other European newspapers in greater detail, if not always free of the condescending asides typical of Euroamericans. Indians' thoughts and commentary are therefore more in evidence. Later still, as Indians trained in the English language at government and private schools began to travel with the shows, the Show Indians would speak for themselves.

3

THE WILD WEST OF LONDON

*"They're a fiery lot of Indians
as I think you'll all agree"*

Buffalo Bill Cody, decorated with the honorific "Colonel" as "Aide-de-camp" on the governor's staff of the Nebraska state militia, sailed from New York on March 31, 1887. Eighty-three saloon passengers, thirty-eight steerage passengers, and ninety-seven Indians, many of them camped on the deck, accompanied him aboard the State Line steamship *State of Nebraska* bound for England. Animals included 18 buffalos, 2 deer, 10 elk, 10 mules, 5 Texas steers, 4 donkeys, and 180 horses of various temperaments and hues. As the *Nebraska* warped away from the dock, the

Cowboy Band, assembled on the forecastle, played "The Girl I Left behind Me."[1] The voyage ahead troubled many in the Indian troupe. They had come far from their homes to be at quayside that morning. They had farther still to go, across "the Great Water" or "the Big Water" as they sometimes called the ocean, before they would again see their kin and country.

Many in the Indian party had joined the Wild West show for the first time. A few harbored doubts, believing that disaster would befall them if they crossed the ocean. When a fierce storm struck a couple of days out on the eastward passage, some of the Sioux sang their death songs. The ship rolled unmercifully for forty-eight hours until the crew repaired a damaged rudder. Thereafter, most passengers recovered from seasickness. Other things besides seasickness and the fear of drowning unnerved the Indians. Red Shirt (*Ogilasa*), who represented the star of the Indian contingent, believed that in crossing the ocean his flesh would become corrupt and fall from his bones. Each morning of the voyage, he examined his arms, legs, and torso for signs of decay.[2] His and the spirits of the other Indians improved, however, when the *Nebraska* dropped anchor off Gravesend in Kent on April 16. All the members of the show had survived an unusually rough crossing.[3]

After a brief quarantine on board, Cody's Wild West loaded onto three trains to make the short trip to Kensington in the west end of London. Three railroad lines served the sprawling complex of the American Exhibition at Earl's Court. Their proximity to the Wild West show arena eased somewhat the task of re-creating the landscape of the Wild West. Workers unloaded seventeen thousand carloads of rock and earth in constructing the simulated Rockies. Mature trees brought in from the midlands took root in the new West of Kensington. In ten days the workers had completed the project and the troupe had practiced their routines. The London *Observer* urged Britons to visit the camp to study "the wilful ways of the children of the prairie before popular favour and superfluous luxury render them civilized and effeminate."[4]

Reporters, American expatriates, and English nobles and commoners flocked to the encampment. Albert Edward, Prince of Wales (who later reigned as Edward VII), asked for and received a special performance before the official opening. He became the show's greatest fan. John Burke seized upon the prince's comments and transformed them into endorsements to embellish posters and broadsides.[5] Crowds gathered around the Indians wherever they went. They were the most interesting members of an otherwise interesting group of exotic Americans.

Red Shirt, as the most prominent Sioux leader among the troupe, became the spokesman for the Show Indians. His handsome features and stately bearing caused reporters to hang on his every word. He became the most quoted Show Indian of Cody's trip to England. Red Shirt explained to a reporter from Sheffield:

I started from my lodge two moons ago knowing nothing, and had I remained on the Indian Reservations, I should have been as a blind man. Now I can see a new dawn. [I have seen] the great houses [ships] which cross the mighty waters, the great villages which have no end where the pale faces swarm like insects in the summer sun. . . . Our people will wonder at these things when we return to the Indian Reservation and tell them what we have seen.[6]

He expressed eloquently the need and willingness of the Show Indians to adapt to a changing world.

Steele Mackaye had incorporated much of "The Drama of Civilization" into the show at Earl's Court. Symbolically, it represented the triumph of Anglo-American civilization over Native Americans. Buffalo Bill himself later echoed this theme in his autobiography. He remembered the pride he felt when sailing for England: pride in himself, his show, his country, and his civilization. He recalled the Indians who accompanied him as "that savage foe that had been compelled to submit to a conquering civilization and were now accompanying me in friendship, loyalty, and peace, five thousand miles from their homes, braving the dangers of the . . . great unknown sea, now no longer a tradition, but a reality." Indians and other rough riders combined in an exhibition "intended to prove to the center of the old world civilization that the vast region of the United States was finally and effectively settled by the English-speaking race."[7]

Indians, however, did not necessarily adopt the part of a conquered race. They might play one in the arena, in the mock defeats suffered at the hands of Buffalo Bill and his cowboy compatriots; but their words and actions do not appear to be those of a chastened and, therefore, wiser foe.

Indians had joined the shows for the money and the adventure. They received both in sufficiency. Black Elk (who appears on the contract under the name "Choice") remembered that during the dangerous ocean crossing, he had to remind himself that he was "there for adventure."[8] Rita Napier suggests that Black Elk enjoyed performing his part; but he disliked the roles played by the whites. She quotes with added emphasis from *Black Elk Speaks.* "I liked the part of the show we made, but *not* the part the Wasichu [whites] made."[9] Black Elk may very well have disliked

7 : "The Noble Red Shirt." Ogilasa *toured with Cody as "Chief of the Sioux." While in England in 1887, he became the most quoted member of Cody's troupe. By the Columbian Exposition (1893), he was the most famous Show Indian in the world. (Smithsonian Institution, National Anthropological Archives, Washington, D.C.)*

the whites playing warriors triumphant. He just as easily may have disliked all the riding, roping, wrestling of animals, and trick shooting of the principals in the show. Raymond DeMallie quotes Black Elk differently in this regard. The holy man comments about the show in New York the previous winter: "I enjoyed the Indian part of the shows that we put on here at Madison Square Garden, but I did not care much about the white people's parts."[10] How then could he revel in "playing" Indian if that part called for him constantly to be defeated? Perhaps his enjoyment came (as he alluded to it even in times of great danger) in the adventure of it all, in re-creating brave deeds, and in getting paid for it. In addition, he and the other Show Indians traveled, something they enjoyed, as they had never traveled before.

Show Indians became tourists as well as entertainers.[11] As one reporter observed, "some of Buffalo bill's [sic] Red Indians are 'doing' the sights of London. They have paid several visits to popular resorts, and despite their proverbial stoicism, they are as much attracted by the curiosities on view as the public are pleased by the ornate appearance of the visitors."[12] On another occasion, shortly after their arrival at Earl's Court, forty Sioux visited the Congregational Chapel at West Kensington, where they were seated in the transept. They enchanted the congregants by singing "Nearer My God to Thee" in Lakota. The Reverend Alfred Norris expressed his gladness that they had joined him in common worship. The Sioux repaid the compliment, with some in the party remarking through their translator that it made their hearts glad to be welcomed with considerable kindness and respect.[13]

Because many in the troupe had joined the Wild West show for the first time, Cody and company rehearsed the routines daily in preparation for the premier in early May. Visitors from London and environs flocked to the encampment where Cody permitted them to wander at will. The Indian village complete with canvas tipis proved to be, except for Buffalo Bill himself, the most popular attraction. Just as the tourists infested the grounds at Earl's Court, so also did the Indians wander about Kensington and greater London in their free time.

---

8 : Red Shirt, photographed at the arena in Earl's Court, West Kensington, during the jubilee spring of 1887. The painted canvas tipi has been erected on a mountain of dirt. The mountain, in turn, has been decorated with boulders, shrubbery and small trees to create an illusion of the rugged western landscape. Red Shirt wears a Ulysses S. Grant peace medal. (Buffalo Bill Historical Center, Cody, Wyoming)

RED SHIRT AND TEPEE.
Buffalo Bill's Wild West

ELLIOTT & FRY   Copyright.   55, BAKER STR, LONDON. W.

Show Indians, however, as Rita Napier observes, were tourists with a decidedly non-Western perspective on what they saw and experienced. Although they left few records of their own, considerable information can be taken from the reports on their behavior, especially when that behavior is viewed from the perspective of Lakota culture. Napier suggests that one can discern the Indians' well-bred politeness, frequently mistaken for arrogance, their pleasure at receiving esteem, and the spiritual vision that infused their language.[14]

Red Shirt and other Indians attended a performance of the actor Henry Irving's production of Goethe's *Faust* at the Lyceum Theater. The London *Times* reported that the Sioux were greatly frightened by its horror. Irving romped through his portrayal of Mephistopheles with malevolent glee. The actor himself described the scene at the Lyceum in the theatrical paper *Era:* it was a novelty "to see Indian chiefs in the full panoply of war-paint, holding the scalp-fringed banner in one hand and eating sugar plums with the other."[15] The Lyceum's manager seated Red Shirt and his companions in a place of honor, the royal box. This may have been a concoction of Irving and Cody to garner publicity for the soon-to-open show. Red Shirt and friends nevertheless accepted the deference accorded them with perfect aplomb. When asked what he thought about the play, Red Shirt answered that it seemed to him like a big dream.[16] The Sioux, who did not believe in a hell, took the fantastic scenes of Hades, according to their interpreter, "for what it was worth," a *Wasichu*'s dream.[17]

For persons familiar with visions and constant communication with spirits, Goethe's fantasy appeared quite normal if no less interesting. On another excursion in London, this time to Westminster Abbey, Red Shirt did receive a vision. This vision revealed a Lakota's perspective on the world of the English. He had been seeking, in his own way, to comprehend this alien world. He told the reporters who accompanied the party that "the Great Spirit speaks to me sometimes since I have been here." Red Shirt and companions, Black Elk among them, received knowledge and wisdom through dreams and visions. They might observe life around them wandering the streets and alleys of London; but understanding came through the spirit world that was itself a part of everyday life.[18] Red Shirt explained to the reporters:

> The white man['s] lodges for the Geat Spirit, whose pinnacles reach the sky, and which have stood for more seasons than the red man reckon, all strike me with a terrible wonder, and the Great Spirit speaks to me sometimes since I have been here. When I was in the Great Spirit

Lodge where the kings are buried . . . , I laid my face upon my hands. The words of the preacher I did not know but they sounded like the soft winds through a leafy forest and my eyelids were heavy. Then I heard soft music and sweet voices, and a great cloud came down towards me, and when it nearly reached me, it opened and I saw in a blaze of light the girls with wings and they beckoned me. And I was so certain that what I saw was true that I called out to my young men who were with me "Come and see what this is," and the young men replied, "You have been dreaming." But what I saw was true, for when I looked round the great lodge afterwards I saw on the walls the same girls with wings as I saw in my dreams. Our people will wonder at these things when we return to the Indian Reservation and tell them what we have seen.[19]

Reporters may have scoffed at his vision, believing instead that he had simply fallen asleep for a moment during the ritual. His compatriots knew, however, that he had been "dreaming." One did not have to sleep to receive visions. His friends did not share his dream; but that did not make the dream any less real for the other Sioux. To Red Shirt, the stone angels on the abbey's walls had come alive and beckoned him to a greater understanding. As he claimed repeatedly throughout his stay in England, he would share his experiences with his people once he returned home. They might also share his wonder.

Red Shirt also displayed his skill as a diplomat. Visits by royalty and aristocrats to Earl's Court provide examples of his tact. William Gladstone and his wife visited the show grounds on April 28. The former prime minister and current leader of the opposition in Parliament engaged Red Shirt in pleasantries about the weather and national heritage. Red Shirt found that, despite the rain, "he had not much to complain about so far."[20] *Ogilasa* charmed the "Grand Old Man" of British politics, so much in fact that Gladstone toasted the Sioux at a luncheon held in his honor. The London *Evening News* cited the "manly frankness of this splendid specimen of American backwoodsman" as the reason for Gladstone's keen interest.[21]

On first meeting Gladstone, it had taken Red Shirt a few moments to take the measure of the man. As they talked, and Red Shirt discerned the politician's oratorical skill, a trait he and other Sioux greatly admired, Gladstone persuaded Red Shirt that he was in the presence of an exalted man. The *Times* reported his summary of the meeting:

When I saw the great White Chief I thought he was a great man. When I heard him speak then I felt sure he was a great man. But the White

Chief is not as the big men of our tribes. He wore no plumes and no decorations. He had none of his young men [warriors] with him, and only that I heard him talk he would have been to me as other white men. But my brother [Mr. Gladstone] came to see me in my [lodge] as a friend, and I was glad to see the great White Chief, for though my tongue was tied in his presence my heart was full of friendship. After he went away they told me that half of this great nation of white men have adopted him as their chief. . . . If he were not both good and wise, so many young men of his nation would never have taken him for their leader.[22]

Red Shirt had become a celebrity second only to Buffalo Bill. His fame in the British press, already considerable after his reported colloquy with Gladstone, increased following his meeting with the Prince and Princess of Wales.

On May 5, four days before the grand opening, the Prince of Wales visited the grounds. His party included Princess Alexandra and their three daughters, Louise, Victoria, and Maude; Princess Alexandra's brother, Crown Prince Frederick of Denmark; the Comtesse de Paris; the Marquis of Lorne; and other nobles and their attendants.[23] The special performance was a smashing success. The royal party became excited from the moment the Indians, "yelling like fiends, galloped out from their ambuscade and swept around the enclosure like a whirlwind." The effect, according to Cody, was "instantaneous and electric. The prince rose from his seat and leaned eagerly over the front of the box, and the whole party seemed thrilled by the spectacle."[24] Afterward, the royal party toured the encampment.

Princess Alexandra welcomed Red Shirt and the Indians to England. *Ogilasa*, through his interpreter, replied with characteristic courtesy. "Tell the great chief's wife," he said, "that it gladdens my heart to hear words of welcome." Impressed, the prince gave Red Shirt, somewhat condescendingly, the contents of his cigar case. Had the prince offered *Ogilasa* a cigar, then it would have been equals sharing the pleasure of a good Havana. Otherwise, it was a little like giving candy to a child. All that was missing from the scene was for the prince to have patted Red Shirt on the head. The Sioux leader immediately distributed the cigars to his followers in a traditional display of Lakota generosity and good manners. He said to the prince, placing his hand on his breast, that it "made his heart glad that one so high above other men should visit him. Though his skin was red and the pale-faced chief's was white, their hearts were one."[25]

In an interview with a reporter for the Sheffield *Leader*, Red Shirt com-

9 : John Y. Nelson, driver of the Deadwood Stage in Buffalo Bill's Wild West, and his family. His eldest son, Yellow Horse, performed for many seasons in the show; and his youngest child, Rose, the smallest of the children in the photograph, proved to be a favorite of the Prince of Wales during Cody's London engagement of 1887. Rose later appeared professionally as Princess Blue Waters, carrying on the family show-business tradition well into the twentieth century. (Buffalo Bill Historical Center, Cody, Wyoming)

mented on the treatment of Indians in the United States. "The red man is changing every season," *Ogilasa* observed. Indians "of the next generation will not be the Indian[s] of the last. Our buffaloes are nearly all gone, the deer have entirely vanished, and the white man takes more and more of our land." But, he continued, "the United States government is good. True, it has taken away our land, and the white men have eaten up our deer and our buffalo, but the government now gives us food that we may not starve. They are educating our children and teaching them . . . to use farming implements. Our children will learn the white man's civilization and to live like him."[26]

Readers in either the United States or England, confident in the inexorability of progress, could applaud such a sentiment. The promoters of

10 : *Nate Salsbury, Buffalo Bill, John Burke, and others seated with Red Shirt, at the Wild West arena, Earls Court, London, 1887. (Buffalo Bill Historical Center, Cody, Wyoming)*

Cody's Wild West confidently reported the inestimable educational value for "blanket Indians" performing in the show. It is easy to understand why, at first glance, Red Shirt's testimony could be read as endorsement; but the chief never said that Indians would cease to be Indians if they learned to live as whites did. American Indians, just as other humans, changed from one generation to another. Indian identity, however, remained. Recognition of that eluded other Americans, and a significant number of Europeans, for generations.

Cody's Wild West opened to thunderous praise on May 9. The London press frothed with exaggerated expressions to describe the first public performance;[27] but the central event of Cody's first European tour was the queen's golden jubilee. Queen Victoria, according to John Burke, officially ended her public withdrawal since the death of the Prince Consort by visiting Earl's Court two days later for a command performance.[28] Black Elk left an intriguing eyewitness account of the jubilee from an Oglala perspective. When Queen Victoria visited Earl's Court on May 12, Black Elk remembered that "one day we were told that Majesty was coming. I did not know what that was at first, but I learned afterward.

It was Grandmother England . . . who owned Grandmother's Land where we lived awhile after the Wasichus murdered Crazy Horse."[29] About the performance, Black Elk reminisced:

> In the show we had to shoot at times, but this time we were not allowed to shoot. We danced the Omaha grass dance then. I was one of the five dancers at this dance. We stood right in front of Grandmother England. I was a boy now and so I was a pretty good dancer. We danced the best we knew how. I was limber at this time and I could dance many ways.
>
> After the show was over they put all of us Indians in a row according to size. I was next to the youngest boys and girls. Then Grandmother England came out and shook hands with us. She made a speech, saying that she was seventy-five years old. She said: "All over the world I have seen all kinds of people, and I have seen all kinds of countries too and I've heard about America as being a great country. Also I have heard about some people that were in America and I heard that they called them American Indians. Now I have seen them today. America is a good country and I have seen all kinds of people, but today I have seen the best looking people—the Indians. I am very glad to see them. If I owned you Indians, you good-looking people, I would never take you around in a show like this. You have a Grandfather over there who takes care of you . . . , but he shouldn't allow this, for he owns you, for the white people to take you around as beasts to show to the people.[30]

Red Shirt, on the other hand, remarked that he was pleased that the queen, whom he called "Great White Mother," came to visit the Indians without her warriors around her. When introduced to Victoria, Red Shirt said that "I have come many thousands [of] miles to see you. Now that I have seen you, my heart is glad." At this display of politeness, according to a reporter for *The Graphic*, the queen only nodded.[31]

Rita Napier has examined the exhibition in Kensington and a subsequent command performance that took place at Windsor Castle. She notes the poetry in Black Elk's description, but describes his political naivete. The Oglala holy man was a person searching for salvation for his "defeated and disunified people," and so the queen's solicitude gratified him. Perceptive as he was, Black Elk missed the subtleties of the phrase "If you belonged to me . . ." Napier concludes that he was not aware that Queen Victoria and the other nobles in her entourage who welcomed the Sioux with such courtesy and affability probably did so because the Indians were part of a great public spectacle. Also, Black Elk could not have known that Queen Victoria, at that very moment, presided over an empire in which native people of Africa, India, and Asia were treated very much like the colonized Indians in the United States.[32]

Black Elk may be forgiven if, in the years before he recounted his experiences to John G. Neihardt, he failed to remember the queen's exact words. The events of the day may have blurred. One can easily imagine Queen Victoria talking to the Indians and using such words as "If I owned you Indians" or "If you belonged to me." Her jubilee coincided with the glory years of empire. Indeed, many people of darker color and exotic culture "belonged" to the diminutive monarch. Would she, however, have addressed the Sioux performers in such a fashion? When introduced to Red Shirt, the recognized leader of the Indian contingent, she spoke no words; but with Black Elk's remembrance, there is genuine warmth in her comments, and this from a person who, until only recently, had remained aloof and withdrawn from her own subjects. Plenty of commentators back in the United States, and contemporary with Black Elk's travels with the show—missionaries, reformers, and congressmen—had complained about the Indians being displayed as "beasts" or "animals." Black Elk would have known this. Queen Victoria, in Black Elk's memory, became the ruler who, unlike so many *Wasichus* of the ruling class, appeared friendly and solicitous. In Neihardt's editing of Black Elk's remembrances, she becomes the foil for the unfeeling Great Father. She is "Grandmother England," who had once offered Black Elk and other Lakotas sanctuary in "Grandmother's Land" (Canada) from the Great Father's wrath following Custer's defeat and death. Neihardt has Black Elk muse, "Maybe if she had been our Grandmother, it would have been better for our people."[33] And what did the queen have to say about her visit to Earl's Court?

Upon her return to Windsor Castle, the queen recorded in her journal the events of the day:

> We sat in a box in a large semi circle. It is an amphitheatre with a large open space, all the seats being under cover. All the different people, wild, painted Red Indians from America, on their wild bare backed horses, of different tribes,—cow boys, Mexicans, &c., all came tearing round at full speed, shrieking & screaming, which had the weirdest effect. An attack on a coach & on a ranch, with an immense deal of firing, was most exciting, so was the buffalo hunt, & the bucking ponies, that were almost impossible to sit. The cow boys, are a fine looking people, but the painted Indians, with their feathers, & wild dress (very little of it) were rather alarming looking, & they have cruel faces. . . . Their War Dance, to a wild drum & pipe, was quite fearful, with all their con-

torsions [*sic*] & shrieks, & they came so close. "Red Shirt" the Chief of the Sioux tribe, was presented to me & so were the squaws, with their papooses (children), who shook hands with me.[34]

With their cruel faces and nakedness, one can just as easily imagine the queen relieved to find that these people "belonged" to somebody else.

Queen Victoria saw the exhibition again by special arrangement on June 22. The Lord High Chamberlain had informed the troupe of the queen's royal command to perform the Wild West at Windsor castle, twenty-two miles from London. At Windsor station, the Show Indians formed a double file and walked through the village. On the way, Rocky Bear espied an American flag about three inches wide and torn from some sort of paper package. He picked it off the ground, folded over the ragged edges, and slipped it on his buckskin shirt. "He wore the flag at the reception at the castle and back to his teepee in Earl's Court," Sergeant Bates recalled, "and was as proud of his national emblem as a freshly commissioned 2d Lieutenant."[35] The queen watched from the castle's East Terrace as the troupe performed below and at easy distance.[36] Cowboys and Indians regaled European royalty who had gathered for the formal celebration of the jubilee; but the show performed alike for royalty and commoners. From May until October thirty thousand to forty thousand people daily crowded the encampment and packed the arena at Earl's Court. Buffalo Bill and his compatriots became the toast of London; and when they went on to Birmingham, Manchester, and Hull, they repeated their successes. The show's triumph that season has become the stuff of legend. It is a story that has been told by a number of chroniclers and historians;[37] but what of the Indians who shared in the enterprise, if not the lion's portion of praise?

One historian has suggested that because of the obvious pleasure first experienced by the English in the presence of "Red" Indians in London in 1887, and subsequently by other Europeans once the Wild West toured the continent, Buffalo Bill and his partners developed a more benevolent attitude toward Indians as expressed in the show's programs.[38] Actually, this occurred at least by the time the show performed at Erastina months before the jubilee engagement. That is not to say, however, that Cody and company were not quick to take advantage of unprecedented European public interest in American Indians. John Burke never let a promotional opportunity escape his teeming brain and heavy hand; but whereas in New York, Indian visits to churches, museums, newspapers, and statehouses pointed up the educational value of the shows for the Show Indians, in

WA-KA-CHA-SHA (RED ROSE),

The Girl-pet of the Sioux.

BUFFALO BILL'S WILD WEST.

London and environs the visits of Indians were planned to whet the public's appetite for more.

Even such an accomplished promoter as Burke outdid himself when Red Shirt, Fly Above, and Little Bull attended the weekly house dinner of the Savage Club that met at the Savoy. Back in the States, the newspapers would tell with obvious satisfaction about the "Savages at the Savage Club."[39] In London, the same humor obtained, but many people reading about the visit in their newspapers would have appreciated the irony. The literary club was named for the poet Richard Savage.[40] On the occasion of the visit, both Buffalo Bill and Red Shirt addressed the members. Speaking in Lakota, Red Shirt hailed the London Savages as brothers, thanked them for the food, and promised to repay their generosity by sending them a pipe from his home to hang on their dining-room wall.[41]

Indians in Parliament's gallery made good press copy. At the House of Lords, when asked by Baron Henry DeWorms what he thought about the August body of nobles and commoners, Red Shirt replied, Not much! Laws, as he observed about his own country—not the Dakotas but the United States—passed through Congress more quickly. A diplomat doubtlessly would have dissembled a little. Not Red Shirt. Those who heard him that day roared their hearty approval and pronounced him a good fellow. His honesty, rather than his quaintness, accounted for his appeal.[42]

Indians so enchanted Londoners that it would be impossible to determine what excited them more about their visits to Earl's Court—a tour of the Indian encampment or the show itself. This is certainly reflected in the newspaper accounts of reporters' visits to the American Exhibition, and still later when the Wild West played in three other English cities. Even when the reporters adopted a mildly derisive tone, more often than not they used the customs of the Indians to tweak the manners of certain Britons. As one music-hall songwriter put it, playing up the image of the "wild" west end of London:

> They're a fiery lot of Indians as I think you'll all agree,
> And to meet 'em on the war-path might not prove a Jubilee;
> But a fiercer lot of savages we very often see
> In the Wild, Wild West of London. [second chorus]

---

11 : Another photograph of Rose Nelson, or Wakachasha, *described in couriers and newspaper accounts as the "Girl-pet of the Sioux." (Buffalo Bill Historical Center, Cody, Wyoming)*

They're a racy lot of beauties as I think you'll all agree
And I heard a British matron say their style was much too free;
But much trickier little maidens, in their war-paint we can see,
In the Wild, Wild West of London. [fourth chorus][43]

Other writers sang the praises of the show and its performers, and far more directly.

In Manchester, for example, a reporter describing the December 17 opening of the show at the racecourse found the "new form of entertainment, at once exhilarating, instructive, and delightful." In the opening parade, audiences could observe the "noble Red Shirt, conspicuous by the luxuriance of his feathery adornment, [who] led his gorgeous warriors through mazy evolutions." Perceptions of the audiences had obviously changed with the country. In the summer of 1885, when Sitting Bull toured with Cody, supposedly men hissed and "ladies swooned." Two years later and thousands of miles away, a reporter could write that "these Indians keenly enjoy their mimic warfare. They rush into it with such a zest and with such fearless skill in horsemanship that the audience is not only amused, but almost carried away with the realism of the scene." In Manchester this time, however, the mock attack by the Indians hardly represented the "big sensation [as] in London. . . . It was exciting enough on Saturday; but it was hardly the supreme sensation of the entertainment." He reserved that dispensation for the Show Indians themselves.[44]

Cody's Wild West played dates for the remainder of the winter and into the spring of 1888. The show's final performance in England took place in Hull in Yorkshire on May 5. The following morning at three o'clock, the troupe set sail for home, aboard the *Persian Monarch*. The weary travelers arrived to wild applause at Staten Island, New York, at daybreak on May 20. Some of the Show Indians boarded a train for the Great Sioux Reservation. Others, however, were far from done with performing for cheering crowds. Almost at once, the show opened again at Erastina. The "Hero of Two Continents," or so the New York *Evening Telegram* described Buffalo Bill, had come home.[45] So had his Indian companions.

Cody's triumphant tour of England with the Wild West has been viewed by historians as a symbolic coming of age for the republic torn from the mother country by revolution a century before. They quote Buffalo Bill himself, who sounded this theme. Cody explained that his tour announced to the Old World that the vast region of the United States had been finally and effectively settled by the English-speaking race. Symbolically, instead of a prodigal son returning home and thereby admitting failure in the larger world beyond his sire's domain, it was a proud and profane son announcing to a parent that he had conquered new worlds and had come home only to display his trophies. For the Show Indians, their esteem in England raised their status from caricatures to persons of character. In fact, they may have been conquered in every way except character; and that realization would have different meanings on either side of the Big Water.

4

REFORMERS AND THE IMAGE OF THE SHOW INDIAN

"Teach him to labor for his own support."

It is no coincidence that protests against the employment of Indians in Wild West shows mounted in the wake of Buffalo Bill's English triumph. Even before Buffalo Bill began to take Indians abroad, criticism increased. This is explained, in part, by significant changes in federal Indian policy.

The same winter in which Indians in Buffalo Bill's employ entertained the crowds at Erastina, Congress passed the General Allotment Act, which brought to fulfillment the dreams of reformers first envisioned in the post-Civil War decade. The story is a familiar one for students of American Indian history.

After the Civil War, a new idea seemed to take hold concerning the West. Whereas once it had appeared to be limitless, perhaps needing centuries of growth and development by hardy pioneers, now it seemed a bounded land, a finite resource. Indians who had been pushed and prodded to the permanent Indian frontier were found once again to occupy land judged desirable by other Americans. Land claimed by the tribes seemed to be in excess of their individual needs. As warfare subsided between Indians and the frontier constabulary army of the United States, questions arose among humanitarians about how best to solve the Indian problem. Commissioner Hiram Price, a prominent Methodist layman, established in October 1881 an agenda for some time to come. "The greatest kindness the government can bestow upon the Indian," the commissioner wrote in his annual report that year, "is to teach him to labor for his own support." All those people who had studied the situation had learned most forcefully the lesson of three hundred years of confrontation with savagery: "Savage and civilized life cannot live and prosper on the same ground. One of the two must die."[1]

Extermination was not, however, the solution to the vexing puzzle. Indians nevertheless would cease to be Indians, once their cultures had been transformed. To "domesticate and civilize Wild Indians," Price proclaimed, "is a noble work, the accomplishment of which should be a crown of glory to any nation." To fashion such a diadem, the nation must first refashion the way Indians used their lands. Price concluded:

I am very decidedly of [the] opinion that ultimate and final success never can be reached without adding to all other means and appliances the location of each [Indian] family, or adult Indian who has no family, on a certain number of acres of land which they may call their own and hold by a title as good and strong as a United States patent can make it. Let it be inalienable for, say, twenty years; give the Indian teams, implements, and tools amply sufficient for farming purposes; give him seed, food, and clothes for at least one year; in short, give him every facility for making a comfortable living, and then *compel* him to depend upon his own exertions for a livelihood.

Implementing such a policy would make Indians a "blessing instead of a curse" to themselves and their country.[2]

Price and his allies, like-minded men and women of conscience and conviction, would arouse public sentiment to persuade Congress to act. Convinced of the superiority of their own culture, and unable to see value in Indian cultures aside from a common humanity and worthiness to be saved, reformers organized themselves into associations to agitate on behalf of Indian-policy reform.

Almost simultaneously, as Francis Paul Prucha explains, there appeared a number of organizations that took up the challenge of Indian reform. Concerned over white encroachment into Indian Territory, a group of Philadelphia women eventually established the Women's National Indian Association to petition Congress for redress. In time, women throughout the country organized over eighty state and local chapters, largely under church sponsorship. In 1882, a number of prominent men in Philadelphia formed the Indian Rights Association. The influential IRA focused its efforts on discovering practical methods to correct injustices to particular Indian groups. It would then lobby the national government for general legislation that would attempt to provide solutions to the Indian problem. These associations worked closely with the Board of Indian Commissioners, first established during President Grant's administration to end fraud in the disbursement of government annuities to Indians. The board, made up of solidly middle-class men urged on by philanthropy, continued to serve as a clearinghouse for humanitarian concern. It met annually in Washington; and its individual members also met more frequently with religious missionaries and other groups interested in Indian welfare.[3]

In 1883, Albert K. Smiley, member of the Board of Indian Commissioners and part owner with his brothers of the Lake Mohonk Lodge in upstate New York, invited disparate groups to meet with board members in more leisurely surroundings at the resort. These annual October convocations became the Lake Mohonk Conference of the Friends of the Indian. The good people of Lake Mohonk thus defined Native Americans in the singular. The solutions to the "Indian Problem" offered by the reformers lacked subtlety when it came to making distinctions among the cultures.[4] The conferences became a powerful influence in the formulation of Indian policy. People of stature, including senators, congressmen, and their wives, gathered together with representatives of the separate groups and created a platform for the next year. They would mold public opinion and apply political pressure so as to see the proposals into law.[5]

Confidence in their rectitude filled the sincere men and women of the Lake Mohonk conferences with fierce purpose. Their Christianity grew muscular through its frequent exercise against iniquity and sloth. They placed their faith in the transformation of Indians from savages to citizens by three means: first, to break up tribal relations and the reservations that sustained them, and to place individual Indians on 160-acre homesteads; second, to make Indians citizens and therefore subject to and beneficiaries of the laws of the states, the territories, and the nation in which they lived; and third, to make available a government educational system designed to create self-reliance and self-sufficiency. Education would be provided for adults, if they were willing to submit, and their children regardless of either's wishes.[6]

In February 1887, Congress finally created the legislation called for by Commissioner Price and others. The General Allotment Act (Dawes Act) put into effect the program for civilizing Indians. Reservations, at the president's discretion, would be subdivided and the surplus land sold to homesteaders. The proceeds from such sales would fund a greatly expanded education program for the allotted tribe. "Detribalized" Indians would become citizens. The men presumably could vote. After twenty-five years, the allottee would receive clear title to the land. The principal concern for Indian-policy reformers after the passage of the Dawes Act was that nothing must interfere with its orderly implementation.

Beginning with the first Cody and Carver performance in Omaha, in 1883, Wild West shows presented an image of the Indians judged by reformers and their allies in the Indian service as unsuitable for public consumption. Indian-policy reformers also denounced the exhibitions as contrary to the best interests of the Indians. Arguing that the shows encouraged unsettled habits and brought Indians into contact with disreputable characters, reformers lobbied the Bureau to ban Indian participation in the shows. The government, however, could not legally interfere. Following the Standing Bear decision of 1879, peaceable Indians on reservations were free to come and go as they pleased.[7] The Indian Bureau possessed no statutory authority to force Indians to stay on their reservations. Special legislation would be required of Congress to overturn the legal principle; but Congress had more pressing concerns, even for Indians. Yet even if Indian participation in the shows could not be banned on principle without the necessary legislation, it could nevertheless be significantly reduced.

Starting in the winter of 1886, the Indian Bureau began to regulate Indian employment in the shows. It required owners to place their Indian employees under contract. Employers had to provide their Indians with adequate food, shelter, and medical care; to pay "fair and reasonable" salaries; to hire chaplains and interpreters to accompany the performers; and to return the Show Indians to their reservations at the close of their contracts. Violation of the contract carried the penalty of forfeiture of surety bond (usually ten to twenty thousand dollars, depending upon the number of Indians) and the inability again to employ Indians.[8] No Wild West show ever forfeited its bond as a punitive measure.[9] There were, however, numerous attempts by reformers to marshal enough evidence of misdeeds to force the commissioner's hand. Furthermore, proving allegations of mistreatment and exploitation might even lead Congress to ban Indian employment in the shows altogether.

Accusations against the shows that reached the Interior Department and the Indian Bureau caused the various secretaries and commissioners to be concerned down to the 1920s about the shows' effects on assimilationist programs, on the image of Indians in the public mind, and on the bureaucrats' careers should the reformers once decide that they were also part of the problem. Although the Indians' physical welfare remained a paramount concern of these humanitarians, the major issue revolved around the question of the image of the Indian. Reformers claimed that the shows played up the Indians' savagery by celebrating their martial spirit. The days of freely roving bands of Indians had ended. The natives had been sufficiently disciplined by the army so that they no longer posed a general threat to lives and property. Reformers believed that Indians would soon embrace Euroamerican views of civilization. Thus, the image that they hoped to create was one of an assimilated Indian who came into being through allotment of reservation lands, education, and industry. Ironically, the approach of Cody's Wild West organization was not unlike that of the reformers: both favored assimilation of the first Americans. Indeed, Buffalo Bill continually emphasized that Indians should adapt to a modern world. So did the Show Indians themselves. Red Shirt, for example, explained to an English reporter during the jubilee tour that "the red man is changing every season. Indians of the next generation will not be the Indian[s] of the last. . . . Our children will learn the white man's civilization and to live like him."[10] Cody, promoting *Ogilasa* as a representative of his race, claimed that Indians' innate virtues would make them as honorable in their citizenship as they had been in their struggles to preserve their cultures.

Wild West shows created vivid images of Indians—as in their ambushes on wagon trains or attacks on settlers' cabins—which persist to this day; but it was never Cody's intention to offer the public only this history lesson. Cody consciously stressed the educational value of his show for both the public and the Indian performers. Part of his reasoning was undoubtedly due to his desire to deflect criticism by reformers. The Indians whom he employed were to be admired and understood. Let the people be con-

12 : "Immigrant Act." Sioux attack emigrant wagons in the 101 Ranch show, Kansas City, 1930. This feature had been a regular part of Wild West shows, in one version or another, since the 1880s. (E. M. Botsford Papers, Southwest Collection, Texas Tech University, Lubbock)

cerned instead for Indians forced by the government to farm or run cattle on marginal lands with only meager assistance to fall back on should crops fail or cattle sicken and die. Cody argued that traveling would enable the Show Indians to appreciate the inevitability of progress as represented in the numbers, achievements, and technology of "the white race." Further, when they returned to their reservations, Show Indians would serve their people as advocates for change. Cody never denounced the right of Indians to retain their cultural and ethnic identities. Those unique characteristics would become apparent to audiences once they observed Indians' skills in the arena.

Perhaps conscious of some of the criticisms from reformers and missionaries, Cody began to forward to the Interior Department, as early as 1886, unsolicited endorsements. Later, as criticism intensified, he solicited praise from powerful and influential friends. The earliest on record came in the summer of 1886 from the Reverend J. Robinson, a missionary at Pine Ridge agency. As Cody explained to Secretary Lamar, he had sent the Sioux home for a few weeks and then, "if you [find] no objection, to bring them back with me."[11] Reverend Robinson reported that the Indians arrived back at Pine Ridge "safe and sound" on September 30,

. . . and everybody was surprised & pleased to see how finely they looked. I have been teasing some of them telling them that they did not want to see their wives & families but only wanted to go back to the Wild West.

From Rev. Mr. Maul's letter & from what some of the boys have told me since their return I feel satisfied that I can safely trust my Christian Indians to your care. Indeed I must confess that for morals & good behavior the baptized boys (baptized a few weeks before they left here) have done a great deal better while away with you than their comrades who remained here have done. While their work was "play" & the amusing of others yet even [the] weakest minded of them feels himself a great deal less of a monkey (parties claim that your show makes monkies [sic] of Indians) than he did before he left here. And men like Rocky Bear have added many fold more to their former abilities & influence with this people.[12]

The idea that Indians improved themselves by going with Buffalo Bill would become more important as charges to the contrary began to multiply at the Indian Office.

Indians demeaning or making "monkeys" of themselves represented a portion of the broadside directed against Cody's Wild West by Congressman James. With the shift in policy signaled by passage of the Dawes Act, commissioners began to concern themselves more with images. In March 1887, Commissioner Atkins, in direct violation of the spirit and the letter of the Standing Bear decision, informed his agents that taking Indians from reservations for exhibition without the formal consent of the government was strictly prohibited. The commissioner ordered his agents to convey the contents of his letter to the Indians. Experience had persuaded Atkins that when "irresponsible persons" enticed Indians away for exhibition or other purposes, they sometimes abandoned them without clothing, subsistence or the means of returning to their reservations. "When the Great Father thinks it best for Indians to leave their reservations," he wrote, "he will grant them permission and notify their Agent."[13] Atkins admonished his agents to keep close watch.

A few spectacular instances of abandonment fueled the other pressing issue, mistreatment of Indians. Agent Hugh Gallagher at Pine Ridge reported one of the more important cases in molding attitudes at the Bureau. In December 1886, he informed Commissioner Atkins that all but two of his charges, *Hampa Naspa* (Wet Moccasin, also known as Whirlwind) and Eagle Horse, had arrived back at the Great Sioux Reservation.[14] They and the other Sioux had been taken from the reservation without permission. Although their names appeared on the return list provided by F. H. Partridge, an American agent for European circuses, *Hampa* and Eagle Horse had disappeared.

Months later, in March 1887, at the request of an Oglala named White Eyes, Gallagher next asked the commissioner to enlist the assistance of the State Department in locating a third missing Indian who had apparently accompanied Partridge to Europe. White Eyes's son Yellow Blanket was, according to some of the returned Show Indians, being held against his will in Christiana, Norway. The State Department investigated. United States ministers and consuls scattered throughout Europe made inquiries. A year and seven months later, the State Department informed the commissioner of the results of the investigation. It was discovered that Yellow Blanket, *Hampa*, and Eagle Horse (or "Horn" as he was sometimes listed) had joined the Circus Krembser in Kiel, Germany, during the summer of 1887. Next, *Hampa* and Eagle Horse, without Yellow Blanket, performed in Kiev, Russia, during July 1888. In October, the secretary of state received information—which he forwarded to Commissioner John Oberly, who had replaced Atkins the month before—that both Sioux had been admitted to an infirmary in Jitomir, Russia. *Hampa* and Eagle Horse appeared "quite ill and in destitute circumstances." Yellow Blanket still could not be found. Oberly passed the information along to Agent Gallagher and assured him that all measures were being taken to locate and return the prodigals to their homes.[15]

Just before Christmas 1888, the Indian Bureau forwarded information recently obtained from the vice-consul at Hamburg, Germany. Eagle Horse, the report to Gallagher stated, had died of tuberculosis in Lodz, Poland, and had been buried there in the Protestant cemetery. The search for *Hampa* and Yellow Blanket continued. Finally, in April 1889, it ended. Robert V. Belt, acting commissioner of Indian affairs in the newly inaugurated Harrison administration, reported to Gallagher that Eagle Horse, buried in Poland, was actually the missing Yellow Blanket. It seemed that the clever proprietors of the Circus Krembser had given Yellow Blanket what they considered to be a more "Indian-like" name and that F. H. Partridge had failed to record that information. *Hampa* had also been found. As of March 1889, he was living in Odessa on the Black Sea, performing in a circus, and appearing "quite alive, well paid and seemingly content." The United States consul at Odessa assured the Bureau, through the State Department, that *Hampa* expressed no desire to return to the United States.[16] *Hampa* then disappeared from the record for more than twenty years. He surfaced briefly in the summer of 1909, when sources in the State Department reported that he was being held against his will in London. Upon further investigation, however, it was discovered that he had been working continuously for various circuses throughout Europe and, according to the United States consul at Leipzig, "most emphatically . . . does not want to return to . . . the United States."[17] Thereafter, *Hampa* disappears from the record. The odyssey of Yellow Blanket and *Hampa* became a testimonial supposedly to neglect. The Interior Department began to monitor contracts more closely; reformers began to report incidents to the commissioner; and agents began to watch over the comings and goings of their charges.

Another common theme that appears in Bureau correspondence is the necessity to impress upon Indians the consequences of their irresponsibility. Although the reformers' arguments against the shows are better known, what is less appreciated is that the particular *form* of the show—that of a nomadic circus—only confirmed for them and certain members of the Indian service what they regarded as the worst tendencies of the plains tribes. Where Indians had once, in freedom, seasonally crisscrossed the prairies and plains in search of bison herds, now they traveled oceans and continents in search of audiences. And the company they kept! Out from under the watchful eyes of their agents, Indians were again free to do as they pleased. Polite, middle-class reformers already harbored deep anxiety toward the unsettled gypsy life of traveling entertainers. Constraints that bound others to civilized society's conventions failed to subdue show people. Unless they were compelled to stay home, Show Indians might be lost to assimilation, the reformers reasoned. They might never be tamed and then tethered by Euroamerican customs. Worse still, once returned to their reservations they might contaminate their people with unhealthy ideas or worse. Ruined lives followed upon the employment of Indians in the shows.

In September 1888, an anonymous correspondent living near Pine Ridge agency and calling himself "a Friend to the Indians" wrote the commissioner that half of the Indians who toured with Cody became infected with gonorrhea.[18] Commissioner Oberly asked Agent Gallagher to investigate. By December, Gallagher had completed his inquiries. He had experienced some difficulty in determining the extent of venereal disease on the reservation attributable to the Show Indians "as every precaution was taken by those affected . . . against promoting the fact to be made known." Although no direct evidence could be established linking a recent outbreak, circumstances suggested otherwise. Two of three recent returnees had died, presumably from venereal disease. Prior to their return, no cases of syphilis had been reported by the agency physician; after their return, "several cases of syphilis, among both men and women, have developed." If that were not enough, according to Gallagher, they had returned to the reservation penniless. The majority of Show Indians contracted to Cody were still absent from the reserve; yet in that time the agent had never witnessed a dollar of wages sent home to their kin. Because Cody's Wild West provided them with room and board, "might it not, therefore, be that they made a worse use of their money than if they had indulged in an occasional spree and squandered their money foolishly in drinking carrousels?"[19] Questions and coincidences abounded, but answers proved to be rare.

Granting formal permission to such enterprises as Cody's Wild West for the employment of Indians seemed inconsistent with the larger aim of assimilation then being advocated by the Indian Bureau. Having pledged itself to advancement through education, Christianity, and agriculture, it seemed inappropriate, as far as reformers were concerned, for the Bureau to allow Indians to work for shows that glorified their "heathenish ways." Commissioner Oberly, a man whose reputation for integrity went unquestioned among reformers, explained in 1889 the philosophical lines of opposition to Wild West shows:

> The effect of traveling all over the country among, and associated with, the class of people usually accompanying Shows, Circuses and Exhibitions, attended by all the immoral and unchristianizing surroundings incident to such a life, is not only most demoralizing to the present and future welfare of the Indian, but it creates a roaming and unsettled disposition and educates him in a manner entirely foreign and antagonistic to that which has been and now is the policy of the Government.[20]

The cause of their civilization would be better served, the commissioner believed, if Indians would stay on their reservations and apply themselves to making their homesteads habitable. The problem, however, was how to make them behave.

Unlike his predecessors and descendants down to the 1920s at the Bureau, and despite his own aversion to the shows, Commissioner Oberly understood that Indians nevertheless had rights which, according to his biographer, "were not subject to the whim of federal officials." He may have disliked the influence of Wild West and other exhibitions on Indians; but he was loath to forbid Indians to participate if they wished to do so.[21] Rather, the commissioner devoted his attention to overseeing more closely the granting of contracts.

In February 1889, Secretary Vilas authorized a change in Bureau procedures. Thereafter, each Indian would sign an individual contract with the show, he informed Oberly,

> specifying fully all that is to be done by him, and all that is to be done for him, his care and keeping, and this should be approved by the Agent and your Office before the Indian leaves the reservation. I think it would be well for you to prepare a form for such a contract, and see that it contains all such provisions as are requisite to properly secure the welfare of these people, in sickness and in health, morally and physically, and their return to the reservation. Especial attention should be given to the case of minors, if any such are sought for or permitted to go.[22]

Oberly accordingly drew up a standard agreement form and submitted it to the agents. Individual contracts became accepted procedure at the Bureau, beginning with the request by Adam Forepaugh of Philadelphia to employ twenty-five Sioux in Forepaugh's All New Feature Show.[23]

Under the provisions of this "Forepaugh Agreement," as it came to be called, Show Indians signed on with Dr. William Frank Carver's Wild America (twenty-five Sioux) for a tour of Europe and the Oklahoma Historical Exhibition Company (twenty-four Sioux, Pawnees, Shawnees, and Kaws) for a tour of the United States. Owing perhaps to the number of Indians he employed (over one hundred Sioux in 1889 alone), Cody was permitted to sign a single contract—though all other provisions of the Forepaugh Agreement remained in force. Eventually, even Buffalo Bill came to issue individual contracts regardless of the number of Indians employed.[24] The commissioner also ordered each company to hire a chaperon for the Indians. His name had to be submitted in advance for approval along with affidavits about his character.[25] The secretary of the interior, in the case of the Oklahoma Historical Exhibition Company, insisted that the person be "a white man." Chaperons had to report under oath about every two weeks to the commissioner describing the conditions of the Indians.[26]

Commissioner Oberly made clear in the Forepaugh Agreement that agents must oversee the individual contracts; that no Indian be unwillingly taken away from the reservation; and that "each Indian engaging himself or herself, clearly and fully understands and agrees to the terms of employment."[27] Only after the commissioner had been satisfied that all the provisions of the agreement had been met, would he then grant the Indians permission to leave the reservation. As Secretary Noble explained to the commissioner, the Interior "department in these matters exercises only its guardianship and to such extent as the law allows; and while it does not intend to encourage such employment of Indians, it will endeavor to protect them as fully as possible."[28]

Employment of Indians by unauthorized shows proved to be particularly troublesome. The worst offender appears to have been the Kickapoo Medicine Company. The company originated in a partnership in 1881 between Texas Charlie Bigelow and Colonel John Healy to sell, among other cures, Indian Sagwa, a "blood-liver renovator" powered by alcohol. The company traded on eastern fascination with the American West. Although no Kickapoos ever traveled with the show, Iroquois, Pawnees, and Sioux did, to lend an air of authenticity to the thirty itinerant company groups traveling in the East.[29]

In the spring of 1889, representatives of the patent medicine company scoured the Sioux agencies looking for potential employees. At Pine Ridge alone, Agent Gallagher reported that sixty-two Oglalas had signed up; but eventually the company hoped to employ fully two hundred. When the commissioner learned of this, he instructed Gallagher to call a council of Indians and inform them that their leaving the reservation without permission greatly displeased him. Furthermore, the commissioner would regard such action as open defiance of the regulations adopted by the Bureau for their welfare, protection, and "the good of the Indian service."[30]

No adequate protection could be provided, the commissioner believed, while Indians remained off the reservation and in the charge of persons having no authority to employ them or giving no proper guarantees for their compensation and care. Agents should advise Indians that it was degrading to travel around the country advertising for the Kickapoo Medicine Company. Without the friendly care and protection of the government, they would be at the mercy of employers whose greed nowhere equaled their concern for employees' health and morals. Henceforth, no Indians would be allowed to leave the reservation without proper authority.[31] The warning apparently went unheeded. Another fifty-three Oglalas joined the company.[32] The number of Sioux who traveled that year with the Kickapoo Medicine Company is unknown. Other Sioux agents, perhaps not wishing to offend the commissioner, did not inform the Indian Office, despite the occasional request for information, about the number of Indians absent.[33]

13 : Samuel Lone Bear, ca. 1898. Lone Bear wears a scarf around his neck, a fabric shirt, a fully beaded vest, arm bands, a bone hairpipe breastplate, and a blanket with bead work wrapped around his lower torso. The photograph was inscribed "Gertrude Häsebier, photographer." (Buffalo Bill Historical Center, Cody, Wyoming)

Reformers chided Oberly for his apostasy. Stung by criticism during his last months in office that he had failed to protect his charges, the commissioner had to remind reformers that peaceable Indians had every right to come and go as they wished. If they subscribed to allotment under the Dawes Act, they could, therefore, be justly regarded as citizens. In a letter to Senator Henry L. Dawes of Massachusetts, sponsor of the legislation upon which Bureau programs were then based, Oberly remarked that, as commissioner, he could not "restrain the liberty of the law abiding person or citizen because in [my] opinion or the opinion of someone else that person or citizen will make an injudicious use of his liberty."[34] Oberly, as Francis Paul Prucha writes, recognized the reformers' dilemma. They agitated against government action when they thought it was oppressive or inequitable, and yet they advocated government force when they considered such action to be in the Indians' best interest.[35]

By the early summer of 1889 a new commissioner had arrived in Washington. Thomas Jefferson Morgan was not content simply to protect Indians from unscrupulous and unauthorized employers. Morgan, a Baptist minister and educator, entertained few doubts about his mission. Unlike Oberly, he was prepared to use the coercive powers of his office—which were never that great to begin with—regardless of whether his actions violated individual rights.

Morgan began to attack Indian employment in Wild West shows in public and in print. He could do nothing about the contracts already in force; but he could focus considerable attention on the seeming failures to meet the obligations specified in the contracts. He may not have possessed the statutory authority to prohibit Indians from joining the shows; but he could act as if he did. At the first opportunity he had to review a contract, he in effect turned it down. An application had been made by the St. Joseph (Mo.) Exposition authorities to hire Indian participants. The commissioner placed as a condition of the contract that "civilized Indians" also be engaged so that "the best phase of Indian civilization may be shown." Apparently, the St. Joseph Exposition Company rejected the provision. Morgan used the occasion of an interview with a newspaper reporter, about the recently completed negotiations of the Crook Commission[36] to the Sioux, to explain further that he "was averse to allowing Indians in a savage state to be made an object of attraction at expositions."[37] He told the reporter that "when the lowest type of Indian, with his war dances, paint and blanket is exhibited the public mind accepts him as typical of the Indians of today. This . . . is misleading."[38]

To discourage Indians from joining Wild West shows, Morgan threatened aspiring showmen with the loss of their allotments, annuities, and tribal status. He likewise threatened entrepreneurs with the loss of their bonds should they fail to uphold the letter of their agreements with the government.

His intentions for the Indians become more apparent when one examines his first annual report, with its ringing declaration in favor of forced assimilation. In his cover letter to the secretary of the interior, Morgan wrote that: (1) the anomalous position of Indians in the United States must of necessity cease; (2) the logic of events demands absorption of the Indians into mainstream society; (3) Indians must be treated exclusively as individuals and not as members of bands or tribes; and (4), in the most quoted phrase from his tenure as commissioner, "Indians must conform to 'the white man's ways,' peaceably if they will, forcibly if they must." Finally, in a declaration filled with menace and promise, Morgan concluded that "this civilization may not be the best possible, but it is the best the Indians can get. They cannot escape it, and must either conform to it or be crushed by it."[39]

The next month, Morgan sent a circular to his agents, explaining that he wanted a full examination of the effects upon Indians of appearing in Wild West shows and other exhibitions. That information might suggest changes in the current policy of the Interior Department in granting licenses to "reputable" enterprises. Morgan wished his agents would give their immediate and careful attention to the subject and report to him:

> *First.* The names of each and every Indian who has been connected with these shows at any time during the last five years, giving the name, age, sex, and condition, how long absent, and with whom. If still absent let that fact appear.
>
> *Second.* What manner of life those persons are living who have returned to the Agency.
>
> *Third.* What their influence is, so far as you are able to gather it, upon those with whom they associate.
>
> *Fourth.* What the health is of those who have returned, as well as what diseases they have brought back with them. On these points I desire that you will have a careful inquiry made by the physician at your Agency, and that you will submit with your own report his official report concerning the matter.
>
> What in your judgment should the Government do about such shows? Please state in full the reasons for the opinions you express.[40]

Most agents, either out of conviction or taking their cue from the commissioner, pronounced the Wild West shows as bad. Most, however, had little direct experience with either the shows or Show Indians.

Agent C. R. A. Scobey at Fort Peck, Montana, explained that "I don't allow Indians to join Wild West shows"; but, nevertheless, "the effects of leaving the reservation are almost always bad."[41] Charles A. Barthalomew, at the Ignacio, Colorado, agency replied that no Southern Utes or Jicarilla Apaches had joined Wild West shows. The shows' effects, however, could not help but be pernicious because the Indian appeared "in all his savage nakedness practicing in almost a reality his devilish acts of cruelty, rapine and murder."[42] William McKusick, agent at Sisseton, South Dakota, observed that "Indians here are too far advanced in civilization to join Wild West shows."[43] From the Nevada agency at Pyramid Lake reservation, S. S. Sears wrote the commissioner that no Paiutes had joined Wild West shows.[44] Robert A. Ashley, agent at the Omaha and Winnebago reservation, Nebraska, offered no opinions, though he did report that twenty-one Winnebagos had been employed with a Dr. Powell selling patent medicine. Another twenty-one Omahas had been variously employed with P. T. Barnum, with the Kickapoo Medicine Company, and with a J. Meyers in Europe.[45]

The agent for the Navajos wrote that none of his charges had joined circuses. Nevertheless, he professed that no Indian under the control of the government should be allowed to travel with the shows under any circumstances. "As their name implies," the agent wrote, "these shows are intended to exhibit the Indian as he is pictured in dime novels and blood and thunder stories, and to make them more attractive in that direction [when] the ideal cowboy is added."[46] In the same vein, D. J. M. Wood at the Otoe subagency, Indian Territory, reported that nineteen Indians had traveled for a few months in 1886 with a show managed by a Captain Stubbs. Abandoned in Tennessee, the Indians returned home only after great difficulty. Agent Wood concluded that "traveling with a show only encourages an Indian in his already strong habits of idleness and vice."[47] And from the Colorado River agency, western Arizona Territory, Henry George informed the commissioner that "in my opinion there is not an Indian on this reservation that ever heard of such a show."[48]

Agent Gallagher at Pine Ridge wrote the longest response to the circular. He, of course, had to account for the largest number of Show Indians. Remarkably, however, he had little to say against the shows. He included the names of 42 Oglalas absent from the reserve with the Kickapoo Medicine Company and 73 returned; 29 veterans of the Carver and

Whitney Wild America show that returned briefly to their homes before, as planned, continuing the tour through Europe; and 79 Oglalas currently under contract with Cody and 101 former employees returned from the show.[49]

Agent John L. Bullis of San Carlos, Arizona Territory, was the only other agent to report a significant number of Indian participants in Wild West shows. He ascertained that forty-seven women and men during the previous five years had been off the reservation traveling with shows. His attitude toward the shows, however, could not have pleased the commissioner. "Their manner of life since their return," he wrote, "is the same. In my opinion, their influence upon those with whom they associate is good: and has a tendency to enlighten those who have remained at home, on the ways of the white man." Reservation Indians, the agent concluded, were "profiting by those Indians who have been out in the world."[50]

Clearly, Commissioner Morgan did not share Agent Bullis's views. With enough contrary evidence and opinion gathered from the agencies, Morgan, late in January 1890, refused Doc Carver permission to take the twenty-nine contracted Oglalas to Europe after their brief Dakota sojourn. Carver protested to the secretary of the interior, whose sympathies were fully on the side of the "Evil Spirit of the Plains." In this instance, the secretary acted as a restraining influence on Morgan's good intentions.

John Noble, secretary of the interior during the Harrison administration (1889–1893), accepted the principle established in the Standing Bear decision. A rarity among bureaucrats involved in Indian affairs, Noble even foresaw favorable results emerging from Indian participation in the shows. Noble advised the commissioner:

I suppose, on the one had, it is a matter for public instruction to have the Indian exhibited where he is fairly treated and is enabled to make some money by this, to him, important industry, and if it can be done without very great attendant evils, I see nothing in it that would prevent its continuance, which must have, I imagine, but little effect upon the tribes of Indians, as the numbers of the exhibited are at best but very small; but if we do not keep control of the matter to the extent I have endeavored to do, the Indians will be stolen for the purpose, in any event, and we should find a great deal of trouble, legally, in compelling them to return to their reservations. It has been held, I believe, that an Indian can get a writ of habeas corpus against anyone endeavoring to confine him, as will be done by attempting to seize and return him to his reservation. I recall no particular law at present that would punish anyone exhibiting him by the Indian's own consent.[51]

Accordingly, Noble lifted the ban against the Carver and Whitney show once it had been determined that the Indians had been well treated and that their "sanitary condition" had suffered no ill effects. He also reminded the commissioner that the applicants had understood their contract, granted in May 1889, was written to last for two years. Carver and Whitney had invested sixty thousand dollars in their business. It would be destroyed by a refusal to renew the licenses.[52]

Morgan, however, would not be so easily diverted. He began to collect evidence of mistreatment of Indians by Wild West and similar shows. He remained convinced that such shows harmed Indians individually and generally. In early March, he reminded his agents that in the interest of Indian civilization and advancement, it was the Bureau's duty to use all of its influence to prevent Indians from joining such exhibitions. Because Morgan's reasoning is important to understanding both his defiance of Secretary Noble and his issuing unilaterally a ban on Indian employment in October, his March circular is quoted at length:

You will please inform the Indians of your agency that this Office has given the subject careful study and is fully convinced that the practice of leaving reservations to join exhibitions is evil in its tendency and results.

Among other things:—

1. Traveling about the country on such expeditions fosters idleness and a distaste for steady occupation.

2. The Indians are brought in contact with people of low character, and learn the worst habits of the white race.

3. As a result they frequently return home wrecked morally and physically.

4. In such case, after their return home, their influence and example among the other Indians is the worst possible.

5. During their absence their families often suffer for want of the care and assistance which they should be on hand to render.

6. Those who, without authority, entice Indians from their reservations to join exhibitions are apt to be unprincipled persons who care only for making money and who, in case of illness or misfortune, might abandon the Indians far from home, penniless, among strangers. This has occurred several times.

You will therefore impress upon the Indians the importance of their remaining at home and devoting their time and energies to establishing comfortable homes, cultivating farms, building houses, and acquiring thrifty, industrious habits and surrounding themselves with the comforts of a worthy type of civilization.

If, on the contrary, they ignore these suggestions, which are made wholly for their best interests, and join exhibitions, they must not look to this Office for favor or assistance.[53]

If employers abandoned their Show Indians, so also would the Bureau abandon them. They had no one to blame but themselves.

What sort of displays, according to Morgan, would signal a worthy type of civilization? Morgan is perhaps best remembered for his emphasis on American Indian education; but his agenda for transforming the savage into citizen went well beyond the three Rs. On the very day when Secretary Noble informed his commissioner that Wild West shows might actually benefit Show Indians, Morgan sent a circular to agents and superintendents of Indian schools telling them that they were to designate a day to be known and observed thereafter as Arbor Day. The only accommodation the commissioner would allow would be in choosing the date best suited to the climate and locality, and allowing the children to name the trees in honor of Indians. On Arbor Day, every child, so far as practicable, would plant one or more fruit, ornamental, or forest trees. In this way, children and their parents, under strict supervision, would have awakened in them "as deep and intelligent an interest as possible" in tree culture. Then the young foresters would learn other valuable lessons in responsibility as they watered, mulched, wrapped, fastened to supports, and protected their saplings from injury by humans or animals.[54] Nothing was said about the pleasure—or the time required—of seeing certain trees bear fruit. Planting and tending yielded the lesson. It was acceptable to Morgan to honor deceased Indians by giving their names to trees that adorned the landscapes of schools and agencies. It was unacceptable to Morgan to honor a way of life, real or imaginary, created by Show Indians in arenas. Names of famous Show Indians might ornament posters or marquees, but they were better left off trees whose planting represented a worthy type of civilization.

The only way that Show Indians could achieve status in Morgan's view was to quit the shows. They were incapable of seeing the errors of their ways, so the commissioner would make them behave. To this effort, the commissioner devoted considerable attention in his first full year in office.

While reformers and Indian Bureau personnel in 1889 and 1890 discussed the sorry influences of Wild West shows, Show Indians again sailed for Europe. Buffalo Bill, at the time of Queen Victoria's jubilee, had found audiences eager for a glimpse of the American frontier. That enthusiasm had not diminished as he began his second European tour.

5
INDIANS ABROAD, 1889-1890

"These are certainly the best looking, and apparently the best fed Indians that I have ever seen."

Buffalo Bill, welcomed in New York by the *Evening Telegram* as the "Hero of Two Continents," and his Show Indians opened Memorial Day 1888 at Erastina.[1] Although scheduled to play there in the month of June, the show remained until the middle of August because of the large crowds. The show then gave performances in Philadelphia, Baltimore, and Washington before ending the season in October at the Richmond Exposition. Afterward, Cody's troupe went into winter quarters for the first time in over two and a half years.[2] Before Cody returned to his home in North Platte, Nebraska, and the Show Indians to theirs in the Dakotas, they went to the Capital. From the galleries, they watched the Senate and House of Representatives in action. At the Indian Bureau, Red Shirt, Rocky Bear, and others smoked the pipe. On their final courtesy call, the Great Father, about to lose his bid for reelection early the next month to Benjamin Harrison, received the resplendent Indians in the East Room of the White House. President Cleveland called them majestic in their bearing.[3]

Since leaving the Pine Ridge agency, Cody's Show Indians had performed for other Americans, crossed the Big Water twice, met the queen of England and her heir, observed the befeathered monarchs of Europe on parade at the queen's anniversary, shared their camp with English lords and ladies, attended sessions of Parliament, visited the theatre, observed the stone angels at Westminster Abbey frozen in their flight, and even dazzled President Cleveland with their finery just before going home. Yet to reformers and their allies, they would have been better off had they stayed on their reservations and performed instead as government Indians. They had been to places made inaccessible by circumstance or finances to most other Americans, let alone to Indians. They had experienced firsthand some of the dimensions of the world. As far as reformers were concerned, however, keeping Indians on the reservation and out of the arena would at least improve their public image.

The ambivalence of the Show Indians' position in the debate between reformers and people like Cody reflects their predicament. Reformers supported everyone's interest except theirs, if that meant ultimately the right to sell their labor to Wild West shows. Looking at the records, one is struck by how often Show Indian opinions were asked and given and then ignored. Despite the ethnocentrism of the period, it is still difficult to understand why nobody among the reformers and within the Indian service listened. Even though the Show Indians often spoke eloquently about the necessity of adapting to a modern world, the Indian Bureau and reformers disregarded the message. Like many historians, they did not take the Show Indians seriously.

It rained the afternoon Buffalo Bill's Wild West sailed from New York for France. Cody had signed a contract the previous year to appear at the *Exposition Universale* in Paris, a ready-made crowd at the celebration marking the century since the French Revolution. As seamen singled up all lines in the rain and the ship swung out into the East River from the Twenty-fourth Street pier, the Cowboy Band on the deck of the *Per-*

sian Monarch played first the plangent air of "Auld Lang Syne," and then the more cheerful "The Girl I Left behind Me." Black Heart, Little Chief, and Kills Plenty, veterans of the 1887 tour of England, joined Red Shirt in his cabin. Others in the company lined the starboard rail and sang their own songs of farewell.[4] Although the transit of the Atlantic was less stormy than in 1887, it was no less exciting for most of the 102 Indians who had never before been to Europe. The ship docked at Havre the first week of May. Cody's Wild West would spend the next six months in Paris, "the capital," as John Burke enthused, "of the how-truly-named La Belle France."[5]

The Wild West, encamped in the Parc du Neuilly, began performing on May 19, 1889. President Sadi Carnot, his wife, several members of his cabinet, and the American ambassadors to France and England favored the event with their presence.[6] Things American quickly became fashionable, first in Paris and then throughout France. Major Burke encouraged this by sending cowboys wearing their sombreros and Indians wearing their headdresses into the streets each day before the performances. Cody recalled that "fashionable young men bought American and Mexican saddles for their rides in the Bois [de Boulogne]. Cowboy hats appeared everywhere on the street. Relics from the plains and mountains, bows, moccasins, and Indian baskets sold like hot cakes in the souvenir stores." The venerable Rosa Bonheur visited the camp and found its inhabitants so enchanting that she returned again and again, painting a dozen or so canvases of the arena's action or portraits of its principal actors.[7] Others found fascinating the painted designs the Indians applied to their bodies. Parisians, one reporter explained, examined closely the costumes of the warriors to determine if they were wearing "really nothing thicker than paint; the colors are so vivid and so boldly applied to all parts of the body that the all but absolute nudity of the Indians is invisible."[8]

On the centennial of the fall of the Bastille, Major Burke and a group of Show Indians ascended the Eiffel Tower. Rocky Bear, Red Shirt, Featherman, and others found the elevators noisier than those they had ridden in the United States. A reporter accompanying the group on the lift mistook their awe for cowardice. About halfway up the tower, Featherman remarked that if they should mount much higher he would "go crazy." The reporter explained that Featherman had "positively showed the white feather." The phrase, however, even in translation, had nothing to do with insanity. When Red Shirt said that he might go even higher without making himself much "crazier," or ecstatic, he and Featherman completed the ascension in a "rejoicing frame of mind."[9] From the observation plat-

14 : *Photograph taken in front of Buffalo Bill's tent at the show encampment,
Paris, July 1889. Rocky Bear appears on Cody's right. The artist Rosa Bonheur
(seated), famous for her animal and nature paintings, spent many hours at the
encampment painting portraits of Buffalo Bill and the Indians during the show's
seven-month stay at the Paris Exposition. To Bonheur's left are Red Shirt and
William "Broncho Bill" Irving. Broncho Bill, married to a Lakota woman, served
on occasion as one of the troupe's interpreters. Cody's inscription of "Paris 1899"
is in error. (Buffalo Bill Historical Center, Cody, Wyoming)*

form, Red Shirt, surveying Paris below him and the sky above, remarked,
"If people look so little to us up here, how very much smaller they must
seem to One [*Wakantanka*] who is up higher." [10]

In traveling about the streets of Paris one day, Rocky Bear came upon
what must have been a political meeting. A reporter for *Le Petit Journal*
learned of this and sought out the showman for an interview. He found
Rocky Bear with a few of his companions one evening smoking and talking
while reclining around a campfire. The Oglala showman explained that,

while walking around, he and Nate Salsbury heard loud noises coming from an open window. Peering in, Rocky Bear saw what Salsbury estimated were two thousand people, many of whom were smoking, shouting, and waving their arms in dramatic fashion. One person making broad gestures with his hands and arms climbed onto a table, while another rapped on the table with a baton or cane. Rocky Bear asked Salsbury, "what is it they want? One would think it was a whole troupe of birds in the same tree all singing at once." Salsbury replied that they had gathered to choose a deputy to the French assembly—a "headman" or "chief," as he explained it. At this point in the story, the reporter interrupted Rocky Bear to ask what he thought about the political meeting. Rocky Bear compared the scene in that room to what typically occurred in his own band. Members, whether in a lodge or in the open air, set themselves in a circle. They passed the pipe around, and each in turn gave his opinion. A Lakota would never speak before another person had finished. In the political meeting he witnessed, however, "you smoke all at the same time, you speak all at the same time, and you understand anyhow." [11]

As Rita Napier observes, Rocky Bear stressed the Lakota approach to political life. The traditional education of a young person underscored those qualities so often demonstrated in public by Rocky Bear and Red Shirt. Non-Indians may have focused much attention on the education of a warrior; but the Teton Lakota encouraged self-control, generosity, tact, wisdom, and responsibility toward the poor or helpless as well as courage and prowess in battle. Those who demonstrated such civic virtues became, in time, *wichasha yatapika* ("men whom all praise"). Such persons embodied the ideal and became role models for the young. On a number of occasions during their trips to Europe, Red Shirt and Rocky Bear had the opportunity to observe and practice the requisite behavior. They showed in their quiet demeanor, stately bearing, politeness, and ability to converse with prominent people that they were Lakotas who honored their heritage. It is no wonder, then, that Rocky Bear seemed so amazed by the behavior of the French in choosing their deputy. They talked all at once and yet, somehow, they understood. [12]

One of the more remarkable, though unheralded, events occurred while the Wild West completed its stand in Paris. Black Elk had missed the boat when Cody's show left Hull, England, the previous year. Hearing that the Wild West had returned to Europe, he made his way to Paris to rejoin the troupe. Black Elk explained to Buffalo Bill that he and three of his companions had become separated from the troupe and were left behind. They made their way to London, where they came across two other Sioux, one of whom could speak English. They all joined Mexican Joe Shelly's (in some documents "Shelbey") Wild West, which was then in London; it was one of the many imitators inspired by Cody's success abroad. The refugees remained with the show throughout its schedule of performances in France, Germany, and Italy.[13]

Cody offered Black Elk a place in the show; but the young, aspiring *wicasa wacan* (holy man and healer), rather homesick, decided to return to the United States. Cody bought him a ticket, gave him ninety dollars, and hired a Paris *gendarme* to escort him to the boat train. By autumn Black Elk was back among his people at Pine Ridge.[14]

Just before the show ended its Paris engagement in early October, another person joined Cody's Wild West. Red Shirt's wife, one of about fifteen spouses who accompanied their husbands on tour that year, gave birth to a son on September 28. There had been much excitement in the Indian camp that day, and it spilled over into the arena when the announcement was made.[15] From the time that Cody began to employ Indians for exhibitions, women had been included. Only wives, however, were allowed to join their husbands on tour. At no time did Cody's show employ unmarried Native American women as featured performers. This also appears to have been the policy of other shows. When Representative James charged that the Show Indians frequented saloons and bought the company of prostitutes, John Burke explained that corporate policy dictated that only married women participate so that there could never be a hint of impropriety.[16] The expanded program introduced in "The Drama of Civilization" allowed women to perform in the show itself, from the opening parade to re-creating domestic scenes of camp life. Beginning with the stand at Erastina, Cody encouraged the public to tour the Indian encampment. As women assumed roles other than those of traveling companions of their husbands, Cody began to pay them. Their names also began to appear on contracts. Well into the 1890s, women who accompanied the show received ten, and occasionally fifteen, dollars a month (a little less than half the pay of an arena performer). They received the same considerations for medical care, food, and clothing as their husbands. Red Shirt's son may have been the first child born in Cody's Wild West; but he was not the last.[17]

In early October, Cody's show quit Paris for a swing through the south of France. From Marseille, in December, the troupe took ship for Barcelona. Always the pitchman and promoter, John Burke had the Show Indians photographed in front of the statue of Christopher Columbus. "There," Burke cheered, "stands our advance agent, four hundred years

15 : Buffalo Bill and cast members of the Wild West Show during their visit to Naples, Italy, in January or early February 1890 (although the inscription reads 1889). No Neck appears standing at the left. The Show Indians seated left to right are Rocky Bear, Black Heart, and Red Shirt. Annie Oakley sits to the right of Red Shirt. The unidentified Indian standing behind Red Shirt may be Has No Horses. (Buffalo Bill Historical Center, Cody, Wyoming)

ahead of us." An unidentified Indian in the group is supposed to have replied, "It was a damned bad day for us when he discovered America."[18] The show's arrival in Barcelona also marked a bad day. Crowds never materialized. One set of authors suggests that the Wild West show could not compete with Spain's national blood sport, unless by inference Buffalo Bill were willing to slaughter one of his twenty American bison brought to

Europe for added authenticity.[19] Crowds also may have stayed away because of the partial quarantine placed upon the city. Influenza and typhus ravaged the population. Contagion also reached the camp. A number of sources suggest that four or as many as seven Indians died in the epidemic. There is no reference, however, in official correspondence to suggest that any Indians in Cody's employ died in Spain. Seven Indians eventually did return to Pine Ridge in ill health; but that came later in the year.[20] Frank Richmond, the show's popular announcer, contracted pneumonia as a result of influenza and died. Annie Oakley became ill and barely survived. It was with few regrets and fewer gate receipts, therefore, that the show left Spain in early January 1890, once city officials lifted quarantine.[21]

To Naples, by way of Sardinia and Corsica, the show came next and opened on the afternoon of January 26. An enterprising Neapolitan counterfeited two thousand reserved-seat tickets, which produced even greater confusion than normal for an opening performance. Yet compared to those in Spain, the crowds showed great enthusiasm. Buffalo Bill's show redeemed its losses sustained during the Spanish interlude.[22]

In Rome by early March, Major Burke made special arrangements for the Show Indians to attend the twelfth anniversary of Pope Leo XIII's coronation. Cody gave the impression to newspaper reporters that he was Catholic. Such a claim perhaps could only help his business. It did not help, however, when Cody asked for a private audience for him and his Show Indians with the eighty-year-old pontiff. Papal retainers explained to the showman that there were just too many of them to be received; but, through the good offices of Monsignor O'Connell of the American College in Rome and Archbishop Corrigan of New York, Buffalo Bill and the Indians were admitted into the Ducal Hall the morning of March 3. His Holiness had to pass through it on his way to the Sistine Chapel for the ceremony marking his coronation. The pope even vouchsafed a concession, owing to special circumstance. Neither Cody nor his Indians had to wear the traditional swallow-tailed coats appropriate for state occasions before the Holy See. The pope would have been pleased to know that the Indians specifically dressed in their finery to meet such an important person.[23]

Rocky Bear led the Sioux delegation upon its entrance into the *Sala Regia*. Pope Leo, preliminary to his procession through the Ducal Hall, had just concluded a speech in his apartments about current labor unrest brought on by miserable wages and unsafe jobs. In anticipation of his meeting the delegation of first Americans, he likened the occasion to the return of Columbus to the court of Ferdinand and Isabella.[24] Major Burke, who was indeed Catholic, described the scene wherein the pope and his train gave a "dazzling fête" for the troupe: "The grandeur of the spectacle, the heavenly music, the entrancing singing and impressive adjuncts produced a most profound impression on the astonished children of the prairie."[25] Borne above the crowd on the *Sedia Gestatoria,* and with the tiara on his head, the pontiff entered the hall "preceded by the knights of Malta and a procession of Cardinals and archbishops."[26] There had been some concern that the Show Indians, overcome by enthusiasm, might let out whoops, or worse. Burke, however, had prepared them well. "For a week before this day," Nate Salsbury reported, "John Burke . . . had worked on the Indians to impress them with the solemnity of the occasion." He told them that they were going to see the representative of "God on Earth, and to those of them who had been under Catholic instruction at the Reservation, the coming event was of great interest."[27] The Lakota showmen behaved admirably. Rocky Bear, baptized by Catholic missionaries at Pine Ridge agency, knelt and made the sign of the cross. The pope leaned forward in his sedan chair and blessed the throng.[28] He seemed, Burke remembered, genuinely touched by the sight.[29]

When they left the hall, however, their grave deportment deserted them. They laughed and showed great amusement at the fantastic uniforms of the Palatine Guards, papal gendarmes, private chamberlains, and especially the Swiss Guards armed with their halberds and two-handed swords.[30] They had seen nothing like them before in their encounters with soldiers. Such gaudy warriors could have been dropped by arrows or a shot from a treasured Winchester before they could heft such blades over their heads.

To some commentators, the Indians' behavior in the Ducal Hall appeared as superstitious, primitive, amusing, or simply quaint.[31] These interpretations, however, fail to consider the religious beliefs or values of the Indians themselves. A visit to the person believed by Catholic millions to be God's vicar on earth of necessity became a grand occasion. Although the idea of a human intercessor may have been foreign to Lakota thinking, the notion that such a man had received the power of God was bound to be attractive. Everything about the pope and his immediate world interested the visitors. The Vatican itself invited exploring. Denied the freedom of the buildings and grounds, however, the Show Indians concluded that it was not honorable for God's representative to exhibit such a lack of hospitality. They compared their own traditions of conviviality with that of the papal court. To the plains Indians, it was unfortunate to be called ungenerous or inhospitable. The pope's failure to provide proper hospitality no doubt reduced his authority in their eyes.[32] An occurrence at the camp, upon their return, further diminished their belief in the pope's powers.

Little Ring (*Depostas*), about thirty-eight years old, and the only member of Cody's troupe to remain behind while the others visited the Vatican, died at midnight on March 2. In the official language of the consular service, Little Ring had been found dead in his bed and a post mortem revealed the cause as heart disease.[33] Nate Salsbury explained that his death "had a peculiar effect on the Indians' minds, for they immediately called a council among themselves." They sent for Major Burke and asked him to explain "why the Representative of God had not protected their comrade while they were away from him, and if he had so much power on earth why he had not exerted himself to shield their comrade from death in their absence."[34] Burke tried to quiet the Indians' doubts, but could not persuade them otherwise that "god should send another man to represent him if he expected the Indians to believe anything the missionaries might tell them in the future."[35]

Power preoccupied plains Indian societies; but their definition of it differed considerably from that of Catholics and, by extension, other Christians. Without power a person's life might trail off into insignificance. Possessed of it, a person might accomplish anything. People sought power to heal, to succeed in warfare or the hunt, to survive a great ordeal, to attract game, or to ensure that their people would flourish. A person in seeking power also sought rapport with a universe that was likewise filled with power. Such a quest would put a person in accord with the universe. Plains people held in high esteem those who had visions and received power and understanding from them. They expected such people, in turn, to use their power for the good of others. Therefore, in this context, as Rita Napier observes, the Indians rejected the pope's authority because he either possessed no real power or refused to use it responsibly. If the latter were true, then from their point of view Leo XIII was not a proper representative of *Wakantanka* because he refused to use the power he had to aid another.[36]

Rocky Bear expressed his disappointment to an American newspaper reporter who encountered him, a few days, later emerging from the ruins of the Roman forum. He spoke about his displeasure in such a way that even Commissioner Morgan would have been proud had he been listening. "The more I see of other countries," the Sioux leader remarked, "the more I like America." Among some of the petty annoyances, Rocky Bear found that "the cabdrivers are very bad men. When you give them one piece of

16 : During the Italian tour of 1890, Show Indians at Naples await their cue to enter the arena for the attack on the settler's cabin. It appears as if the riders in the arena are completing the segment usually described as "Cowboy Fun," with riding "wild" horses as one of the amusements. (Buffalo Bill Historical Center, Cody, Wyoming)

money they hold out their hand for more. Everyone hold his hand out for money here. That makes my heart heavy. It is not so in the land where the sun goes to sleep."[37] Rocky Bear picked up a piece of broken marble. Many of the once-magnificent Roman buildings had tumbled down into rubble. Turning to his companions, he said:

> I want you to remember that these men who ask money from us through the streets and laugh at us will all die like the people who used to live here and their houses will fall down like these you see around you. . . . This country is no place for an Indian. The government gives no rations and there are too many soldiers. . . . We will all be very glad

to go home. We throw our tobacco on the ground here, and don't care if we lose it. In our own country we did not do so. Then why do we waste the tobacco of this city? It is because the tobacco is not good. That is all I have to say, my people.[38]

There is no evidence that any Italian journalists interviewed the Show Indians. No clear Show Indian personality emerged in the Italian press.[39] Instead, as Rocky Bear indicated, the people of Rome laughed at the Indians. They were not so much fascinated as amused by their presence in the *piazzas* and along the *vias*. Crowds were much friendlier outside Rome.

The Wild West next toured northern Italy, with Florence, Bologna, Milan, Venice, and Verona among the cities visited. In Florence, an officious customs agent delayed the opening of the show. He wanted to place entrance duties on the animals, according to their weight.[40] Huge audiences turned out in Milan for the show's eleven-day stand. Giacomo Puccini attended. He afterward wrote to his brother to tell him that he had enjoyed the show. "They are a company of North Americans," he explained, "with some Red Indians and buffaloes. They perform magnificent feats of shooting and give realistic presentations of scenes that have happened on the frontier. In eleven days they drew 120,000 lire!"[41] Although Puccini got his libretto for *La Fanciulla del West* from David Belasco's play *The Girl of the Golden West*, he must surely have been impressed by what he saw in the Wild West show.[42]

In Venice, Major Burke had a photographer record their progress through a few of the sites. Rocky Bear, Black Heart, and two companions joined Cody in a gondola for a leisurely excursion along the Grand Canal. At the Doge's palace, the troupe stared down from the balcony at the crowds below who returned their gaze. And at St. Mark's cathedral, Cody and the Show Indians formed a tight little island of gaily dressed visitors on the *piazza*'s broad sea of gray stone.[43] But even these feats of press agentry and management were eclipsed in Burke's triumph a few weeks later. In Verona, he actually booked the show into the ancient amphitheater built by Diocletian. John Burke estimated the attendance that day at forty-five thousand.[44]

The financial successes of Italy were repeated when the show traveled north through Innsbruck and the Tyrol to Munich. The summer tour included Vienna, Berlin, Dresden, Leipzig, Bonn, Coblentz, Frankfurt, and Stuttgart.[45] Buffalo Bill and the Indians created a sensation. The enthusiasm in Germany seems to have been greater than anywhere else in Europe.

17 : A black-and-white print of a hand-tinted photograph of Lakota Show Indians at the Doge's palace in Venice, Italy, 1890. The photograph was the work of Paolo Salviati. (Buffalo Bill Historical Center, Cody, Wyoming)

Both Doc Carver's Wild America and Cody's Wild West toured Germany that summer—crossing paths briefly in July. German interest in plains Indians had been whetted by the appearance, in 1886, of a group of fifteen Oglalas touring with a Frank Harvey show followed in 1887 by the first of Karl May's fanciful, though wildly popular, western novels.[46] Cody inspired many of May's stories. As two authors have noted, interest in the American West of legend remains strong among Germans. In the late 1980s, at least seven organizations in Germany were devoted to the study and perpetuation of the "real West." Parks exist where Germans can go, camp, dress as Indians, and imagine themselves back in the Old West.[47] The German press, in 1890, produced far more laudatory accounts of the Show Indians, though surprisingly few quotations.[48]

In marked contrast to the favorable press in Germany, back at home allegations began to reach the Indian Office that Cody had mistreated his Indians. The deaths of five Show Indians traveling with Cody, and another

18 : *Show Indians with Buffalo Bill at St. Mark's Cathedral, Venice, Italy, 1890. Black-and-white print of a hand-colored photograph by Paolo Salviati. (Buffalo Bill Historical Center, Cody, Wyoming)*

who had died in Moscow while touring with Doc Carver's Wild America, coupled with allegations of abuse, prompted Secretary of the Interior Noble on August 4 to reverse his previous position. He ordered that "no more permits be granted for Indians to go with these shows, under any circumstances."[49] Commissioner Morgan sent a list of questions to be answered by Cody and his partners. He also demanded that they provide suitable documentation for their treatment of the Indians. These communications the United States consul general at Berlin delivered by hand to Buffalo Bill.[50] The growing uproar in the press at home and the increasing scrutiny of his operations persuaded Buffalo Bill to cancel a proposed winter tour of the south of France and Riviera, and to bring his Show Indians home.[51]

The controversy's origin can be traced to a series of events that began the previous March. On the fourth, Commissioner Morgan informed Agent Gallagher at Pine Ridge of the deaths of "Chief Hawick" (Swift Hawk) and Featherman in early January. The two Show Indians had been left in Marseilles at Conception Hospital. John Burke had paid in advance for a private room, physician, and attending nurse. Hawick died of complications resulting from contracting influenza, and Featherman of small pox "of the most virulent type."[52] It was on the eighth that Commissioner Morgan issued his circular that urged agents to impress upon Indians the importance of their remaining at home and devoting themselves to "a worthy type of civilization."[53] This circular represented the conclusion to the investigation, begun the previous fall, into the effects upon Indians of traveling with Wild West shows. The effects kept mounting as far as the commissioner was concerned.

On April 1, Morgan briefed the agent at Pine Ridge that four of his Indians had shown up destitute at the Cheyenne and Arapaho agency in Indian Territory. They and thirty-three other Sioux had left Pine Ridge the previous October without the agent's permission. They had joined a Wild West show, probably Pawnee Bill's, and then left when the show encountered financial difficulties while touring fairs in the South.[54] They arrived early in the new year, 1890. Two in the party asked to remain in the Indian Territory. The others wished to return to Pine Ridge. The commissioner directed Agent Gallagher to investigate, "by correspondence or otherwise," whether the Indians might be able to recover what was owed to them in unpaid wages.[55] Within a few weeks of this latest problem caused by Wild West shows, news arrived in Washington that other Show Indians had died in Europe.

The State Department notified the Indian Office of the deaths of two more Indians in Cody's troupe. Goes Flying, age forty-five, died of smallpox on February 15 at the Hospidale Cotugoro in Naples. Italian authorities burned all his effects. And, of course, Little Ring died in his sleep of an apparent heart attack on March 2.[56]

May passed without additional incidents; but then in June, the U.S. Consul in Moscow reported the death of Black Owl from Pine Ridge agency. He had been traveling with the Carver and Whitney show. He too died of heart disease.[57] Finally, five Sioux arrived in New York. They had left the Cody show in Leipsiz. Buffalo Bill had thought them too ill to continue the tour. Accompanied by a representative of the show, they sailed in steerage from Bremen and had their travel by train paid through to Rushville, Nebraska. One of the showmen, Kills Plenty (*Otakte*), had to be hospitalized upon arrival in New York. His health, however, failed to improve. He died at Bellevue Hospital of tuberculosis complicated by blood poisoning.[58] While waiting for their convalescing companion to get well, the four Show Indians shared the company of James R. O'Beirne, the assistant U.S. superintendent of immigration at the port of New York. O'Beirne, a stalwart Republican, had once been employed in the Indian service among the Sioux. His agitation of the issue caused the controversy to explode in the newspapers.[59]

O'Beirne implied that Eagle Horn, White Horse, Bear Pipe, Kills White Weasel, and Kills Plenty had sailed from Europe without an interpreter "or anyone to conduct them."[60] In fact, Fred Matthews, a veteran stage driver, accompanied the showmen.[61] It is easy to speculate how people, upon reading newspaper accounts of the incident, might take exception to what they regarded as Cody's flagrant dereliction of duty toward his employees—who just happened to be wards of the government. One is less certain, however, about why O'Beirne would lie to the press. He perhaps wanted to show how Cody had abandoned helpless Indians to their own incompetence. Yet even if Cody had let the ill showmen travel on their own, one could just as easily imagine that perhaps Buffalo Bill thought them capable of fending for themselves. Some in the party spoke English; and they had, after all, been abroad for more than a year. Throughout the tour, the Show Indians were free to come and go as they pleased as long as they did not violate general rules of deportment—such as sobriety—established in their contracts. Kills Plenty himself had been a veteran of not only the 1887 tour, but also the plains wars. Given the fact that Kills Plenty died soon after arrival in New York, O'Beirne's version of events took on additional authority.

O'Beirne arranged for six pallbearers to escort Kill Plenty's coffin from the barge office to the midnight train bound for Chicago. He purchased a pillow of flowers, as he described it, which he gave to the attendant in the baggage car. "I am very much annoyed at the manner in which these Indians have been treated," he wrote Agent Gallagher at Pine Ridge, "and will lay the matter before the government at Washington." Back in the fall of 1877, when O'Beirne had been employed at Red Cloud agency, he favorably considered Buffalo Bill's application to engage reservation Sioux for his theatrical combination. On that occasion, Cody had agreed to keep the Indians free from demoralizing influences, liquor, and other temptations, and to return them safely to their reservation; but this time, Cody's

19 : *Eagle Horn, Oglala, who, because of ill health, returned with Kills Plenty and three others from Cody's European tour, 1890. This portrait was taken by De Lancey Gill of the Bureau of American Ethnology in 1907. (South Dakota State Historical Society, Pierre)*

Indians "came here without an interpreter, or anyone to conduct them, or to supply their wants, except a boy sent from an imigrant [*sic*] boarding house who fortunately came to me."[62]

Before they left for the Dakotas, O'Beirne had White Horse, from among the returnees, speak to the press. He told a story, with O'Beirne interpreting, of neglect and malnutrition at the hands of Buffalo Bill. "For months past," the article in the *Herald* read, "the warriors have been straggling back in groups of three and five, sick and disgusted with their treatment while abroad. Fully one-third of the original band have returned to this country."[63] Agent Gallagher contributed his voice to the rising clamor by insisting that the Indians had nothing to show for their labors upon returning to the reservation "except shattered constitutions which may or may not be built up again." As O'Beirne and White Horse had, Gallagher declared that the Indians had been treated inhumanely. After they had been "broken down" in the show and were therefore no longer profitable to their employers, they were sent home.[64]

O'Beirne kept up the pressure, reporting early in August that, of the three Sioux who had recently returned to Pine Ridge accompanying the body of Kills Plenty, two had revealed signs of pulmonary disease, and another had developed jaundice.[65] That, apparently, proved enough for Secretary Noble. The next day, he issued a ban on further contracts and ordered that an investigation be made into the condition of Cody's Indian employees.[66]

Commissioner Morgan took advantage of the changing attitudes at the Interior Department. Short Horn, a relation of one of Cody's employees still on tour in Europe, complained to the commissioner that Agent Gallagher had confiscated wagons, plows, other farm implements, and cattle issued by the government to the families of Show Indians. Instead of reprimanding the agent, Commissioner Morgan praised him. He found the agent's actions to have been "for the best interests of the Indian."[67] Whereas Secretary Noble had previously shown himself to be friendly to the shows, restraining Morgan on more than one occasion, now even the secretary had cause for concern. It appeared that Wild West shows did more than create improper images in the public mind. Wild West shows endangered not only the health of Indians, but also their very lives. And the tally of the dead continued to rise.

When No Neck arrived back at Pine Ridge agency in the middle of August, he informed Agent Gallagher that Wounds One Another, also an Oglala, had died the previous month. He had been killed, the agent reported, "by falling from the cars while traveling as [No Neck] thinks through Germany."[68] Stories appearing in the press about Cody's indifferent treatment of his employees compelled Dr. Joseph A. Tonner, a physician who had been present in Paris at the opening of the exposition and had examined the Indians, to counter some of the charges. Dr. Tonner had found them to be generally healthy and well treated. He sent his letter to the commissioner, however, rather than to an editor of one of the newspapers repeating O'Beirne's allegations of mistreatment.[69] At this point in the controversy, there were few voices raised in support of Cody and the Wild West shows.

The consul general at Berlin delivered the commissioner's message to Buffalo Bill. Additional documents were forwarded from Washington, which caused a delay of two more weeks. Salsbury acknowledged receipt of the materials from the consul general in Berlin; but he advised that some time would be required to answer each of the questions.[70] The consul general, the secretary of the Berlin legation, and the consul at Hamburg visited the show, which remained in Berlin through August 22. They found the Indians to be "certainly the best looking, and apparently the best fed" of any they had ever seen.[71] The next week, however, during a performance, Uses the Sword fell from his horse and was trampled by a buffalo. He died from his injuries.[72] That brought the total to seven Show Indians in Cody's employ who had died, two in accidents and five from disease. It was probably then that Cody decided it was best to return the Show Indians to the United States.

Buffalo Bill erred in not taking seriously O'Beirne's charges. He could have better served his reputation and that of the Wild West had he sent Burke to accompany Kills Plenty and the returning Indians. Someone as schooled in press-agentry as "Arizona John" could have diverted much of the criticism. This eventually became clear to Cody and his partners as controversy deepened and the investigation began. Rather than risk additional losses to the show's reputation, and a possible ban on hiring Indians, Cody, Burke, and Salsbury brought the Indians home after first establishing a winter camp, at Benfeld in Alsace-Lorraine, for the remainder of the troupe and all of its baggage.[73]

Burke immediately went into action. He cabled newspapers in New York. He ranted against O'Beirne and other detractors, calling them "notoriety-seeking busybodies" who "without rhyme, truth or reason have tried to stain a fair record."[74] He even sent a copy of the consuls' remarks to the Paris edition of the New York *Herald*. The editor then commented that "It shows the value of an international newspaper that stories wilder than the Wild West itself can be so promptly sat upon and refuted."[75]

20 : *No Neck, who traveled many seasons with Cody's Wild West and then ap-*
peared in "The Indian Wars," filmed by Buffalo Bill on the Pine Ridge reservation
in 1913. (South Dakota State Historical Society, Pierre)

Finally, Burke also cabled the commissioner, explaining that Buffalo Bill had decided to bring the Indians to Washington. Cody would be glad to explain matters personally. Burke implored the commissioner to delay making a judgment. He reminded Morgan that justice to all was the foundation of good government and Christianity.[76] Robert V. Belt, acting commissioner, received the wire.

Commissioner Morgan had left Washington in early September for a tour of the agency schools in the western and southwestern United States. He had wanted to view firsthand the conditions present at each of the reservations for a program of rapid assimilation through education. Commissioner Morgan, as minister and educator, had brought to his position an aggressive Americanism and an exaggerated faith in common schools to serve as engines for Indian advancement. He hoped that one day Indian children, freed from the impediments of family, tribe, culture, and the federal government, would learn their Americanism in public schools rather than at reservation schools.[77] He was not present, therefore, when Buffalo Bill and the Indians arrived back in the country.

Nevertheless, Acting Commissioner Belt had already expressed his displeasure with the shows. On October 1, under his own authority, he issued a circular to Indian agents. He instructed them to remind their Indians of the "ruinous evils" generally resulting from employment in Wild West shows. Agents must urge their wards to "remain at home and engage in more civilizing avocations." Any attempt to leave the reservation for exhibition purposes would be regarded as open defiance of the government.[78] It was no surprise, then, that Belt took special interest in the arrival of Buffalo Bill's Indians.

Knowing that the ship bearing the Show Indians would dock in Philadelphia, the acting commissioner sent James O'Beirne to meet it. He also asked Herbert Welsh, resident of the city and corresponding secretary of the Philadelphia-based Indian Rights Association, to accompany the immigration officer. O'Beirne had traveled down from New York in the company of Father Francis M. Craft, a Catholic missionary who had spent many years among the Sioux and could speak Lakota. Craft had been one of the pallbearers to carry Kills Plenty's coffin from the barge office to the train. Craft would act as interpreter.[79]

When the *Belgenland* tied up at a wharf close by the Philadelphia navy yard on November 13, O'Beirne, Welsh, and Craft were first up the gangway, followed close behind by a group of reporters. John Burke denounced the trio in front of the reporters. Welsh withdrew to another part of the ship and hurriedly scribbled a note to Burke. When a ship's steward returned from delivering the note forwarding more unpleasantries from "Arizona John," Welsh went looking for the manager. He came upon him in the smoking room. Again, Burke refused to speak to the corresponding secretary. Welsh wired the Interior Department that Burke "positively declined to permit an examination [of the Indians] and stated that the matter was none of my business." Instead, Welsh explained, Cody had already left for New York and Burke, Salsbury, and the Indians would start for Washington by the 4:41 P.M. train.[80]

Burke and Salsbury called at the Indian Bureau before noon the following day. Acting Commissioner Belt scolded them for refusing to allow Herbert Welsh to conduct an examination. They countered that "General O'Beirne's" presence prejudiced the proceedings. He had an interpreter of his own selection. They further believed that, given all the bad press inspired by him, the examination would be far from impartial. Instead, they brought the troupe to Washington. Somewhat placated, Belt agreed to see the Indians the next morning at 10:00 A.M.[81]

When they gathered in a room at the Interior Department, Rocky Bear, spokesman for the seventy-nine Show Indians present, announced that President Harrison expected them at the White House promptly at 1:00 P.M. A Mr. Titus from the Bureau acted as stenographer. Chauncey Yellow Robe, a Lakota student sent down from Carlisle Indian School the previous evening, acted as interpreter. Belt first asked them if any in their party had been mistreated in any way. All answered that they had not. Rocky Bear explained, "If [the show] did not suit me, I would not remain any longer." None starved, either. The Indians, Rocky Bear said, stroking his cheek, "eat everything; that is the reason I am getting so fat. When I come back to the reservation I am getting poor."[82]

To the charge that performing in Cody's Wild West show demeaned them, Rocky Bear replied: "If the great father wants me to stop, I would do it. That is the way I get money. If a man goes to work in some other place and goes back with money, he has some for his children." The showman had continually sent money home. What is more, he carried in his pockets that day three hundred dollars in gold coins.[83]

There had been reports in the press that the Indians sometimes appeared naked in the shows. "Did you appear without any clothes on?" Belt asked Rocky Bear. He answered, "There is none needed when not cold, but when cold we wear clothes." Belt pressed him further. "I mean when you were exhibiting before the people, did you go without clothes?"

21 : *Black Heart, here wearing a war bonnet, fabric shirt with stars and stripes, and a bone hairpipe breastplate. During a meeting with Acting Commissioner R. V. Belt at the Interior Department, he gave an impassioned defense of the right of Indians to work for Wild West shows. (Buffalo Bill Historical Center, Cody, Wyoming)*

"When it was not cold we did," Rocky Bear explained, "and when it was cold, we did not." Wearing breechcloth, as far as Belt was concerned, constituted nakedness.[84]

When queried about the specific charges General O'Beirne had made, Black Heart observed:

> What [he] has said, that is not to be listened to. What the great father says, that is to be listened to. . . . These men [Cody, Burke, and Salsbury] have got us in hand. We were raised on horseback; that is the way we had to work. These men furnished us the same work we were raised to; that is the reason we want to work for these kind of men. . . . If Indian wants to work at any place and earn money, he wants to do so; white man got privilege to do the same—any kind of work that he wants.[85]

Black Heart's words were compelling. Convinced perhaps of the falseness of the charges, or believing instead that the Indians had been well prepared, it was at this point in the interview that Belt allowed Burke and Salsbury to enter the room.[86]

Nate Salsbury thanked his employees, congratulating them for their candor. "We knew that you would speak the truth," he said, "that is the reason why we brought you 3000 miles and broke up our business, to answer these charges that have been made against Mr. Cody."[87] In sending them on their way, Belt warned them of changed conditions at their reservations. They would find "some little excitement growing out of the religion of your people," who believed in the coming of a new messiah. They labored, the acting commissioner explained, under a great delusion. The Show Indians, however, had learned many things in their travels. Belt hoped that they would use that knowledge among their people to encourage loyalty to the government. With three cheers for the acting commissioner, the Show Indians and their employers filed out of the room.[88]

O'Beirne was livid when he read accounts in the newspapers which implied that Buffalo Bill and company had been exonerated. He fired off a letter to Belt and the secretary of the interior, demanding to see a copy of the report.[89] Apparently, the acting commissioner also entertained a few doubts. He wrote to the new agent at Pine Ridge, Daniel F. Royer, explaining about the thwarted investigation in Philadelphia and his subsequent meeting with the Wild West show troupe. Although none of the Indians had complained of mistreatment, Belt wanted a further investigation of the matter to be made. He instructed the agent to make a full investigation of the condition of the Indians who had returned from the various shows. Belt required sworn affidavits about their treatment and whether or not they had been fully paid their salaries. Had they also received traveling and incidental expenses? Finally, the acting commissioner instructed Royer to report the names and whereabouts of all Indians who had not yet returned from the shows. "Let your report be explicit on all the points indicated," Belt concluded, "so that this Office may be able to determine whether . . . Cody and Salsbury, Carver and Whitney, or Adam Forepaugh, have violated their contracts with the Indians and are liable therefor under their respective bonds."[90]

Such a request proved daunting for the beleaguered agent at Pine Ridge. Royer could no more easily fulfill the request of the acting commissioner than he could control events at the reservation. From the time he took over from Hugh Gallagher on October 9, he showed himself ill equipped to handle administration of the reservation. The Oglalas of Pine Ridge hung the derisive nickname on him, "Young Man Afraid of His Indians."[91]

Nine days before the acting commissioner sent his directive to Royer, the agent had frantically telegraphed the Indian Bureau with a request for troops presumably to restore order and to overawe the ghost dancers at the reservation.[92] So strained had conditions become at Pine Ridge, at the height of the Ghost Dance, that the investigation was conducted less rigorously. Even Belt said as much when he informed the secretary of the interior on December 1 that, though Agent Royer had his orders, further investigation was unwarranted.[93]

It was into the charged atmosphere of the Ghost Dance among the Sioux that Cody's Show Indians returned from Europe. One of the ironies is that the Indian Bureau, frequently hostile toward the Show Indians, now expected them to act as harbingers of Euroamerican civilization. Another is that the number of Indians who had died on tour, five from disease and two in accidents, was for Morgan and his friends (indeed, for anyone reading accounts in the newspapers) a shocking statistic that they hoped to turn to their advantage. The death toll—from starvation, exposure, and gunfire—at Pine Ridge reservation within a month of their return would shock the nation.

Show Indians had seen London, Paris, and Rome. They had sojourned in the world of the *Wasichus*. And now they must tell some of their people that they deluded themselves in longing after an Indian messiah. More than likely, a great cataclysm would not sweep away the world as the ghost dancers knew it—at least not at the moment anyone anticipated. The Indian Bureau asked the Show Indians, reviled as symbols of a way of life on the verge of extinction, to explain to their people the nature of things to come. As far as the commissioner and his cohorts knew, American Indians could expect much more of the New World rather than a return to old ways, the miracle of the Ghost Dance religion. Acting Commissioner Belt believed that the Show Indians had seen that future—or at least the vastness of the world of the *Wasichus*—and that they must persuade their families and friends to awake from their fevered dreams.

6
GHOST DANCERS OF LONDON, 1891-1892

"Any man who can exercise such judgment is quite
capable of choosing his occupation and profiting by it."

The "little excitement" to which Acting Commissioner Belt referred represented one of the largest social and religious movements among American Indians during the nineteenth century. By late November 1890, newspapers and magazines reported a great religious excitement among western Indian tribes, most notably the Sioux in the Dakotas. Plains and Great Basin Indians, since the late summer, had been dancing a "ghost dance" given to them by a mysterious prophet—some said the "Indian messiah"—who lived somewhere in the Rocky Mountain West.

The November invasion of the Sioux reservations by almost half of the U.S. Army represented the largest deployment since the Civil War.[1]

The Ghost Dance religion of Wovoka, a Paiute spiritual leader and weather prophet, appealed to many Indians in the West. Tribes had been defeated militarily, removed from their homelands, concentrated on reservations, and forced to accept new laws directed by the government of the United States. Broken treaties, land encroachment, depletion of traditional sources of food, epidemic diseases, and relentless attacks upon their religions and cultures by Euroamericans demoralized the tribes. Many members listened attentively to Wovoka's apostles preaching a religion of deliverance.[2]

A time would come, according to one version of Wovoka's prophecy, when all Indians living and dead would be reunited on a renewed earth. Death would have no dominion. Indians would be free forever from destitution, disease, and interference by non-Indians. The faithful could hasten the transformation by performing certain rituals, chief among them a circular dance renowned as the "ghost dance." In their exhaustion from performing the dance, and in their desire to experience visions, ghost dancers would collapse and "die." After returning to consciousness, they would tell about their meetings with deceased relations and friends.[3]

It is not the purpose here to retell the story of the Ghost Dance. Cody's aborted mission to Sitting Bull, the deaths of the Hunkpapa visionary and some of his followers at the Grand River settlement in mid-December—what some Hunkpapas believed then, and since, to be Sitting Bull's assassination—followed two weeks later by the slaughter of Big Foot's band at Wounded Knee are familiar stories.[4] The tragedy that engulfed the Sioux of the Dakotas, however, had other consequences for the Show Indians.

In the aftermath of the slaughter at Wounded Knee, the Indian Office sought to dissociate itself from blame as either participant in, or contributor to, the disaster. To Bureau personnel, military blunders led to the bloodshed. Commissioner Morgan launched his own investigation into the causes and consequences of the Ghost Dance, prompted in part by his desire to fix blame on the army and General Nelson A. Miles, commander of military operations against the Sioux, for Wounded Knee.[5]

Morgan outlawed the performance of ghost dances. He ordered his agents to arrest anyone defying the ban. How various agents responded to the order depended upon their interpretation of the attitude and demeanor of the Indians. Except at the Sioux reservations, civilian or military authorities arrested few ghost dancers.[6]

Acting Commissioner Belt had wished to pursue the investigation into

THE SIOUX OF 1890   PHOTO BY J A ANDERSON

22 : Identified as "Bill Cody's Show Indians, 1890," these would have been some of the Wild West show veterans who, after meeting with Assistant Commissioner R. V. Belt at the Interior Department, were asked to encourage loyalty to the government among the Lakota during the Ghost Dance disturbances of December 1890. (South Dakota State Historical Society, Pierre)

the condition of Cody's Indians, but the "Sioux Outbreak" got in the way. Two days after receiving notice, on January, 8 of his suspension from executive service by the president, Agent Royer at Pine Ridge submitted his report to the commissioner. Remarkably, even in the midst of the Ghost Dance the otherwise hapless agent had been able to carry out an investigation first ordered by Belt on November 24. "Young Man Afraid of His Indians" had actually secured fifty-nine sworn affidavits from the nearly one hundred Show Indians returned to Pine Ridge. None lodged any complaints against Cody's Wild West. Furthermore, it pleased the agent to report that "since the return of these Indians to their reservation they have all used their influence and shown by their actions that they were to be classed on the side of right and stood by their government in the late excitement among their people." They traveled to some of the Ghost Dance camps to advise calm and patience. If the world were to be renewed in the spring, they could afford to be patient just a little longer. If not, the *Wasichus* had too many guns. To the east, beyond sight, *Wasichus* were numberless. Even Commissioner Morgan, who despised the Show Indians, conceded that they had learned much in their travels. He praised them for remaining loyal to the government, for counseling patience, and for not succumbing to the delusion that an Indian messiah now walked the earth.[7] Actually, some of the Show Indians could easily imagine an Indian deliverer. They simply did not believe one then walked the earth, and certainly not the author of the Ghost Dance religion.

General Miles, at the close of military operations, took with him to his headquarters in Chicago thirty Indians identified as the "ringleaders" of the Ghost Dance among the Sioux. He intended to hold them for several months at Fort Sheridan, under his personal observation. Such action, he informed the adjutant general, "is the strongest assurance of success and guarantee of permanent peace." He concluded, in an obvious swipe at the Indian Bureau, that "nothing is necessary now to secure that [peace] other than good government in the future."[8]

Cody applied to the commissioner for a renewal of his contract. He asked for permission to hire seventy-five Sioux. He enticed the commissioner with a promise to make his selection among those Oglalas and Brules who "might be mischievous in the Spring if allowed to remain upon the reservation."[9] Members of the Nebraska delegation to Congress endorsed Cody's request. Writing for the group, Republican Senator Charles F. Manderson, president *pro tem*, assured the commissioner that he had "no question as to *the right* of Indians living on Reservations to contract for employment in which they can be self supporting." Further, if no regulation existed "by which they can obtain such employment, they will enter into it as I believe, even in the presence of opposition from your department."[10] Morgan was nothing if not loyal to his party. Cody received permission.

Cody visited General Miles in Chicago before returning to the Sioux country to hire a group of Show Indians for the upcoming season. Miles suggested that Buffalo Bill take to Europe those Fort Sheridan prisoners willing to accompany him. The general thought it "a most excellent measure" for a number of reasons:

> It would give them occupation for a year and a half without expense to the Government; they would be away from the Sioux country during

23 : Buffalo Bill, American Horse, and Indian police following the formal "surrender" of the Sioux at the close of "The Sioux Outbreak." The photograph was probably taken at Pine Ridge agency, January 1891. (Cody Collection, State Historical Society of Colorado)

---

that time; their experiences would be most valuable to them as they would see the extent, power and numbers of the white race, and when they eventually return, would be entirely different men from what they were when they left the reservation.[11]

Commissioner Morgan enthusiastically supported the decision, although he let it be known that it had been made on the recommendation of the army and not the Indian Bureau. Morgan reasoned that in allowing Cody to take the imprisoned Sioux, who had been described as "restless spirits" in official correspondence, any renewal of the Ghost Dance religion among the Sioux could be postponed for at least the length of the proposed tour. In that two years, Morgan believed, the religion would cease to inspire rebellion among the Sioux.

On this occasion, Commissioner Morgan accepted, and at the same time reviled, the popular image of the Indian that he believed the Wild West show portrayed. He regarded the Sioux prisoners as wild, treacherous, and incapable of civilization. They *belonged* in Cody's Wild West show. And what did the Fort Sheridan prisoners think? If Kicking Bear's comments are any indication, they were ecstatic to be out of the stockade. "For six weeks I have been a dead man," Wovoka's preeminent Sioux apostle told Buffalo Bill. "Now that I see you, I am alive again."[12] Twenty-three of the prisoners, along with an additional seventy-five Sioux, sailed from Philadelphia on April 1, 1891, aboard the Red Star steamship *Switzerland* bound for Antwerp. They joined the show at its winter quarters at Strasbourg.[13]

Reformers responded immediately. Mary C. Collins, a Congregational missionary at the Standing Rock reservation, seems to have initiated the protests. She had become an inveterate opponent to the employment of Indians in Wild West shows. A friend, but occasional adversary, of Sitting Bull, she believed that his tour with Buffalo Bill in 1885 had spoiled the Hunkpapa leader. He had supposedly seen only the vice and corruption of Euroamerican society and therefore wished to have nothing to do with it.[14] She supposed that Sitting Bull, for that reason, had fought the civilization programs of the Indian Bureau. He had become a champion of the Ghost Dance among the Hunkpapas. That fact and his contrariness had gotten him killed.[15]

While visiting the humanitarian retired general Oliver O. Howard in Glenco, Illinois, Collins learned about the Sioux prisoners taken by General Miles. Ironically, some local children of Collins's acquaintance wished to see the imprisoned ghost dancers. She decided that she could accede to the children's wishes and, at the same time, "do [the prisoners] some good by visiting them." She learned from the prisoners that plans had been made to send them to Europe with Buffalo Bill. Afraid that they had been coerced, she asked the Indians, "speaking their language, and they said they were willing to go; that they understood they would be made prisoners there for six months at Sheridan, and that perhaps when they returned west after that time, they might be arrested, and tried by the civil courts and punished." She returned on Sunday, March 15, to hold Sab-

24 : *Nineteen of the Fort Sheridan Sioux prisoners. Blamed for the "Sioux Outbreak of 1890," these Sioux ghost dancers joined Cody's Wild West. (National Archives)*

bath services with the prisoners. On that occasion "some of them begged me to interfere in their behalf, [for they] did not want to go with Buffalo Bill, but were willing to stay there for six months and then return to Pine Ridge."[16] Or so she reported afterward to General Howard.

Howard told Collins that, fortuitously, Commissioner Morgan had arrived in Chicago and planned to address a meeting of the Congregational Club on the following evening. They decided that Collins should go into Chicago. Not only did she speak to Morgan, who reassured her of his opposition to Indians in the shows; but she also persuaded the club to champion the cause. At the evening session, the three hundred ministers and business leaders drafted a resolution protesting against "any man being allowed to go with Buffalo Bill." They appointed a committee of three, with

KICKINGBEAR

25 : *Paroled from the Fort Sheridan stockade by order of General Nelson A. Miles in the late winter of 1891, Kicking Bear, one of the leaders of the Ghost Dance among the Lakota, traveled with the Wild West during its European tour. He and Short Bull were celebrated as leaders of "The Last Indian War." (Buffalo Bill Historical Center, Cody, Wyoming)*

26 : *Mary Clementine Collins (1846–1920), a Congregational missionary among the Lakota, was described by a biographer as a "wary but respectful" friend of Sitting Bull. She opposed the hiring of Indians by Wild West shows. She led the agitation against Cody's taking the so-called ringleaders of the Ghost Dance to Europe in the spring of 1891. (South Dakota State Historical Society, Pierre)*

Collins as its chairman, and sent her to Washington to deliver the resolution to President Harrison.[17]

Other Congregational clubs throughout the East soon involved themselves in a letter-writing campaign to newspapers and governmental agencies. The *Christian Register*, under the title "Stop the Farce," editorialized that permission given by the Interior Department to Cody's Wild West should be immediately withdrawn. "It is the duty of the government to educate the Indian out of his old traditions," the editorial continued, "not to go into partnership with a circus to perpetuate them. Let the friends of the Indian protest loud and strong against this procedure."[18] M. M. Cutter, secretary of the Congregational Club of Boston, sent the secretary of war a resolution adopted by the organization decrying the "unfortunate moral and physical results of employment in Wild West shows."[19] Closer to the late disturbances among the Sioux, the editor of the Gordon, Nebraska, *Independent* wrote that "we have seen these show Indians return home reeling drunk, dead drunk, so drunk it was necessary to carry them to their tepees."[20]

All that the campaign seemed to have accomplished was to put the secretary of the interior into an uncompromising mood. When Collins met with him, he explained his disquietude at all the publicity generated thus far. Why, he asked the Dakota missionary, "did you not write a private letter and state the fact to me, instead of going before a public meeting in Chicago!" More than anything, he added, "I want you to understand, Madam, that I cannot be driven."[21] He saw nothing wrong in Buffalo Bill's Wild West show. He therefore did not object to the Show Indians going to Europe with Buffalo Bill. If Collins and her associates wished the Sioux prisoners returned to the Fort Sheridan stockade, they would just have to take it up with the secretary of war.[22]

Herbert Welsh of the IRA also joined the protest. Still smarting from his rebuff by Major Burke the previous October, Welsh had wanted to press his investigation into the shows' effects on Indians. He sent inquiries to the agents at Pine Ridge and Standing Rock reservations; but owing to the Ghost Dance and other distractions, by the time he received replies the Show Indians had already left the United States.[23]

Captain Charles Penny, acting agent at Pine Ridge, forwarded Welsh's questions to Cody in Europe. From Brussels on May 8, Nate Salsbury answered on behalf of the organization. He told Penny that, upon "a cursory examination of our books," Lakota Show Indians since 1885 had been paid seventy-four thousand dollars. That sum did not include the wages paid to Pawnees and Omahas; neither did it include any part of the expenses for transportation and maintenance. The letter represents a creative summary of Show Indian employment in Cody's Wild West:

You can also add to this sum the cost of a good substantial suit of clothes which we invariably present to each Indian at the close of each season of service with us and which is entirely outside of our contract with them. We give the clothes as a sort of premium for good conduct and saving habits. I am sorry that no record has been kept of the money sent home by them. . . . We do not pretend to control the disposition of their wages. In the first place we have no shadow of a right to do so. In the next place we find that an Indian knows the value of a dollar quite as well as a white man. Of course we constantly urge upon them the value of saving habits and we exercise a constant vigilance that they do not fall into the hands of tradesmen who are sharpers. This is hardly necessary as we find that they have as good a knowledge of relative values as any Jew or Gentile with whom they may come in contact.

They transmit their money home through the various agencies of Post Office Orders, Bank checks, and express companies. And as each man is a free agent in his personal affairs we have no means of knowing what sums they send without direct inquiry of them. This inquiry we will not make as it would be a direct violation of our rule to treat them with the same personal consideration as we do our white employees. We believe that the application of this rule adds to their self esteem and dignifies the relations between us.

It would interest you, I know, to be present on a pay day to note the careful scrutiny each man gives to his account. They are honorable to a degree in paying their debts and equally careful to get all that belongs to them, some of them going so far as to enquire the rate of exchange between a foreign coin and the American dollar. I assume that any man who can exercise such judgment is quite capable of choosing his occupation and profiting by it.[24]

Salsbury concluded by describing Agent Penny as a "real friend of the Indians in our employ." He resented, however, having to suffer the abuse and impertinence of people "who know no more about the real character of an Indian than they do about a degraded Hottentot."[25] His resentment was about to increase dramatically.

On her way back to Chicago from Washington, D.C., Mary Collins visited Welsh in Philadelphia. Welsh then prepared a statement for publication in the New York newspapers.[26] They both hoped, as Collins explained to her sponsors in Chicago, to persuade "the best people of our country" to help them bring pressure on the government. "I fully believe that our work has not been in vain," Collins reflected, "and that He who knoweth the end from the beginning will bring our desires to pass."[27] Welsh's letter appeared in the New York *Evening Post* of April 27, under the title "Demoralizing the Indians." Whereas Nate Salsbury had stressed the Indian as free agent in his communications with the Indian service, Welsh emphasized governmental paternalism.

"Let it be remembered by those who read this story," he observed, "that the Government's acknowledged relation to the Indian is that of guardian to ward." That relationship implied governmental protection and guidance until the Indian had reached an advanced condition of mental and moral development. Welsh explained how the inordinate pride of Sitting Bull, stimulated by his employment in Cody's Wild West show, had led him to urge rebellion against good order during the Ghost Dance. That example should have served as a cautionary tale; but the government had made a mistake. It had assisted a "private speculation" by allowing Indians, against their best interest, to join a Wild West show. Worse, in freeing the prisoners, the government had rewarded them for "treason, thieving, and possibly murder, while the peaceable man remains at home in poverty and contemplation as to the true significance of the white man's ways!" Although nothing could be done at the present time to rectify the situation, perhaps a large public protest would prevent future abuse. Welsh concluded that because their appeals to governmental authorities had been in vain, they would now court public opinion.[28]

When Nate Salsbury read Welsh's remarks in the *Evening Post*, he sent a scathing reply to the secretary of the IRA in care of the editor of the newspaper. He questioned both the intelligence and credibility of Mary Collins, whose "active exertions" would do little more than "take bread out of the mouths of people who are anxious to be self supporting and independent of Missionary Boards—or Boarders." He also questioned whether working in the Wild West had indeed "stimulated" Sitting Bull's "inordinate pride," as Collins described. "It was stimulated" instead, Salsbury explained, "by his confidence in himself and his hatred of the white men who had been robbing and abusing him for years." Finally, in courting public opinion, Salsbury asked Welsh:

to insist that all treaties made with the Indians shall be vigorously observed; [and] that they shall no longer be robbed and starved; that Congregational Clubs shall not take the unsupported testimony of female cranks as a basis for their interference with the material welfare of Indians who seek honorable employment.[29]

For his part, Welsh would just as soon let the matter "be passed over in silence" were it not for the fact that Salsbury had challenged Collins's statements on a number of key issues.[30] Her "exertions" had placed the secretary of the IRA in an awkward position. Worse still, Agent James McLaughlin, at Standing Rock, informed Welsh that Collins had erred in several of her statements. Although the agent disliked the shows, he knew that Cody's organization had never mistreated the Show Indians, had never given them whiskey, and had never taken them to "low places."[31] In mounting anxiety, Welsh wrote to Collins, all but begging her to provide him with documentary proof of her allegations against Cody's show. She claimed to have newspaper clippings that would corroborate her assertions. "If that is the case, can you not secure me copies of them?" There is no record that Collins ever complied with Welsh's request.[32]

Welsh's investigation and Collins's agitation had no immediate consequences. Cody's Show Indians, including the Fort Sheridan ghost dancers, performed successfully in Europe throughout the summer and fall. Collins and Welsh, however, did contribute to a growing conviction among the opponents of Wild West shows that they must create their own alternate version. As Hazel Hertzberg writes, Wild West shows were anathema to the Christian reformers, "a perpetuation of everything they were trying to eliminate. They greatly preferred the Indian exhibitions showing modern Indian accomplishments."[33] As of the spring of 1891 no such exhibitions existed. By the late summer, however, the Indian Bureau, with the active support of reformers such as Welsh and Collins, would be making plans to celebrate the proper image of the Indian at the forthcoming Columbian Exposition.[34]

Cody, Burke, and Salsbury had only to count their gate receipts each evening to reassure themselves about public opinion. The 1891 European tour began with performances at Karlsruhe, Germany, and then proceeded to Mannheim, Mainz, Weisbaden, Cologne, Dortmund, Duisburg, Krefeld, Aachen, and Berlin.[35] Something new had been added to the show.

Nate Salsbury, in anticipating the possibility of an Interior Department ban on the employment of Indians, revised the show so that it "would embody the whole subject of horsemanship." He recruited equestrians from around the world: Syrian and Bedouin horsemen, British lancers from the Prince of Wales regiment, German guards from the German emperor's Uhlan regiment, French chasseurs, Russian cossacks, Argentine gauchos,

Mexican vaqueros, and former troopers from the U.S. Sixth Cavalry. With the cowboys, cowgirls, and mounted cowboy band already well established in the troupe, Salsbury created the Congress of Rough Riders of the World.[36]

It was during the spring swing through Germany that the old Prussian high command became interested in the logistics of the show. "We never moved without at least forty officers of the Prussian guard standing all about with notebooks, taking down every detail of the performance," Annie Oakley wrote in her diary. "They made minute notes of how we pitched camp—the exact number of men needed, every man's position, how long it took, how we boarded the trains and packed the horses and broke camp; every rope and bundle and kit was inspected and mapped." The traveling kitchens intrigued them. Little did Oakley realize that twenty-five years later Americans would learn about the "marvelous traveling kitchens of the Teuton army, serving meals piping hot on the road to Brussels—an idea gained from the Buffalo Bill Wild West show when we toured Germany!"[37]

The route next took the show to Holland and Belgium. Following a side trip to the battlefield at Waterloo, Cody's Wild West sailed from Antwerp to Grimbsy on the North Sea where a tour of provincial England commenced the last week of June. The troupe gave performances in Liverpool, Manchester, Leeds, Sheffield, and Birmingham, and then in Cardiff, Wales, by September. Salsbury revived Steele Mackaye's indoor pageant for the upcoming winter stand in Scotland. To the Congress of Rough Riders, he added certain novelty acts: Sam Lockart's performing elephants, fresh from their triumph in France; and a group of Zulus brought to Europe by explorer, journalist, and sometime American Henry M. Stanley.[38] In Glasgow, the Zulus met the Sioux for the benefit of the photographers. One of the cowboys in Cody's contingent called on Rocky Bear to try his sign language on the South Africans. A Zulu leader apparently understood some of the gestures and answered him.[39]

For some of the Sioux prisoners, their absence of more than eleven months from their homes seemed sufficient punishment. They informed Buffalo Bill that they wanted to go home. Because he himself was tired and ready for a break from the daily grind of performances, he decided to take a short vacation by returning to North Platte, Nebraska.[40]

On the last night in Glasgow's East End Exhibition Building before sailing for home, Kicking Bear tarried as his compatriots filed out of the arena. He recounted in Lakota his deeds of valor. George Croger, the interpreter for the Sioux, thought Kicking Bear's actions in the arena

signified connivance. Croger had often found the ghost dancer talking in hushed tones with Short Bull, another Sioux apostle of Wovoka. Whenever whites came around, the interpreter explained, the Indians would cease their conversation.[41]

Cody and the Indians sailed for home on March 4, aboard the Atlantic and State Line steamer *S. S. Coreau*.[42] Days before, Nate Salsbury had written to General Miles, trying to explain his predicament. "I have exhausted every argument in seeking to keep [the Sioux prisoners] here — but led by Kicking Bear they have resolved to return." Kicking Bear apparently believed that he and his compatriots would be allowed to go straight to their reservations. Salsbury explained:

> After an experience of eleven months with Kicking Bear, I am forced to the conclusion that . . . [h]e is turbulent and lawless. Has no fear of consequences and will promote trouble on the Reservation *sure* [*sic*]. The war spirit is evidently on him at present. . . . Short Bull is a religious enthusiast, but is a decent fellow, amendable to reason and has a sense of honor utterly lacking in Kicking Bear.[43]

News of the prisoners' forthcoming return to the United States also troubled leaders in the military and the Indian service. Major General John M. Scofield, Headquarters of the Army, recommended that the Indians, upon arriving in New York, be returned immediately to Fort Sheridan. The secretary of war concurred.[44] General Miles, like Croger, hinted at a conspiracy. It had been understood that the Sioux prisoners would be occupied and kept in Europe until the fall of 1892, but influences had been at work on the reservation to draw them back. Miles therefore recommended that Kicking Bear, Revenge, and a few others remain under army control.[45] The remaining ghost dancers would be permitted to go home. Accordingly, Adjutant General J. C. Kelton ordered that all but the "plotters" be allowed to return to South Dakota.[46]

George Croger would turn over the prisoners to the military in Chicago. Cody's company covered expenses for one noncommissioned officer and three enlisted men to serve as guards.[47] The party arrived by limited express train at the Baltimore and Ohio depot in Chicago at noon on March 13. Omnibuses conveyed the travelers to the Northwestern Railroad depot, where Croger divided the Indians into two groups. A detach-

---

27 : Annie Oakley, years after leaving the Wild West, in "Indian Costume." (Buffalo Bill Historical Center, Cody, Wyoming)

28 : Kicking Bear (L) and Short Bull (R), Wovoka's preeminent Lakota disciples, who brought the Ghost Dance to the Sioux reservations in the spring of 1890. Speaking to a reporter after he joined the Wild West, Short Bull said of Buffalo Bill, "He never fought us except when we needed it." (National Archives)

ment of troops dispatched from Fort Sheridan took into custody Kicking Bear, Short Bull, Long Bull, One Star, Revenge, Brings the White (sometimes Brings White Horse), High Eagle, Standing Bear, Knows His Voice, Brave, and Wounds with Arrows. Croger kept with him the other prisoners, among them Both Sides White, White Horse, Bear Lies Down, Charging Thunder, Has No Horses, Holy Bird, Kills Crow, Pulls Him Out, Short Man, Shooting Star, Medicine Horse, Her Blanket, and Plenty Blanket. They left for Pine Ridge early in the evening.[48]

Perhaps mindful of the close scrutiny that their business would receive in the wake of recent investigations, or perhaps indeed out of genuine concern, Cody and his partners went to extraordinary lengths to meet the needs of their employees. Indians who had taken ill on tour received the best medical care regardless of the expense. Those too ill to continue were returned to the reservation.[49] One performer, Eagle Bird (or Eagle Star), had to have his leg amputated following an accident. Tetanus set in and Eagle Bird died. Buffalo Bill sent his widow 500 dollars plus his back pay of 120 dollars; and he also agreed to pay her 25 dollars a month for the rest of her life.[50]

29 : The Oglala Has No Horses, wearing for the studio portrait his war bonnet, fabric shirt, arm and wrist bands of ornate quill work, Bone hairpipe breastplate and heavy wool blanket wrapped around his lower torso. Another portrait by Häsebier. (Buffalo Bill Historical Center, Cody, Wyoming)

Allegations again reached the secretary of the interior that Cody and company had mistreated Indians and that the Sioux prisoners had returned in deplorable condition. Secretary Noble ordered an investigation into the condition of the repatriated Sioux.[51] He received no corroboration of the charges. Accordingly, on April 14, Noble granted Cody permission again to employ an additional fifty Sioux. Commissioner Morgan would not authorize the employment of Indians under his signature. He had the assistant commissioner sign and send the appropriate letters.[52]

When Commissioner Morgan learned that General Miles planned to release some of the ghost dancers from confinement at Fort Sheridan, he sent strong protests to the War Department. The tone of his letters has an almost frantic quality about them. "Affairs at Pine Ridge agency have been in a very unsettled and unsatisfactory state ever since the [late] disturbances," he reminded Secretary Noble, whom he had saddled with the responsibility of granting permission to employ Indians.[53] He doubted the wisdom of allowing prisoners to return at present to Pine Ridge. He feared that they "and their stories will have a very decided tendency to unsettle the minds of the Indians and to interfere with the forces now at work which make peace."[54]

Secretary Noble referred the commissioner's letter to the War Department; but unlike Morgan, Noble explained to Secretary of War Stephen Elkins that he was not at all apprehensive about the ghost dancers' return.[55] General Miles, therefore, released all of the prisoners except Short Bull and Kicking Bear (and they were freed in October).[56] As an added gesture, he sent one of them "to visit some of the jails or court rooms and to the State Penitentiary at Joliet, Ills." He hoped that this would impress upon Brings the White, onetime student at Carlisle, "the restraint and punishment for evil doers, and then to send him back to his tribe quietly and alone."[57] No one, least of all the commissioner, expressed any objections. What Brings the White thought is unrecorded.

Commissioner Morgan succeeded in thwarting one of the Wild West shows that season. The Carver and Whitney show ran afoul of the Pine Ridge agent in the late spring of 1892. Carver, after leaving his partnership with Cody, had teamed with Fred C. Whitney of Detroit. Captain Brown, an army officer recommended to the post at Pine Ridge by General Miles, accused Carver of bad faith and kidnapping. Carver's company used the services of James A. Asay, part owner of a store in Rushville, Nebraska, as a contracting agent. Captain Brown charged Asay and his employees of coming to the reservation and spiriting away potential Show Indians to the rail line at Rushville. There they plied the Indians with whiskey, got them arrested by the local constabulary, and then arranged for their bail, apparently set at one thousand dollars. The Indians could avoid paying the bond if they agreed to join the cast of Doc Carver's Wild America.[58] Despite Asay's sworn denial, Commissioner Morgan had all the evidence he needed. He forbade permission to the Carver and Whitney circus to employ Show Indians.[59]

At the time of the ban, Doc Carver's Wild America was appearing in San Francisco. A few members of the company performed "The Scout" at the grand opera house each evening. During the day, in Golden Gate Park the entire company performed the program which included: Indian races on ponies and on foot; a reenactment of the Pony Express; bronc riding and driving Texas steers; feats of marksmanship; a camp of Cheyenne, Apache, Pawnee, Washo, and Sioux "fresh from the Pine Ridge reservation" (thus lending credence to some of Brown's charges that Indians had left the reservation without permission); an Indian attack on the Overland Stage; scalp and war dances; and a "Ghost Dance by those who performed it."[60]

Standing Bear, an elderly Brule leader and, until only recently, one of the Fort Sheridan prisoners, told a reporter that "my feet ache here; I cannot breathe."[61] He had been among the last of the prisoners released by General Miles.[62] He told the reporter in San Francisco that he did not think that he could restrain his warriors if they decided to return to the "warpath." The Indians appeared to the newsman to be "a pretty solemn bunch." Doc Carver, on more than one occasion, had to implore the Show Indians to yell even louder during some of the battle reenactments. Standing Bear, however, was not all that solemn. He smiled considerably when he watched a New York actress named Miss Harris mount her horse from the wrong side.[63] Standing Bear and the others in the troupe would be the last Indians employed by Carver for some time to come.

Commissioner Morgan's ban against the Carver and Whitney show included a directive. He ordered agents to tell the Indians that should they defy the ban against Carver, join the show, and then find themselves stranded far from home, the Bureau would not aid them.[64] Morgan's directive acquired even more authority when certain incidents became known about Indians apparently employed by Doc Carver and then abandoned in Australia.

In April 1893, the U.S. consul at Sydney, New South Wales, wrote the agent at Pine Ridge that two Sioux, Eagle Elk and American Bear, had been stranded in that province. "They were set adrift," William Kapus told the agent, "and they sank to the lowest levels of demoralization and degradation." The Sioux had been arrested repeatedly for vagrancy and drunkenness.[65] Kapus received authorization from the State Department to book passage for the two men on a steamer bound for San Francisco. At San Francisco, the collector of customs received instructions to place Eagle Elk and American Bear on a train to South Dakota. Morgan, just before surrendering his office to Democratic successor Daniel M. Browning, used the incident as "a good illustration of the usual outcome of Indians who allow themselves to be enticed away" by Wild West shows. He ordered his agents to read the Kapus letter to those Indians who still looked longingly beyond the boundaries of their homesteads.[66]

How the two Sioux had actually gotten to Australia remained a mystery. Carver, for example, had taken his show to Australia in October 1890, and it had remained there well into the new year. Eagle Elk and American Bear, however, had been members of the Pine Ridge group hired by Cody for his 1891–1892 European tour. According to a *Chicago Tribune* story, the two had "escaped" from Cody and then "turned up in Australia."[67] If indeed the escapees had joined Carver, he remained silent about it. By the time the story became widely known, Carver and Whitney were already under ban by the Bureau. They may have thought it wise to be quiet and not risk further punitive action. Cody, for his part, refused responsibility since "escaped" showmen did not constitute violation of the agreement with the Interior Department. As far as he was concerned, it was he who had been bonded for "faithful performance" of the contract. Eagle Elk and American Bear, in leaving the show, had proved unreliable.[68] With Morgan out of office, the incident passed quickly from public scrutiny. Remarkably, given all the agitation by Indian-policy reformers after the employment of the Fort Sheridan prisoners, the odyssey of American Bear and Eagle Elk caused hardly a stir by comparison.

At the end of the 1892 season, Doc Carver returned the Indians to their homes. The Interior Department refunded his ten-thousand-dollar bond.[69] He thereafter quit the Show Indian business for a number of years. Buffalo Bill returned to England for another triumphant season. His show enjoyed great popularity at home and abroad. He numbered the powerful and influential among his friends. It turned out that persons opposed to his show could do little to hurt him. Letters, petitions, memorials, and newspaper editorials had slight effect. Knowing that the secretary of the interior approved of Cody's employment of Indians, and that Buffalo Bill seemed to have friends in high places, Richard Henry Pratt of the Indian Industrial School, Carlisle, Pennsylvania, wondered aloud to his reformer friends, "what's the use."[70]

The 1892 season marked a return for Buffalo Bill's Wild West to Earl's Court. This time the show would be the centerpiece of the London International Horticultural Exhibition. Cody opened the new season on May 7, 1892.[71] The troupe gave one performance a day, two on weekends, throughout the summer at Earl's Court. As in their previous visits to London, Show Indians toured the city. Newspaper reporters found them as quaint and quotable as ever. At St. Paul's Cathedral, Two Elks showed great interest in the Duke of Wellington's imposing carved stone sarcophagus. "Those who put him there," Two Elks commented, "must not have wanted him to get away again."[72]

Much of the 1887 show would be repeated. The new equestrian acts of the Congress of Rough Riders ensured great enthusiasm from the crowds who traveled out to the west end of London. The Russian cossacks, led by Prince Ivan Rostomov Macheradse, proved to be particular favorites with the crowds as well as royalty.[73] Once more, Queen Victoria arranged for a command performance. On June 26, the troupe transformed the tennis courts at Windsor Castle into an arena.[74] Whereas the Indians had fascinated the queen during the performance five years before, this time the cossacks captured her attention.[75] As a token of her appreciation, she bestowed gifts on Cody, Salsbury, and Burke at the conclusion of the performance.[76]

The show suffered only one casualty that summer. On June 11, Long Wolf died, probably from pneumonia, at the West London Hospital. Attending physicians described the cause of death as partly due to old wounds as well as to a current illness. Dr. Maitland Coffin said that Long Wolf "was a complete mass of [old] gun-shot wounds and sabre cuts." Cody and the Show Indians conducted a graveside memorial at the West Brompton Cemetery.[77] Others in the troupe found the London climate difficult. A woman reporter for the London *Morning* visited the Sioux encampment later in August. The Sioux had constructed a sweatlodge out of canvass and logs. The reporter referred to it as a "bathing tent," and likened it to a Turkish bath. She found in the lodge the daughter of Blackheart singing to her child, who appeared quite ill. The mother sang soothingly in Lakota (and in translation), "Swing, swing, little one, lullaby, sleep my little one, sleep." The reporter was astonished at the woman's tenderness and "motherly concern." Indians, she discovered, shared some of the same human emotions as good British subjects.[78]

The season at Earl's Court closed on October 12, 1892. Although not as grand as the jubilee year tour, Cody and his partners nevertheless labeled it a smashing success. Cody and the Indians landed in New York on October 24. Their arrival marked the end of almost four years of touring Europe. The next spring would inaugurate the show's most successful season, yet as part of the Columbian Exposition.[79]

On November 1, the returning Show Indians arrived at Pine Ridge agency. They had traveled that afternoon by wagon up from the railroad at Rushville, Nebraska. All signed the agency register. Some signed their names; others made their marks. Under the column designating "occupation" they are listed as "Showmen."[80] Some in the party like Little Wolf and Good Elk had completed only their first tour with the Wild West.[81] Others, like Ghost Dog and Little Iron, had been to Europe twice. Still others, like Star, had been among those identified as ringleaders of the Ghost Dance. All would be there in the spring when Cody again canvassed the reservation, looking for Show Indians to commemorate the first Columbian voyage.

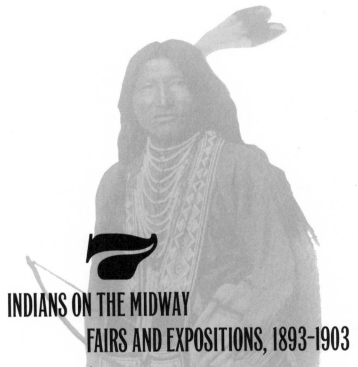

INDIANS ON THE MIDWAY
FAIRS AND EXPOSITIONS, 1893-1903

*"To be picturesque and impressive . . . the
primitive Indian must be presented."*

A financial panic early in 1893 descended into an industrial
depression by the next winter, the likes of which the American people
had never before experienced. Banks closed, jobs disappeared, immigration dropped, suffering increased, and doubts about the immutable laws
of progress swept the country. Whereas many in the nation agonized over
the economic collapse, at least in Chicago a few citizens prospered.[1]

On May 1, 1893, the Columbian Exposition opened. A brief, but severe,
thunderstorm preceded the formal ceremonies. Despite an ominous sky,

nearly 200,000 people filled Jackson Park, the site of the fair.[2] President Grover Cleveland addressed the multitude. Those near the ceremonial stage could hear him extol the power of the dormant machinery awakened by electricity, and liken it to hope awakening forces that would transform society.[3] In unison with the choir's singing of the Hallelujah Chorus, the thundering of cannon, and the screeching of whistles from boats on Lake Michigan, the president closed the electric circuit that energized the exposition's machinery.[4]

Chicago's White City spread over 664 acres on the shore of Lake Michigan. Among its myriad attractions, the U.S. Government Building housed, beneath a bunting-draped ceiling in its north wing, the Smithsonian Institution exhibit. "Once in the federal building," a guidebook read, "if true enjoyment is to be found anywhere, surely it is here." Visitors entered a little world of interest. They could gaze upon the "facial characteristics of Indian races, as also their dress and occupations; whole [families] are represented in cases, or singly, both men and women engaged in some useful art."[5] Many, but not all, of the Smithsonian's exhibits were ready by opening day. A separate Anthropological Building on the fairgrounds housed most of the ethnological exhibits authorized by the World's Columbian Commission. The building and its exhibits were largely the creation of Frederick Ward Putnam, curator of the Peabody Museum of American Archaeology and Ethnology at Harvard University.[6]

In May 1890, Putnam had proposed that, as part of a celebration marking four hundred years of progress since Columbus, the stages of the development of mankind in the Americas should be demonstrated. Such a grand collection of specimens, he insisted, could be placed afterward in a permanent museum, which would then grow in importance and value over the years. It would be a lasting monument to Chicago and its fair, or at least that is what Putnam told the Chicago business leaders whom he asked to help finance the project. Parties would be sent into the field to collect materials from the Inuits of Baffin Bay, the inhabitants of Tierra del Fuego, and others in between. The fair commissioners approved Putnam's plan and he, not so coincidentally, became chief of the Department of Ethnology and Archaeology.

The trustees of Harvard granted Putnam a leave of absence in 1892. He and his able assistant, Franz Boas, who had recently resigned from Clark University, organized both museum exhibits and "outdoor, living exhibits" of indigenous peoples from North and South America. The project grew to such an extent that over one hundred assistants eventually worked on it.

The fair commission authorized a separate building to house the museum collection. Putnam insisted that it be named the "Anthropological Building" and the directors concurred. Putnam thus introduced the newer term to the American public. It was not until July 4, 1893, two months after the fair opened, that the building and its exhibits accepted visitors. Putnam's contribution to the exposition, including the Smithsonian exhibits, did much to popularize anthropology in the United States.[7]

In the decade preceding the 1893 World's Columbian Exposition in Chicago, Buffalo Bill's Wild West created images of Indians for public consumption that challenged those fostered by the Indian Bureau. First Cody, and then many of his imitators, re-created, after a fashion, the theme of "the winning of the West." American Indians assumed roles that portrayed them as heroic warriors of a vanishing culture. The Indian Bureau, by contrast, consciously projected Indians as on their way to "productive citizenship." This rivalry in the creation of popular images found its literal expression at the American world's fairs beginning with the Columbian Exposition.

Clearly, the images the shows had been projecting conflicted with those traits encouraged by Christian humanitarian reformers and their Indian service allies. Indian-policy reformers had condemned Wild West shows as injurious to the sober image of Indians embracing Euroamerican civilization. The gypsy life of show people had proved "to be hostile to those settled habits of industry which it [is] the purpose of the government to foster as a necessary basis of the Indian's civilization," as Herbert Welsh had written in the wake of the imprisoned ghost dancers joining Cody's Wild West.[8] How could Indians develop the proper attitudes toward work and citizenship if the shows used gold to entice them away from their reservations to play? At best, the reformers claimed, Wild West shows celebrated the heroism of the independent warrior, and at worst, they exploited the idea of Indian menace. Either way, audiences had been receiving the wrong message. The Bureau of Indian Affairs, with the encouragement of reformers, consequently designed its Indian display at the Chicago world's fair to counteract the image projected in the shows.

A third, closely related force in the marketing of Indian images was the ethnological exhibit—also beginning at the Columbian Exposition with Putnam's displays. It presented not only the works of anthropologists, but also the Indians themselves as the objects of anthropological inquiry. These living specimens, displayed to the fairgoers, embodied both evolutionary theory and the comparative method of anthropology.[9]

Among professional anthropologists in the United States, many of whom worked for the Smithsonian Institution's Bureau of American Ethnology (BAE) in the late nineteenth century, the belief prevailed that civilization arrayed itself hierarchically. According to Lewis Henry Morgan, whose theories dominated the BAE for many years, societies developed through various evolutionary stages, from savagery through barbarism to "civilization." Each stage found expression in kinship, types of property, technology, aesthetics, and religious beliefs. One of the tenets of the comparative method maintained that, by studying "primitive" societies, a person could restore the lost or "conjectural history" of civilized societies at the same stage of development. The comparative method rested on the assumption of "the psychic unity of mankind," a belief that human minds in every place and every culture were similar. Because of psychic unity, the past cultures of any people could be reconstructed through close observation of the "survivals" of past cultural traits. Through the comparative method, the discoveries made about present Indian societies would contribute to a greater understanding of the evolution of more sophisticated cultures. Thus, in a sense, Indians were mirrors of modern Americans at a much earlier stage of development.[10]

In Chicago's White City, patrons could tour Indian encampments along the midway or browse through museum displays in the anthropological and U.S. government buildings. There, they could marvel at both the observers and the observed: the adventurer-anthropologists who brought back from the field trophies of their scholarly pursuits, laying them out in such a fashion as to confirm evolutionary progress and the superiority of white-skinned peoples; and the American Indians at work or play, those living anachronisms whose societies verged on extinction. Fairgoers might even take some comfort in the knowledge that anthropology, or "the Science of Mankind," might someday unravel the mysteries of human history and behavior.[11] In time, however, both the ethnological exhibits and the Indian Bureau exhibits took on the trappings of Wild West shows. For his part, Buffalo Bill, in turn, promised anthropological displays of "real Indians" living and occasionally fighting as they had *since* the arrival of "civilized" Old-World people.

The difference in interpretation showed up clearly during planning for the Chicago fair. Progress in technology, science, government, the arts, and human relations since 1492 served as the themes of the Columbian Exposition. In designing the exhibits, the Board of Fair Managers planned to group natives of the continent in villages that, when compared to the main exposition buildings of the neoclassical White City, would demonstrate their lack of development and show fairgoers what life must have been like at the moment Europeans effectively discovered Americans. It was one thing to portray docile natives who had not progressed much since the late fifteenth century; but it was quite another matter to portray some of them as armed and dangerous. The managers regarded Buffalo Bill's Wild West as unseemly and not up to the educational standards of other exhibits. They would not dignify an exhibition such as Cody's that supposedly demonstrated, with plenty of shooting, what Indians had been like until only recently. Accordingly, they refused permission for Cody to locate his show within the fairgrounds.[12]

Originally, the Indian Bureau had agreed to sponsor and supervise the Columbian Exposition's American Indian exhibit, including an Indian encampment. A model Indian school to be situated near the midway would serve as a counterpoise to the natives in their imitation villages. According to the original plan, the exhibits would include "specimens of the handiwork of the North American Indians, showing their native self-taught industries in comparison with the accomplishments in the arts of civilization and the methods adopted in the management of Indian schools." The school itself would re-create life and labor in a typical reservation boarding school for fifteen to thirty students. "The windows," according to Commissioner Morgan, "will be filled with transparencies showing scenes on Indian reservations and pictures of Indian life and customs." Groups of Indian students drawn from reservation boarding schools in the western United States would visit Chicago at intervals throughout the fair. Each group would remain a week or two, becoming part of the exhibit and, in their leisure time, seeing the sights. The school, however, represented only the "civilized" and "becoming-civilized" side of Indian life. "To be picturesque and impressive, to satisfy the curiosity and philanthropic and scientific interest of people," Morgan concluded, "the primitive Indian must be presented, living in his own habitation and carrying on his own avocations, such as making baskets, blankets, jewelry, bead work, pottery etc. This part of the exhibit is not to be omitted."[13]

The Bureau, however, withdrew its sponsorship of the ethnological portion of the exhibit early in 1892. The fair's Department of Ethnology and Archaeology, under Putnam's directorship, assumed responsibility for the Indian village. To some extent, finances dictated the withdrawal; but other considerations influenced Commissioner Morgan as well. He feared that a display including the sale of Indian handicrafts, such as the one planned for the Midway Plaisance, might create a conflict of interest and generate criticism of the Bureau. As he explained in a meeting with Putnam, sales of handicrafts

> would involve us in difficulties and possible scandals. That is to say, everybody is critical about anything the Indian Office does. It would be charged that somebody is making money out of that, somebody is getting privileges and concessions that other people don't and I would prefer that the Government as such would not have anything to do with that.[14]

Instead, Morgan used his portion of the Interior Department's appropriation to build and run the model Indian school. He did not decry the purpose of the midway's Indian village, but he hoped that it would be located near enough to the school that no one could miss the work the United States was doing in raising the Indian through education. "There," he imagined, would be "the native Indians, customs, etc.," and "here are the educated Indians, and it is to be so arranged that everything shall put forth the school in its best light." The commissioner even suggested that Putnam organize the American Indians in their separate encampments according to an evolutionary scheme. The school would represent the "apex—as the culmination" of the progress of civilization. For instance, Morgan continued, "Suppose you have some of the Yumas there. Follow . . . with those [Indians] that are a little higher, until here is a group of people living very much as white people live, and from that to the school would be only a step."[15] Such a display would also serve as an antidote to the impressions Buffalo Bill created outside the fairgrounds.

Putnam, however, organized his ethnological village geographically and situated it at a considerable distance from the school, making it of little value in establishing the school's place in Morgan's hierarchy. Nevertheless, Morgan continued to cooperate with Putnam in securing "persons or materials" from the reservations. The Bureau paid transportation expenses for bringing Indian delegations to participate in the running of the school, but other Indians had to pay their own way to Chicago.[16] The Indians at the school, therefore, became the government's "Show Indians."

Meanwhile, Nate Salsbury had leased a fourteen-acre parcel of land near the main entrance of the fair, and the company constructed stands around the arena to seat eighteen thousand spectators. Cody contracted seventy-four men and women from the Pine Ridge reservation to perform in the show. As an act of generosity, and partly to show up the Indian Bureau, Cody also brought an additional one hundred Sioux from the Pine

Ridge, Standing Rock, and Rosebud reservations. These Lakota visited the fair at his expense and took part in the formal opening ceremonies.[17]

Buffalo Bill received permission to take his friends and employees to the highest balcony of the fair's administration building to view the opening festivities, of which they inadvertently became a focus. Amy Leslie, whose column "Amy Leslie at the Fair" appeared regularly in the *Chicago News* and was later published as a book, effused about the scene on May 1:

A very pretty accident gave an unexpected American tinge to the climax of the interesting ceremonies. . . . By an unintentional gauge of time that seemed strategic just as . . . the magnificent chorus intone[d] 'My Country, 'Tis of Thee' these Indians in their resplendent war paint, gorgeous necklets [*sic*] and representative American savagery appeared on the north abutment of the building, a blazing line of character moving along with high, flaunting crests of feathers and flaming blankets which stood out against the gleaming white of the staff dome like a rainbow cleft into remembrances of a lost, primitive glory.

The scene concluded with "this fallen majesty slowly filing out of sight as the flags of all nations swept satin kisses through the air, waving congratulations to cultured achievement and submissive admiration to a new world."[18]

It is highly unlikely, in retrospect, that the group including the ghost dancers Kicking Bear, Two Strike, Jack Red Cloud, and Short Bull actually filed out in anything that resembled fallen majesty or, like the flags of other nations, waved in submissive admiration to Euroamerican spectacle. When asked what he thought about the opening ceremonies, Rocky Bear remarked that Grover Cleveland "must be a good president because he is fat and looks so prosperous." Young Man Afraid of His Horses and Spotted Bear said they rather liked the merry-go-round on the midway.[19]

The Chicago fair board had initially resolved to keep the midway from becoming a sideshow by selectively choosing exhibitors; but as the opening date drew closer and expenses mounted, this resolve evaporated. Easing their restrictions, fair managers granted licenses to concessionaires, including some Indian shows, along the Midway Plaisance for a cut of the profits. As the fair opened, it was along the midway, the marketplace of pleasure, that the educational ideals of ethnological villages competed for attention and dollars with snake-oil salesmen.[20] What patrons thought while wandering the midway cannot be determined. One may safely assume, however, that they knew little or cared less about the fine distinctions between what truly represented the spirit of the enterprise and

30 : *Some of the Show Indians who appeared with Cody's Wild West during the Columbian Exposition, Chicago, 1893. The negative has been reversed. (South Dakota State Historical Society, Pierre)*

what represented crassness. Novelty probably intrigued them. And there was much to dazzle them.

Historian Robert W. Rydell argues that it was on the midway at the Columbian Exposition that evolutionary theory, ethnology, and popular amusements interlocked as "active agents and bulwarks of hegemonic assertion of ruling-class authority."[21] He has noticed in Putnam's arrangement of the Indian encampment near the midway a "fundamental flaw" which "immediately degraded" the Indians because of the association. He also writes that the Indians who participated in the exhibits did not benefit from the exposition. "Rather," he concludes, "they were the victims of a torrent of abuse and ridicule."[22] Certainly, Putnam's arrangements contained many flaws. The Indian Office, once the fair began, went to great lengths to disassociate itself from responsibility for the midway, and in retrospect, the evolutionary theory of developmentalism appears to be both racist and wrongheaded. Indians may also have been abused and ridiculed, but neither the newspaper accounts nor the agency records containing comments by and about Indians bear this out.[23] Finally, how is one to judge whether or not Indians benefited from visiting or participating in the exhibition? Some may just have had a good time. It would be better to examine that topic from the perspective of the Indians themselves. Seeing or participating in the pageantry of Chicago's White City probably did not change their lives significantly, but few Euroamericans were transformed by their visits either. In the end, Buffalo Bill's Show Indians may have benefited the most, for they at least had their salaries to show for their stay at the fair.

Over two million patrons saw the Buffalo Bill show. Although Commissioner Morgan, his successor, and the fair managers detested Cody's show, the patrons loved it. To most fair visitors, the Wild West show located near the main entrance appeared as an integral part not to be missed.[24] A newspaper reporter commented that "every line of transportation leading to the World's Fair first stops at the entrance to Buffalo Bill's Wild West grounds." Some visitors assumed they were at the entrance of the fair itself.[25] The Chicago *Globe* summed it up with a banner headline: "All Roads Now Seem to Lead to Buffalo Bill's Big Show."[26] A few journalists also saw the show as part of the larger ethnological exhibits on the fairgrounds. One reporter for the *Chicago Reform Advocate* claimed that Cody's site served as "an object lesson of incalculable value showing as it does the Red Man camped in primitive style on the same ground where one hundred years ago his forefathers lived and battled with the advance guard of caucasian settlers." During that century of progress, the Indian tipis had been replaced by "sky-scraping brick and mortar wigwams."[27] To many Americans, Indians had become the vanishing Americans. If Cody and his imitators had their way, however, they would survive for a few more seasons.

Increasingly after the Chicago Exposition in 1893, Indian agents and Bureau personnel began to refer to Indians employed in Wild West shows and other exhibitions as "Show Indians," thereby proffering them a kind of professional status. Even the Bureau's policy of requiring individual contracts between individual Indians and their employers represented a subtle shift, a grudging recognition that they were professionals and

31 : The residential encampment near the arena, Chicago, 1893. The Show Indians are dressed, not for the performance, but to receive visitors. Cody encouraged the public to come out early and to visit the back lot of the Wild West. The tipis and tents are cordoned by a rope barrier. Indians, who slept in both types of enclosures, were not segregated from the rest of the troupe. John Burke, Buffalo Bill, Sergeant Bates, and Nate Salsbury (in top hat) appear in front of Buffalo Bill's tent, always adorned with the mounted buffalo head. (Buffalo Bill Historical Center, Cody, Wyoming)

should be treated as such. In 1893, Cody signed one contract to employ seventy-five Indians. In 1894, he signed one hundred contracts with one hundred Indians.[28]

The term *Show Indian* probably had its origin among newspaper reporters and editorial writers. In early 1891, for example, when the editor of *The Independent* (Gordon, Nebraska) protested the decision by the secretary of the interior to permit Cody to take the imprisoned Sioux ghost dancers from Fort Sheridan to Europe, it may have been the first recorded use of the term.[29] By 1893, however, the term appears frequently in Indian Bureau correspondence, but without the opprobrium or derision implicit in the remark by the *Independent*'s editor.

Not all Indians who joined Wild West shows or performed for concessionaires, however, did so under contract. At Chicago, a number of Indians appeared with various shows along the midway; none apparently possessed a contract, which violated Bureau procedures. P. B. Wickham of Mandan, North Dakota, ran a show called "Sitting Bull's Cabin," in which nine Oglalas rather than Hunkpapas acted. The centerpiece was Sitting Bull's house brought piece by piece from the Grand River settlement.[30] Henry ("Buckskin Joe") De Ford of Topeka, Kansas, employed another sixty Indians, many of them Sioux, in his "American Indian Village" (separate and distinct from Putnam's exhibit).[31] Because of the popularity of the Indian ethnological village at Chicago as well as Cody's great success, individual concessionaires at subsequent fairs in the United States would apply to Indian agents for permission to hire individual Indians. Less-reputable shows simply hired them without permission from the agent or the Interior Department. As stories of their mistreatment appeared in the press, the situation stimulated renewed criticism from Indian-policy reformers, who denounced the Bureau for failing to act as guardian to its wards.[32]

Buffalo Bill had won a victory against reformers and their sympathizers at the Bureau in the controversy over the treatment of Indian performers.[33] Wild West shows had achieved such great popularity before and during the Columbian Exposition that many of the later world's fairs incorporated their features. By granting licenses for concessionaires who staged miniature versions of the shows along the midways, fair managers gave tacit approval to their portrayals of American Indians. Fair officials had originally considered it unseemly to sanction entertainment of such dubious educational or ethnological value, but the midway concessionaires who employed Indians (who most often were identified as famous warriors) enjoyed considerable success. Fair managers ultimately shared in their profits. In American world's fairs after Chicago, fair managers would incorporate the Wild West shows themselves as major attractions, disguising them on occasion as Indian congresses, each one more elaborate than its predecessor.

Even as it fought the images the Wild West shows projected, the government became involved in the "Show-Indian" trade. At Chicago, Commissioner Morgan had hoped to contrast "long-haired blanket Indians" (essentially the "real" Indians of the Wild West show) with uniformed and disciplined Show-Indian students drawn from the government schools.

Owing to the expense involved, however, he consigned the "untamed" Indians to the ethnological village and the fair's Anthropology Department. For Morgan and many others, long hair represented the old ways of Indians. When John Shangreau, a Sioux of mixed heritage and a former student at government schools, wished to accompany Cody to Chicago as an interpreter, the Indian Office ordered him to cut his hair. When the agent at Pine Ridge informed Cody of the commissioner's wishes, he added:

> I am willing to allow John to join your Troupe in Chicago, providing he has his hair cut. I want to say Colonel, in this connection, that I have no objection to long hair, 'per se': on the contrary, believe that it is often ornamental and attractive; but, as representing the advanced Indians, and on account of his English speaking ability, and his white blood, I believe that John should have his hair short.[34]

Cody, who wore his hair to his shoulders, could only have been amused. John's hair grew out in Chicago.

That season, Cody's Show Indians made good money, toured Chicago, took boat rides on Lake Michigan, ate peanuts and popcorn until they could eat no more, bought boutonnieres and funny coconut-fiber hats and wore them proudly, and on occasion rode the merry-go-round by the hour. One evening in the high summer of Chicago's White City, fifteen Lakota led by Rocky Bear and No Neck mounted the painted ponies. As the carousel picked up speed, No Neck, holding the reins in both hands, gave a full-throated yell. Others in his party joined him. The *News-Record* placed the scene in its proper context. The Show Indians, observed the *Record*, "seem to like being jerked around on a carousel. They prefer it to art galleries, and some people who are not Indians feel the same way."[35] In all, about twenty-seven million people, a few hundred Indians among them, visited the fair. Most, Indians and non-Indians alike, probably had a glorious time.

Buffalo Bill's Wild West enjoyed its most profitable single season during the Columbian Exposition. Although his enterprise had reached its zenith, it would remain successful and lucrative well into the next century. Cody's Wild West, as seen in Chicago during the world's fair, would retain as its core the scenes involving cowboys and Indians; but over the next ten years it would incorporate newer scenes from the nation's immediate past.[36] Other shows would challenge Cody's in the coming decade for supremacy in presenting, according to press-agent hyperbole, the greatest entertainment extravaganza of the age. Numbers of Wild West shows and circuses competed directly with Cody. As a result, between 1894 and 1903,

Show Indians toured the United States, Canada, and parts of Europe in record numbers with Wild West shows. In addition, Indians also participated in "Indian congresses" at trade fairs and international expositions in the United States, usually with the encouragement and open support of the Indian Office.

Two commissioners presided over the Indian Bureau between 1893 and 1903. The period began with a commissioner who remained largely indifferent to the operation of Wild West shows (a marked contrast to his immediate predecessor), and ended with another who for the first time "banned" the government's participation in the contracting of Indians with the shows. Indians still joined circuses, medicine shows, and Wild West shows, but without the approbation of both the commissioner and the secretary of the interior.

Ironically, however, for these years of extensive Indian participation in Wild West shows there is the least amount of information available. Never that identifiable as individuals anyway beyond a few prominent participants, the Show Indians all but vanish from the records. This may be explained partially as a result of the novelty having worn off. For ten years the press had reported the antics or quaintness of the Show Indians in the United States and abroad. With so many shows now competing for audiences during the summer and early fall exhibition seasons, perhaps the Indians were not as newsworthy as once they had been. Their uniqueness had disappeared.

The amount of official correspondence concerning Show Indians also decreased. Commissioner Morgan had wanted data about every aspect of Indians' participation in the show. As a consequence, a great amount of information appears in the records for the period 1889–1893. Despite his hatred of the shows expressed throughout his tenure as commissioner, even Morgan could not compel Indians to stay at home and cultivate what he regarded as "a worthy type of civilization." Reformers continued to write at the tops of their voices about the shows; but they lost an ally when Morgan resigned at the end of Harrison's administration, only to be replaced in April 1893 by a spoilsman of sorts, Judge Daniel M. Browning of Illinois.[37]

Browning, as so many of his predecessors, came to his office without interest or training in Indian affairs. He had hoped to become the commissioner of the General Land Office.[38] Finding himself as the nation's chief guardian, he showed himself to be far more relaxed—his critics would have suggested derelict—in his approach to his office. Whereas Morgan inveighed against Wild West shows on every occasion, Browning displayed considerable indulgence. Morgan had gone as far to suggest legislation prohibiting "the exhibition of Indian in shows of any kind."[39] Browning, on the other hand, voiced no opposition to Indian employment in the shows. On one occasion, he even permitted Billy Great Bear, an Oglala, to tour with the Kickapoo Medicine Company as a juggler and slack-wire walker.[40] Morgan, who despised "medicine shows" and never tired of using the title as a synonym for Wild West shows, would have refused permission. Of course, Billy Great Bear might have traveled with the medicine company anyway, but without the goodwill and cooperation of the commissioner. Failure to receive the commissioner's permission could create problems when it came to him or his family receiving annuity payments, rations, or any services provided by the government under its treaty obligations.

William A. Jones replaced Browning. He likewise had no interest or experience in Indian administration; but whereas Browning cared little whether Indians joined Wild West shows, Jones cared a great deal. His hostility toward the shows almost equaled Morgan's. It led him in early 1900 to ban government participation in the contracting of Indians.[41] The Indian Office would neither supervise the writing of contracts nor regulate Indian employment. Shows were no longer required to post surety bonds. The Bureau therefore had nothing officially to say or do about the shows. As a consequence, as in Browning's tenure as commissioner but for different reasons, there is little information available in official correspondence during Jones's term—the longest of any commissioner up to that time—relating to Show Indians.

It is also during these same years that the government's alternate version of Show Indians, introduced at the Columbian Exposition, appeared regularly at the larger fairs and expositions. Indians mostly went to smaller trade and agricultural fairs as spectators rather than as participants. Commissioner Morgan had encouraged Indian participation in the fairs. In the same report where he talked about the possibility of recommending special legislation to Congress banning Indian participation in Wild West shows, he observed:

> In a few cases authority has been granted for Indians to attend industrial expositions, not only in response to the urgent request of the responsible parties having the expositions in charge, but because the office fully believed in the beneficial influences of such industrial expositions, fairs, etc., upon the Indians themselves as an educative force.[42]

Concessionaires and sponsors received the same authority accorded to Wild West show entrepreneurs. The Indian Bureau imposed certain re-

32 : The Smithsonian Institution Bureau of American Ethnology exhibit in the U.S. Government Building, Tennessee Centennial Exposition, Nashville, 1897. It represents the Kiowa camp circle at the time of the signing of the Treaty of Medicine Lodge, 1867. The model tipis, painted on hides by Kiowa artisans, stood about three-feet tall. These exhibits, sometimes planned in conjunction with ethnological encampments, showed visitors what American Indians had once been; and when displayed alongside the BIA-sponsored demonstration schools, fairgoers could also measure the progress of Indians on their way to Euroamerican civilization. (Smithsonian Institution, National Anthropological Archives, Washington, D.C.)

strictions to keep Indians "away from bad company."[43] It was a small step to take for Indians to go from being visitors to becoming participants. All the Indians had to do was take up residence on or near the "midways." This was true for small agricultural and industrial fairs and for the larger world expositions.

The 1895 Cotton States and International Exposition in Atlanta and the 1897 Tennessee Centennial Exposition in Nashville featured Indians to a considerably lesser extent than did Chicago in 1893. The entertainment avenues—Midway Heights in Atlanta and Vanity Fair in Nashville

—hosted small Indian villages. True ethnological exhibits, despite the claims of midway concessionaires, could be found in the Smithsonian Institution exhibits in the U.S. government buildings at each fair. Life-size figures depicting various Native Americans and other "primitives" filled the displays.[44]

Buffalo Bill's show played the Atlanta fair but did not remain for the duration as it had at Chicago. In 1895, Cody's show began extensive national tours, often stopping in a city to give a single performance before moving on. Nate Salsbury had become ill in the fall of 1894. Unable to manage the show, he and Cody negotiated an agreement with James Bailey of the Barnum and Bailey Circus to oversee scheduling the performances and laying out the route. Bailey provided transportation and expenses in return for a share in the profits.[45] His influence, according to Sarah J. Blackstone, was pronounced. Using standard circus practice, Bailey routed the show through a series of one-a-day stands for much of the 1895 season. The show traveled nine thousand miles to cover 131 stands in 190 days.[46]

By the last years of the decade, Wild West shows and ethnological exhibits had merged in fact. In the 1897 season, press agent "Arizona John" Burke billed the shows as "An Ethnological, Anthropological and Etymological Congress—Greatest since Adam."[47] The next year at the Trans-Mississippi and International Exposition in Omaha, the Indian Office agreed to cooperate in creating an Indian congress that professed to be an ethnological exhibit but, in actuality, became a Wild West show. In the words of its originator, *Omaha Daily Bee*–owner Edward Rosewater, the congress would be "an extensive exhibit illustrative of the life and customs and decline of the aboriginal inhabitants of the western hemisphere." Designed as an assembly rather than a mock legislative body debating the concerns of the moment, this "grand ethnological exhibit undoubtedly would be," Rosewater claimed, "the last gathering of these tribes before the bronze sons of the forests and plains, who have resisted the encroachments of the white man, are gathered to the happy hunting ground."[48]

Rosewater planned to bring representatives of all the tribes of North and South America to Omaha. Such a plan proved to be wildly impractical and too expensive. Instead, organizers brought representatives from American Indian tribes in the trans-Mississippi West to live and work in a large encampment located near the midway. The Indian Bureau and the War Department (some Chiricahua Apache prisoners of war, Geronimo among them, inhabited the village) chose Captain William A. Mercer, acting agent at the Omaha and Winnebago reservation, to super-

vise the congress. Rather than staging Indian ceremonials and demonstrations of native industries, Mercer scheduled a series of sham battles.
The first skirmish on August 10 featured a fantastic coalition of cowboys and "friendly Indians," played by members of the midway Wild
West show recruited for the occasion and a few local white business-
men who belonged to a fraternal organization called the Improved Order
of Red Men. They arrayed themselves against the real Indians of the
thirty-one tribes participating in the congress. In subsequent battles,
the Sioux delegates usually stood alone against other unlikely confedera-
tions.[49] Although scrupulously planned by Captain Mercer, the battles frequently ended ahead of schedule when the participants ran out of blank
ammunition.[50] There was always, according to an ethnologist from the
Smithsonian Institution, "a great deal of shooting & yelling & about fifty
of them roll around on the ground and pretend to be dead. Success is measured by the amount of noise and by ticket sales."[51]

Both the commissioner of Indian affairs and the secretary of the interior, who had endorsed the idea of an Indian congress, came to regret
their decision, for the sham battles quickly became popular, and elements
of the fair continued into 1899 as the Greater American Exposition, also in
Omaha. In this second year, Colonel Frederick T. Cummins managed the
congress, in which seventy-five Sioux from Pine Ridge fought it out with
cowboys and "friendly" Indians. The Bureau had decided to support the
Indian congress at Omaha in order to scale back its own exhibits. From the
Bureau's point of view, a group of long-haired Indians engaged in native
industries would have contrasted nicely with its own relatively inexpen-
sive display of photographs, foodstuff, and handicrafts illustrating the role
of Indian education. Instead, the congress had become a Wild West show,
and as could have been expected, the Bureau's apparent connivance in
staging sham battles ignited further criticism from reformers. From the
reformers' point of view, fairgoers could easily overlook the achievements
of American Indian education when they were secreted away in a series
of photographs that hung in the government building. Criticism of the
Omaha exposition led Commissioner Jones to refuse any more contracts
for Indians to perform in shows. Indians could still participate in the 1901
Pan-American Exposition in Buffalo, New York, but without either the
blessing or sanction of the Indian Bureau.[52]

At the Buffalo exposition, according to Robert Rydell, aesthetics and
anthropology combined to present the most powerful visual statement
about American progress.[53] As at the Omaha exposition, but to an even
greater extent, the Pan-American Exposition acclaimed an imperial

vision of peace, prosperity, and paternalism. Ideas about race and progress inspired the arrangement of buildings and the color scheme that gave the Buffalo exposition the name "Rainbow City." Visitors crossing the Triumphal Bridge on the exposition grounds would first encounter buildings and structures painted in bold primary colors representing the earliest human state and primitive nature. Farther up the avenue, the colors became more refined and less contrasting, until finally, the Electric Tower at the head of the Court of Fountains suggested the triumph of human achievement in ivory and gold. Rainbow colors also linked ethnological exhibits to the larger theme of evolution. For example, the Ethnology Building, placed at the center of the exposition grounds, had its exterior colors arranged halfway between "crudity and artistic refinement." Colors, according to the Buffalo *Enquirer,* moved in an ascending pattern. "In accordance with the general color scheme, which placed the harsh, bright colors at the southern end of the grounds and in the lower part of the buildings, red will predominate near the base, gradually merging toward the top with a pale yellow and then to bright ivory." The Ethnology Building displayed artifacts arranged geographically, together with oil paintings of various racial types set against a pyramidal backdrop of colors decorating the interior walls. "The gradual change from an earthy red at the base to an ethereal blue at the top," the article in the *Enquirer* continued, "at once signifies the artistic sense and prompts the analogy between it and the ascent of man from savagery to civilization."[54] When visitors ascended the spiral staircases to the galleries, they followed the progression of human evolution from savagery to enlightenment. A sign in the galleries informed the guests that additional lessons about racial progress and human evolution could be found on the Pan, the exposition's midway, where the ethnological villages both delighted and educated.[55]

Living exhibits of non-whites appeared along the Pan. Frederick Cummins, manager of the Indian congress at the Greater American Exposition received the concession for American Indians at the fair. His Indian encampment, known officially as the Indian Congress and Village Company, shared the avenue with the Filipino, "Eskimo," Hawaiian, and Japanese "villages," Darkest Africa under the direction of the French explorer-scientist Xavier Pené, the Old Plantation concession where "genuine negroes" strutted the cakewalk to the beat of a bass drum, the Streets of Mexico, and The Evolution of Man exhibit, linking the varieties of humans to the color scheme of the fair and the reassuring lessons of evolution currently in vogue.[56]

Mary Collins visited the fair and Cummins's Indian Village on the Pan.

As she strolled through the displays, the hyperbole of a sideshow barker upset her. For an additional ten cents, she could come into the Indian theater and watch the performers dance, sing, and shout their war whoops. The shill explained it this way: "We are not making anything by this; it is for the Indian little ones. The Government does not take the children into school until they are 10 to 14 years old, (!) and then they have become so accustomed to the old camp life that it is impossible to forget it. This is to get them a chance earlier." On the billboard for the show were the words in large letters: "The Redeemer is the Government."[57]

That sentiment, if not the exact wording, should have pleased the Christian missionary in Collins. It did not. In portraying themselves, the Show Indians at Buffalo offered, according to the carny barker, an object lesson of the need to educate Indian youth beginning before the age of ten. Yet Collins appreciated the inconsistency of the message. The show itself put a premium "on the old time savagery, encouraging the continuance of the old customs," but, at the same time, the Indian was being told that "the 'Great Father' wants him—even requires him—to put away all this."[58] Show Indians were performing, not to remind the audience about the recent past, and not to encourage a feeling of racial superiority in the observer, but to suggest that the Show Indians themselves must of necessity vanish from the earth. At least on that matter, Mary Collins and the barker presumably shared the same sentiment.

Between the Columbian Exposition and the Pan-American Exposition, Cody's Wild West and those who followed his lead changed considerably, for no longer were they just cowboys-cum-soldiers and Indians. At Chicago in 1893, Buffalo Bill had introduced his Congress of Rough Riders of the World to an American audience. During the next few years, not only did the other shows add "rough riders" (soldiers or other equestrian riders) from Europe, South America, South Africa, and central Asia, but after the Spanish-American War and the scramble for empire they featured depictions from the Boer War, the Boxer Rebellion, and the Charge at San Juan Hill. Despite these additions, the number of scenes depicting mayhem between Indians and Euroamericans actually increased. For example, Buffalo Bill's Wild West "programme" during its 1893 Chicago run featured nineteen scenes. Indians appeared in ten of them, and only three involved conflict: (1) Buffalo Bill, his fellow scouts, and some cowboys repulsed an Indian attack on an "Emigrant Train Crossing the Plains"; (2) in an Indian attack on the Deadwood Mail Coach, Buffalo Bill and his "attendant Cowboys" rode to the rescue; and (3) a re-creation of the Battle of the Little Bighorn, or "Custer's Last Charge," featured Buffalo Bill again

33 : "Bringing Home the Dead." Cody's Wild West in Brooklyn, 1907. The conclud-ing scene from the "Attack on the Deadwood Stage." (American Heritage Center, University of Wyoming)

---

arriving on the scene too late either to help or to add his body to the harvest of the dead. The fight at the Little Bighorn replaced the show's vintage "Attack on a Settler's Cabin," which had already proved to be a crowd pleaser in the United States and Europe. Those Indians and sol-diers pretending to be dead at Custer's last rally rejoined the cast for the conclusion, a salute to the audience.[59]

After the 1893 Chicago season, Buffalo Bill's show not only re-created Custer's Last Stand, but it also featured the Indian attack on the settler's cabin. Four instead of three firefights with Indians became the new stan-dard for Wild West shows. Overall, the amount of shooting in the shows increased as the "Winning of the West" theme received less prominence alongside U.S. Marines fighting their way into Peking, Colonel Teddy Roosevelt shooting a Spaniard in the charge up San Juan Hill, or pastoral Boers bedeviling British carbineers in the Transvaal.[60] And so popular were the sham battles, the most spectacular features of the Wild West show, that they became permanent features of the U.S. world's fairs held in the years 1893 to 1903.

At Chicago in 1893, Commissioner Morgan consigned the "untamed" Indians to the ethnological village and the fair's Anthropology Department.[61] At St. Louis ten years later, however, Samuel McCowan, head of the government's exhibit, with a larger budget from the Interior Department, would combine Show Indians with Indian students "on show" to make an effective display. In the hands of the Indian Bureau, the Indian Cody's Wild West portrayed heroically and sympathetically as a vanishing American became either a barbarian best forgotten or a measure of the progress made by worthy members of the Indian race. Thus, at the world's fairs, the image of the vanishing Indian was set beside the aspiring Indian who, through the government's efforts on behalf of civilization, would also presumably vanish one day into mainstream society.

The Louisiana Purchase Exposition of 1904 became the last of the great fairs in the United States before World War I. Even more than the Buffalo fair, it would signal the fact that Show Indians had won the battle of images.

SHOW-INDIAN STUDENTS IN ST. LOUIS, 1904

*"This trip would be very profitable for your Indians, as
you would get to see the whole world in a small space."*

      The Louisiana Purchase Exposition commemorated the na-
tion's acquisition of a vast, continental domain one hundred years before
and celebrated the recent seizure of an overseas empire. It dwarfed all
previous world's fairs. St. Louis's city of dazzling light spread over more
than twelve hundred acres. The fair managers returned to the gleaming
white city first enshrined in Chicago eleven years before. In the words of
President Theodore Roosevelt, spoken on opening day near the base of
the Column of Progress, the fair signaled that the American people had

taken their place "among those daring and hardy nations who risk much with the hope and desire of winning high position among the great powers of the earth."[1]

Directors of the exposition, according to Robert Rydell, created an "anthropologically validated racial landscape" that made the appropriation of the Philippines, Hawaii, Puerto Rico, and other Pacific islands and the proclamation of the Open Door in China seem as much a part of the manifest destiny of the nation as had the acquisition of Louisiana.[2] At St. Louis, the Indian Office, with the cooperation of the Anthropology Department, returned to the concept that it had only imperfectly realized at the Columbian Exposition. The model Indian school at the Chicago world's fair was situated far from the native villages. At St. Louis, the federal government planned to construct a model Indian school and around it place an Indian congress, a gathering of America's native race. Indigenous people from around the world would also share space in what would then become a grand ethnological village. These gathered races would represent living exhibits that demonstrated the otherwise imperceptible sequence of past, present, and future.[3]

Visitors to the fair could not help but learn at such a "University of the Future," according to William F. Slocum, president of Colorado College. Pictures and living objects would substitute for textbooks. The fair would make accessible a world that even the ordinary traveler might otherwise fail to experience.[4] And what fresh insights might the visitor to the model U.S. Indian School gain? According to the director of the exhibit:

Visitors will see with their own eyes that Indians are ordinarily endowed, physically, mentally, spiritually; that they are not abnormal in any sense; that both boys and girls are well favored; that they can talk; that they can sing; that they can learn; that they are docile and obedient; that they are human. Verily, the St. Louis Indian School may well be called the Hall of Revelation.[5]

It was safe to assume, the director proclaimed, that no visitor would leave the school without a better opinion of the Indian and the Indian service.[6]

Commissioner of Indian Affairs William A. Jones originally wanted to depict the progress since 1804 of only those Indians living in the Louisiana Purchase.[7] The fair managers, however, soon expanded the geographic limits to include Indians living outside the boundaries of the purchase. Jones then appointed Samuel McCowan, forty-year-old superintendent of the Chilocco Agricultural Training School in Oklahoma Territory, to administer the Indian Bureau exhibit. Sam McCowan, from Elmwood, Illinois, had entered the Indian service in 1889 as superintendent of the day schools on the Rosebud reservation. In subsequent years, the service transferred him to Fort Mohave School, Arizona; the Albuquerque Indian School, New Mexico; and then back to Arizona for a six-year tenure as superintendent of the Phoenix Indian School. From there, he transferred to Chilocco, where he established the first and only agricultural school for Indian youth.[8]

At the Omaha exposition, where he had managed the Indian Bureau display in the government building, McCowan had been critical of the Indian congress and the sham battles staged by Captain Mercer. Perhaps for that reason, McCowan joined forces with W. J. McGee,[9] former ethnologist-in-charge at the BAE and the director of the fair's Anthropology Department. McCowan became McGee's assistant and the person charged with supervision of the ethnologic encampment. In this way, McCowan could borrow some of the "life groups" from the settlement without having to turn to the "ethnologic villages" along the midway (called the "Pike" in St. Louis). McCowan's plan represented a variation on Commissioner Morgan's suggested scheme for the Columbian Exposition. The "primitive ways" of the Indians from the encampment would highlight the achievements of the boys and girls in the school.[10]

A year before the scheduled opening of the fair, Commissioner Jones sent a circular among his agents, describing the purpose of the Indian Office exhibit. The display would show, so far as practicable, the work accomplished in the schools, the usefulness of that education in the careers of the returned students, and the progress made by older Indians in agriculture and the mechanical arts. These were to be portrayed "vividly and concretely." Displays might include:

> School room papers, articles manufactured by pupils in schools shops, specimens of crops raised at schools and especially by Indians on their own farms—and of work done by Indians outside of schools will all be wanted; also photographs of Indian homes and farms and schools, interior and exterior views.
>
> To give an Indian setting to it all, specimens of the native arts, foods, implements, utensils and other products will be needed.[11]

Shortly after his appointment, McCowan began canvassing the agencies for some of the people and items to set in the exhibit. He wished to inform the public about "not only living Indians in native dress, settings, and environments, but such display as will illustrate the Government's policy,

34 : Samuel M. McCowan, superintendent of Chilocco Indian School and assistant
director of the Department of Anthropology at Louisiana Purchase Exposition,
1904. (Archives and Manuscripts Division, Oklahoma Historical Society)

methods of instruction, and progress being made by the Indians themselves."[12]

McCowan had expressed interest in obtaining "Old Indians" who could work at their "native industries," such as building birchbark canoes, manufacturing stone implements, chipping arrow points, weaving blankets, fashioning jewelry, or making baskets. Numbers of agents and superintendents responded cheerfully, describing those items as well as those Indians who might be helpful. John H. Seger, the semiliterate superintendent of the Seger Colony Indian Training School, Colony, Oklahoma Territory, sent the most humorous response. "I will have to say," Seger wrote, "that I do not know an old Indian in this district who can make a basket." He did know a few young men who were adept at constructing stone walls, but that was "an acquired art with them." Besides, these were young men rather than the preferred older men. Seger explained that he had spent the last thirty years of his life trying to get Indians to forget the old ways. Indeed in competing with whites at some of the local fairs, Colony students had won a number of premiums and diplomas. "I did not enter in my exhibit any oldtime golf belts or music rolls, or the warclub which captain Smith was not killed with. I leave those kind of exhibits to the frontiersmen from Boston and other frontier places." He concluded that he was not the type of exhibitor for whom McCowan was searching. Still, he imagined, old Indians might contrast nicely with the "educated Indians" who would share space on the building's first floor.[13]

Originally, the model Indian school was to be housed in Cupples Hall No. 1, one of the imposing stone buildings of nearby Washington University.[14] A separate Indian Industries Building would be constructed behind Cupples Hall with labor recruited from the Indian schools. The plan grew so large that Cupples Hall could no longer accommodate the school. The Industries Building, placed at a special site, would be expanded to include space for the school, student lodging, and a dining hall.[15] All of the interior finishing and plumbing would be done by student labor.[16] In mid-August 1903, the secretary of the interior directed McCowan "to erect the required building, perfect the details of the transfer of Indian families and pupils from their homes and schools to St. Louis, install and conduct the exhibit and supply the Indians with necessary food, shelter, and medical attendance."[17] For the conduct of the exhibit, the fifty-seventh Congress appropriated forty thousand dollars, to which the fifty-eighth Congress added another twenty-five thousand dollars.[18]

Unlike the model Indian school at Chicago, stuck off in a remote corner of the exposition grounds and far from the ethnologic encampment, St.

UNITED STATES INDIAN SCHOOL, BUILDING FOR EXHIBITS OF INDIAN INDUSTRIES.

35 : The model Indian school at the Louisiana Purchase Exposition, St. Louis, 1904. The building was constructed using Indian laborers drawn from the various off-reservation boarding schools. (Western History Collections, University of Oklahoma Library)

Louis's Indian school would be built upon a hill. "Primitive peoples" would be symbolically arrayed in a semicircle around the base of the hill. When completed, the "old mission style" building measured 40 feet by 205 feet along a north-south axis with an addition that projected eastward from the grand entrance another 80 feet. This wing would serve as a recitation and concert hall. The building stood on a promontory raised about ten feet above the surrounding landscape. Including its windowed basement, the school rose three stories, with six towers reaching higher still (one on each corner of the main building and one on each side of the main entrance). The covered front portico ascended by two flights of stairs overlooked a plaza, upon which were constructed the native habitations of the "Old Indians" and their compatriots from throughout the hemisphere and the more distant reaches of the new American empire.[19]

The "Old Indian Exhibit," as it came to be called, had the potential—just as in Omaha and, to a lesser extent, in Buffalo—of turning into a Wild West show. The superintendent, of course, had already expressed his criticism of the previous efforts of the Bureau that had degenerated into sideshows. As McGee's assistant in the Department of Anthropology, McCowan likewise tried to influence the granting of licenses to concessionaires along the Pike. Early in his tenure, he wrote to Frederick J. V. Skiff, director of exhibits, expressing his concern over "well-founded" reports of licenses being awarded to shows of "a Wild West character." He complained that the "Navajo village, the reproduction of the Zuni village, the Hopi Cliff-dwellers, together with the Hopi snake dance," had but one purpose, to make money for the concessionaires.[20]

Concessionaires, he presumed, possessed the right to reproduce "alleged Indian dances, customs, and rites, which, if they ever existed, have long since been outlived and forgotten by the Indians themselves." Such ceremonies would, necessarily, be "farcical, nonrealistic and barbarous." The shows were without any educational or scientific value. They would misrepresent the real Indians and their lives to such an extent as to destroy the value of the government's more authentic exhibit. McCowan reminded Skiff that "the Government Indian Exhibit will be large and realistic, strictly educational, and entirely free from barbarous features that do not now exist." Any exhibit other than that would be superfluous.[21] Neither Skiff nor the exposition management retreated, even with McCowan's subtle threat to withhold the disbursement of additional funds to the anthropological exhibit.[22] At the time, they, if not McCowan, could see both the educational value and the potential for profit from the various Indian villages. Even McCowan came to appreciate the drawing card of the Wild West–type display.

Frederick Cummins, professional exhibitor at world's fairs, would be along the Pike with his Indian congress. So too were a number of enterprises that planned to sell Indian curios. The Cliff Dwellers Exhibit Company, W. Maurice Tobin managing, included such special features as "The Ruins in the Mancos Canon," a mammoth cliff over one hundred feet high, built up on one side of a walled enclosure. Within the hollow square, visitors would find "The Pueblo of Taos" oddly enough inhabited by three hundred Hopi and Zuni men, women and children, and an exhibit of Australian Aborigines described as members of the "Tribe of Marvelous Boomerang Throwers." The Zunis received billing as "The Last of the Aztecs." Visitors might also witness the Hopis' "dramatically sensational Snake Dance."[23] Apparently, Tobin bore no animosity toward McCowan for all the superintendent's maneuvers. The manager of the Cliff Dwellers Exhibit gave McCowan a season pass.[24] Still, on opening day of the government's Indian exhibit, McCowan had one of the Chilocco salutatorians remind the crowd that the Indians taking part in the present program must not be confounded with the "show people, or performers, but are here as an educational exhibit only, and their exercises this afternoon will be the same sports and past times they would enjoy when in their native homes."[25] It is difficult, however, without their direct testimony to judge whether the visitors ever made the distinction.

McCowan himself came to relax somewhat his strictures against employing Show Indians. He soon appreciated their skill, fame, and potential for attracting otherwise blasé customers to a government Indian exhibit. On the one hand, he discouraged, to the point of rudeness, persons who offered to bring a delegation of older Indians of certain renown. He also wrote unfriendly letters to the Indians themselves. Charles S. Bush, for example, the non-Indian chief of police at Fort Yates, North Dakota, offered to bring veterans of the Custer fight and survivors of the shoot-out following Sitting Bull's assassination in mid-December 1890. McCowan explained that it was "not the purpose of the Government nor of the Anthropological Division of the Exposition to expend money in bringing large bodies of old Indians to the Fair."[26] Eighty-three-year-old Blue Horse, a "made chief" of the Oglalas and, as one of the "Laramie Loafers," an unflagging supporter of government programs, asked for employment "as one of your show Indians." McCowan curtly replied: "I have made all arrangements for Indians for exhibition purposes at the Worlds Fair, and will not therefore have any use for you."[27] He did, however, have some interest in persuading a few "patriot chiefs" to join his exhibit.

Long before he had written to Commissioner Skiff, McCowan had hit upon the idea of bringing to his exhibit such notable resistance leaders as Geronimo of the Chiricahua Apache prisoners of war at Fort Sill, Oklahoma; Chief Joseph of the Nez Perce; and Quanah Parker, Comanche leader and principal advocate for the peyote religion. Having previously dealt with Quanah Parker over allowing Comanche children to attend Chilocco, McCowan genuinely liked the chief. His favorite example of Parker's wry humor was the great leader's insistence that the white man was superior to God, because at least he could make ice in the summer time and God couldn't.[28] To Chief Joseph, he wrote that he wanted to secure a number of prominent and "representative Indians" to come to the World's Fair. "It has occurred to me that you," the director coaxed, "as an intelligent and progressive man, would like to attend this Fair. . . . I can also take three or four more members of your tribe who do some kind of native work well, and afford an opportunity of earning considerable [money]."[29] He assured the superintendent at the Fort Lapwai Reservation, Idaho, where Chief Joseph occasionally visited, that in bringing the famed leader to St. Louis, "nothing of a wild west nature is contemplated, but we do desire to secure the *best types* [McCowan's emphasis] of Indians only for this exhibit."[30]

For Geronimo, McCowan reserved special consideration. Along with Naiche, son of Cochise, he was the last of the great leaders to be held by the government as a prisoner of war. Even the Ghost Dance leaders, veterans of the "last Indian war," had long since been released from military custody. Not so Geronimo. McCowan secured from the War Department the release of Geronimo and nine of his compatriots.[31]

Of all the old Indians, Geronimo alone would have his own booth in the exhibit building. McCowan had bargained for much more than he got. For some reason, he had imagined Geronimo to be about as "conservative" and unregenerate as any former renegade. Captain Farrand Sayre, the officer in charge of the Apache prisoners at Fort Sill, had to explain to McCowan that his charges "live in houses and have no tents or teepees. . . . These Apaches dress and live like white people."[32] No matter, McCowan decided. He had Cheyenne artisans near Colony, Oklahoma, construct a special tipi for Geronimo and his band.[33] Geronimo as a Show Indian par excellence deserved such special consideration. Once ensconced in the school building, he earned his keep not so much by selling native manufactures, but rather by signing his name. Geronimo had learned to write just enough English to make it useful.[34] As McCowan found, the "old gentleman is pretty high priced, but then he is the only Geronimo."[35]

Owing to his many years of service as superintendent of various Indian schools, McCowan hoped to recruit matrons and industrial arts teachers from the alumni. From both alumni and current students, he put together a choral group, and a "first-class band" that he hoped would surpass even the famed Carlisle Indian School Band that had won renown at Chicago back in 1893. To Richard Davis, former Dog Soldier and currently special interpreter for the Cheyennes at Colony, Oklahoma, he promised an opportunity to sell handicrafts on the grounds if he would put together a picturesque display of ten or so "conservative full-bloods," none of whom could be drunkards or renegades. As before, only the "worthy Indians" were to be displayed. "This trip would be very profitable for your Indians," he coaxed Davis, "as you would get to see the whole world in a small space. The cost would be very small and you would see things that would give you pleasure throughout life."[36] Ironically, he attempted to entice certain graduates and former students who could perform in the chorus or the band to leave their jobs for the promise of a summer in St. Louis.

Andres Moya, a cornetist working in a paint shop in Old Albuquerque for twelve dollars per week, worried about giving up certain employment for the uncertainty of joining the World's Fair Indian Band. "State me how much you can give me per Mont during the Fair," Moya asked his former principal, "and also tell me what instruments or Bandmen you want in the Band, and I try and get them from here."[37] McCowan, occasionally trading on old loyalties, collected his musicians. Moya and many others in like circumstance left their jobs. McCowan offered only to pay their travel expenses, and provide them room and board. He had an easier time with those alumni who held jobs in the Indian service. At least he could request for them a leave of absence and temporary reassignment to the model Indian school.[38]

McCowan, working closely with exposition architects, had designed a building that would showcase the new Indian along with the old. He divided the first floor of the school on its longitudinal axis with a wide hallway. On either side of the hallway stood two "long apartments which are subdivided into rooms or booths." "Old Indians," who worked at their native industries, occupied a space appropriately situated on the west side of the hallway. Beginning at the south end of the building, visitors would find Pueblo women grinding corn and making wafer (*piki*) bread in the traditional manner; the next booth contained Geronimo working occasionally on bows and arrows, but more frequently signing photographs which he sold to the visitors; next came Pueblo potters, Pueblo weavers, Pomo basket makers from northern California, Pima basket makers and Maricopa potters from Arizona, Navajo blanket weavers, Sioux pipestone carvers, Sioux bead and buckskin workers, Jicarilla Apache basket makers, Navajo silversmiths, Chippewa (Anishinaabeg or Ojibwa) blanket, bead, and mat workers, and finally Cheyenne bead and buckskin workers.[39]

On the east side of the hallway, McCowan placed the booths housing the manual training and industrial exhibits. These included a class in "Domestic Science" re-created from Chilocco Indian School consisting of a model dining room wherein Indian girls demonstrated daily the "intricacies of good cookery and housekeeping"; a laundry class also from Chilocco under the charge of a Miss Daugherty; a class in printing that produced daily *The Indian School Journal;* classes in painting, blacksmithing, and fashioning wagon wheels from Haskell Institute, Lawrence, Kansas; a manual training (carpentry) class and domestic art (sewing) class, also from Haskell; and finally a class in harness making staffed by students and teachers from Genoa Training School, Nebraska. The Show-Indian students, like their "Old Indian" counterparts, performed each day between the hours of 9:30 to 11:30 A.M. and then from 2:00 to 4:00 P.M. "These workers," McCowan explained to his superiors in the Interior Department, "were changed constantly in order to give variety and maintain interest."[40]

In the assembly hall, "recitations" by kindergartners and seventh graders took place each morning and afternoon, while the band played on the portico and the workers applied their craft. The noise must have been deafening. When the band struck up "The War Dance," McCowan had planned at first to have some of the Old Indians dance. He thought better of it. He informed his wife that "the dancing may cause some harsh criticism from some quarters and I think we had better not lay ourselves liable."[41] Later in the spring, when some of the Lakotas from Rosebud reservation wanted to institute "a dancing school," as he called it, among the inhabitants of the ethnologic village, McCowan also demurred. As a result, some in the party, including Scott Charging Alone and Yellow Hair, returned to South Dakota.[42]

McCowan, however, seemed to reverse the ban on dancing when it appeared that a group of Hopi priests might actually agree to visit St. Louis and perform the Snake Dance, presumably one more authentic than the one being executed daily at the Cliff Dwellers Exhibit along the Pike. Officials in the Anthropology Department enthusiastically endorsed McCowan's suggestion, whereupon he wrote to Superintendent Staufer of the Keams Canyon Indian school to bring "say twenty to thirty of your Antelope and Snake Priests from one or more of your Hoopa [*sic*] villages to come here in August for the purpose of giving a realistic . . . Snake ceremony." McCowan justified reversing his position by insisting that such a ceremony, "if given realistically, and by old priests, would be intensely interesting from an educational and scientific view point." McCowan also insisted that it would be a good thing for the Hopis as well. "The Hoopa tribe is very exclusive," he observed, "and if a large party of these influential old men could be brought to this World's Fair to view the strange people and the grand creations of handiwork, they would go back with entirely different views of the whites and live differently." Remarkably, the Indian Office granted its approval, even going so far as to suggest that if the Snake Dance were to be given at all in 1904, let "the priests give it here instead of at home at the usual time and with the same environment."[43] In the next two weeks, however, all hell broke loose in the Hopi villages, especially on Second Mesa, not among The People, but among the "white folks," as Staufer described them.

The Snake Order at Shongopavi talked favorably of going out to St. Louis; but before they could decide one way or the other, the white missionaries got wind of the plan. One of the missionaries wrote to the super-intendent, "I would be sorry to connect your name with anything of this kind." Another warned that Staufer would "be working against yourself and against the progress of the Hopis to persuade them to go to St. Louis and I prefer that no employee be concerned with this affair at all. The Commissioner is opposed to it and only acquiesces because of superior authority."[44] Faced with such opposition, and the apparent defection of the commissioner, McCowan backed off. As he explained to Staufer, "we will let the matter of the Moki delegation rest for the present."[45] The "dance order" dating from the early 1880s still held sway in the Indian Bureau, despite the "educational" value, even for white folks, of the ceremony. McCowan's record remained pure despite his intentions.

Although in operation since the middle of May, the model Indian school opened officially on June 1.[46] One has simply to read the daily schedule of the school to appreciate how industrious everything must have appeared to visitors on the hill.

DAILY PROGRAM

Reveille	6:00 A.M.
Flag Salute	6:45
Breakfast	7:00
Children's Irrigated Gardens	7:30–8:30
Band Concert	9:30–11:30
Industrial work	9:30–11:30
Kindergarten	9:30–10:30
Literary Class work	10:30–11:30
Dinner	12:00 P.M.
Band Concert	1:30–3:30
Industrial work	2:00–4:00
Kindergarten	2:00–3:00
Literary Class work	3:00–4:00
Literary and Musical Programme	4:00–5:00
Flag Salute and Dress Parade	5:30
Supper	6:00
Taps	10:00 P.M.[47]

McCowan touted the enterprise as a practical illustration of the government's work for the betterment of Indians. "It embraces the results of the ripened experience of the Indian Office," he enthused; "it illustrate[s] . . . the evolutionary stops of progress—from timid, halting ignorance toward confident knowledge and competence."[48]

Ida Little Pifer, a student attached to the printing department that produced the *Indian School Journal*, described soon after opening day the typical crowds at the model school. Before the industrial work began in the building, the first arrivals usually toured the Indian encampment west of the school, ranged in a semicircle about the plaza. "The visitors poke into these dwellings," she explained, "which are real homes of these Indians, built in their own way, where they cook, eat, sleep, visit and amuse themselves after their own fashion." The tourists asked numberless questions, which invariably few of the villagers understood. Sightseers peeped into kettles and cooking pots, and generally oppressed the rules of hospitality common among American Indians. Sometimes the villagers displayed mild resentment; but usually they received all comers with elaborate courtesy.[49]

At the sound of a bugle at 9:30 A.M., work began. Pifer recounted the scene:

> A motley crowd swarms into the building—the industrial workers of the old school, in moccasined feet and blankets, straggle in, some with papooses on their backs, some with cradles in their arms, some with their material and tools for work, many untidy, but all picturesque; the industrial workers from the Government schools neat as new pins, with cheerful, intelligent faces, march into the building as orderly as trained soldiers; and the day's work begins. Just the ordinary day's work—the old Indian in his old way, the educated Indian in the new way. That's all. But it tells the whole story, and "he who runs may read." . . . They gaze at the baskets, rugs and the large wall glass cases of Indian School work. So they begin to grasp the idea, purpose and plan of the Indian Industrial Exhibit. And then the real enthusiasm begins.[50]

The rugs, baskets, and beadwork hanging on the wall and priced to sell intrigued some, whereas the "the home life of the old Indians" engrossed others. Still others found their curiosity aroused by the "sociologic problems" of the old Indians; but the greatest interest "of each and all is centered in the bright young Indian students from the schools and the work they are doing." For those people who never before had enjoyed an opportunity to view firsthand anything of Indian life and character, the exhibit proved to be a revelation.[51]

Again and again, observers and commentators returned to the literal divide between the two sides of the exhibit. The metaphor of young and old, the new and the antiquated was made still more poignant by the self-loathing of one who had made the passage in her own life. "On one side of the main hall are the old types of Indians," Pifer explained. "They dress in their usual costumes, use their primitive tools and looms and do their regular work in their old fashioned way." On the other side of the cultural frontier, one would find "children from the same tribes—born in the same kind of homes—many of them related to the very Indians opposite them, yet so great is their refining influence of even a few years of school training that strangers coming into the building are often heard to say: 'Why, these children are not really Indians!'"[52] And in that discovery, another revelation. Indians had been tested and found capable of civilization, education, and culture, if not as the mirror image of middle-class Euroamericans, then at least in the guise of their potential servants.

Surrounded by the magnificence of the great buildings of the fair, and far enough removed from the sideshow ambience of the Pike, the Indian school appeared as a decided contrast. "Its simplicity pleases as the simple truth always does," Pifer observed. The sincerity of its purpose could not be overlooked. "Its exhibits are living, human creatures," with their daily lives laid bare. The honest, mundane labors of old and new Indians alike served as a subliminal object lesson. Superintendent McCowan did not need to lecture or schedule sermons in the school's chapel to drive the message home. The crowds preferred late dinners over missing dress parade at six o'clock. They learned, as even Ida Pifer thought she had learned, that "in the natural order of things the Indian as an Indian cannot exist"; but after a few regimented seasons in the schools of the Indian service, the Indians "come into the nation, not as savages or underlings, but as civilized, educated, law abiding people."[53]

Sam McCowan believed that the hundreds of thousands of visitors who traipsed through the Indian school came to understand the Indian problem as it actually existed, and perhaps delighted in the fact that the government and its social scientists had discovered the correct solution. The Indian as living exhibit encouraged Ida Pifer. McCowan, on the other hand, trusted that the painting hanging at the northern end of the central hallway would, as the cliche suggested, speak louder than words to the educated and ignorant alike.

In the allegorical composition, a mountain reared its snow-capped head in the distance. On its topmost peak, amid the sparse fir trees and down its timbered sides, wild animals gloried in their habitat and assumed picturesque poses. A freshet boiled from beneath the rocks and forced its way in merry haste to the mountain's base and then out across the thirsty plain. About halfway up the corrugated sides of the mountain, and in its roughest, wildest part, an Indian tipi materialized out of the tall spruces — "typical of the old Indian and the old life." McCowan continued:

> The old Indian clings with death-like tenacity to the old life. As civilization approaches he scowls, growls a little, paints the war-black over his face, then perceiving the hopelessness of resistance, wraps the blanket of silence about him and moodily retires to the woods and silent places. He will have none of it.
>
> Down at the mountain's base is an 20 acre farm properly laid out in regular modern fashion — the home of the educated Indian, and the son of the old chieftain on the hill. The son has utilized the water of the spring, and made it grind his corn. He has led it to his thirsty fields where it turns the golden grain into golden dollars. He has a comfortable home and good buildings for his stock. Orchards bloom and bear; cattle, horses and hogs gambol over green fields and an air of prosperity and content[ment] broods over all.[54]

For McCowan, the busy painting illustrated the mighty and uncontrollable influence of civilization, as well as the all-powerful influence of parental love. The old father would have none of the white man's civilization for himself; nevertheless, when it "pursued him and found him out and gripped him hard he saw that it was good — and gave it to his son."[55] The old man erected his lodge in the gloom halfway up the mountainside. Beneath him, in triumph, rested the home of his son if no-longer heir. The lesson, according to McCowan, turned on this truth (though it belied all the tortured symbolism of the painting): "The study of man is of vastly more interest than a study of his works."[56] And out West, the Hopi still danced on their mesas, and welcomed their gods from the mountains.

At the close of the fair, McCowan penned two editorials for *The Indian School Journal*. "A Fair School" and "The Real Indian" repeated the themes stressed throughout the summer and on into the fall. It had been his personal desire to show the public just what the Indian race was capable of doing. "We want to remove the impression that is quite widespread," he had written earlier to one of his teachers, and a sentiment he repeated in his editorials, "that the money spent on educating Indian children is thrown away."[57] The summer of the Show-Indian school at St. Louis also included the end of Richard Henry Pratt's tenure as superintendent of Carlisle, the first Indian industrial academy. McCowan marked the passing with a fleeting reference to Pratt's unwillingness over the years to cooperate with other schools in the government system. As one of McCowan's colleagues trenchantly observed after reading his editorials:

> You are not so hard on Pratt, as he has always been on the rest of us, but you have courage to speak out. The many deaths at Carlisle I used to consider the vicarious sacrifice made in showing Indians to eastern people, Carlisle was of greatest value as a show school, & I wonder what will happen there! Schools elsewhere have not stopped I notice.[58]

Teachers and superintendents who could accept the statistics of mortality at Carlisle and other Indian schools as a sort of vicarious atonement for the sins of the race would not necessarily lament the fact that the schools also aimed at the destruction of native culture.

At St. Louis, the Show-Indian students replaced the Show Indians. It remained to be seen, however, whether their supremacy would continue as they competed for audiences outside the fair's magnet community. It was one thing for customers to visit the Bureau's exhibit at the world's fair; it was quite another matter to sustain that interest once the fair closed. Few Americans planned excursions to Indian schools. The question for McCowan and others in the Indian service became one of how to keep public interest, and therefore public support, at a level commensurate with that achieved at the Louisiana Purchase Exposition. The answer might be to take the Indian school, or at least a part of the school, to the public. Carlisle, the premier institution of American Indian education, offered examples of how to take the liberating message of Show-Indian students to the public.

Carlisle had produced its own groups of Show Indians. Pratt had hoped that the success of its students would inspire confidence in a greatly expanded Indian educational system. Carlisle alumni, however, never achieved the prominence in the public mind that Pratt perhaps anticipated. Instead, the Carlisle band enjoyed considerable success following its stand at the Columbian Exposition. It thereafter appeared regularly at public occasions. The Carlisle football team enjoyed even greater success. It played its first full schedule in 1894. By the early years of the twentieth century, the team performed away from home so often that sportswriters began to refer to its members as the "Gypsies of the Gridiron." At Harvard, Pennsylvania, and Princeton, it drew crowds in the tens of thousands that would have rivaled any of Buffalo Bill's Wild West performances. It did not matter to people that the school offered its students little more than an eighth-grade education. It was an Indian "college." The

Indians of Carlisle were old and talented enough to face the men of the nation's elite institutions. The imagery of the Wild West show inevitably found its way into the Homeric strivings of sports reporters who could not resist descriptions of Indians burning and scalping their opponents, or re-creating the slaughter at the Little Bighorn. Unlike the Wild West show, Carlisle and its Show-Indian football team did not survive the First World War. The school's 311 acres and forty-nine buildings were needed to house the wounded from the last great offensive of the war.[59]

McCowan had no team that could compete in or out of season with Carlisle's. He had, however, created a sort of Indian all-star band. Even before the fair opened, McCowan began to think seriously about taking the World's Fair Band on tour. He engaged the services of Fred Pelham, president and manager of the Central Lyceum Bureau of Chicago, whose stable of lecturers, entertainers, and musicians included Representative Champ Clark of Missouri, Eugene V. Debs, May Parker's Pickaninnies and Concert Company, and the Wesleyan Male Quartette. Unfortunately, Pelham took it for granted that the members of the band would be attired "in full fledged Indian costume and not in regular band uniforms."[60] It proved a considerable disappointment when he learned that the members of the band wore dark green majordomo band costumes. Eventually, it also proved a bitter disappointment to McCowan when he realized that small towns, civic organizations in larger cities, or even certain churches desperate to attract crowds with deep pockets were unwilling to engage the band for six hundred dollars a performance.[61] The "greatest Indian musical organization in existence" passed quickly from a route traveled by other, more successful Show Indians.[62]

William Cypher, a Paiute boy from Carson City Indian School, quit the band and went to work on a road gang of the Santa Fe Railroad in Kansas. He would rather walk all the way back to Carson City if he had to, he wrote his agent, than travel another day with the band or return to Chilocco once the fair and the tour ended. "I dont thinks I would like to served so many yr's at Chilocco are we suppose to be under your yes[?]"[63] When Asbury wrote to McCowan, informing him of Cypher's whereabouts, the master of Chilocco curtly replied that, since "William ran away . . . I have nothing more to do with the boy."[64] And nothing more, apparently, to do with his vision of a traveling Indian show band.

Robert Rydell views the Louisiana Purchase Exposition as giving a utopian dimension to American imperialism. Contrasted with the grades of culture illustrated in the ethnological villages and along the Pike, the White City blazed brightly as the embodiment of racial and material progress in the United States. "Most visitors," Rydell writes, "basked in the glow."[65] But for Frederick Hoxie, the 1904 fair condemned the Indians' future. Euroamericans judged Indians to be so backward that they seemed capable of little more than manual labor. Hoxie quotes from W. J. McGee's assessment, wherein the chief of the Department of Anthropology explained the two lines of narrative to be discerned in the outdoor exhibit and the model Indian school. "It presents the race narrative of odd peoples," McGee wrote, "who mark time while the world advances, and of savages, made, by American methods, into civilized workers."[66] To Hoxie, the exhibits at St. Louis represent a decline in optimism about the capacity of Indians to adapt, to change, and to evolve. If that were true, however, it never occurred to McCowan. His survey of Indian affairs, his evaluation of the whole world in a small space, indicated that, as of 1904, "The Indians are increasing in numbers. Many are also increasing in wealth." Education held the key to a future of health, wealth, and good citizenship. As far as he was concerned, the racial landscape at St. Louis had taught him, "It is a long cry from an Igorotte to an educated Indian."[67]

Show-Indian students of St. Louis, despite the Indian Bureau's best effort, did not alter the image of Indians in the public mind. It was also a far cry from a uniformed student at the 6:45 A.M. flag salute to Geronimo selling his autograph in his private stall. A few spectators would actually arrive early at the fairgrounds to witness the patriotic display; but many more at their leisure paid money to own an inscription as historical as a stone scraped by a sword. Geronimo, the last Indian warrior chief, had passed this way. Many more of those same citizens who could not travel to St. Louis that season to see the sacred and profane of the American celebration could visit fairgrounds, empty lots, or vacant fields transformed into the Wild West in the cities and towns across the nation when the Show Indians and their companions came to play.

THE WILD WEST SHOW IN ITS PRIME, 1900-1917

*"I do like the Show life but I would like
to . . . be a cowboy & my wife a cowgirl."*

From the number of traveling shows alone, the first eighteen years of the twentieth century mark the heyday of Wild West shows and their Show Indians. Whether in Wild West shows, carnival sideshows, trade expositions, or world's fairs, Show Indians found employment, or were displayed, in record numbers. Dozens of Wild West shows and "combines" flourished. Many were small, organized mainly to play modest venues such as county fairs and carnivals. The shows could be produced and routed along the summer circuit without large sums invested in the enterprise. To stage a Wild West show, an entrepreneur needed a string of ponies, a stagecoach, a covered wagon, a few cowboys, fewer cowgirls, and ten or so Indians. It had been nearly two decades since the long drives and the big roundups had ended. Cowboys or would-be cowboys occasionally sought employment in the shows as an alternative to either unemployment or a forced change in their careers.[1]

In the records of the Miller Brothers' 101 Ranch Real Wild West, for example, one is struck by the number of letters from literate and semi-literate cowhands seeking employment in the autumn of each year, touting their skills as riders and their expertise with a lariat, and promising complete satisfaction.[2] And finally, as Don Russell suggests, anyone with a goatee, mustache, long hair, and looks that favored Buffalo Bill's could be a headliner in his own show, if not always a celebrity in the culture at large.[3]

Down to World War I, a number of Wild West shows competed with one another principally in the United States, but a few of the more ambitious organizations as before sought paying customers in Europe, Australia, South America, and, on one occasion, even South Africa.[4] To these enterprises, one can add the smaller medicine shows and the various trade and fair associations that sought to employ Show Indians as unique attractions.

For a percentage of the profits, James A. Bailey in 1895 began providing transportation, paying for local expenses, and planning the route for Buffalo Bill. More and more, Bailey took over the management from Nate Salsbury, whose health continued to deteriorate. There followed years of crisscrossing the nation, sometimes in direct competition with the myriad lesser shows. In 1902, Buffalo Bill completed a coast-to-coast tour. The next season, the twentieth anniversary of the Wild West show, Buffalo Bill again took the show to England. Bailey's strategy was to trade territory with the Barnum and Bailey Circus, which had been touring in Europe between 1897 and 1902. For the next four years Buffalo Bill's Show Indians performed the perennial favorites of attacking the Deadwood Stage, battling Cody and his companions at the Little Bighorn, and appearing as picturesque as ever in performances throughout England and the continent.[5]

It had been more than a decade since Buffalo Bill took the Wild West to England. Although the crowds were as impressive as ever, the excitement and novelty of the first tour were never repeated. As a reporter for the Aberdeen *Daily Journal* observed, men who as boys undoubtedly read Buffalo Bill's recorded deeds with absorbing interest and then saw the splendid feats in the arena now "hurried along with wives and bairns eager to get a good view of Colonel Cody and his Red Indians." Indians

36 : *Buffalo Bill's Wild West in Rome, Italy, March 1906. (George T. Beck Collection, American Heritage Center, University of Wyoming, Laramie)*

"of all tribes, many of them naked," were but one of many types who rode with the Rough Riders of the World.[6]

Actually, the many tribes of "Red Indians" were none other than the venerable Oglala from Pine Ridge who, this time out, only acted the part of others. Back in the United States perhaps an Indian was still an Indian after all; but in England and Europe what novelty remained could be conjured by the names Arapaho, Cheyenne, and Blackfoot added to Sioux. Luther Standing Bear, an alumnus of Carlisle who served Cody's Indians as interpreter, explained that "we were supposed to represent four different tribes, each tribe to ride animals of one color."[7] Even so, "Red Indians" were not as rare as once they had seemed. Just how ordinary Indians had become is suggested by a reporter for the London *Daily Graphic*, who wrote contemptuously about another Wild West show and its Canadian "red men with their squaws and piccaninies [*sic*]" appearing at Earl's Court. They, "like all the red men of the West," the reporter observed, "have fallen in with civilised methods to such an extent that they seem to prefer felt hats of the bowler type to the bonnet of eagles' feathers, sloppy trousers to buckskin leg gear fringed with scalp locks, and cheap brown boots to moccasins, mores the pity."[8] This particular version of the vanishing-American theme, nostalgia for a pristine past, seems to have crossed the Atlantic with Buffalo Bill. Now writers appeared to be more impressed with the size and logistics of the show than with the stories re-created in the arena. Back in Cornwall during June, one reporter went on about the eating arrangements of the show, whereas in Aberdeen another reporter extolled the "remarkable manifestation of the complete organization and preparation for every imaginable contingency." [9]

At one time, Major Burke had boasted that the Buffalo Bill show contained no tinsel or fakery. It represented instead an authentic re-creation of "frontier" life. Buffalo Bill himself had bragged that he constantly changed his Show Indians to keep a freshness about the production and to avoid the humbuggery usually associated with carnivals and sideshows. But by 1903 the shows had changed. Nate Salsbury died in December 1902; Burke, as general manager and press agent, eventually would be forced out by Bailey's heirs. For twenty years with Buffalo Bill, the Show Indians had only to be themselves. The sheer numbers of shows and Show Indians competing for audiences, however, made it inevitable that artificiality crept into the productions. In the early years of Cody's Wild West, "Show Indians" represented a professional status, those whose lives were re-created in the tableau and scenes performed in the arena. It had been the real-life experiences that had made Show Indians; now they increasingly represented just another class of actor.[10] They were authentic because of their "race," if not for their deeds.

Artifice is even evident in the contracting of Indians for the shows. Early on, representatives from the more reputable (which also meant "larger") shows met with agency superintendents to work out the details. By the early years of the century, however, third parties, usually Indian traders, increasingly became contractors for the shows. Although they shared with the show owners the desire for profit, theirs appears to have been an even more relentless pursuit.

In the late 1880s, Buffalo Bill used to employ James F. Asay, former Chicago lawyer and for a time the trader at Pine Ridge. Asay moved his operation to Rushville, Nebraska, south of the reservation line. He served Cody and Salsbury as a recruiter and contracting agent for the show. Asay, however, because of his methods, continually irritated the agent at Pine Ridge. Cody thought he was working exclusively for him when, in fact, Asay also worked for the Carver and Whitney organization and the Kickapoo Medicine Company. When Cody found out, he stopped doing business with the trader. At a time when the commissioner tried to discourage Indians especially from joining the medicine shows, when the companies'

37 : Luther Standing Bear (ca. 1865–1939), one of the first students at Carlisle Indian School (where he was given the name Luther), joined Cody's Wild West as an interpreter in 1902. In 1912 he moved to California and began work in motion pictures. He later earned renown as the author of My People the Sioux *(1928),* My Indian Boyhood *(1931),* The Land of the Spotted Eagle *(1933), and* Stories of the Sioux *(1934). (National Archives)*

representatives were unwelcome on the reservation, Asay would travel through the settlements, careful to avoid the agency, looking for prospective Show Indians or Show Salesmen.[11]

Like Asay, W. H. Barten left one profession to pursue the more lucrative career of Indian trader. Following his graduation from the state normal school in Fredonia, New York, Barten began the study of law at Columbia University, but left there in 1891 to enter the Indian service as a teacher on the Pine Ridge reservation. He married Angelique Cordier in the spring of 1894. He and his wife then ran the boarding school at the agency until 1902, when the family moved to Gordon, Nebraska, where Barten opened a mercantile store. In addition to his other business, Barten became principal outfitter for Wild West shows, rodeos, and eventually movies.[12]

When Cody first began hiring Indians for his show, he would often purchase needed supplies for the families who gathered at Rushville, and later at Gordon, Nebraska, to see their Show Indians off. At the close of each season, just before the Indians returned home, Cody would purchase a new suit of clothes for each member of the troupe. All that had changed by the first decade of the twentieth century. Perhaps it was just too expensive to show such generosity. Still, there is no record in the early years of the show that Cody required his performers to purchase or rent their costumes. Barten, however, did just that. Barten became the principal contractor with the Indians who joined various shows, but not Buffalo Bill's. As Colonel Fred Cummins once complained, Barten gave "the impression that he is the Indian Agent, instead of a store keeper living in a different state from where" the Show Indians came.[13] The shows and the Show Indians signed contracts with Barten, and not under the authority of the Indian Bureau.

Francis Leupp, the commissioner who succeeded William A. Jones, quietly resumed the practice of overseeing contracts and requiring shows to post bond for the faithful completion of their obligations to the Show Indians and the government. As usual, however, not all shows hired their Indians with the official approval of the Indian Office. Barten, for example, contracted with the Shubert Anderson Company that ran the New York Hippodrome, with the Miller Brothers' 101 Ranch Real Wild West until 1911, and with the Young Buffalo Wild West and Colonel Cummins's Far East, to name but a few of the organizations with which he did business. The companies would write to Barten asking to employ a certain number of Show Indians for the coming season. He gladly filled their orders. Barten drew up contracts that, even by the legendary standard of Indian-trader greed, were exceedingly generous on his behalf. A typical contract for the 101 Ranch Real Wild West stipulated that the Miller Brothers would provide their Indian employees "with proper food and raiment, except one set of Indian Clothes, Head Dress, Mocasins [sic], etc." Barten provided the costumes, which remained his property until the Indians had quieted their debts to him. To that end, the contract further specified that most of the money earned by the Indians each week go to Barten. Bear Shield, for example, received $5.00 in weekly wages. Indicated by his mark on the contract, he agreed to surrender $4.00 of it to Barten. His wife received $2.50 a week, of which Barten claimed $1.50. Cody and Salsbury were paying their Show Indians $25.00 a month back in the 1880s. That the wages had not increased, and in fact had declined in certain instances, is testimony to the availability of Show Indians, and the lack of generosity on the part of the owners when compared to Buffalo Bill.[14]

It is not surprising, then, that a number of Show Indians complained of the arrangements when they discovered, much to their chagrin, that they had unknowingly signed away most of their salaries. The contracts contained a clause that specified just such a payment.[15] Angelique Barten, who presumably explained the various clauses in Lakota to the Indians when necessary, witnessed the contracts. Worse still, the debt owed Barten seemed to increase as if by magic. Joe Paints [Himself] Yellow wrote from Kansas City:

> Friend. I am going write you a few lines I owe you nothing in this Show, and you send to show people owe you, and you put in 50.00 dollar, you point me, and, I was, owe you besid mowe[r] and Rake, owe you $5.00, and, if I got mony, I come home Gordon I will paid you some of them, and, I was tell you I got & steel [steer], and, when he get fat this jun[e] or July my Brother he is going to sales and he paid you mowe[r] and I never said I paid you 50.00 in this show.[16]

If that were not enough, the Miller Brothers charged Joe Paints Yellow and others for clothing purchased at Barten's store with 101 Ranch money.

Before Joe Paints Yellow could square his disputed account with Barten, he would first have to reimburse the show for its generosity.[17] According to his contract, Pine Bird owed Barten 130 dollars for food and clothing. He wrote to the storekeeper, with unintended irony, at the end of his first week of employment. Pine Bird called himself Barten's "friend who always make you Plenty money."[18] And when Bear Runs In the Woods informed his creditor that he planned to leave the Miller Brothers for better pay with the New York Hippodrome (with whom Barten provided contracted Show Indians), the store owner reminded him that "by going away from the 101 you would place yourself liable to arrest for getting of me goods under false pretense and also for getting transportation from the 101 show under false pretense." The only safe thing for him to do was to stay with the 101 show. Then he would not get into trouble. "None of the Indians are allowed to go away from the 101 Show. If any of them do they will surely get lots of trouble."[19]

Barten created a type of indentured servitude that would have been the envy of any boss of any company town. He explained to Joe Miller that he first required payment of existing accounts. "The rule with the Government," he explained, "is that all their wages must be sent here for the entire season excepting the allowance of one dollar per week to each Indian for spending money." Actually, no such rule existed; but Joe Miller did not know this. In 1890, Nate Salsbury had boasted that Indians knew the value of a dollar. They were competent to manage their money. Barten, on the other hand, insisted that if Indians were paid a regular salary by the shows, they would "spend it for booze, women, gambling and other harmful purposes and their families at home would suffer." Moreover, if Indians saved their money, they might be apt to buy a railroad ticket and "run away and come back in any moment on any foolish impulse." Long experience dealing with Indians had taught him that indebtedness to the trader "is the magnet that draws together the large number [of Indians] and makes it possible to pick out and get the number required for the show." Without credit, Indians could not survive "as they have no money this time of the year with which to buy food." Finally, there were also a great variety of other debts that Indians owed each other. They paid these "by using my store as a kind of clearing house." He confided to Miller that, personally, he would just as soon quit the Show Indian trade. It paid little and brought a person into contact with unpleasant people.[20]

Profits, as it turned out, could not have been that minimal. He was still in the business five years later. He wrote to Vernon C. Seaver, owner of the Al Fresco Amusement Company of Peoria, Illinois, that he was "not as anxious for this kind of business as I have been in past years. Supplies are higher in price and the profits much smaller." Yet he could still sell "all these kinds of supplies for cash and at prices just as high as the Indians will pay, just as fast as I can buy the supplies."[21]

If an example of exploitation of Indians existed anywhere in the history of the Wild West shows, it was certainly present in Barten's operation. He and the Miller Brothers represent a shift in attitude, or at least a willingness to express openly a callousness toward, or sometimes even contempt for, Indians.[22] Barten charged Indians outrageous sums to carry their accounts. He insisted that the shows pay him before they paid the Indians. And for that, the shows were allowed to retain 10 percent of the Show Indians' wages as a service charge. Indians who did business with Barten and the companies he served returned to their reservations with nothing to show for their months of performing with the Wild West shows except their experiences.

Protectionist associations such as the IRA in the past had been sensitive to charges of Indian exploitation. There are few complaints in these years compared to, say, Thomas Jefferson Morgan's tenure as commissioner. The only ones who complained were the Show Indians themselves, and when they did they usually greeted their tormentors as "friend." They did not complain to the IRA. They did not know the good people of Philadelphia, Boston, Washington, D.C., and New Paltz, New York, who called themselves friends of the Indian. When the Indian Bureau got involved, however, it was usually to remind the Indians to live up to their contracts.

Standing Bear v. *Crook* had allowed Indians to come and go as they pleased; but according to Barten, contracts with the shows made Indians virtual prisoners of their signatures. They appeared as property of the shows. Buffalo Bill would never have dreamed of charging his Show Indians for their clothing, or insisting that they were bound to contracts regardless of their wishes to return home or to go to work for someone else. Cody, compared to other entrepreneurs, took seriously the language in the contract that bound him to guarantee the Indians' welfare. Clearly, Buffalo Bill had a larger definition than others about what constituted "welfare." By the 1900s, the Show Indian trade had become a lucrative business for some people, if not always for the Show Indians themselves.

In some ways, the Miller Brothers were opposites of Buffalo Bill Cody and his Wild West. With the fortune Cody had made with his Wild West show between 1883 and 1903, he bought land, invested in mines, and involved himself in town building and real estate. With the farming, ranching, oil refining, and mercantile empire created by their father, Colonel George Washington Miller, and added to by their own labor, the Miller Brothers, J. C. or Joe, Zack, and George, founded the 101 ("Hundred and One") Ranch Real Wild West. It boasted not only an authentic western ranch to inspire the show and serve as its headquarters, but also real cowboys and real dispossessed Indians from the tall-grass prairie of northeastern Oklahoma Territory. The Miller Brothers' ranch chewed up the better part of four counties, 110,000 acres or 172 square miles.[23]

In June 1905, in something reminiscent of the Old Glory Blowout, the

Joe   George Miller

of the 101 Ranch four miles north of
Bliss, Oklahoma (now ....)

*38 : The Miller Brothers, left to right, Zack, George, and Joe Miller (mis-identified
by the donor of the photograph). From their ranching and oil empire, they
branched into show business in the first decade of the twentieth century. Their
101 Ranch Real Wild West traveled throughout the United States and Europe.
Zack Miller tried to continue the show tradition following the accidental deaths
of Joe and George in the late 1920s; but the show went into decline and collapsed
with the deepening of the Great Depression. (Archives and Manuscripts Division,
Oklahoma Historical Society)*

Miller Brothers staged a roundup for the National Editorial Association.
The organization naturally spread news of the success of the combination Wild West show and roundup. Ranch workers performed what Cody's
organization years before had dubbed "cowboy fun," but would eventually
be known as rodeo. Stars of the show included Lucille Mulhall, an outstanding rider billed as "America's First Cowgirl," Ponca Indian neighbors who played all the Indian parts, and Geronimo, brought up from Fort
Sill for the occasion with a soldier escort. Geronimo shot a buffalo in what
the brothers acclaimed as the old warrior's last hunt. They could just as

39 : The Miller Brothers invited the National Editorial Association to the 101 Ranch on June 11, 1905, for a "roundup." Reminiscent of Cody's "Old Glory Blowout," the roundup served as the inspiration for the 101 Ranch Real Wild West. The brothers employed Poncas for the celebration. Geronimo, a Chiricahua Apache prisoner of war at Fort Sill, arrived under army escort at the 101 Ranch in Bliss, Oklahoma. (Archives and Manuscripts Division, Oklahoma Historical Society)

---

easily have called it his first hunt. Geronimo and his band had never done much buffalo hunting in New Mexico, Arizona, and the Sierra Madre of northern Mexico. It mattered little to either the Miller Brothers or the sixty-four thousand spectators who crowded the arena at the ranch on the north side of the Salt Fork River.[24]

Owing to the success of the exhibition, the Miller Brothers received an invitation to take part in the Jamestown Tercentenary Exposition. Lewis Schauss, manager of the Kansas City Convention Hall, had seen the spectacle staged at the ranch. Upon hearing about the forthcoming Jamestown exposition and the Miller Brothers' participation, he scheduled an exhibition of the 101 Ranch show at the Chicago Coliseum before the opening of the fair. Favorable notices impressed New York promoters, who persuaded the brothers to put together a second show that also played Brighton Beach during that summer. At the close of the fair, the main group appeared at the Georgia State Fair and at Louisville before returning in November to Bliss (renamed Marland in 1922), Oklahoma. Early in the winter, the brothers decided to make the 101 Ranch Real Wild West a permanent institution. The show opened at Ponca City, Oklahoma, on April 14, 1908. From then through 1916, it remained one of the premier traveling shows.[25]

In 1907, J. C. Miller wrote to Barten with instructions for procuring an additional twenty Indians for the show at the Jamestown Tercentenary. "Your being familiar with the Indians," Miller advised, "will enable you to steer clear of the boozers." Once gathered, the Show Indians were to be put on the train. "We hardly think it will be necessary to send a man up there to bring them here," Miller explained. "You can give one of them a letter and put him in charge of the bunch. Give them what money will be necessary to feed them enroute."[26] Miller also wanted a small herd of "good blocky Indian ponies" sent on to Jamestown. Barten answered that whereas the Indians could be found without much difficulty, even though they were widely scattered throughout the reservation, the ponies were another matter. "There have been so many buyers here," he explained to Miller, "that prices are way up." He suggested, instead, that Miller purchase the horses from the white ranchers in the vicinity rather than bargain with the Indians.[27]

The 101 Ranch Real Wild West continued to employ Oglala and Sicangu (Brule) performers from the Pine Ridge and Rosebud reservations; but it also employed in large numbers Cheyennes, Poncas, Sac and Foxes, Comanches, and Kiowas from the former Indian Territory. Like the other organizations, the Miller Brothers occasionally hired former students and graduates of the off-reservation boarding schools as showmen or interpreters. From Chicago, at the first performance away from the ranch, Walter Battice of the Sac and Fox agency wrote his superintendent that unseasonably cold weather had plagued the early performances. The Miller brothers had brought 165 Indians for whom English, however imperfect, was the common language. Battice proclaimed Chicago "a great city—and much to see."[28]

Once at the Jamestown fair, a site about twelve miles east of the original settlement and nearer still to Norfolk, Battice found ample time between afternoon and evening performances to explore the countryside. He enjoyed returning to Hampton Institute, where he had gone to school years earlier. His teachers told him that he "was not the same Walter." He had "changed especially in size," he wrote Agent Kohlenberg. It cost $3.50 for a round-trip train ticket between Norfolk and Washington. Battice decided to spend the better part of a week's wages to make the trip on Sundays, when the show gave no performances.[29] He found a great deal to do in his off-hours outside the grounds—"bathing -fishing & boating. Rates on the water are very cheap to all points on the coast—so one can go to all the larger Cities for little money after once getting here." He thought about returning home in late August, but when the opportunity to join the new show at Brighton Beach came up, he decided to stay.

He worked as the chief of police, ticket taker, and performer. "And you don't know how pleased I am of the change," he wrote Kohlenberg. He found the place beautiful. "We are just between Coney Is. and Manhattan Island = and the show is so far a success." He went bathing every day. He marveled at the throngs of New Yorkers who crowded the beaches and parks during the week and in even greater numbers on Sundays. He estimated the crowds at near 300,000, but added that "of course all don't come to see the show—if we get 3 & 4 thousand a day we are satisfied." He visited New York City on his own, went by Madison Square Garden, "where [Harry K.] Thaw & [Stanford] White had their trouble—also saw where Thaw is confined—and you can bet I saw all the law would allow me to."[30] Just before the show closed, he wrote candidly to his agent that he was not sorry to see it end. A continuous "good time is not an easy life to follow for an old man like me. The show here has been a great success—but the Indians & cowboys are all getting enough of it."[31]

Battice and many other Indians from Oklahoma had joined Sioux performers to participate in the 101 Ranch show. Some of the Oklahoma veterans of the Jamestown stand had joined the Zach Mulhall show for a tour of the eastern United States in 1910. From Knoxville, Tennessee, the Cheyennes Frank Shot Eyes and Frank Red Fish wrote "Friend Joe Miller" to say that they did not like their employer. Frank Shot Eyes informed Miller that "I well lik to come you show if you want me, her[e] six Boys her[e] like to come you show. please let us no if you want us to come and also for women and theree child so if you want us please let us no soon as you can." They did leave the Mulhall show and caught up with the Miller Brothers in Missouri, on their way back to Bliss.[32] The Cheyennes numbered the largest contingent of Oklahoma Indians in the 101 Ranch show. Year after year, High Chief, actually an enrolled Cheyenne from Pine Ridge, and Southern Cheyenne allottees from around Calumet joined the show each spring. He would write to Joe Miller near the end of December,

40 : *Walter Battice, Sac and Fox, who performed in the Miller Brothers' 101 Ranch Real Wild West. (Archives and Manuscripts Division, Oklahoma Historical Society)*

asking that the entrepreneur "send me condtract to go by an I got 25 indians now ready to come."[33] Miller sent the contracts. In fact, he specified that he would pay the "regular Indians" five dollars a week, and four dollars for women who rode. "I would like the men all to be as nearly as possible long-haired or have good wigs and good costumes," he told High Chief. The show train would leave for the East on or about April 10.[34]

Harry Lucas, an Ihanktonwan (Yankton) from Eggleston, Minnesota, joined High Chief and others for the 1911 season. Lucas, in one of the most interesting letters written by a Show Indian, told Joe Miller that "I do like the Show life but I would like to know if I could be a cowboy & my wife a cow girl when I come back. . . . I dont mind to take the part in the show as we did, but my wife like the cowgirl life & I like the cowboy life so please let us hear from you by the return mail." That season, Harry Lucas, his wife, and his friends Minne and Jammie Blue Bird were able to play the parts of Indian cowboys and cowgirls.[35]

Walter Battice and Richard Davis, his Cheyenne friend and sometime business partner from Kingfisher, Oklahoma, also signed on for the 1911 season. Davis had left Carlisle years before to take a job as an agency farmer on the Cheyenne and Arapaho reservation. With changes in political administrations, he lost his job at the agency. He thereafter worked for many years as an informant and interpreter for the Bureau of American Ethnology. That he had quit a job as dairyman at Carlisle was bad enough for Richard Henry Pratt; but that he had been subverted by the "Government Ethnological schemes" and, the denouement, had finally joined a "Buffalo Bill" show, was too much for the cranky, retired headmaster. He wrote to Dr. Carlos Montezuma to say that "Luther Standing Bear went off with 'Buffalo Bill' and lost his character, and from time to time there have been others. There were no better boys in their time at Carlisle than Luther Standing Bear and Richard Davis."[36]

Davis hardly considered himself a failure. He wrote to Joe Miller:

Now Joe, if you want 2 aristocratic Indians this summer just call on me and Mr. Walter Battice—two of your old boys. We are both prepared with the finest Indian outfits and with good real Indian wigs.

My personal outfit is worth something. I still have the eagle feather head dress I wore at the Coliseum Chicago and at Coney Island and have also a new horned-head-dress trimmed with white mink and a new buckskin suit (whole) besides 2 other suits. Battice has also a good outfit and is about to get a Cheyenne eagle feather doubled tail war-bonnet something unusual. You dont see these 2 tailed head dresses often.

I have 8 farms, a good city home and money in Bank and Battice has ¾ interest in a store and money in Bank and we care for no one else only yourself and the other Miller boys and we would like to patronize your show this summer just for pleasure.

But—Battice weighs 230 pounds and I weigh 215 pounds and I think we are too heavy to ride.

Now Joe if you want two of your old boys that will stay with you write at once.[37]

Miller did just that; but he also reduced their pay by ten dollars a month (from forty dollars to thirty dollars) for their inability to ride. Davis and Battice, nevertheless, were able to march in the opening-day parade in Washington, D.C., that April.[38] When the show played Oklahoma in the third week of September, they invited all of their friends to watch, as Battice called it, "the only W. W. show in the world." [39]

The Miller Brothers show prospered in 1911, 1912, and 1913. In head-to-head competition with Buffalo Bill's Wild West, the organization held its own. Part of the show's success may have been its emphasis on the "real" aspects of ranching. For the Miller Brothers, that feature, more than marauding Indians, made the West wild. The show also highlighted trick shooting, as in the Buffalo Bill tradition; but the Millers placed greater emphasis on trick riding, "broncho busting," wild steer riding, and fancy rope spinning, "a cowboy pastime." The Indian scenes included a buffalo hunt, Sioux and Cheyenne dances, and either the "Pat Hennessy Massacre," a re-creation of an 1876 attack on a wagon train in the Indian Territory (always a popular feature in Oklahoma), or the "Mountain Meadows Massacre" of 1857 in southern Utah. In the latter feature, instead of the California-bound emigrants being slaughtered by Mormons and their Indian allies, in this version the cowboys and cavalry arrive in time to drive off the Indians.[40] The show's success on the circuit spread the fame of the ranch. Early motion-picture companies began using both the ranch and its show performers in their films about the West and pioneer life. And in time, as with all successful shows, the brothers decided in 1913 to send their show to Europe. Actually, it was only half the show. With Buffalo Bill's organization bankrupt, there were financial rewards awaiting a premier Wild West show on the American circuit.[41]

The Miller Brothers negotiated for Show Indians to appear with the Sarrasani Circus, "the grandest show ever seen in Europe." [42] The Sarrasani Circus, in addition to its wild animal acts from Africa and Asia, its jugglers, tumblers, and equestrians, boasted a Wild West show of cow-

41 : *Walter Battice during his school days at Hampton Institute, Virginia. Certain leaders in the Indian service lamented that people like Walter, despite their acculturation into Euroamerican society, joined Wild West shows. Battice, through show business and investments, accumulated considerable property. (Archives and Manuscripts Division, Oklahoma Historical Society)*

---

boys, Indians, bucking "bronkos," "buffaloes and bisons," and, incongruously, "Canadian sea-lions." Although it traveled throughout Europe, it based its operation in a six-thousand-seat, covered arena in Dresden.[43]

Hans Stosch-Sarrasani, owner and impresario, asked the Miller Brothers to secure the services of "real Sioux Indians." Fifty Oglalas from Pine Ridge, accompanied by Wayne Beasley of the 101 Ranch, crossed the Big Water to Germany in the spring of 1913. Everything went well until early July, when seventeen of the Show Indians decided that they had seen enough of Germany, Austria, and Belgium. They had been treated badly at frontier crossings by German border police. Only two of the Sioux were citizens (by virtue of their allotments under the provisions of the Dawes Act) and possessed passports. The others, according to J. B. Moore, counselor at the State Department, were not citizens of the United States and therefore could not be issued passports. Instead, he had Joe Miller wire him a narrative description of each Indian, including the person's age, "height, the color of eyes and hair, the shape of the face (whether round, full, or square) and the description of forehead, nose, mouth and chin." With that information in hand, the State Department forwarded a document for Beasley's use at border crossings, which contained a departmental seal and a statement that the United States would appreciate "proper consideration and assistance" extended to its noncitizen Indians. It was hoped that such an official-looking document would fulfill all the requirements of *Deutsche Ordnung*. Joe Miller, of course, had to rely on Beasley for descriptions that, in retrospect, would have pleased a physical anthropologist. Miller, however, was not willing to release the seventeen Indians from their contracts.[44]

Some of the seventeen decided that they might be able to force Beasley's hand by violating the morals clause of their contracts. They began drinking in their guardian's presence. They could purchase all the alcohol they wanted, especially beer, without much difficulty; but, worse, the local inhabitants were quick to treat the celebrities to all of the beer and schnapps they could drink.[45] Dick White Calf was particularly insistent. His daughter had been mauled by a tiger when passing its cage. Although she suffered superficial wounds, they were serious all the same. White Calf and his wife got drunk and stayed drunk, as Beasley thought, so that he would have to send them home. Beasley remained firm. The seventeen finished the season with Sarrasani. Beasley referred to the them as "crumby," to which Joe Miller, in a lame attempt to find humor in the situation, replied that Beasley "did not say whether they were United States crumbs or natives of Germany." The seventeen did not reenlist for the tour the following year, although others from the troupe did.[46] Those Sioux returned to Germany in December 1913.

The remainder of the Miller Brothers group sailed for England, in April 1914, to appear at the Anglo-American Exposition in London, whose theme proclaimed one hundred years of peace between the two great English-speaking nations.[47] It was the same organization (though in a different incarnation) that had been running annual trade fairs at Earl's Court in the west end of London for more than a quarter-century. Sixty-five Show Indians, most of them Oglalas, accompanied the London group.[48] Both the Sarrasani Circus and the Miller Brothers show did well until summer. In the aftermath of the assassination on June 28 of Franz Ferdinand, first Austria-Hungary, then Russia, then Germany, and finally France and Britain mobilized their armies for war.

With Britain's declaration of war against Germany, communication was cut off between the London and Dresden groups of performers. Zack Miller, with the London bunch, thought that perhaps Joe Miller, back in the United States, might be able to get in touch with the Sarrasani group; but Britain controlled the cable to the continent and the U.S. government took over wireless communication in the United States. The Dresden Indians, it seemed to Joe and Zack, got lost in the fog of war. On August 7, British military authorities, under section 115 of the Army Act, seized the horses and transport of the 101 Ranch Real Wild West. They paid for the material in British pounds at "fair market value," but the seizure nearly bankrupted the organization. Zack began to look for ways to reunite the groups and then get them all out of England.[49]

Prince Lucca and his cossacks were first to leave. They caught a cross-channel packet to France and began their long journey to Russia where, it appears, most perished.[50] Joe Miller learned that about forty other Americans, stranded in London because of the closing of other entertainments, had virtually joined his organization. In the rush to find passage out of fortress England, none of the steamship companies were willing initially to sell tickets to Indians.[51] The War Department intervened and began to organize transport for the stranded Americans; but it was estimated that the ships would not be able to leave Newport News, Virginia, for at least a month. Zack, as best he could, arranged passage piecemeal for all of the non-Indian performers.[52]

Days stretched into weeks. Zack Miller booked space on every possible ship leaving England and bound for any place in the Americas. Finally, in mid-September, he secured berths for the remainder of his troupe, including the sixty-five Show Indians, on the U.S. Mail packet, *St. Paul.* Seven hundred frightened refugees stuffed the staterooms and cabins below-decks of the ship that had been designed to carry 250 first-class passengers. Then, just two days before the *St. Paul*'s westward passage, the missing Show Indians from Germany turned up in London with fantastic stories to tell.[53]

At the onset of the war on August 3 and 4, Sarrasani had started his Show Indians moving by passenger train toward the coast. In Denmark, they joined another group of expatriates from the Colonel Cummins's Wild West, who had just barely escaped with their lives from the authori-

42 : *A poorly focused photograph of Bill Arthur and a group of Oglala Show Indi-*
ans, July 1914. This group was arrested by Hamburg authorities shortly after
the outbreak of war. They made their escape to London through Denmark and
Norway. (Wyoming State Archives, Museums, and Historical Department, Chey-
enne)

ties in Hamburg. Dressed in civilian clothes, some with short hair (they
wore braided wigs in the arena), and all without passports or papers,
they were arrested as Serbian spies. Bill Arthur, hired by Cummins as
both interpreter and chaperon in charge of nine Oglalas, got word to the
American consulate. H. H. Morgan, the American consul general in Hamburg, persuaded the authorities to release the band, pending review by a
military tribunal. Morgan did not wait around in Hamburg for justice to
be realized. With official seals and enough vellum to befuddle the wariest
bureaucrat, Morgan took the fugitives by rail to Copenhagen, where they
joined the Sarrasani entourage. Only later, after Germany's defeat, would
Morgan write to Arthur with some humor about "the good old times in
Hamburg when the Germans tried to shoot the feathers off the aggrega-
tion of Indians which you had with you."[54]

Arthur and the Show Indians made their way to England in circuitous
fashion, sailing first to Norway, then Holland, and eventually to England.
The Show Indians were not too sure where they had been; but when the

Sarrasani group saw Zack Miller at Victoria Station they all laughed, hugged, and patted their employer.[55] The entertainers from Germany were allowed to board with the London group. Performances continued at Earl's Court, though with numbers of features excluded or considerably modified because of the absence of livestock. The Sarrasani refugees performed in the dance numbers of the show. They thought they were going to be paid; but safely back in the United States, Joe Miller refused to compensate them. As he explained to the agent at Pine Ridge, they went into the dance "as a matter of pass-time while they were waiting for an opportunity to return home." As far as he was concerned, they were not entitled to any pay. "Your own experiences with Indians will tell you," he reminded Agent Brennan, "that if you would issue each Indian on the Reservation a big fat cow, there would be several who would kick because they had no calf."[56]

Show Indians from Europe arrived back in the United States on September 21, without much notice. Four ships docked in New York that day, disgorging their desperate cargos of 4,498 Americans.[57] Some of the Indians joined the main group of 101 Ranch performers, which toured until closing in Houston on October 28, whereas the others simply went home to Pine Ridge, South Dakota, or the flyspeck towns of southwestern Oklahoma. For some of these, "a dollar a day and feed" was not enough inducement to remain entertainers. It was one thing to risk life and limb in the arena. It was quite another matter, however, when potential customers became instead actual adversaries.[58]

The losses the Miller Brothers sustained from the 1914 European show season were considerable, but not catastrophic. True, they had lost much of their livestock and gear, and efforts to rescue the stranded performers had cost an additional twenty-five thousand dollars.[59] Still, most of the troupe remained intact, and the organization put a small show on the road for the 1915 season, with Joe Miller taking the role of a Buffalo-Bill style character. The next year, however, the show hired the real, if aged, item. Buffalo Bill Cody traveled for the last time on the circuit with the Miller Brothers.[60]

Buffalo Bill's Wild West had remained in Europe for the show seasons between 1903 and 1906. Late each fall, the show would go into winter quarters (in England in 1903 and 1904 at Stokes-on-Trent), and Cody and the Show Indians would go home for a rest. Many would return with the colonel in the spring. Iron Tail, an Oglala later advertised in exaggerated fashion by the Miller Brothers as the model for the Indian-head nickel, now headlined the Show-Indian troupe. The show was still popular enough to bury the competition. Writing from Bordeaux in the fall of 1906, Cody boasted that the J. T. McCaddon Show, going head to head with the Congress of Rough Riders, "went bust" outside Paris. Buffalo Bill and his Indians took up a collection to send McCaddon's Indians and some of their faithful cowboy adversaries home.[61]

Cody's show visited France, Italy, Austria, Hungary, Germany, Holland, and Belgium in its last year of the European tour. In the section of southern Poland controlled by Austria, Russian Jews flooded the towns. They had fled the latest pogrom in Russia. "Well I simply done no business," Cody explained to a friend, "and had worlds of trouble. I lost my socks, but not my courage, for I knew if the old show could live to get out of there she would right herself and she is doing it. Germany so far is simply immense."[62] Cody was right. The show broke its previous records for a stand in Germany.

In Dresden, a reporter found the nighttime performances spellbinding. "One sees the electric flashing on the bare skins of the Indians, sees their wonderful adornment of feathers silhouetted against the dark background." In language that could have anticipated the productions of Albert Speer in Nuremberg a generation later, the writer experienced the "weirdness" and sensed a certain "mysticism in the lurid flames" at the Custer massacre.[63] Cody had been performing Custer's Last Stand since the first engagement at Erastina, back in the fall of 1886. How many times had Buffalo Bill arrived too late to avert the destruction of the Seventh Cavalry? There may have been a tinge of wistfulness to go along with the melancholy and mysticism in the dramatic gesture of Cody doffing his hat and hanging his bare head in arch remorse. His hair, as long as ever and once a robust brown, now hung thin and gray. He commented, late that season, that "all my old friends are dying off." He was looking forward to going home for a season or two of touring the United States before retirement.[64] But his planned retirement proved to be as elusive as the riches from his varied investments.

James A. Bailey died unexpectedly on March 22, 1906. Among his effects, his wife and heirs found a twelve-thousand dollar note signed by Cody and dating from the 1903 show season in London. Although Cody insisted that he had already paid the debt, the colonel honored the outstanding loan. The note, his other debts, and Mrs. Bailey's desire to abandon show business hung over Cody's head. Instead of one more good season before retirement, he now anticipated perhaps five. That would make him sixty-four, the mandatory age for his army friends, at the time he hung up his hat and guns. Unfortunate for him, he had no one to rely upon with the business acumen of either Bailey or Salsbury.[65]

When Buffalo Bill and the Indians arrived back in the United States in November 1906, the Lakota entrained for Rushville and home, and Cody remained in New York to plan his next season in the arena. He returned to first principles. He scrapped the Charge at San Juan Hill, the Siege of Peking, and some of the sideshow features. In their place, he substituted a new spectacle, the Battle of Summit Springs (1869), where two white women were saved from having to live with Indians. He also added an attack on the Union Pacific train (a modified automobile dressed up as a locomotive and pulling a string of passenger cars) by bandits.[66] This feature may have been unique in another respect as well. As one newspaper account recorded early in the season, justice triumphed in rough western style "when the train robbers, even their woman [*sic*] accomplices, were all killed." [67]

The tour opened at Madison Square Garden and then went on the road for two years. As in the heyday of Bailey's management, the show made numerous one-day stands. The Bailey estate, anxious to unload the property, approached Gordon W. Lillie about a possible merger. Although a complicated deal, exacerbated by Cody's numerous creditors, Buffalo Bill's Wild West joined Pawnee Bill's Great Far East for the 1909 season. Its personnel referred to it as the "Two Bills Show" and remembered it fondly as a "happy" organization.[68]

Gordon Lillie, who started out with Buffalo Bill as interpreter, had been touring off and on since 1889 with his own Wild West show. He even took his show to Europe for two seasons of mixed success. By the early years of the twentieth century, many of the Show-Indian personalities who had once been objects of curiosity in the various Wild West shows were either dead or, frequently, too old to travel. Survivors of the late plains wars no longer starred in columns of newsprint. The competitive nature of rodeos had yet to develop. The Wild West format, in many respects, lacked variety. Hence Buffalo Bill and his competitors were always changing features to remain current or to increase the novelty of their performances. Lillie's solution was to restyle his show as Pawnee Bill's Historic Wild West and Great Far East. The Far East doubtless got its inspiration from Buffalo Bill's Congress of Rough Riders of the World. Pawnee Bill's Far East included Hindu magicians, Singhalese dancers, Madagascar oxen cavalry, Australian Aborigines with boomerangs, Boers, "Kaffirs" and

43 : *Buffalo Bill and a group of Show Indians at Ocean Beach, just south of the Cliff House in San Francisco, ca. 1908. (Buffalo Bill Historical Center, Cody, Wyoming)*

"Hottentots" (Bantu-speaking South Africans), Zulus, Abyssinians, Chinese and Japanese cavalry, cossacks, gauchos, and Arabian horsemen.[69]

In the actual show, the Great Far East received considerably less emphasis than the billing suggested. It represented the seventh act of an eighteen-act extravaganza. Of the seventeen other episodes, only one offered anything new to patrons of Buffalo Bill's Wild West. Indians played "Football on Horseback" against cowboys. They used a five-foot-diameter ball. It proved as popular a feature as any in the history of the show, and was a refreshing change from all the gunfire usually associated with the traditional adversaries.[70]

In 1910, Cody began a series of farewell performances which extended well into 1912. The profits for the show that latter year were considerably less than in the two previous years. Cody's mine in Oracle, Arizona, had proved to be a bottomless shaft into which he sank a considerable portion of his earnings with the show. The gold and tungsten ores of Oracle were insufficient to finance his retirement. Although he had been able to reduce his debts with the success of the Two Bills show, he still owed too much money to quit show business.[71]

He took out a loan from Harry H. Tammen, former bartender and, at

44 : Buffalo Bill at Mexican Joe's cedar log house on Gordon "Pawnee Bill" Lillie's ranch, ca. 1910. Buffalo Bill teamed with Pawnee Bill between 1909 and 1913. (Archives and Manuscripts Division, Oklahoma Historical Society)

the time, the co-owner of the *Denver Post*. The story of Cody's association with Tammen, filled with deviousness, intrigue, high drama, low morals, and considerable comedy, is told elsewhere.[72] It is sufficient here to note only that Cody's loan of twenty thousand dollars allowed the unscrupulous Tammen to claim, by intricate design, a controlling share in the Two Bills show. He then wrecked it so as to acquire exclusive right to Cody's name for use in his other show interest, the Sells-Floto Circus. Buffalo Bill's Wild West, which had traveled the nation and much of Europe for the better part of thirty years, went under the auctioneer's gavel on September 15, 1913.[73]

Buffalo Bill traveled for two more seasons with the Sells-Floto Circus, serving largely in the capacity of announcer for the various acts. In 1916, he acquired rights to his name from Tammen and joined the Miller Brothers organization. Billed as the "Miller & Arlington Wild West Show Co., Inc., Presents 'Buffalo Bill' (himself) Combined with the 101 Ranch Shows," it included a "preparedness" pageant that highlighted the nation's readiness for war. Cody's health limited his role. He participated in the parade and the grand opening, wherein the ancient scout rode around the arena in a carriage or sometimes in an automobile.[74]

The season closed on November 4, 1916. Cody, at his sister's home in

Denver since early December, took ill shortly after the New Year. On the afternoon of January 9, May Cody Decker summoned a Catholic priest. Father Christopher Walsh of the Immaculate Conception Cathedral baptized Cody. The next day, just after noon, Cody died. The funeral that followed was filled with respectful remembrances and gaudy pageantry as befitted a consummate showman, though no Indians attended. Major Burke also could not attend. The ailing press agent followed his idol in death on April 12, thirteen weeks later.[75] Just six days before, and in a much more somber mood than was ever suggested by Cody's Pageant of Preparedness, the United States declared war on Germany. No Wild West show traveled the circuit during that tense and troubled spring.[76] The heyday of the Wild West show and its Show Indians had passed.

The *New York Times*, in marking the death of Buffalo Bill, limned a nostalgic theme. "Will there ever be anything to equal the Wild West Show," the editor wrote, "or is it to confess one's self the child of a simpler time so to ask?" Cody's Wild West had been a "grand show," providing its audiences with glimpses of "an extinct civilization."[77] In the same vein, the editor of *The Outlook* observed about Cody:

> Alas for the boy of to-morrow! He was the last link clearly visible to the boy of today between the golden age of American romance and the commercial present. . . . Does that name mean anything to you, O Reader? Does it not mean the smell of sawdust and popcorn, the sight of a high-pooped coach hard pressed by galloping Indians clinging to the sheltered sides of their ponies (piebald, please) as they empty across the withers of their trusty mounts the contents of equally trusty Winchesters. . . . In his Wild West Show Colonel William F. Cody was not playing the part of a mimic. He was reliving his actual past. Hence the boys and girls of Cody's own generation who had seen those galloping redskins when their Winchesters spat real lead got more thrill from the Wild West Show than even the younger boys and girls. . . . When the Indian wars had ended, Cody's fairness and tact won the friendship of the very chiefs who had been his bitterest enemies. Some of them entered his Wild West Show . . . , a university, a traveling course in the history and social life of the United States at one of its most interesting eras. Buffalo Bill helped to lay the foundation for the civilization of our modern West.[78]

Commenting on his funeral, another writer for the *New York Times* described how Buffalo Bill had employed "all sorts of tawnies." Most important of all were the Indians of "fine feather and ferocious paint." Buffalo Bill and his Show Indians created a grand spectacle. Let the "slaves of the movie habit say what they will," the reporter concluded, the Wild West "pictured an extinct civilization and barbarism. It was honest, [and] courageous . . . like its master."[79] In truth, however, Show Indians were not representatives of an extinct civilization, but of one in transition.

For more than three decades, Indians traveled throughout the Western world (with at least two or three shows appearing in Australia), offering audiences glimpses into the recent American past, and providing the Wild West show with its most distinctive features. They also served occasionally as spokespersons for the rights of Indians to be themselves. They had survived the original contest on the Great Plains. Many of them later earned a good living by re-creating portions of their lives and cultures that they and, later still, their children could celebrate.

Indians survived "Winning of the West," both in reality and then as portrayed in the shows. Whether on or off the reservations, they drew strength from their cultures to sustain them. It is testimony to their remarkable resilience that, given the hostile environment created by governments and Euroamericans between 1883 and 1917, the time of Buffalo Bill's career in the Wild West, Indians and their cultures endured.

10

FEDERAL POLICIES AND ALTERNATE IMAGES, 1900-1917

"As long as there is no expense . . .
the government has no objection."

By the first decade of the twentieth century reformers had largely ceased their steady assaults on Wild West shows. A few actually came to appreciate the value that Indians held as popular entertainers. Certain voices in the Indian service or among reformers began to notice the value of Show Indians whom, they knew or quickly learned, could attract crowds. Indians could participate, to their way of thinking, in legitimate and wholesome entertainments. "No possible objections can be made," one reformer wrote, "to Indians taking part in local historical plays and pageants designed to correctly portray historical or ethnological facts, when under the auspices of colleges and historical societies in localities near their reservations."[1] One therefore could determine the appropriateness of the show on the basis of "correctness" and "proximity." Indians could stay close to home and still serve as object lessons for other Americans. Had Buffalo Bill and his theatrical heirs erred only in taking their Indians far from home? Historical reenactments might stimulate "the white man to acquaint himself with the real red man of the past" and to learn about "the Indian of to-day as he is."[2]

Fair associations also found it lucrative to feature Show Indians. Although certain dangers existed in "commercializing the Indian," according to Sioux reformer Chauncey Yellow Robe, the risks nevertheless were worth the benefits. Local, county, and state fairs could provide the American public with examples of Indians on their way to productive citizenship.[3]

During his years as commissioner (from May 3, 1897, to January 1, 1905), William A. Jones opposed, on principle, Indian employment in Wild West shows. It seemed inconsistent to support programs of "civilization" that at least emphasized the trappings of conformity, and yet also allow Indians to join shows that glorified the unregenerate or unrepentant Indian as adversary or "freedom fighter."[4] Indians continued to find employment during the Jones years, but without the approval of the Indian Bureau. Jones's successor, although continuing to avow departmental policy that frowned on employment in the shows, nevertheless resumed a policy, which dated to the Forepaugh agreement of the late 1880s, of administering contracts of the Show Indians.

Francis Leupp (January 1, 1905, to June 15, 1909), unlike his predecessors, had worked in Indian affairs, first as an advocate for civil-service reform and later as Washington agent for the IRA in the 1890s. During that decade, he also served as a member of the Board of Indian Commissioners. He encouraged assimilation, but according to a more reasonable timetable when compared to other commissioners. As a Washington journalist involved in reforms, and as the confidant or friend of many social scientists, he had some understanding, according to Donald Parman, of anthropology's cultural-disparity theories. He therefore did not accept the simplistic and remorseless view that Indian cultures could be transformed in single life spans. Likewise, he rejected the notion that all distinctions between Indians and whites would or should disappear. He believed that Indians of middle or advanced years, who would never be absorbed into the dominant culture, nevertheless had the right to be themselves—to remain "Indians."[5]

These issues dominated Leupp's and reformers' attention during his tenure: continuing federal financial support for sectarian schools; expanding and strengthening civil service in the Indian Bureau; suppressing the liquor traffic on reservations; and administering the provisions of the Burke Act of 1906. That legislation amended the Dawes Act of 1887. Like the severalty act, it did not apply to Indian Territory. Instead of holding Indian allotments in trust for twenty-five years, the act authorized the secretary of the interior to grant patents in fee simple to Indian allottees judged competent to manage their affairs. The new legislation, unlike the Dawes Act, withheld citizenship from subsequent allottees until they received clear title to their lands.[6] Of all the policy concerns during his commissionership, employment of Indians by Wild West shows ranked fairly low on his list. Indeed when questions arose, if at all, they appeared as almost humorous asides from much more important issues.

The responsibility of overseeing the contracting of Show Indians rested with Charles F. Larrabee, former chief of the land division. Leupp had him appointed assistant commissioner. Larrabee saw to it that printed contracts—five copies instead of the previous three—were executed at the agencies and the necessary bond or cash deposit provided to secure the provisions. The agent, the company representative, the commissioner, the interpreter who accompanied the troupe and served as a BIA employee, and, for the first time, the Show Indian all received copies. The failure in August 1906 of the J. T. McCaddon Company just outside Paris highlighted the effectiveness of the policy. Although Buffalo Bill and his entourage, touring the continent that summer, had to take up a collection to send the stranded entertainers home, the Bureau submitted the matter to the Justice Department to force the American Bonding Company of Baltimore to pay the Indians' claims. As a result, the Indians received their unpaid salaries.[7] The failure of the McCaddon show also brought about greater precautions in allowing Indians to travel outside the United States. For all the precautions, however, shows that took Indians abroad failed at a rate greater than some of the more spectacular incidents from Thomas Jefferson Morgan's regime at the Bureau.

Earl B. Gandy, manager of "The Red Man's Syndicate," approached the Indian Bureau about hiring Oglalas from Pine Ridge and Navajos out of Fort Defiance, Arizona Territory, to appear with the Exhibition Company, Ltd., at Earl's Court, London. Leupp sought testimonials from Americans in England. Ambassador Whitelaw Reid answered that the syndicate promoters always fulfilled their engagements in "a thoroughly satisfactory manner."[8] On the other hand, Robert J. Wynne, the consul general, informed the commissioner that the proprietors were British professional showmen (actually Gandy was American) without the slightest interest in the United States "except to use our flag and people for catch-pennies." For shows such as Buffalo Bill's or Barnum and Bailey's, "where the managers are personally known to us, and where the Indians and their habits are understood," Wynne could cite not a single objection; but "if you will remember that Earls Court is but another Coney Island (inland), where liquors of all kinds are sold in various parts of the grounds, you will see the reason why I write to you instantly and frankly."[9] Leupp decided to increase the requirements placed on the show.

A surety bond would not do. Leupp required Earl Gandy to leave with the agents a cash deposit equal to the full salary of each contract, including all transportation expenses. Because Indians would be taken out of the country, the persons with whom they contracted would therefore "not be within reach of our courts and have no property which the courts can seize."[10] Gandy, on behalf of the exposition company, accepted the provisions. Due to the expense involved, however, he opted to hire only Sioux. Commissioner Leupp sent two letters to Pine Ridge, informing Agent John Brennan of the arrangement. The first, granting formal permission, spelled out the provisions including the cash deposit. Conditions at Earl's Court were such that the Indians would encounter more than a "minimum of temptation." Leupp therefore admonished the agent to take special care in selecting the Indians and their chaperon.[11]

In the second letter to Brennan, marked "personal," the commissioner wrote more candidly. He explained that he had made the conditions "as severe as possible so as to protect the Indians." Because Gandy had agreed to all of the provisions, Leupp felt honor bound to extend formal Bureau permission. Yet he also pointed out that "under the law we cannot prevent any Indian from leaving the reservation if he wishes to go." In matters of "show business," the most the department could do would be to withhold its permission from organizations that appeared less than reputable. "I get a great deal of attack, first and last, from would-be philanthropists who do not know what the law is, and who keep finding fault with me" over Indians joining Wild West shows.[12]

His unofficial position had always been that show business, properly conducted, was just as respectable as any other business. Were he to express such sentiments openly, however, his critics would become apoplectic and every "low-lived show in the country" would lure Indians to their doom. He had to "keep up the fiction outwardly of having control" of the matter, even at the risk of attracting criticism from his erstwhile friends in reformist circles, or risk greater harm to the nation's wards.[13]

Criticism from the IRA doubtless inspired his defensiveness. His former employers condemned his peremptoriness in dealing with Indians and his proposed legislation to force fee simple titles on allottees who refused to send their children to school. Exhausted by his many battles, Leupp resigned in mid-June 1909 in favor of Robert G. Valentine, former confidential clerk and, since the previous year, assistant commissioner of Indian affairs.[14]

In 1910, Leupp published what Francis Paul Prucha has called his long apologia, *The Indian and His Problem*.[15] He reminded his readers that no matter what the Bureau did, Indians were free to seek employment in Wild West shows. The disreputable shows, even if banned from the reservation, could if they chose "gather bunches of Indians" by nefarious means. "So the Department has been faced with the alternative of sitting still and letting the low class of showmen outstrip their respectable rivals," he wrote, "or minimizing the possible dangers in these transactions by the exercise of a little paternalism." Although not the most "exalting" vocation, show business nevertheless did give its votaries a chance to see something of the country and the world. When they returned home, they did so with money in their pocket. The provision of the "hold back," first adopted by Buffalo Bill in the 1885 tour, became part of the contract for all shows during Leupp's tenure, wherein the Show Indians received upwards of a third of their wages once they returned home. They thus learned, according to the commissioner, the "practical wisdom of saving a few dollars."

He dismissed the complaint that Wild West shows degraded Indians. Critics were an odd lot. They found fault with Indians who, having taken "a few steps up the path of civilization," nevertheless donned their "fanciful toggery once in a while" to earn some money. Those same critics raised not a whimper of protest against plays like "Samson" or "Macbeth," or any others which depicted the "life and manners of our own race when it was still in a semi-barbarous state."[16] Leupp had known a good many Show Indians. None ever failed to appreciate the difference between the old and the new, the real and the artificial, "in spite of the fact that twice a day he puts on buckskin leggings, sticks feathers in his hair, and gallops his pony around an ellipse of tanbark."[17]

All went well that first year for Earl Gandy and "The Red Man's Syndicate." Gandy paid the Indian performers a dollar a week more than the competition. As he reminded Brennan at Pine Ridge, "I, too, am an American, and all I want in this world is a fair chance, and I think by leaving this large cash deposit with you, that I am certainly proving that I mean the right and honest thing in every respect."[18] He was as good as his word. When some of the Oglalas wanted to travel about the streets of London unescorted, Gandy insisted that none could leave Empress Hall, the headquarters for the Wild West show, without permission. This they had to obtain from Red Shirt, back in England for the first time in many years, Frank Goings, the government chaperon of the troupe, or Gandy himself.[19]

Gandy exceeded the requirements of his contract. When Red Shirt and other prominent members of the party decided that Charley Yellow Wolf and Alfred Running Bear had to be sent home because of chronic drunkenness and insulting behavior, Gandy booked their passage on the White Star liner *Oceanic*. He arranged by cable with people from Cooks Tours in New York to meet the ship and escort the returned showmen to the train for Rushville. He also put American dollars and English pounds in their pockets for incidental expenses along the way.[20] Frank Goings, an Oglala, wrote to Agent Brennan weekly. Late in the summer, he explained that, except for the incessant rain, the "Indians [are] all well and fat as Pigs as they get all they can eat and more too." A woman employed at Empress Hall had "taken to" Thomas Brown Eyes, a Carlisle alumnus whose language skills later won him government employment as an interpreter. Every morning, Goings found her teaching Brown Eyes how to type on the No. 5 Oliver Standard Visible Writer. Goings reported that he had tried his fingers on the keys, but unfortunately he would "never be able to run it." Brown Eyes typed the letter.[21]

The show finished its run at Earl's Court on October 2, and on the morning of October 6 the Show Indians sailed aboard the *Majestic* of the White Star Line. Gandy's brother, Franklin, took them all the way to Pine Ridge. The adults in the party brought back at least two trunks, each full of clothes purchased in London. Red Shirt, Little Wolf, and Spotted Weasel each had five trunks.[22] John Brennan informed Commissioner Valentine that the thirty-seven Show Indians were "all well, look prosperous, and have no complaints to make about their treatment."[23] As a result, Gandy again received permission to employ Indians for the "Red Man's Syndicate," renamed the American Wild West Show Company, to perform at the international exhibition in Brussels, Belgium. Gandy left a bank draft of five thousand dollars with Agent Brennan as security.[24] As it turned out, Brennan would need all of it to settle the claims against the company.

The American Wild West Company was unable to repeat the success of Earl's Court.

Crowds proved disappointing almost from the opening of the exposition in May 1910. The company never met its expenses. By the first week of June, Gandy sent eight of the forty Show Indians home. He contemplated sending others. Business "here is terrible," he advised the commissioner, "not only for the Wild West Show but every attraction in the Brussels Exhibition." Gandy received a regular salary as manager. He pledged to use his own money, if necessary, to get the Indians home.[25] Frank Goings advised Agent Brennan to cash the bank drafts immediately and hold the money as "silver or Gold or Bills as they may send a cablegram to head it off." The company had already cut the salaries of its other employees and was pressuring Goings to circulate an agreement to be signed by the Indians to relinquish a third of their weekly salaries. Goings disapproved. The petition "dont suit me," he wrote the agent, "and I cant see my way clear. If I did get the Indians to sign it they would never forget me or you would not forgive me either."[26]

The Indians hired themselves a Belgian lawyer for twenty-five francs (about five dollars) and brought suit against the Continental Amusement Co., Ltd., for two-weeks back salary and damages of ten thousand dollars. If they needed to, they were willing to abandon the Brussels exposition, "get out of here," as Goings put it, "on cover of darkness." Although Earle Gandy supported the suit "in silents," as Goings explained to Brennan, his brother Frank believed that it was only a ruse to hasten their departure for London, perhaps to salvage the remainder of the season. Some of the cowboys and cowgirls had gone to see the American consul, but he had offered no satisfaction. He informed them that he had no money to send them home unless they were "sailors, or seamen, or Indians." So "we are safe if this be true," Goings continued. The other actors, however, were a little worried. "These cow-boys and Girls," Goings observed,

> are fighters from Fightersville and they beat up a East Indian nigger from which the man died. than a few nights latter one of the cow-Girl named Marry Ann Malone knock down two German gentlement with a right-swing on one and a short jab to the point on the jaw on the other and put them down for the count. They try touching her and kiss her and it was to their sorrows. A few nights ago they knock out a Turk peddler Two of theses cowboys done this. Indians behaving well and mind their own business. Cowboys are out with a chip on there shoulder both night and day.[27]

But nothing came of the suit because Gandy and the owners "skipped" to London and left Goings "keeping the tram cars pretty hot" between the exposition grounds and the consul general's office.[28]

June turned into July with the Indians still stuck in Belgium. As Goings told his former employer hiding in London, "if I ever get back to America, you never see me here no more in this country."[29] He explained to Commissioner Valentine:

> We cannot depend on none of the officials of the Wild West Show company or Des Plaine Attractions Company. . . . Their storys dont meet together very well one official tells me some thing than the other says different from the other party, so I got so I dont pay no attention to any one only figuring on getting the Indians home.[30]

Accordingly, Goings, with money forwarded from Agent Brennan, booked passage on the White Star liner *Oceanic* because it had brought them safely to Europe.[31] At New York, they transferred to a through car on the Erie Railroad, which changed again to the Chicago and Northwestern Railway.[32]

Gandy wrote to Brennan requesting the remainder of his cash deposit. Hoping that the agent would take his word "as a white man," he reminded Brennan that the Show Indians under Frank Goings's care had "taken the most expensive road and boat that there was from Brussels to New York. This was also very much against my wishes"; but it pleased the Indians immensely.[33] They arrived back at the reservation tired, poorer, hungry, but not necessarily wiser for the experience.[34] Their misadventures had not dampened their enthusiasm for working in the shows. Most went out again. Even Frank Goings, contrary to his Brussels oath, joined a European show the very next spring. This time, however, he truly should have stayed home.

In April, Goings and forty-seven Oglalas from Pine Ridge signed contracts to perform for fifteen weeks in Paris at the Jardine Acclimation.[35] The show belonged to Fernand Akoun, a twenty-five-year-old Algerian who had begun his career in show business with his brother. For a while, the brothers had built and operated mechanical amusements. Only recently had they branched into performance. Their recent efforts won the endorsement of the office of the mayor. Akoun's exhibition at the zoological gardens was, according to one report, "appreciated by the inhabitants of Neuilly, and for that matter all of Paris. Not only is it instructive—it is appreciated by the poor."[36] Apparently paying customers found it neither instructive nor entertaining. In September, Akoun, out of money, closed the show and demanded that the U.S. consul general at Paris send the Show Indians home. He referred the diplomat to the five thousand dollars he had deposited with the Indian Bureau.[37] It was not until March, however, long after the Akoun troupe had returned to Pine Ridge, that Agent Brennan was able to get some of the money released by the Bureau to pay off the show's debts to the Indians and the agency trader.[38]

Such developments annoyed Commissioner Valentine. Twice in two years, the Bureau had had to involve itself in the tangle of Indians stranded in foreign countries. Although events underscored the wisdom of Leupp's policy of requiring the shows to deposit cash to guarantee their contracts, the collapse of Earle Gandy and Fernand Akoun reflected badly on the Bureau. Valentine had continued Leupp's lenient policy toward the employment of Show Indians. As he wrote on any number of occasions when impresarios or their well-placed friends asked permission to employ reservation Indians, "as long as there is no expense to the government, the government has no objections."[39]

In a commissionership that had stressed efficiency and honesty as its goals, efficiency had died amid many controversies that engulfed the Bureau in 1912. Exhausted and dispirited, Valentine resigned on September 10 before revising a policy for the employment of Indians abroad.[40]

When Frank Goings joined Fernand Akoun for the 1911 season, his friend Thomas Brown Eyes instead decided to see Australia. He contracted with a John P. Tiffen to perform for fifteen weeks in Sydney. Brown Eyes was the only Indian in the show. Tiffen paid him a premium salary of five dollars a week.[41] The Oglala showman and Carlisle alumnus returned to Pine Ridge in the fall. The following year, when another Australia-bound show received permission to employ Indians (within a month of Valentine's resignation), Thomas Brown Eyes became the obvious choice of Agent Brennan for the position of interpreter and government representative.[42]

For the eight Indians who joined the Bud Atkinson show, it seemed to be the perfect job. Not only would they get to travel to an even more exotic place than before, but also they would receive premium wages. Bud Atkinson paid his Indians, men and women alike, eight dollars a week.[43]

After wandering around San Francisco for five days, the party sailed for Australia on November 19, 1912. Just after Christmas, Brown Eyes reported that they had a "splendid voyage coming over and all [are] well at the present date. And this show is first-class and we are treated well which I hope it will continue." The party found the countryside beautiful.[44] M. C. Smith, the show manager, wrote to Brennan early in the New

Year that the show was "making a big hit" in Sydney. "All the boys are doing well," he explained, "and are satisfied except Henry [Janis] and he is a bad egg." Janis had been drunk once and chafed under a reprimand from both Smith and Brown Eyes. He ran away for a day or two, but then came back. Smith did not think that anything serious would result from the scolding. "It is very warm here," he concluded, "and the natives do not like *Yanks* very much which makes it still hotter."[45] He was right about the weather and social climate, but wrong about Janis.

Janis ran away once the show reached Wellington, New South Wales, on January 30. "I dont think they can find him this time," Brown Eyes confided to Brennan, "but I think he'll stop in Sydney." Smith blamed the interpreter for Janis's defection. "On account of him," Brown Eyes continued, "I had little trouble with M. R. Smith and he discharged me, but I dont have enough money to go to Sydney so I am staying with the show yet." Brown Eyes put down his pen as government employee and put on Henry Janis's warrior costume. He made less money; but, as he and Janis knew, Australia was no place to be without food, friends, or a way home.[46] Within a short time, all the Indians shared their compatriot's predicament.

Janis wrote to his agent to explain his troubles. He had left the circus for the second time. The first time was because he "was not payd for some days now and still not payd yet. Second was not treated properly . . . off corse I have had my wages deduce on account of getting drunk but I have no kick against that but as for the rest treatment I will not stand for any longer." Janis went to the American consul, told him of his plight, but he "would take no heed of it." As one of the provisions of the Atkinson contract, Brennan held return tickets from the steamship company for each of the Show Indians. Janis asked the agent to forward one to his Sydney address, a rooming house.[47]

In Melbourne the crowds disappeared. "I am sorry to say that events have taken a decided turn," M. R. Smith informed Brennan, "and I think we are ready to return." The manager, however, did not stay around to see the Indians safely aboard a steamer bound for California. He left them in the care of the American consul at Sydney, who arranged for their food and lodging. With just "enough money to bring myself and wife back to Frisco," Smith caught the first eastbound steamer.[48] The consul wired Brennan to release the money for the relief and return of the destitute Americans.[49] It was not until June that the Indians reached San Francisco. Thomas Brown Eyes had numerous misadventures to report since taking ship.

Henry Janis, while still in Australia, had been arrested three times for public drunkenness. Each time, Brown Eyes had to bail him out with what money he could scrape together by working day jobs around the town. The Union Steamship Company received payment in Australia for the transportation and care of the Indians all the way to Rushville, Nebraska. The group sailed from Sydney on April 19. When they docked at Wellington, New Zealand, Henry Janis left the ship. He got drunk and ended up in jail. Brown Eyes paid five dollars from his own money—about all he had left— to get Janis released just before the ship sailed.[50] In San Francisco, the local office of the company had not been advised as to the arrangements made in Australia. Officials refused to provide rail transportation to South Dakota and the agreed-upon fifteen dollars of "meal money" for each of the Indians. As a result, the four found themselves stranded again until, as Brennan explained to the commissioner, the next steamer arrived from Australia and its captain confirmed the arrangements.[51] The Indians remained in San Francisco from May 15 until June 2. Brown Eyes kept close watch on Henry Janis. On the train trip home, however, Janis fell in with a group of cowboys, got drunk, and left the cars in Cheyenne, Wyoming. Brown Eyes caught up with him and put him to bed. The next morning, the interpreter, perhaps looking for a job, looked up the Irwin Brothers, circus veterans and currently the owners of Irwin Brothers Cheyenne Frontier Days Wild West. When he returned to the rooming house, Janis had gone. Thoroughly frustrated, Brown Eyes left a ticket at the depot and boarded the next eastbound train.[52]

Brennan wanted to charge the steamship company for the Indians' bills for food and lodging in San Francisco. It had been the company's mistake, after all, and not that of either the Indians or the Bureau. The new commissioner, Cato Sells, who assumed his office on June 2, wanted to settle the matter without more fuss. Brennan accordingly paid the proprietor of the rooming house out of money from the Atkinson deposit; but he did not like it.[53] The matter was closed.

Within his first seven months as commissioner, Sells resigned himself to the fact that Indians would appear in Wild West shows. He had no power to stop the practice. Every commissioner—even William Jones, who chose to ignore the matter—had come to the same conclusion. He could, however, encourage displays that portrayed Indians as competent farmers and workers. In this way, Indians would not display themselves, only the products of their fields and workshops.

This type of display had already been tried at world's fairs and international expositions in New Orleans, Nashville, Atlanta, Jamestown, Portland, and Seattle. The work of Indian schoolchildren became the focus of the Bureau's displays. There were a number of reasons to recommend this type of exhibit over the more elaborate Indian congresses, ethnological villages, or model Indian schools. Foremost, it saved money. At Seattle's Alaska-Yukon-Pacific Exposition, the Bureau spent nineteen hundred dollars on the entire display, including three hundred dollars set aside for Indians to attend the exhibit to explain its significance.[54] Compared to the more than sixty-five thousand dollars spent at St. Louis, one can see how commissioners would enthusiastically endorse the smaller expenditure. Through a series of photographs, the present could be highlighted along with the past, thereby suggesting the distance traveled by the schoolchildren on the road to civilization.

When it came time to plan for the Panama–Pacific Exposition, Commissioner Sells found it just a small step to expand the theme of basic literacy to a more comprehensive display that included "the nature and scope of instruction given in Indian schools and homes. It should be chiefly a display of the results of home economy, agricultural, industrial, and academic instruction." Sells also desired that the work of agricultural fairs be featured.[55] These had their origins during Leupp's years as commissioner.

For some time, Bureau permission had been solicited by the boards of managers of state, county, and town fairs, to feature Indians as part of their regular attractions. The Colorado State Fair and Exposition in Pueblo, for example, had hoped to feature an Indian village in 1905. The Indians would appear for one week in Pueblo, and then move on to the Western Slope Fair at Montrose for another week. Including travel to and from the reservation, the Indians would be gone in the fall for up to four weeks. Commissioner Leupp, in this instance, refused permission. The president of the fair association probably made a mistake in suggesting that "we expect many tourists from the East and desire to give them as much 'wild west' as possible."[56] Yet the next year, the acting commissioner granted permission to the Elks Club of Denver to stage a Wild West show and parade, including Indian dances, at its annual reunion of July 16–19, 1906. It appears that much depended on the recommendation of the Indian agents closest to the venture. In the case of the Pueblo fair, Superintendent Burton B. Custer at the Southern Ute agency objected because it would disrupt the Indians' farmwork. Only recently, he explained, and for the first time the Southern Utes had failed to hold their annual Bear Dance. They had been too busy tending their fields. How then could the agent sanction such a distraction from worthier pursuits?[57] No plausible explanation has been found to explain Custer's sanction of the Wild West show sponsored by the Elks Club of Denver, which received Bureau approval.[58] Perhaps he was a brother Elk.

Acting Commissioner Larrabee learned from Denver members of the National Indian Association that the Utes attending the Elks reunion planned to perform a Bear Dance. He reminded Custer by telegram that the department had granted authority "upon condition that Indians not engage in hurtful or degrading practices or customs."[59] To the Utes, the bear epitomized the bravest of all animals except the mountain lion. It possessed wonderful magical powers. They felt a kinship with the bear. The original ceremony occurred usually in March, where symbolically the singing of the people aroused the bear from its hibernation. Proffering food for the ravenous bear in the ceremony helped ensure that it would help its friends, the Utes.[60] Larrabee had no such understanding of the ceremony. He instead learned that "the Indians dance for several days until exhausted; that the last night of the dance the men and women sleep together; and the request is made that this most pernicious old-time practice be forbidden."[61] The Bureau would tolerate no improper dancing; and the best way to accomplish that was to ban all dancing.

For Larrabee, Leupp, and others, the question became how best to encourage Indians to remain close to home, yet receive the benefits associated with the friendly competition of state and county agricultural fairs. The reservation fair became the answer. Indian fairs at the Southern Ute agency, for example, started in 1907 and then lapsed in 1912; but it resumed a few years later. Locally financed, the Ute fair was started by Agent Custer to promote Euroamerican agriculture within the tribe.[62] He took as his model the Crow fair that began in 1905.

The Crow fair originated in the ideas of Superintendent Samuel G. Reynolds, who tapped into a far older tradition of trade and communal ceremony. As Reynolds explained to a 1909 convention of Indian superintendents, "a very few years ago practically all the Crows were living in communities and drawing full rations, which entailed large expenditures each year." As with many Euroamerican middle-class reformers, time and its proper use obsessed Reynolds. The Crows, the superintendent believed, squandered theirs at dancing, horse racing, gambling, and searching for rations. "It was also their habit to go to adjoining towns whenever there happened to be a fair, circus, Fourth of July celebration, or other public gathering," Reynolds noted. These trips took them away from their homes for weeks at a time. The lands of the Crow reservation had been allotted. The "fair scheme was originated," the agent explained, "as a means of interesting them in the work of home building and earning their living from the soil, as well as to give them opportunity to enjoy themselves at gatherings other than those of the detrimental sort." As far as he was concerned, the great benefit of the fair "has been in the doing away with ration issues. Not an Indian has drawn rations at Crow in four years."[63]

Reynolds divided the reservation into six farm districts to accommodate his plan. District farmers, all government employees, visited their assigned Indians, explaining the superintendent's scheme and enlisting the support of each allottee. Farmers impressed upon the Indians the idea that they should compete against one another. "This friendly rivalry," Reynolds boasted, "was, and is to-day, kept constantly before them."[64]

Crows did not respond immediately to the blandishments of the district farmers, and as a result there were no industrial exhibits that first year. Reynolds blamed it on incomplete understanding because in succeeding years the exhibits had "been astonishing in number and quality." Since the first fair, the superintendent blanketed the reservation with premium lists, showing the cash prizes to be paid for the best exhibits. In 1909, for example, the Crow Fair paid 574 dollars in premiums. "The most noticeable benefit," Reynolds exulted, "is the growing interest among the Indians in their individual homes and farm work."[65]

Reynolds's idea had been to hold a fair "by and for the Crow Indians." To that end, he allowed as many Indians as possible to assist in the management. Distribution of the many offices among the Crows encouraged them to their best efforts, he believed, and thus increased their experience in business practices. Indians sold tickets, collected license fees for concession privileges, paid the bills, awarded the premiums, tended the grounds and buildings, arranged the exhibits, and managed the refreshment stands and lunch counters. At the end of the fair each year, the Crows held a convention and elected a president, secretary, and treasurer of the fair association for the following year. Next, Indians of each farm district likewise met and elected a vice president, two judges, five committeemen, five policemen, two gatekeepers, two starters, two criers, a secretary, a treasurer, and a ticket seller. When the fair took place the following summer, the fair association provided large gaily colored ribbon badges for the officers. Participants also received ribbon badges printed with the word *Exhibitor.* Each person having an exhibit thus wore his own advertisement which, according to Reynolds, "rendered [the person] somewhat distinguished."[66]

Indians paid a twenty-five-cent admission, whereas non-Indians paid double. Everyone paid twenty-five cents to enter the grandstands. The Crow fair committee sold concession privileges to Indians only. They assessed fees from ten dollars to twenty-five dollars depending on the location. The committee also printed and distributed daily programs. A band of Indian boys, trained in the schools, furnished the music. The boys played on instruments purchased with profits from previous fairs.[67]

The fair grounds consisted of forty acres of reserved land at the agency, located about one mile from the Little Bighorn battlefield. At the first fair, the Crows used a large tent as a meeting place. Each year, the fair profits allowed for improvements. By the fifth year the grounds included an agricultural hall one hundred by thirty feet for farming and industrial exhibits; a barn one hundred feet long for livestock and poultry; a barn two hundred feet long for horses; a grandstand seating eight hundred people; and a good half-mile track, well fenced, laid out for horse racing.[68]

Reynolds found all of this—the management, the premiums, the participants, the grounds—to be of great benefit to the Crows:

As I have said, since the inauguration of the fair no rations have been issued—not a single ration in four years. And I find that the Crows are staying at home; that there is less wandering. Formerly many of them could be kept track of only with the greatest difficulty; but now most of them are satisfied to stop in one place and work. I give the fair credit for a good deal of this.[69]

The Indian Office gave its unqualified endorsement. It pointed to the inauguration of the Navajo fair held at San Juan School, Shiprock, New Mexico Territory, as further evidence of the applicability of the Crow experiment.

The Navajo fair took place over two days, October 20 and 21, 1909. It had not been decided definitely to have the fair in the first place until about two weeks before the opening. There had been little opportunity to advertise and little time for the Navajos to prepare exhibits. Nevertheless, 290 general exhibits were listed, containing from five to sixty articles each. Superintendent Shelton counted 185 exhibits of corn, 73 of wheat, 47 of oats, and so on through a long list of specials. Also featured were Navajo blankets and silver work, which "lent to this fair color and a unique art tone." Instead of cash premiums, the winners received agricultural implements. *Attsose Bitcilly*, whose silver-inlaid bracelets took first prize, received a cultivator; *Clahetsoue*, who drew a first place in corn displays, won a corn planter; and first and second premiums for wheat received grain cradles. Superintendent Shelton also awarded prizes for the "prettiest baby" and the "cleanest Navaho baby." Sports and recreation included horse races, foot races (the longest, five and one-half miles), various games, and dances in the evening. To illustrate the spirit with which the Navajos embraced their first government-sponsored fair, the superintendent noted that exhibitors came by wagon and horseback from as far away as seventy miles.[70]

Commissioner Valentine pronounced the Indian-fair movement "a good thing for the individual allottee and for the service." He, like many at the Bureau, had absorbed the rampant stereotypes that pronounced Indians as gregarious people who liked to visit, to gather in bands, to dance, and to revive old customs, "all of which invite to a roaming life away from allotments and authority." Unlike many of his predecessors, however, Valentine saw some value in Indian dances. The "dance is probably most popular," he observed, "because it brings the Indians together." By combining Indian amusements and ceremonies with an "educational exhibit," such as a tribal fair, "some practical benefit must result."[71]

Valentine believed that for too long the Indians had "spent" themselves in excitement, with little to show for their purchase. Yet their keenness for sport could lead easily to healthy competition. The Crow fair harnessed the competitive spirit, giving Indians an incentive to work their farms as well as race their horses. It established a place for a "legitimate gathering," provided sport "of the cleanest kind," and maintained the spirit of friendly rivalry throughout the succeeding year. In time, the indolent might learn from the example set by their friends and neighbors who were making great strides "toward a higher state of civilization." At the last Crow fair, even sixty-eight-year-old Chief Plenty Coups had been active in the exhibit. He had not ceased warfare against his enemies until the age of forty. "It may seem unromantic," the commissioner declared, "that this veteran of the warpath should show several varieties of potatoes, beets, mangels, corn, sugar beets, watermelons, muskmelons, tomatoes, [and] cucumbers of his own raising, instead of scalps." Valentine proclaimed the change for the better, ascribing much of the credit to the fair which both encouraged and rewarded good behavior.[72]

These Show-Indian farmers, unlike their Show-Indian brothers and sisters of the arena, remained under close governmental observation. They did not have the same opportunities—the pernicious freedom—that allowed them to use their time unwisely. Their rewards came as ribbons, implements, cash, and the realization that their reach perhaps exceeded their grasp. Fair Indians, like school Indians, were another version of the

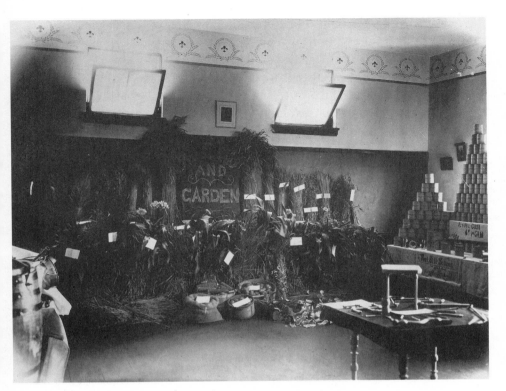

45 : *Agricultural exhibit from the Fort Sill School, Indian Territory, Kiowa-Comanche Fair, celebrating the harvest from "field and garden." Indian agricultural fairs, which came into vogue during Thomas Morgan's tenure as commissioner, offered to the public images of success in the government's programs of forced assimilation. The larger Indian fairs that began during Robert Valentine's service as commissioner countered the popular public images of Indians as portrayed in Wild West shows. At the Kiowa-Comanche fair, the students served chilled buttermilk to the visitors. (National Archives)*

government's ideal, a corrective to the "promiscuous employment" in Wild West shows.

The Show Indians had only their pay, their purchased clothing and finery, and their experiences to account for their labor in the arena. Their efforts would never win a premium for displaying skills on horseback, in battle, or in the dance. Chief Plenty Coups had stopped counting and instead planted beans, melons, and corn. His people, nevertheless, remembered him for who he was and not for what he grew. Red Shirt of the Lakota did not plant his allotment with tomatoes, cucumbers, and mangels; instead, he continued to travel the show circuit. His people likewise remembered his generosity when he returned home each fall, and not what he did for pay in the cities of the *Wasichus*.

Even the best-planned Indian fair, however, offered occasion for backsliding. As Commissioner Valentine learned, a few non-Indian missionaries and reformers were certain to find fault with features of the Indian fairs—"the dances, old camp life, and the congregation of large numbers of white visitors, who only wish to view the Indian at his romantic worst, and who constantly encourage dancing." Strict regulations would prevent Indians and non-Indians alike from thinking that "these are the chief features of the fair."[73] The commissioner nevertheless understood that it would be disheartening to ask Indians to support a fair that included only industrial displays. Added to the grave industrial exhibits, which Valentine endorsed along with the social dances, were the comical "fancy prizes." At the third annual Lower Brule fair (1912), for example, managers awarded fancy prizes for the best Indian costume, male and female, the oldest Indian, the fattest Indian, the largest Indian family, the prettiest Indian baby, and the Indian coming the longest distance to the fair.[74] In a sense, these recipients of the fancy prizes were the Show Indians at the fair, in some instances the comic interlude among more sober scenes. Their friends and neighbors who won the cash premiums for their harvest of field and garden represented the true aristocrats. "The transfer of interest," Valentine mused, "must necessarily be accomplished slowly." Indians would become self-supporting once they thoroughly understood and appreciated "improved agriculture and the better modes of life"; and awarding implements instead of money would dramatize the point.[75]

From just two in 1909, Indian fairs flowered like late-blooming perennials. Within five years, Indian fairs were being held between September 1 and December 30 on thirty-eight reservations and as special features at four state fairs. By 1915, fifty-four reservations staged fairs and eleven state fairs included Indian expositions.[76]

Cato Sells continued the practice of Indian fairs. Unlike Leupp and Valentine, he had no experience in Indian affairs. He nevertheless threw himself into his work with all the merciless enthusiasm that only a progressive Democrat from Texas could muster. He steadfastly accepted the canon of national Indian policy of the previous generation that called for the allotment of Indian land and the destruction of tribal governments. His prohibitionist tendencies found release in redoubled efforts to halt illegal liquor traffic. He immediately implemented programs for Indian self-support through stock raising and an agricultural program which, with congressional support, included reimbursable loans for seed, wagons, implements, and blooded stock. During his tenure, the twenty-five-year trust period of the first allottees under the Dawes Act ended. His was to be an administration of Indians emancipated from Indian affairs, with the trust responsibilities of the Bureau reduced accordingly.[77] Indians in Wild West shows did not fit into his idea of self-support. Sells thundered against the shows; but he continued his predecessors' policies all the same. If, as commissioner, he had no power to forbid Indian employment in Wild West shows, he could nevertheless support more deliberately a different ideal of showmanship.

When Sells found out early in his tenure how many Indians were actually away from their reservations or allotments and with the shows, his vexation turned to sterner stuff.[78] Colorado congressman H. H. Seldomridge wrote to the commissioner hoping to grease the skids on behalf of a Colorado Springs fair company looking to obtain the services of some Southern Utes. Sells disapproved. He found it detrimental to both the best interests of the Indians and the service to allow participation in exhibitions that recalled "conditions existing fifty years ago, and giving the public false impressions as to their present status." Instead, exhibitions in which Indians participated should demonstrate "what the government is trying to accomplish for them and give evidence of their progress." Such presentations would encourage Indians who had given "evidence of an effort to adopt civilized Manners and customs." So that none might misinterpret his message, Sells announced that the "Indian Service is endeavoring in every way possible to discourage the promiscuous employment of Indians in wild west Shows and other similar enterprises." There would be no objection, however, if the proposed celebration "be in accordance with the ideas outlined above."[79]

When Representative Carl Hayden of Arizona asked permission for a group of Hopis to accompany Edgar A. Brown of the state corporation commission to a planning session in San Francisco for the Panama–Pacific Exposition, Sells again refused. He mistakenly believed that the Hopis would perform in some sort of show. He explained to Hayden that it was not the Bureau's policy to allow Indian participation in any sort of exhibition "which emphasizes their early habits and customs at the expense of our efforts to encourage progress looking towards the Indian putting behind him the things of the past and taking on the betterments of the whiteman's civilization." At places in the immediate vicinity of a reservation, however, "we favor industrial exhibitions of Indian accomplishment." Such displays harmonized with the Bureau's intentions.[80] Neither Hay-

den nor Brown pressed the matter. Given the problems at Hopi during the Leupp years, when the government sentenced elders to hard labor for refusing to send their children to the hated government schools, agents and certain Arizona politicians encouraged a greater cosmopolitanism among the traditional Hopi leadership.[81] Although disappointed in not getting to see the city named for the patron-founder of some of the brown-robed missionaries (a few of whose bodies, legend had it, had been salted around the mesas as warning to other intruders), the Hopis stayed on their reservation safe within the confines of the Four Sacred Mountains. Eventually, however, they got to visit San Francisco.

A little more than a year later, the Babbitt brothers, a renowned mercantile family of Flagstaff, Arizona, who traded with the Indian communities in the vicinity, won permission from the Bureau, under the signature of Assistant Commissioner Edgar B. Meritt, to take a group of Hopis, Apaches, and Navajos to the Panama–Pacific Exposition. The Babbitts, prominent Democrats, probably learned from Representative Hayden how *not* to approach the Indian Bureau. The Babbitts made their request through Walter Runke, superintendent of the Western Navajo School at Tuba City, a reservation settlement about seventy-five miles northeast of Flagstaff. The agent explained that the Indians would be displaying their pottery, blankets, and jewelry—thus exemplifying their "industrial pursuits." Better still, none of the Indians would be dancing for the gathering masses along the "Joy Zone," the midway at the San Francisco fair. On the fact that no dancing would take place, Meritt advised the superintendent that the "government has no objections."[82]

It had been one thing for Sells to forbid a few Hopis or Southern Utes from leaving their reservations to appear in inappropriate fairs or carnivals; it was quite another matter when one of the larger and more powerful organizations—with friends in high places—approached the commissioner about hiring Indians. Early in 1914, the Miller Brothers asked to employ eighty Indians. The commissioner initially balked; but eventually he yielded. Because Indians would leave the reservation with or without his permission, he explained to Agent Brennan, it was better that govern-

---

46 : Red Shirt in later life. He still wears proudly his Grant Peace medal. He also wears badge No. 25 identifying him as a Chief in Cummins's Indian Congress of Forty-eight Tribes. Cummins's Indian Congresses appeared at worlds' fairs and international expositions from the 1890s through the Panama–Pacific Exposition in San Francisco in 1915. (Buffalo Bill Historical Center, Cody, Wyoming)

87

17682—By the Zuni Pueblo in the "Painted Desert," Panama-California Exposition, San Diego, Calif., U.S.A.

47 : A black-and-white stereoscopic print of a group of unidentified Zunis at the Panama-California Exposition, San Diego, 1915–16, which ran concurrently with San Francisco's Panama–Pacific Exposition. The group inhabited "Zuni Pueblo," as part of the larger "Painted Desert" exhibit along the Isthmus—the exposition's midway—financed by the Atchison, Topeka and Santa Fe Railroad. In keeping with the ethnological theme of the San Diego exposition, the several pueblos and villages of the Painted Desert, were to give visitors "a little sermon" about progress. With the stereo cards, visitors could recall the lessons, and non-visitors could learn them perhaps for the first time. The text on the back of the card explains that one feature of the San Diego exposition was the "habitat groups" of Southwestern Indians, "Living Pueblo Indians in a reproduction (as far as conditions permitted) of their natural surroundings." The text includes references to the theme of the vanishing American. "The primitive life of the Pueblos is fast disappearing, and to see it in its inherited simplicity we must go to the villages farthest from the railroad." But even the Zuni were changing. They had not escaped progress. Tourist dollars supposedly had tempted the Zunis to sacrifice their "native good taste on the altar of popular demand." Government policy of establishing training schools "with conscientious but uncomprehending teachers has grafted eastern ideals on [their] ancestral ways, with resulting disaster to both." Such group displays as at San Diego were valuable reminders of a "fast-vanishing phase of American life." (Buffalo Bill Historical Center, Cody, Wyoming)

48: A Colonial Pageant at Seger School, Colony, Oklahoma, June 19, 1913. In these years the federal government tried to refine images of American Indians through its schools, at expositions, and Indian fairs. Cheyenne and Arapaho students performed the pageant, inspired by Dora Porterfield, one of the female teachers at the school. The photograph's caption reads: "The Indians plan an attack on the Puritans," wherein Wampanoags, showing the influence of Wild West shows by sporting traditional plains attire, prepare to attack a settler's cabin while other students, dressed as dotty Puritans, wait in ambush. Such a pageant, ubiquitous in other American grammar schools at festive or patriotic times of the year, takes on added irony when compared to Wild West shows. The "attack on the settler's cabin," a set piece in Buffalo Bill's Wild West, was often criticized as celebrating Indians' martial spirit. At the Seger pageant, the Indians will likewise be bested by their Euroamerican opponents; but this time, the Indians—presumably well on their way at being transformed into cultural Euroamericans—play both the victors and the vanquished. (National Archives)

ment maintain some kind of control. He found eighty Indians "too large a number"; but if their home conditions made it necessary for them to seek outside employment "in the absence of other means of obtaining a livelihood," he would not stand foolishly on principle. Still, he encouraged Brennan to do all in his power to reduce the number of Indians leaving their reservation and homesteads.[83]

Sells refined the system of Indian fairs. These reflected his sober progressivism. He eliminated dancing, horse racing, and the occasional sham battle, and ordered that the larger reservations hold their fairs during the same week. This would end the practice, the commissioner insisted, of Indians going from one fair to another to the great neglect and injury of their stock and standing crops.[84] Indians would be protected from "the degrading or demoralizing influences" of alcohol and gambling. Every effort would be made to direct their attention to the agricultural and industrial exhibits. Indians could have fun, but not at the expense of their regular "amusement features" typically associated with fairs.[85]

How did the agencies respond to the commissioner's directives? The superintendent of Standing Rock reservation, for example, proudly reported that, from the viewpoint of "the more progressive Indians," the fair was all that could be desired. A few malcontents expressed their disappointment at not being allowed to dance; but most Hunkpapas fulfilled the commissioner's vision of Indians having fun. Indians had made no attempt to dance, noted Superintendent Kneale, "and the sound of the 'tom-tom' was not heard throughout the fair."[86]

Commissioner Sells ordered that fairs be financed locally from receipts at the gates and grandstands, the sale of concessions and privileges, and cash bonuses given to the fairs by local non-Indian communities. He also encouraged participation in county fairs. They offered certain advantages over purely Indian fairs, which unfortunately emphasized Indians' separate identity "from a racial standpoint—rather than their community of interest with the whites as does the country fair."[87]

Sells adjusted his policy to fit the occasion; but there was a consistent element, as it turned out. Claude Covey, the new superintendent at Standing Rock Indian School, on one occasion reported that little in the fair program beyond the "industrial and agricultural exhibits" interested the older Indians. Even the prominent "amusements," consisting mostly of "modern games and sports, moving pictures, [and] merry-go-rounds," offered insufficient allure. The old people insisted that they ought to be allowed to dance. The superintendent assured the commissioner that, were permission granted, such dances would be held in the evenings between the hours of eight and eleven; there would be neither advertising nor the "featuring" of dances as attractions at the fair; and schoolchildren and "educated young Indians" would be barred from participation.[88] Sells relented. Indians would be allowed to participate in "harmless dances" as long as the superintendent enforced the restrictions.[89]

Sells also allowed Show Indians to participate in a historical reenact-

49 : "The Puritans are Saved!" Goodmen and women from the Bay Colony behold the grim harvest. One of the girls at right clasps her hands as if in prayer of thanksgiving. In the extreme right of the picture, one of the "hostile" Indians, as if waiting in ambush, is accidently caught in the camera's lens. The proper image of American legend, whether in the Wild West show arena or in school pageants for students everywhere to celebrate, was the triumph of light-skinned people over people of color who inhabited a savage wilderness. Buffalo Bill's most criticized reenactment, "First Scalp for Custer," wherein he mimics his alleged scalping of the Cheyenne Yellow Hand (or Yellow Hair) at the Battle of War Bonnet Creek, is no more horrific or indeed lamentable than the pantomime slaughter staged by the schoolmistress at Seger Indian School. (National Archives)

ment commemorating the centennial of Fort Wayne, Indiana. For four nights, the Fort Wayne centennial featured a tableau depicting life before the era of industrial progress. The commissioner consented because the Indian part in the pageant was largely passive. There would be no battles, war whoops, or raised tomahawks—in fact, the Indians would appear stationary.[90] In contrast, when Harry Cochrane, production manager at Madison Square Garden, approached the Indian Bureau with plans for a convention to feature "Indian Progress," Sells denied the request. Assistant Commissioner Meritt explained the line of opposition. Cochrane had wanted to feature both Show Indians and those of a "progressive" tem-

50 : *"The Colonial Pageant Parade" at Seger School. Some of the children participated in tableau that supposedly re-created life in colonial Virginia. A few, depicting slaves, appear in black face. The male student just left of center in the procession played a dual role: as colonial judge and as a modern student, who had exchanged his old life for the responsibilities of modern citizenship. (National Archives)*

---

perament. Meritt recited the party line that the Indian Office viewed with disfavor the active participation of Indians in exhibitions of any nature that detracted from their industrial advancement. The Indians who would portray their barbaric ancestors were themselves "unprogressive." They, according to Meritt, "as a general rule, have little attachment for their homes." Yet their roving and dissolute ways had to be discouraged. The "good" Indians required at Madison Square Garden, on the other hand, were to be drawn from "the progressive members of the tribes, who have stock and growing crops and other home interests." Not only would it be injurious to their progressivism to attend such a convention, but the display of their unprogressive kinsmen would undo all the good efforts of the Bureau.[91]

51 : "*The Colonial Pageant: The Virginia Reel.*" *Dora Porterfield, senior teacher at Colony, introduced this feature "new to the Indian Schools of this section." The children, dressed as ladies and gentlemen from the Old Dominion, are waited upon by their servants, in black-face masks. The four are Lucy Arey, Mary Hadley, Mamie Bear Bow, and Nancy Boynton. Re-creating the conqueror's dance was perfectly acceptable. Traditional dances of the Cheyenne and Arapaho, of course, had long been banned. (National Archives)*

Indian fairs continued through the First World War. The Council of National Defense encouraged war exhibits at state fairs. It was a measure to sustain public morale and to subscribe Red Cross and war-bond drives. The National Emergency Food Garden Commission, for example, offered five-dollar premiums and certificates of merit for the best canned vegetables at each of the Indian fairs during the war.[92] The commissioner lauded such worthy examples of progressive-citizen Indians farming their allotments and showcasing their bounty each harvest.[93]

Cato Sells considered the occasional historical reenactment, along with agricultural and industrial fairs, as worthy enterprises. The Indian Office, as it had done with Show-Indian students, came to sanction an authorized, and perhaps sanitized, version of Show Indians. At the fair, they displayed their crops, livestock, needlework, breads, jams, jellies, fattest babies, prettiest babies, and oldest members of the tribe. And having displayed these, Commissioner Sells reasoned, Indians might win the admiration of their fellow citizens, along with the occasional premium, and stimulate a healthy competition among "their own kind." In historical tableaus, as at Fort Wayne, they became mannequins frozen in history. In the Wild West, the Show Indians rode, raced, shouted, and danced. They made the past "come alive." They sent the wrong message to the audiences that the past lived on in the lives of the Indians. In the tableaus, at least, the barbaric past remained lifeless. The future belonged to those Indians who abandoned their past.

11

FILMING THE WILD WEST, 1896-1913

"For history and fact . . . carry often a greater thrill than the wildest dream of the writer of fiction."

Thomas Edison's New Jersey laboratory of magic and invention produced the first motion pictures in 1896.[1] Hailed as an educational device that would enlarge a viewer's world to unimagined vistas, few people at the time could conceive of the potential of motion pictures to tell stories and entertain the masses through suspended disbelief.

Buffalo Bill Cody and his Wild West appeared early as subjects for factual "shorts," as they eventually came to be called. The earliest recorded images of Buffalo Bill and the Wild West date from the second half of the

1890s. Years later, when Cody tried to recoup his fortune following the bankruptcy of the Two Bills show, he turned to motion pictures. He filmed himself, his real and imaginary exploits, and re-created scenes that would have been familiar to audiences schooled in the historical reenactments of Wild West shows. By 1913, however, when he began the Col. W. F. Cody (Buffalo Bill) Historical Pictures Company, the "Western" had already emerged as a staple of popular entertainment. Cody's epic, two-and-one-half-hour film *The Indian Wars* failed to draw crowds. Flickering images of white and gray, light and shadow, starring Buffalo Bill himself, could never duplicate the glamour, perhaps even the authenticity, of the arena. Buffalo Bill the legend, as large as life, became on the screen Buffalo Bill the towering ancient showman too old to play the part.

During film history's first decade, according to Steven Mintz and Randy Roberts, movies represented little more than novelties, often used to signal the end of a show in a vaudeville theater. Unlike anything seen today — except perhaps the ubiquitous music video — they lasted less than ten minutes, and told simple stories, if they were stories at all. Performers rather than actors appeared anonymously. The camera stood far back from the action in the field of view, making it impossible to distinguish the actors' faces. Movie performers received little pay and no credit for their appearance on the screen.[2]

Within ten years of Edison's showing his first film — of surf breaking on a beach, a mock prizefight, and two women dancing — at Koster and Bial's Music Hall in New York (where Macy's Department store now stands in Herald Square), hundreds of small movie theaters opened. Called nickelodeons, in reference to the price of admission, by 1908 they numbered nearly ten thousand across the country. Patrons other than immigrants, the working class, the poor, or the young filled the seats. From the beginning, film impresarios built their theaters in middle-class neighborhoods as well as in working-class ghettos, and in towns as well as cities. Regardless of their location, movies attracted audiences of unprecedented size in the aggregate. Admission prices remained low, seating arrangements unreserved, and schedules convenient. Lack of spoken dialogue did not inhibit immigrants from sharing the experience. Although narrative began to turn films into art, most still emphasized stunts, chases, and actual events. Subjects mattered little. Nickelodeon owners rented or purchased films by the foot. The assembled footage, scene by scene, became a larger and longer show.[3]

Film historians disagree on the sources of inspiration for early films. Some argue that the films, beyond the real-life footage, incorporated almost exclusively working-class settings and expressed the interests of the poor in their struggles with the rich and powerful. Others have claimed that movies drew largely upon popular conventions, stock characters, and routines derived from vaudeville, melodrama, Wild West shows, dime novels, and comic strips. Because thousands of films reached theaters and nickelodeons in these years, and furthermore because relatively few have survived, it is dangerous to generalize, as some film historians have warned, about the nature of movie content.[4] Less difficulty exists, however, when discussing the emergence of "Westerns."

Westerns meant action. Chases, races, Indian attacks upon wagon trains or settlers' cabins, the cavalry's charge against the Indians, stampedes of cattle or bison, and shoot-outs—all the staples of Wild West shows became regular features of the Westerns.[5] Western images behind that action came into being before the advent of moving pictures. The movies drew upon the novels of James Fenimore Cooper, dime novels, and Wild West shows for their themes.[6] Owing to Cooper's novels, Indian heroes antedated the cowboy hero by a few years. And Buffalo Bill Cody proved, as Natasha and Ralph Friar observe, that the West was not the real West without Indians. Moviemakers soon realized this too.[7] As proclaimed countless times in print by Buffalo Bill, Indians were noble, wise, and trustworthy even unto death. The silent, imperturbable Indian, whose face remained impassive despite horror or pain, began as a positive stereotype. That face had been used to sell all manner of products. Eventually, it would also be used to sell movie tickets.[8]

The same Edison Company that, in 1896, had filmed a variety of everyday scenes to be shown to a public awed by technological innovation, just two years later made what some historians regard as the first Western, a vignette entitled *Cripple Creek Bar Room*. Without plot or action, it depicted nevertheless a western barroom haunted by a dandy, miners, cowhands, a woman, and a barrel of whiskey labeled "red eye." Five years later, the company made a major contribution to the development of the Western with the release of *The Great Train Robbery* (1903), directed by Edwin S. Porter in feral New Jersey. In view of all the vignettes that had preceded it, *The Great Train Robbery* was hardly, according to William Everson, the first "Western," let alone the first "story" film. But it was the first Western with a recognizable form: it established the essential pattern of crime, pursuit, showdown, and justice. Within its ten-minute running time, in addition to the train robbery itself, it included fistfights, horseback pursuit, gunplay, and saloon bullies forcing the city dude into a dance by shooting at his feet.[9]

The Great Train Robbery prompted outright imitations. Yet, prior to the arrival of D. W. Griffith and Thomas Ince five years after *The Great Train Robbery*, neither the direction nor the story pretended to be art. Early directors, such as Porter for example, often operated the cameras themselves. Good, clear images for the screen interested them more than plot or story line. Initial scripts, at the Edison Company and elsewhere, were little more than a page or two on which the director had typed a list of scenes or "shots." These scene titles or "shot lists" provided no information to the performers (hardly actors) as to motivation, or the duration of a shot, or even ways to concentrate audience attention on the character or action. Using shot lists, most directors assumed that it would be a simple matter to transfer those images to the screen. Given the simplicity of plots, this may have been understandable early on. Sometimes the screen was so busy with movement, all in medium or long shot, that the audience never knew where or at whom to look. Titles, inserted arbitrarily or infrequently, did little to assist understanding of the flow of action. Whereas this problem plagued early narrative films, it was far more vexing to the Western. By its very nature, the Western involved considerable physical movement. Audience understanding was not automatic. In the early years, however, the technology itself was so entertaining that few audiences registered their complaints by not attending the "flickers."[10] In time, as audiences grew more sophisticated, they would patronize those films that told stories and told them well.

Missing from the early films was a character around which the action could revolve and with whom audiences could identify. In 1908, Gilbert M. Anderson (Max Aronson), a beefy former photographer's model with aspiration to acting and directing, made a short Western entitled *Broncho Billy and the Baby*. Anderson had played several small parts in *The Great Train Robbery* and, in the years since, had turned his hand to other Westerns. None proved successful. In *Broncho Billy*, Anderson played the lead himself. The film became a hit. Its action and unbridled sentiment pleased audiences. The story involved an outlaw, or a "badman," who sacrificed his chance for freedom in order to aid a stricken child. The story became a familiar one as directors continued to reincarnate it as *Three Godfathers*.[11]

Until *Broncho Billy*, Anderson considered himself more as a director and executive than as an actor or a "star." With his partner George Spoor, Anderson created the Essanay Film Company (the *S* for Spoor and the *A* for Anderson), originally incorporated in Chicago. Eventually, the company relocated to San Francisco's East Bay, in the town of Niles. The Westerns, increasingly shot in the West, had their first identifiable hero-star. Others, in large number, followed Anderson's lead.[12] When Buffalo Bill Cody decided to make his own films, he turned to Broncho Billy Anderson's company for assistance.

Two other filmmakers in these early years influenced the art of the Western. Thomas Ince and D. W. Griffith introduced a more self-consciously artistic style and a level of professionalism unprecedented among early film directors. Both made a great number of one- and two-reel Westerns between 1908 and 1913. Ince made them because he was showman enough to realize that they could be easily marketed. Relying on the personnel and livestock from the Miller Brothers' 101 Ranch Real Wild West, he created "Inceville" in the canyons around Santa Monica, California. He built standing sets of Western towns, ranches and saloons, and hired a permanent company of 101 Ranch cowboys, Indians, and trick riders, with accompanying wagons and livestock—all for twenty-five hundred dollars a week, for the winter camp season.[13] Eventually, the Miller Brothers made some of their own films; but to begin with, they served the film industry of southern California in the same fashion as W. H. Barten of Gordon, Nebraska, served the Wild West show: as outfitters and purveyors of livestock and performers.

To Ince's credit, he was the first to try to create stars of some of his Indian players, such as William Eagleshirt, an Oglala.[14] The experiment did not last very long. William Everson writes that, apart from ceremonials and dances, Indians had no acting tradition, and make-believe came hard to them. Perhaps, instead, the rich heritage of both Native American ceremonialism and spiritualism escaped early directors like Ince. Given the tradition of elaborate stage-managing among Cody's Lakotas, which dated back at least to Steel Mackaye's extravaganza in Madison Square Garden, Indians' acting ability could have been easily adapted to the rigors of the two-reelers. Indians obviously played themselves very well. A portion of their filmic value, just as in the Wild West shows, came in the very authenticity they brought to the production. Even though Ince and others considered that Indians brought with them their "classic" features, the larger Indian roles, even in the earliest productions, nevertheless went to such pretend Indians as Sessue Hayakawa, Francis Ford, and Ann Little.[15]

Both Ince and Griffith influenced Western films in significant ways. Griffith experimented with action format and elevated cinematic techniques, according to Jon Tuska, to a level approximating genius. Ince, though more prosaic, nevertheless systematized production. Until his work, Westerns remained rather haphazard. He depended increasingly on the "scenario"; he incorporated in the shooting script everything from action directions, facial expressions, plot, set design, camera setup, and even dialogue to be mouthed by the actors.[16] Both Griffith and Ince made Westerns in which whites and Indians appeared as villains. They also made films that were sympathetic to Indians and critical of federal Indian policy.[17] Two of Ince's more important films appeared in 1912: *War on the Plains* and *Custer's Last Stand*. Early the next year Griffith released his most ambitious short Western, *The Battle of Elderbush Gulch*. He had been impressed with Ince's large-scale battle sequences, made possible by use of the 101 Ranch troupe.[18] These three films, all widely popular moneymakers and all featuring warfare between plains Indians and cavalry, probably influenced Buffalo Bill Cody to record his own exploits and, in a sense, to become just like Broncho Billy Anderson.

When Henry Tammen, proprietor of the Denver *Post* and part-time scoundrel, forced Buffalo Bill's Wild West and Pawnee Bill's Far East into bankruptcy in the summer of 1913, creditors sold the Two Bills outfit at a sheriff's auction on September 15. The Miller Brothers and their partners in the Bison Picture Company purchased some of the equipment and most of the livestock. Cody had already signed an agreement to tour the following season with the Tammen-owned Sells-Floto Circus. He had no money to retire on either to Cody, Wyoming, or North Platte, Nebraska. He had little money to live on even for the few months until the beginning of the next season. As most sources suggest, the devious Henry Tammen, ever amiable even though he had done all in his power to smash the Two Bills show, suggested to the elderly colonel that he appear in motion pictures. Cody refused; but the offer perhaps set him to thinking. Why not make a film of his own, "The Last Indian War," about the events of the Ghost Dance religion and the massacre at "the Creek Where the Man Who was Wounded in the Knee was Buried"? Indeed, why not bring together the original participants as much as possible?[19] The principals in the bankrupt show could flesh out the troupe of actors; besides, they could certainly use the employment. All had been caught in strained circumstances when the show closed.[20]

As an abused child will nevertheless sometimes seek succor from its tormentor, the occasionally gullible Buffalo Bill approached Harry H. Tammen for financing. Tammen, ever interested in spinning straw into gold, along with his partner Frederick G. Bonfils, agreed to bankroll the Cody Historical Pictures Company. Cody would receive a one-third interest for his services and for the use of his name in the company's title. He would also receive his own copy of the printed film to do with as he pleased. Tammen approached the Essanay Film Company for production assistance. President George Spoor assigned his top producer and director, Vernon M. Day and Theodore Wharton.[21] The company provided the cameras, film stock, and costumes. Wharten, described as "stage manager," handled the actual filming of the project. Distribution would be left to the Cody film company that used Essanay's Chicago address.[22]

Cody met with Secretary of War Lindley M. Garrison who happened to be visiting Denver in August and pitched the story to him. Cody would shoot the film on Pine Ridge reservation. His Show-Indian friends would provide the talent; he needed only the cavalry to complete the scenario.[23] Cody persuaded Garrison that re-creation of the Indian wars, using real soldiers, would remind the forgetful public of the army's vital role in winning the West. He further promised to secure the services of retired army officers, including former Chief of Staff Nelson A. Miles. Officers who had figured prominently in the Indian campaigns would help to make the film historically accurate. Garrison allowed soldiers from the Twelfth Cavalry stationed at Fort Robinson, Nebraska, to participate in the filming.[24]

Fortuitously, Secretary of the Interior Franklin Lane was also visiting Colorado at the time. Buffalo Bill met with him in Colorado Springs. The sixty-seven-year-old showman promised Lane that, in addition to the inherent value of historical reenactment, the last reel would include a visual record of Sioux progress since their surrender at Pine Ridge back in January 1891. He would film exemplary Indians at work and play, learning the white man's way in their schools. Cody also promised to provide the secretary a copy of the movie for the government to use in silencing its critics.[25] Lane likewise endorsed the project, but left final approval to the Indian commissioner, who, in turn, deferred to Agent John Brennan at Pine Ridge.

Cody wired Brennan his plan:

> ... to have moving pictures taken of Wounded Knee Massacre and last surrender. Also the last grand council, in order to preserve the sign language which took place in 1890 and 1891. These films will be preserved at Washington. ... This will not involve removing Indians from reservation. All pictures to be taken on reservation. It means reunion of participants who are surviving and preserving for future generations of great events by aid of the camera. All expenses will be paid by financial men. Indians will be fed and well taken care of, all under your direct supervision.[26]

Brennan offered no objections. Accordingly, Commissioner Sells wired his approval on August 27, noting that none of the activity should interfere

52 : *Buffalo Bill, retired General Nelson A. Miles, General Marion Maus, Johnny Baker (the mature "Cowboy Kid"), and unidentified Sioux actor at Pine Ridge during the filming of "The Indian Wars." (Brennan Family Papers, South Dakota State Historical Society, Pierre)*

with "the industrial or educational pursuits or training of the Indians engaged."[27]

A potential problem did exist, however. Brennan warned that two hundred troops arriving from Fort Robinson on September 9 might upset the Oglalas. It had been almost twenty-two years since Wounded Knee, but dreadful memories died hard.[28] Sells blanketed the reservation with his letter that announced the arrival of two hundred troops on "a friendly visit" to participate in a moving picture "under the direction of Col. Cody and General Miles."[29]

For about three weeks the participants rehearsed while Cody, General Miles, and Wharten perfected the script. Filming finally began on October 11 and ended seventeen days later. Cody then spent another month or so in postproduction editing of the film and in writing titles. Very little footage remains of the finished product, *The Indian Wars.* It became just one among a myriad of films from the silent era lost through the decomposition of nitrate stock. Apart from a few minutes of actual film to survive, all that remains of the eight-reel epic is a "scene list," or script, from which Wharten shot the story. The film as planned originally included twenty-seven scenes (further broken down into incidents and settings). Once in production, however, Cody's vision grew. "The Last Indian War" became, instead, "The Indian Wars." Why not add other excerpts from his life? Cody had been performing autobiographical vignettes for decades anyway in the arena, so he added the battles of Summit Springs (1869) and Warbonnet Creek (1876). The original "scene list" included:

First—Indians in their natural condition, showing Indian life, habitations, occupation, devotion, amusements, sports, etc.

Second—Distressed condition of Indians, great poverty, causing disaffection and hostility.

Third—Receiving intelligence of the return of the Messiah to the earth, and the starting of emissaries to see him in response to his summons.

Fourth—Their journey toward the setting sun to meet the so-called Redeemer.

Fifth—Received with great solemnity by the Messiah. His revelations, prophecy, and admonitions.

Sixth—Return of the emissaries and consternation in the Indian camps. Demonstrations of great joy and thanksgiving.

Seventh—Great war council. War dances. Hostile demonstrations.

Eighth—Rush of the Indian tribes to the bad lands. Hostile demonstrations.

Ninth—Occupation and hostile demonstrations in their strongholds in the Mauvassas or Bad Lands.

Tenth—Charge of mounted Indians.

Eleventh—Cavalry charge.

Twelfth—Arrest and death of Sitting Bull.

Thirteenth—Troops in order of battle.

Fourteenth—Surrender of Hump and his warriors to Capt. [Ezra P.] Ewers.

Fifteenth—Council between the division commander and the Indian chiefs.

Sixteenth—Movement of large camp of Indians toward the agency to surrender.

Seventeenth—Engagement at Wounded Knee.

Eighteenth—Engagement on White Clay Creek near [Drexel] Mission.

Nineteenth—Final surrender of the Indians and close of the Indian wars.

Twentieth—Officers viewing large hostile camp.

Twenty-first—Final review of the troops before their dispersement.

Twenty-second—Surrender of leaders of the hostile Indians as hostages for the permanent peace of the Indian tribe.

Twenty-third—Return of hostile Brules under Capt. [Jesse M.] Lee.

Twenty-fourth—Return of the hostile Cheyennes under Capt. Ewers.

Twenty-fifth—Indians in peaceful condition of industry and prosperity.

Twenty-sixth—Portraits of prominent Indians.

Twenty-seventh—Portraits of men who were distinguished in Indian wars and rendered important service in securing permanent peace.[30]

Part of the rationale for "The Last Indian War" had been its authenticity in every detail except the ages of the players, with the actual participants filming on the very ground where events had occurred. Ryley Cooper, hired by Tammen to shill for the picture, blazoned in the pages of the Denver *Post* and other newspapers, "correctness, historical correctness, that is the slogan of the men who are working today."[31] With all the equipment and Oglalas present, however, Cody could not resist. He decided to use his Show Indians to portray Cheyennes in earlier encounters than the "Ghost Dance War."

Historical correctness had its limit in other areas as well. Cody wished to present the fight at Wounded Knee as a massacre down to the last detail, including the slaughter of women and children. General Miles balked. Although Miles himself proclaimed the butchery unwarranted, he nevertheless thought it contrary to "the public interest" and the "welfare of the Indians, to have such exhibition presented in its objectionable phases." He remained at the agency during the filming, having decided not "to take part in the affair." He appealed to Agent Brennan to use his authority as titular supervisor of the project to intervene.[32] It must have worked because when Cody and Wharten shot the "Battle of Wounded Knee" from three different angles, using three cameras, women and children were absent from the synthetic bloodletting.[33]

Short Bull, the great disciple of the Ghost Dance prophet and a veteran of the Wild West, along with No Neck and Woman's Dress led the group of Oglalas and Brules that would perform for the camera. They greeted their old friend warmly.[34] Cody explained a few months later in *The Moving Picture World*, perhaps adding his own press-agentry, that he had to use all

53 : Agent John Brennan and Buffalo Bill at Pine Ridge during the filming of "The Indian Wars," October 1913. (Brennan Family Papers, South Dakota State Historical Society, Pierre)

54 : From the filming of "The Indian Wars," 1913. The scene reproduces the capture of Big Foot's band of Minneconjous at Porcupine Butte, on the Pine Ridge reservation, in December 1890. John Brennan's photograph captures one of the movie camera positions in the left foreground. (Brennan Family Papers, South Dakota State Historical Society, Pierre)

of his persuasiveness to ease their fears. Seeing the Hotchkiss guns, the soldiers dressed in blue, the diminutive village of stacked rifles, and the boxes of ammunition, Short Bull and the others thought the Twelfth Cavalry just might try to finish the job begun with such earnestness by the Seventh Cavalry twenty-three years before. Cody explained that the filming was being done for posterity's sake. The Sioux had a chance to set the record straight about how the shooting started and who did the killing.[35]

Buffalo Bill also intimated in the pages of *The Moving Picture World* that some among the Lakotas planned to substitute real bullets for blanks in the guns issued to them for the sham battle.[36] Although animosities lingered, it was pure buncombe to suggest that the Indians would conspire one last time to commit a glorious suicide rich in retribution. Cody wrote the story to heighten the drama of the "historical film" and to promote its distribution around the country.

On Monday morning, October 13, a hundred or more automobiles and

ounded Knee Battle, Pine Ridge, So. Dak.

55 : Agent Brennan's photograph of the "Wounded Knee Battle Scene," October 1913. (Brennan Family Papers, South Dakota State Historical Society, Pierre)

many teams of horses parked on "Spectator Hill" southwest of the site of Big Foot's encampment, separated by a ravine that itself became a killing field once the firing had started. Without question, one reporter remarked, "it was the largest crowd of visitors that Pine Ridge had seen for some time."[37] They had come from all points in Nebraska and South Dakota, "from Chadron to Valentine, and from Rapid City to Interior," as another reporter noticed.[38] Along the foot of the hill, hundreds more Oglalas gathered to bear silent witness to their memories. The two hundred or so others led by Short Bull (who was not present at Wounded Knee in 1890) would re-create the surrounded deaths of Big Foot's band.[39] Richard J. Walsh, one of Cody's biographers, writes that an itinerant merry-go-round arrived to create in part a curious, carnival scene with "its tinkling music and its gaudy horses."[40]

Rehearsals had been carried on for several days at the main encampment about a mile and a half south of the battlefield. On the final day of

56 : Another view of the reproduced "Battle of Wounded Knee," October 1913: The fight in the deadly ravine. (Buffalo Bill Historical Center, Cody, Wyoming)

---

shooting, a wooden platform had been raised about fifteen feet on a farm wagon and braced by ropes. Operating the camera, Wharten tried to catch each movement below. An Indian impersonated Yellow Bird, the original Ghost Dance orator who harangued the men in Big Foot's band. Then there was the sound of a single shot, and the fight was on. As a reporter described it, "backed with a perfect knowledge that it was all harmless play, it was an interesting, awe inspiring sight, but it represented a terrible tragedy."[41] Some of the Show Indians had to be reminded to play dead until the director signaled the end of the scene. A few had repeatedly disrupted the filming by raising up, propping their chins on their hands, and watching the action.[42] Much was made of this in later publicity, which certainly challenged the image of the more belligerent and conspiratorial Indians identified by Buffalo Bill in other promotions. Once-dead warriors reanimated as recumbent voyeurs suggested a far more relaxed atmosphere, and even introduced an element of comedy into an otherwise somber re-creation. The filming was completed without incident.

Two days later, Wharten finished shooting the fight at the Holy Rosary Catholic Mission—the Drexel Mission, about four and one-half miles below Pine Ridge agency—which had occurred on December 30, 1890. Angry Brules of Two Strike's band, who had already come into the agency to surrender, bolted the settlement when they learned of the butchery at Wounded Knee.[43] Although neither Cody nor Miles figured in the engagement, nevertheless Cody had decided, and Miles agreed, that the Drexel fight would be shown. As Ryley Cooper explained to the readers of the Denver *Post*, at Wounded Knee,

> the white man was the aggressor, they far outnumbering the Indians. ... But at the battle of the Mission the Indian was the aggressor and the Indian fought in his own style. There his pony circled and swung. There he sang to the cutting wind, there his rifle cracked with far greater effect than it did at the battle of Wounded Knee. The Indian was fighting in his own Indian way ... ; different, far different was Wounded Knee.[44]

Other differences remained unrecorded. At Wounded Knee, the Sioux died in large numbers. At the mission fight, casualties included an officer and a ranker killed and five troopers wounded. More remarkable perhaps, no Sioux apparently died in the skirmish. Yet even among the Lakota players, their wives and mothers sang mourning songs. One by one, Cooper wrote, the warriors came "forward to lay their heads upon the shoulder of some weeping Indian woman, then stalk on again. Again there were the tears and the clasping of hands, for memory and grief can live long in the heart of an Indian."[45] Perhaps they remembered the grief and torment of the fifty Brules who sought revenge that day against the poorly led Seventh Cavalry. In any event, Cody and Miles witnessed the re-creation and seemed genuinely enthusiastic over the results. "Even Wounded Knee outclassed," Cooper wired Tammen in Denver. "Pictures immense."[46]

The entourage split up. Some ventured into the badlands, out near Cuny Table and about fifty miles north of Pine Ridge, to film the occupation of "The Stronghold" by Short Bull's ghost dancers. They were joined in the Stronghold by Oglalas who had fled Pine Ridge after the arrival of so many troops, and others, Hunkpapas who had escaped the bloodletting at Sitting Bull's camp on Grand River. The other motion picture unit remained at Pine Ridge to film sequences about "The Indian of Today," and to complete the "historical" vignettes of Short Bull's meeting with

57 : *Wovoka, the "Indian Messiah," preaches to his disciples in a scene from "The Indian Wars" that tries to depict the gathering of delegates in Mason Valley, Nevada, during the summer and fall of 1889. The actor playing Wovoka appears to be a Euroamerican wearing makeup and a wig. (Buffalo Bill Historical Center, Cody, Wyoming)*

Wovoka, the "Indian Messiah," and the death of Sitting Bull. Finally—though far from the scenes of the original conflict—the battles of War-bonnet Creek and Summit Springs were filmed near the agency. "So, you see," Cooper wrote, "there will be the thrill and the excitement of history in the battles which are to come—for history and fact . . . carries often a greater thrill than the wildest dream of the writer of fiction."[47]

Wharten completed filming on October 28. Ryley Cooper had written on three separate occasions during the seventeen days of filming that the gods of weather had smiled benignly on the enterprise, allowing the production to go forward without delays.[48] Buffalo Bill, relieved to be finished, predicted that "the pictures will be a great success. Certainly, there is everything to make them a success. The Indians all worked well, the soldiers did excellent work and the hearts of everyone were in their tasks."[49]

Although press releases were largely favorable, given Cooper's daily

58 : *Another view of Wovoka preaching to the Indian disciples. As promotional copy for the film suggested about the sequence depicted in this photograph, "From the words spoken from a towering cliff, the pictures become one splendid panorama of brave deeds—donning the ghost shirt." (Buffalo Bill Historical Center, Cody, Wyoming)*

---

dispatches, the project did not escape criticism. Chauncey Yellow Robe spoke before the third annual conference of the Society of American Indians in Albany, New York, within days of the October 13 re-creation of the Wounded Knee massacre. The *Rapid City Journal* picked up the Brule-reformers story and ran it on October 21. Yellow Robe claimed that Cody and Miles had deliberately allowed themselves to be filmed as if they had been participants at Wounded Knee. Their presence thus defiled that sacred place "for their own profit and cheap glory." Cody and Miles "who were not even there when it happened," Yellow Robe told his audience, "went back and became heroes for a moving picture machine. . . . You will be able to see their bravery and their hair-breath escapes soon in your theaters."[50] Yellow Robe's denunciation may have inspired others.

A story with the dateline of "Pine Ridge Agency, South Dakota," ran in the New York *World* on November 29, a month after filming ceased.[51]

59 : Chauncey Yellow Robe, Indian-policy reformer, member of the Society of American Indians, and an inveterate foe of Wild West shows. (South Dakota State Historical Society, Pierre)

Other newspapers picked up the story over the next two months. The story took on a life of its own. Some of the charges, all false, have worked their way into the historical record.

The unsigned article appears to have been the work of Melvin R. Gilmore, curator at the Nebraska State Historical Society. Even if Gilmore did not write the article, he nevertheless is quoted extensively as the principal source. The story claimed that the Indians were "kicking" about not only the way in which the film belittled their prowess in battle, but also about how the director deliberately distorted reality. Gilmore repeated Yellow Robe's charge that General Miles and Colonel Cody allowed themselves to be filmed as if they were participants at Wounded Knee. Worse still, the celluloid rendition of Wounded Knee presented the Sioux as well mounted, armed with army rifles, and equal in number to the soldiers they faced. The Indians insisted, according to the author, that the Sioux at Wounded Knee, mostly women and children, numbered fewer than four hundred. All were on foot during the fight. What few men were there had already surrendered their guns and were therefore defenseless. The two or three rifles they retained were old-fashioned muzzle loaders in decrepit condition. Indians had not been the aggressors. And finally, as for the claim that many survivors of the Wounded Knee Battle had taken part in the "filmed" version,

> the Indians say there were no Indian survivors. . . . Only one Indian, a lame one, came through without a scratch or got past the line of soldiers. . . . At least, in the big grave into which all the dead Indians were thrown there are more than 350, a majority of whom were women and children.[52]

Gilmore insisted that Cody and his associates had "beguiled" the Indians. The Lakota participants did not know they were reproducing the Wounded Knee fight. Rather, they believed they were simply taking part in a sham battle for the movies. In their indignation, they called "a meeting of the grand council of the tribe, which will frame a formal protest to the Government."[53]

Indignation also seized Generals Miles and Baldwin when they read Gilmore's statements. Both independently sent copies of the New York *World* column to Agent Brennan at Pine Ridge. Brennan pronounced Gilmore a "nature fakir from Lincoln." The agent reassured Miles that the Indians at Pine Ridge had never discussed the matter in council; neither had they entered a protest at the agency.[54] Brennan even elicited support from prominent people in Indian-policy reform. He wrote to Warren King

Moorehead at Philips Academy to commend Cody's contributions to the economy of the reservation. Brennan explained to the educator and amateur anthropologists that filming *The Indian Wars* had employed about three hundred Indians and spent close to thirty thousand dollars in wages and other expenses at Pine Ridge.[55]

Brigadier General Frank Baldwin, a captain on Miles's staff in 1890, found the charges rather ironic because Miles himself had protested against staging the battle. Baldwin, who *was* present at the re-creation of the battle, confirmed that "the Indians understood perfectly what they were doing."[56] Both Miles and Baldwin planned to review the completed film in Chicago sometime in January 1914. Baldwin insisted that neither he nor Miles would "O.K. anything that is not all correct and true."[57]

Vernan R. Day, production manager for Essanay films, saw the story in the Chicago Sunday *Examiner* of December 7. He quipped that someone was taking a lot of pains to give the project publicity. He wrote to Brennan the next day:

> The only thing that will not be authentic in the Wounded Knee Battle will be the fact that the picture will not show the men and women being slaughtered as they really were.
>
> The Indians knew that we were reproducing the Wounded Knee Battle and the interpreters informed them. . . . If these Indians should go to Washington we would be pleased to have them stop in Chicago as our guests and we would show them, at the time, these pictures. We might save them some money by ending their trip here rather than going to Washington under misapprehension.[58]

Philip Wells, a Sioux of mixed heritage, served as Colonel Forsyth's interpreter during the "Ghost Dance War." He noted in a letter to the editor of the Rapid City *Daily Journal* that Lone Bear from the Medicine Root district, who played the part of Big Foot, and the interpreters—Joe Horn Cloud, Ben American Horse, Jacob White Eyes, and Jim Grass—explained in detail to the Show Indians in the project that they were reenacting Wounded Knee. Joe Horn Cloud was himself a survivor of the fight. "To deceive them all so completely, as [Gilmore] states," Wells wrote, "would lead one to believe that we are living in the age of miracles."[59]

As it turned out, the only protest from the Indians, except for Chauncey Yellow Robe's, came from the Oglala council over an unrelated matter, although it did concern Buffalo Bill. One of the "made chiefs" of the Oglala Lakota, Good Lance, hoped to recover the body of his son who had died in hospital in Garden City, Kansas. The Cody show had left him there, presumably on its way to its last stand before bankruptcy in Denver. When Good Lance's son died, the Garden City health authorities, instead of returning his body to Pine Ridge, buried it in the town cemetery. The Oglala leaders wrote to President William Howard Taft, even though Woodrow Wilson had been in office since the previous March, asking that the Great Father do something:

> Our Indian Agent, Mr. Brennan, said "I don't want this show," but you Indians wanted and cause some boys sickness and he said let the Oglala Council talk about this (boy died body). So the Council had meeting about it, and they wanted this (boy's) dead body to be send over here and they wrote a letter to Buffalo Bill's show. . . . Oglala council said . . . they don't want Buffalo Bill show to get contract from you, and we don't want them to come to Pine Ridge Reservation after show boys again. We don't want any boys to go of show again. We don't want them as they got allotment and they got to work on their allotment. But the Buffalo Bill's show bother them all the time, and we don't want no other show to come over here after show boys again. There are several boys died on account of show, they had small wages, and they don't do them any good.[60]

No other protest was made, and certainly not one concerning the filming of *The Indian Wars*. In this instance, the Oglala council internalized the official BIA position against the show, whereas their agent, John Brennan, had cooperated with the project and spent considerable time during the last month of the year in challenging the allegations of Yellow Robe and Gilmore against the production.

Other historians have suggested that the matter did not end there; that indeed the Indians' protests by inference led to either a ban on the film by the government, or a six-month delay in the commercial release of the film.[61] Neither case was true. Bob Lee explains that one "rather nebulous report" about the film asserted that "the government suppressed it because it depicted the Indian wars too realistically, and not to the credit of the frontier army. . . . But this hard-to-trace rumor has never been substantiated."[62] Kevin Brownlow quotes Ben Black Elk (whose father supposedly appeared in the film) as asking: "Do you know what happened to that motion picture? The government put a ban on it. A friend went to Washington, D.C., to see the movie, but they had destroyed it."[63] Brownlow explains that Cody spent six months editing the film—an unprecedented effort for the time. The premier then took place in April (actually it premiered in February); but then the government suppressed the film— for which it had no right—and held it for an additional six months.[64]

The truth seems to be far less dramatic. After finishing shooting at Pine Ridge, Cody went to New York and then back to Chicago and the headquarters of Essanay Films to work on the project. He was still there on December 13, when he wrote to R. Farrington Elwell, a western artist whose lithographs appeared as advertisements for Buffalo Bill's Wild West. He explained to Elwell that he was busy putting together five miles of film.[65] He went to his home in North Platte, Nebraska, for Christmas. A newspaper story reported that he planned to shoot additional scenes, some of which would include Inspector James McLaughlin, agent at Standing Rock reservation during the Ghost Dance troubles.[66] A little more than two weeks later, Cody traveled to Lawton, Oklahoma, with plans to film several scenes at Fort Sill. He negotiated for soldiers from the Fifth Field Artillery and a large group of Comanches to depict scenes of thirty years before. Rather than show warfare, these scenes would contrast the "various stages of civilization." He wished to show modern Indian schools, farms, houses, stock, implements, and vehicles "with the idea of portraying the actual progress the Indians have made and are making, and what the government has done for its wards." Cody explained that the pictures would be first sent to Washington and "passed upon," after which they would be shown throughout the country.[67] Unclear was whether these would form part of *The Indian Wars* or would be distributed as a separate film.

There is no evidence extant in "scene lists" or correspondence to determine whether the scenes filmed in the former Indian Territory were included in the "Indians Today" segment of *The Indian Wars*. Nellie Snyder Yost writes that Cody offered a copy of *The Indian Wars* to the Interior Department in December 1913—the timing coincides with his editing work in Chicago before returning home for Christmas. No record of its receipt by the Interior Department or any other governmental agency exists.[68] Bob Lee learned from officials at the Library of Congress that Cody never copyrighted the film. That left it particularly vulnerable to piracy.[69]

No prints, or even decomposed remnants of the highly flammable nitrate film, have ever been discovered in a government archive. The loss of the film, however, seems to have little to do with sinister motives. If indeed Cody gave the promised copy to the BIA or the Department of the Interior, it may simply have been disposed of as a safety measure.

In December 1919, the chief clerk at the Interior Department asked his counterpart at the BIA what films that agency possessed. C. F. Hauke, chief clerk of the BIA, reported the following month that the Bureau owned but one film, *The Moqui Snake Dance*, stored in vault 4005. Hauke explained that given the combustibility of the stock, it posed too great a danger to keep nitrate films around so much stored paper. To conserve such films, the Bureau would need to modify its existing storage with considerable venting, something that was beyond the budget of the agency.[70] *The Indian Wars* disappeared, not because the government suppressed it, but because it failed to gain an audience. Decomposition did the rest. Had it been more successful, other prints would undoubtedly have been made. As it is, what snippets exist usually came from stock footage used in other films with Indian subjects. William Cody could not have anticipated this in the early months of 1914. For all he knew, and hoped, *The Indian Wars* would restore his fortune.

Miles joined Cody for the first screening of the completed motion picture at the First National Bank Building of Chicago on Wednesday, January 21, 1914.[71] A month later, the film premiered in Washington, D.C., at a special screening in the Home Club of the Department of the Interior and sponsored by the National Press Club. On the evening of February 26, members of Congress and Interior Secretary Franklin Lane joined Cody at the club to watch what was later described as an epic depicting "the closing Indian wars of North America."[72] The next evening, the film began its run at the Columbia Theatre in the district. In the brochure produced for the first public presentation, Cody boasted that the scenes he filmed would be "as valuable a hundred years from now for the entertainment and enlightenment of future generations as they are today."[73] The next day, a review in the Washington *Herald* explained that "many of the scenes are beautiful, many are inspiring, [whereas] others impress through the terrible realism they show. All defy a detailed description."[74] A poem by John A. Joyce appeared in the *Washington Post:*

> The Indian Wars for fifty years
> On stream and vale and hill
> Are now produced with moving slides
> By brilliant Buffalo Bill![75]

It appears that the film opened at various places around the country during March and April 1914, which belies the controversy with the Indian Bureau and its suppression of the film. As the critic for the Omaha *World Herald* recorded:

It was a happy inspiration to close the show with pictures of Indian schools and industries and Indian life of the present day. There is nothing to be learned from the pictures as to the causes of these Indian wars, but they will likely lead many to search the historical records to find out the causes.[76]

A reporter for the San Francisco *Star*, however, feared that the motion picture might arouse public opinion against Indians. "The moving pictures are here to stay," he wrote to the commissioner, "they will be a great force for good or evil, and so they are entitled to receive consideration at the hands of the best brains in the nation." He hoped, however, that Congress might soon pass a law "forbidding the exhibition of scenes of cruelty" that would prejudice the minds of other Americans concerning Indians.[77]

The day before the film opened at Denver's Tabor Grand Opera House on March 8, John Burke told a newspaper audience that he had been moved to tears by Cody's film. The realism stunned him. He reminisced about the Ghost Dance and taking the Fort Sheridan prisoners to Europe after the close of the "War of the Messiah"; and how he took Short Bull, Kicking Bear, and others to art galleries, theaters, cathedrals, and Windsor castle.[78] He concluded, with all the fustian of an enraptured press agent: "It is war itself; grim, unpitying and terrible; and it holds your heart still as you watch it and leaves you, in the end, amazed and spell bound at the courage and the folly of mankind."[79]

Advertisements appeared in the trade publications of the burgeoning movie industry. As copy from one of these touted, "State Rights Now Ready. Get Busy! . . . Exhibitors—Write or wire us at once and if your state has not been sold, we will book you direct."[80] "State rights" referred to the fact that distributors could obtain exclusive use of the movie in their respective states or groups of states. Distributors who acquired such rights had the privilege of changing the film title if they so desired.[81] Exhibitors then arranged for showings at their theaters through the distributors, or booking agents. As of November 1914, five such distributors had purchased rights for eighteen states.[82] How many others purchased rights is unknown.

Despite a number of favorable reviews, Cody must have been disappointed with box-office receipts within the first month of the premier in Washington. Cody's son-in-law, Fred Garlow (his daughter Irma's second husband), as Nebraska agent for the Buffalo Bill Historical Picture Company, reported that he did only fair business in Blair. From there, he planned to show two days at Wahoo and then back to the Star Theater in

60 : Wovoka, or Jack Wilson, "The Indian Messiah," with perhaps his grandson, near Schurz, Nevada, ca. 1917. (Special Collections, University of Nevada, Reno)

Omaha for another two days. Next, he would show in Hooper for one day and in Oakland for two days.[83] This may have been typical. One source has claimed that the film only made enough money to recover the costs of the production.[84] Garlow himself may have unwittingly described the film's downfall. In copy written to entice theater managers to book the film, he boasted that "these pictures . . . appeal to the best classes of people, the Clergy, Board of Education, City Officials, School Teachers, and people who as a rule do not patronise Motion Pictures to any extend [sic], which means a big add."[85] What the film needed was mass appeal.

Cody's film may have been successful, however, in encouraging others to attempt moviemaking among the Sioux. During the next few years, the Indian Bureau received numerous requests for permission to hire Indians and to film on the Dakota reservations. Whereas once the commissioner had discouraged—though not forbidden—Wild West shows from hiring Indians and thereby disrupting their cultural transformation, now he did the same for aspiring filmmakers. And if, despite the best efforts of the commissioner, films were to be made, then official policy declared that moving pictures should demonstrate "what the government is trying to accomplish for the Indians along educational and industrial lines and not exhibit their old time customs."[86] Indians might otherwise get the wrong impression that whites were more interested in "old-time customs and habits of a relatively small proportion of the Indians," the Show Indians, rather than in the less spectacular accomplishments of the great majority along the lines of "modern civilization."[87] Joe P. Yellow, a veteran of the Wild West shows who lived in Pine Ridge reservation's Porcupine district, knew what he and his friends wanted. He wrote to W. A. Brooks of the 101 Ranch Bison Moving Picture Company, "I wants to work. The Company going have Indian. Many man wants to go with you next time."[88]

Cody's Arizona mines yielded no wealth; and neither did the Buffalo Bill Historical Film Company. Cody, in debt to Henry Tammen, contracted in 1914 and 1915 with the Sells-Floto Circus. In the off-season, he toured and lectured with *The Indian Wars*. In 1916, he talked about reviving Buffalo Bill's Wild West. As Rosa and May write, by that year the Wild West seemed quaintly out of place. The war in Europe had lasted almost two years. Preparedness campaigns swept the country, despite the fact that Woodrow Wilson campaigned for reelection by reminding voters that he had kept the nation out of war.[89] Cody approached Major General Hugh Lennox Scott, army chief of staff, with an idea for a Pageant of Preparedness that would combine the Wild West spectacle with military drill and weaponry demonstrations. Scott approved, and Cody searched

61 : Show Indians arrive in London to promote The Covered Wagon *in 1924. E. J. Farlow, of Lander, Wyoming, and Colonel Tim McCoy talk to reporters as a group of Northern Arapahos led by Goes in Lodge—who wears two feathers, a breastplate, and a peace medal—wait to be taken to their hotel. (Fremont County Pioneer's Museum, Lander, Wyoming)*

for a patron or an organization with which to tour. The Miller Brothers, backed by circus impresario Edward Arlington, joined with Cody to form "The Miller & Arlington Wild West Show Co., Inc., Present 'Buffalo Bill' (himself) Combined with the 101 Ranch Shows." For a while, early in the show's tour, crowds again filled the arenas. Toward the end of the season, however, interest waned and profits dropped. So ended William Frederick Cody's last season as Wild West showman. He died in Denver shortly after noon on January 10, 1917.[90]

Within days of Buffalo Bill's death, the Essanay Film Company placed advertisements in such trade papers as *The New York Dramatic Mirror*

62 : *Show Indians who appeared in "The Covered Wagon" (1923) making camp in New York City en route to the London premier of the film. (Fremont County Pioneers' Museum, Lander, Wyoming)*

and *Motion Picture News* about its latest feature film, *The Adventures of Buffalo Bill*. Supported by a cast of thousands, real Indians and real U.S. troops, Buffalo Bill, "the most romantic figure in American History—the idol of every man and boy," could be seen fighting battles on the western plains, including his duel to the death with the Cheyenne warrior Yellow Hand. "BOOK IT NOW," the advertisement encouraged, "WHILE HIS NAME IS ON EVERY TONGUE."[91] It was nothing more than *The Indian Wars* edited to a length of an hour and fifteen minutes. It had a limited run.

For a while, the burgeoning movie industry continued to employ real Indians in its Westerns. It had been the heritage of the Wild West show to employ real Indians in historical reenactments. Certain directors continued to honor this tradition. They took their actors and film crews on location, to Bishop, California, or Wind River, Wyoming, or Monument Valley, Utah.[92] They engaged Show Indians or their children to play the parts. Occasionally, however, producers and directors encountered resistance from BIA superintendents in hiring Show Indians to appear in their films.[93] In time, it proved cheaper and more convenient to create the West on a back lot or, after 1927, on a sound stage. As filmmakers discovered, it was easier to employ pretend Indians. With a little makeup, a braided wig, a feather bonnet, a blanket, a strung bow, or maybe even a Winchester carbine, the Hollywood director could create the western American Indian by getting an extra to play the part. For more than a generation, however, and including the first years of motion pictures, real Indians had been the Show Indians.

12

DECLINE OF THE WILD WEST SHOWS, 1917-1933

"If sanction were given to all the requests received
for so-called Indian pageantry . . . , large numbers of
the Indians would be on the road much of their time."

        With Buffalo Bill's death early in 1917, and the United States entry into World War I later that spring, the "golden age" of outdoor show business ended. All attempts to revive it met with limited success. Although rodeos increased in popularity in the decade after the Armistice, the Wild West Show which had spawned it went into pronounced decline.[1] The Miller Brothers tried to continue the tradition by reviving the large, elaborate, and railroad-borne Wild West show in 1925.[2] It had a couple of good years; but even before the Wall Street crash, it acquired huge debts that contributed to the downfall of the 101 Ranch empire by March 1932.[3] Although the number of Show Indians did not necessarily decline, the nature of their employment changed. Whereas Wild West shows and circuses had once employed an average of about four hundred a year, by the mid-1920s fewer than one hundred found full-time employment. Competition had become so keen that, instead of seeking other forms of livelihood, it made Show Indians try even harder. Those who were left behind, the agent at Pine Ridge explained, "feel that if they had been a little bit better dancers, had a prettier costume, or had painted themselves a little more carefully, that they would have been chosen." Consequently, Indians spent much of their time practicing their dances, "another waste of time."[4]

The suppression of Indian dancing, organized by the Bureau in 1882 with the "Rules Governing the Court of Indian Offenses," had been inconsistently enforced at the reservations. Even at the height of the Ghost Dance, for example, agents were unable to suppress every performance. The Sun Dance, regarded by Euroamericans as among the most "barbarous" of all American Indian ceremonies, continued to be performed on citizen allotments, free from interference by the agents. With the arrival of Commissioner Charles Burke, however, there were renewed attempts to outlaw dances considered either as immoral or as vestiges of savagery. It was Burke's infamous "dance order" (and supplements in 1923), issued soon after becoming commissioner, that John Collier and others judged as attacks on Indian cultures. A new generation of Indian-policy reformers, more respectful of American Indian cultures, would level considerable criticism of the Bureau throughout the 1920s.[5]

Persons in the Indian service continued to rail against the shows, but, when pressed, nevertheless cooperated in the contracting of Indians. Official reticence, however, led some of the smaller shows to forego the employment of Indians altogether. As one enterprising showman explained to the agent at Pine Ridge, he found the rules and regulations governing Show-Indian employment too cumbersome and expensive to suit his taste or budget. He would rather just employ Indian regalia. He could hire all the people he needed off the reservation to dress up in leggings, buckskin shirts, and feather bonnets and play Indians.[6]

Correspondence concerning Show Indians all but ceases between 1917 and 1920. State and local pageants, fairs, and stock shows requested permission for Indians to participate; but there were few opportunities for employment. Even then, the Bureau continued to discourage what it described as the wanton display of old Indian customs, particularly dances.

63 : *Agent Brennan took this photograph of "Buffalo Bill Indians dancing at Pine Ridge preliminary to leaving for Rushville." As competition grew keener, Show Indians would compete with one another for the attention of the employers. These competitions share many similarities with the modern powwows. (Brennan Family Papers, South Dakota State Historical Society, Pierre)*

For example, when George H. Hazzard, secretary and general manager of the Minnesota Territorial Pioneers, asked permission to use Indians in a pageant marking the one-hundredth anniversary of Fort Snelling, Assistant Commissioner Edgar B. Meritt—whom Francis Paul Prucha describes as one of those persons left over from the Progressive era who took seriously his charge as guardian of the Indians[7]—answered that the Bureau had no objections "as long as there is no dancing."[8] Hazzard regretted exceedingly that "we have been boxed up with cowboy shows and Buffalo Bill ideas." He explained to Meritt that the Minnesota state fair "is for the uplift not only of cattle, but American citizens." The participation of Anishinaabeg and Sioux would demonstrate to the thousands of people in attendance that "your bureau and the reservations haven't allowed the Indian race to stay where Ft. Snelling found it a hundred years ago." As for any dancing, the general manager noted for the record, "both my feet are Methodist on the line of that pastime for whites, reds or blacks."[9]

Gone were the days when Indians would simply play themselves. In the 1920s, historical tableau gave way to greater emphasis on rodeo features, or comical interludes in circuses. Texicole-Charley's Troupe of Wild West Performers and the Sells-Floto Circus wanted Indians who could perform as fancy ropers and bronco riders. In 1921, Charles Cole hired seventy-five Sioux for two weeks, whereas in the following year the Sells-Floto Circus employed "ten good Indians—half men and half women"—for the season, April through October.[10] In his letter to Texicole-Charley discouraging Indian employment, Agent Tidwell at Pine Ridge put an economic twist on a familiar refrain. The Indian Bureau was making every effort to educate and civilize the Sioux as well as other Indians. "Congress is appropriating large sums of money for this purpose," the agent explained, "and should these Indians continue to take part in wild west scenes and wild west shows the public at large will soon become convinced that it is useless to appropriate these large sums of money and accomplish nothing whatever."[11] To "Colorado Cotton" Smith of the Sells-Floto Circus, Tidwell remarked that the Bureau's attitude had changed in the last few years "so that official sanction is seldom, if at all, given."[12] Cole accepted discouragement with aplomb and abandoned plans to hire Indians for the summer of 1921. Smith, however, got the support of Senator James E. Watson. The Indiana Republican called upon the commissioner, who then advised Agent Tidwell to choose only "such Indians as have not home and industrial interests that will suffer by reason of their absence during the period of the contract."[13]

As Commissioner Burke discovered soon after assuming his duties on May 7, 1921, the Bureau had been inconsistent in granting permission to some and denying it to others who wished to hire Indians.[14] The recent participation of Indians without Bureau permission in the Billings and Mandan fairs had sparked protests from missionaries and harried agents. "The fact is," Burke explained in an office memorandum of May 24, "we do not seem to have any real *authority* [Burke's italics] to prevent the Indians from attending such fairs." It had been the policy to discourage attendance in groups although nothing could be done about Indians visiting the fair individually. Discouragement usually took the form of denials of specific requests. Yet, if the petitioning party wished to go ahead and hire Indians anyway, there was nothing the Bureau could do except bar them from the reservation. Even this would not thwart the persistent company. People on occasion complained about the apparent inconsistency in Bureau policy, that some companies received permission and others did not. Some companies never bothered to ask permission. The only way to explain the apparent inconsistency of policy would be to admit that the Bureau possessed no real authority. Such an admission would be "inadvisable at least officially and in writing."[15] The system worked reasonably well as long as prospective employers did not engage political influence. Then the commissioner, in true partisan fashion, shaped his policies according to party discipline.

Eleven Sioux who hired on for work with the Sells-Floto Circus did not last the season. In separate letters, Philip Poor Bear and Bat Shangreau asked Agent Tidwell to intervene on their behalf with Zack Terrell, manager of the show. They wanted their "hold back" so they could buy train tickets home. Neither of them was making any money. Both remarked that they knew it would be wise to put up some hay for the winter. Bat Shangreau also needed a new saddle.[16] Tidwell sided with management. No matter. By the middle of July all the Indians had been returned to the reservation after they had struck for better working conditions. They resented Terrell's insistence that they perform manual labor in setting up and tearing down the big top. This labor certainly varied with Show-Indian traditions. In warning off prospective performers, Tidwell explained the labor insurgency of the Sioux contingent with the Sells-Floto Circus. "It seems that show companies require certain manual labor of the Indians in connection with their demonstrations and exhibitions," he observed, "which is not particularly to the Indians' liking; hence there is not a great deal of enthusiasm among our Indian people for a show life."[17] The last statement, however, was wishful thinking on Tidwell's part.

Pageants, fairs, stock shows, and "powwows" collectively continued to employ the largest numbers of Indians, but for much shorter periods of time—a week rather than a summer, a month rather than a year.[18] The going rate appears to have been two dollars a day for a run of a week or two; a lesser daily wage for a month's employment. Monthly salaries averaged between thirty dollars and forty-five dollars. As always, contracts included food, lodging, and transportation to and from the site.[19] The fact that salaries remained largely the same for thirty years, at the same time that the demand for full-time Indian performers after 1910 declined, suggests that the status of Show Indians had also been diminished. In a sense then, as Gretchen Bataille and Charles Silets assert, by the 1920s Show Indians had become firmly established as stock characters like the stage Irishman and the comic Jew.[20] The largest employer of 1923 was Denver's

Pageant of Progress between July 2 and 15. Frank Goings served as interpreter and chaperon. He remarked wryly that of the fifty Indians brought from Pine Ridge, Rosebud, Crow Creek, Cheyenne River, and Lower Brule reservations, each wanted to be head chief. When the pageant officials tried to feed them "weenies and nice ham," the Indians "kicked" and demanded beef. They got their preferred meat at every meal.[21]

As a publicity stunt, the pageant organizers took a contingent of Show-Indian veterans to Buffalo Bill's grave on Lookout Mountain, west of Denver. Denver's Chevrolet dealers provided the automobiles that carried the troupe to Buffalo Bill's Memorial Museum. All the press-agentry in Denver, however, could not replicate the genuine outpouring of emotion. A number of veterans spoke in Lakota. Johnny Baker, the former "Cowboy Kid" and Cody's foster son, translated. Flying Hawk laid his war staff of eagle feathers on the grave. Each of the Indians placed a buffalo nickel on the imposing stone as a symbol of the Indian, the buffalo, and the scout, figures since the 1880s that were symbolic of the early history of the American West. Speaking slowly, Spotted Weasel recited at length the virtues of his deceased friend. He told how Buffalo Bill, once an enemy of the Lakota, became in time their best friend among the *Wasichus. Pahaska* ("Long Hair") had clothed, fed, and given money to many of them, in friendship and the generosity that obliges it. To many others, he provided good jobs. "With his voice shaking with emotion which he made no effort to conceal," a reporter for the Denver *Post* wrote, Spotted Weasel "ended his eulogy with an appeal to his benefactor's spirit to be with him and his tribe."[22]

From Denver, some of the group went on to the Cheyenne Frontier Days, and afterward appeared at the Colorado Springs' fair for four days beginning the third week of August. It was only "piecework," but Frank Goings noted that the troupe was "getting pretty good feed now [and] plenty of meat."[23] While in Cheyenne, some of the Show Indians signed on for the Knights of Columbus Rodeo for July 28 in Denver. Goings noted that many in the party had been sending money home to their families. The troupe had eaten four beeves thus far, he told the agent. Indians were "looking good and getting lazy."[24]

So great were the number of requests for Show-Indian participants at pageants and fairs in 1923 and 1924 that Commissioner Burke became involved. He complained that Americans were receiving the wrong messages about American Indians, first in exhibitions that celebrated the Indian past, and then in other ways that tried to mark the Indian as unique and special. Attempts by the Society of American Indians to set aside the second Friday in May as a national "Indian Day" were met with hostility.

Burke wrote to missionary and other influential organizations reproving the proposal. A governmental policy of unity and Americanization demanded that no class or race distinctions be observed, and certainly not by presidential proclamation. The Bureau itself "is now quite liberal," Burke explained. It already permitted reservation Indians "to hold meetings or convocations in which customs and traditions peculiar to their race are celebrated and enjoyed." That liberality, however, did not extend off the reservation.[25]

When P. H. Marshall of Gallup, New Mexico, proposed taking a group of Zunis, Navajos, and Hopis on a tour to re-create the annual intertribal ceremonial, Burke sent a letter of discouragement, if not a denial of permission. "If sanction were given to all the requests received for so-called Indian pageantry lasting several weeks," he wrote to the would-be showman, "large numbers of the Indians would be on the road much of their time with little at home of any value when they returned." All such demonstrations portrayed the "earlier customs of tribal life."[26] That the commissioner found intolerable.

Burke's letter to Marshall represents a synopsis of prevailing attitudes at the Bureau, largely unchanged since the 1880s, that would be challenged by such critics as John Collier and the American Indian Defense Association. The commissioner acknowledged that a tour of the Gallup Inter-Tribal Ceremonial might prove educational for the Indians; but he doubted that "such benefits would offset the objectionable consequences." The most popular Indian shows and performances appeared to be those that exhibited "old-time habits and pagan ways which place[d] the more progressive Indians in a false light." This led the public to conclude wrongly that the spectacle they were witnessing was typical of present conditions. "Too many whites are attracted by gaudy paint and feathers and war whoops who would take little interest in an Indian display of successful farming or business pursuits." Burke claimed that the Bureau had made it plain that "the Indian is not to be deprived of his occasional feast days, his periods of play and recreation, and his religious ceremonials."[27] Just the opposite was true. Indians were to have their "play and recreation" curtailed and their religious ceremonials, or "pagan ways," restricted if not banned. The commissioner and his compeers failed to realize that dancing represented not simply "old-time habits," but also present expressions of culture. It never occurred to them that these, as well as industrial pursuits, might prepare the Indian "to cope," as Burke described it, "with the tests that await him as a full-fledged citizen."[28]

Ernest W. Jermark, Tidwell's replacement at Pine Ridge in the summer of 1924, represented the muscular Christian so endearing to Burke and his supporters. Jermark had distinguished himself as the superintendent at the Fort Berthold reservation in North Dakota in curtailing Indian dances and community celebrations.[29] Once ensconced at Pine Ridge in August, he found himself "obsessed" with requests to take Indians from the reservation for exhibition. "I can safely say," he informed the commissioner, "that we have had 15 or 20 requests up to this date for parties of Indians ranging from 10 to 75." Unfamiliar with Bureau policy governing the contracting of Show Indians, he nevertheless echoed his predecessor in outlining ideas for the commissioner. Jermark noted the "vast amount" of money that Congress authorized annually for the "education and civilization" of the Indians. These funds, he remarked, were "largely gratuity . . . provided from the money of the tax payers [sic] of the United States." It puzzled him why these same taxpayers who supported the Indian would nevertheless encourage him "to exhibit himself in the nature of a freak," and to act in ways contrary to the stated objectives of the commissioner and field-service employees.[30]

Jermark found it confusing to allow only the "non-productive" Indians to go with the shows. If this were the sole criterion, it took little effort to become nonproductive. It "requires no effort on their part," he explained, "to defer planting or otherwise acquiring property which would require them to stay at home and give the same attention." Pine Ridge reservation alone held "approximately 150 or 200 professionals, Indians looking for these engagements, willing to travel around the country for little or no salary, so long as traveling expenses and beef are provided." Great "rivalry" existed among the Indians to obtain these engagements. His complaint about "little or no salary" may have been wishful thinking, for he conceded later in his letter to Commissioner Burke that Show Indians indeed received "fair compensation for the 6 to 10 weeks they are absent" from the reservation. He acknowledged the "deplorable" conditions of the Oglalas in matters of health and finances and as viewed from an "industrial standpoint," but he could not fathom how Indians would want to leave the reservation. Only by "the most confining effort" would Oglalas be able to make a living and provide for their families. Neither "they nor we can expect them to do [so] if they are permitted to run to every celebration far and near." Authority or not, were it in his power he would not allow an Indian "to exhibit himself as a freak."[31] As Burke had to explain, in words reminiscent of every commissioner—with the possible exception of T. J. Morgan—from John H. Oberly to Francis Leupp, it was not within his power.

The commissioner repeatedly discouraged application for Indian exhibitions, even those instances "where the pressure was very strong." However, in those areas of the West where "Indians are practically all fee patent citizens, and have been for some time," he noted, "it is difficult to make any effectual restraint." Where Bureau control extended to "noncompetent" Indians, "we should and do object by the strongest moral influence, at least, to this waste of time and neglect of home and industrial welfare."[32] The Bureau had to contend with actions of the Sixty-eighth Congress on June 2 (Public Law 175) granting citizenship to those Indians who had somehow escaped the various citizenship provisions enacted since 1887.

For 1925, Burke outlined a five-year program aimed at the formation on each reservation of Farm-Bureau chapters, women's auxiliaries, and recreation committees to stimulate Indian interest in agriculture, stock raising, and a "more modern community."[33] To support the plan, and at the same time confront the continuing distraction of Indian exhibitions, Eugene D. Mossman, superintendent of the Standing Rock Indian School, composed a circular. He sent it to all fair associations, to towns where rodeos and roundups were held during summer and fall months, and to any organizations that used "Indians as a drawing card to show off their old time dances and customs and their old time finery."[34] He then got the other agents in Sioux country to endorse it.[35]

Mossman explained that if the Indians were to become "efficient capable citizens they must conform sufficiently to the ordinary practices of successful farmers." Many of the Sioux were indeed farming and "making a success of their work." There were, however, "a vast number who travel about during the summer from one rodeo to another, from roundup to roundup and from fair to fair." He described one such person as "addicted to this practice." He had been known to leave a standing field of twenty-five acres of good oats ready to harvest so that he might travel long distances to parade in paint and feathers "while he goes back two generations and dances the old savage dances." Or consider the example of the young woman returned from school. Circumstances forced her to become "one of the rovers and campers to be stared at and remarked about." Everyone was doing it. The white people around her "think her far more interesting in her savage dress than in her proper clothing in which she returned from school." Was it any wonder, then, that she "dons her beads and paint and feathers and joins in with the others?" Even the "better element" among the Indians frowned on such things. It was up to the good Christian people, Mossman insisted, to discourage the antics of barbarism. They should celebrate, instead, the sober, industrious, well-dressed farmer-Indian and pay him with respect and not with money and beef to lure him from his fields.[36]

Jermark so liked the letter that he had Superintendent Mossman initially send him fifty copies.[37] His displeasure did not keep any of the circuses or the Miller Brothers' show from hiring Indians. He did, however, occasionally make things unpleasant for the Show Indians. Edward Brown, an Oglala, had to remind the superintendent that, as an "unrestricted" Indian, he had the "liberty" to contract with whomever he chose. For "40 years," he wrote the superintendent, "I have not received any rations from the Gov't but have always helped myself & still continue to do so." Edward, his wife, and his son were all fine and receiving good money from Bill Penny's circus. When "you answer me," he entreated Jermark, "kindly do not exercise highness or be tyrannical."[38] No record of Jermark's reply has been found. Perhaps he never answered Brown. It is perchance equally dangerous to speculate about the superintendent's thoughts when he learned of Edward Brown's death, apparently from illness, on July 15.[39] At the time, Jermark was busy getting ready to take a group of Indians—"two or three hundred of our workers who can be spared"—to Cheyenne, Wyoming, as guests of Colonel C. B. Irwin and the Frontier-Days celebration.[40]

By the following year, much of Jermark's hostility had subsided. He still did not condone the practice of Indians joining Wild West shows and circuses; but he came to run a smooth operation in the contracting of Indians. He spent considerable effort in arranging for veterans of the Battle of the Little Bighorn to be present to mark the fiftieth anniversary of their victory over Custer and the Seventh Cavalry. They received no pay, though the Custer Memorial Association transported them to and from the battlefield and provided a number of beeves to barbecue.[41] When the association balked at some of the expenses in taking the Indians from the reservation to the railroad in Nebraska, Jermark grew impatient. He explained to J. A. Shoemaker, the association's secretary, that between five hundred and fifteen hundred Sioux joined various celebrations every summer. They all charged for their time. Just then there were Indians in Europe, and Indians with circuses, and requests from another eight rodeos and frontier pageants to hire Show Indians. Jermark let the association know that its members were getting off easy.[42] And finally, even Commissioner Burke relaxed a little. Bombarded by requests to hire Indians, and complaints that he had permitted the hiring of Indians, he reminded one petitioner that "apparently you do not realize that Indians are

A

B

64 : *Composite: Little had changed in over forty years of Show Indian performance. Oglalas who appeared with the Hans Stosch–Sarrasani Circus in Dresden
during the 1920s. A: Sarrasani Circus troupe en route to Germany aboard the
Hamburg-American steamship* Westphalia, *ca. Oct. 1928. B: Sarrasani Circus
troupe, Dresden, Germany, ca. Nov. 1928. Standing at extreme right is Clarence O.
Shultz, who used to contract Indians through the Miller Brothers, and who eventually traveled to South Dakota himself to gather a troupe of Show Indians.
C: Portrait of Mark Spider (L) and Sam Lone Bear (R), veteran Show Indi-
ans. D: John Milk, wife, and two children (unnamed in the record). E: Martin
Red Deer, wife, and son. (Federal Archives and Records Center, Kansas City,
Missouri)*

D

E

as free as other citizens to go and come from their homes or reservations as they see fit."[43]

In 1927 and 1928, Peter Shangreau chaperoned a group of Lakotas with the John Robinson Circus; Frank Goings and a dozen compatriots traveled with the Sells-Floto Circus; the Hagenbeck Brothers and the Sarrasani Circus each kept small groups of Show Indians—less than a dozen—on tour in Europe; and the Miller Brothers employed about thirty-five Indians from South Dakota and Oklahoma. They were smaller outfits. Indians did everything from performing in the rodeos, if that was a regular feature, to participating in the clown acts, usually as dupes for the jesters.[44] For all the commissioner's acknowledgments of citizenship, agents nevertheless made it difficult for any but the "unproductive" to go with the shows.[45] Even Frank Goings noted the changes that had taken place. For the first time, he complained about the Show Indians in his charge as "lazy" (though before he had often used the word *lazy* to indicate contentment and prosperity). Incidents of drunkenness increased markedly.[46] Agent Jermark ascertained that few Show Indians were returning at the end of their contracts with any money to show for their labors. They and their families, the "unproductive element" on the reservations who "get very hard up for foodstuff during the winter months," had become dependent on the shows for their livelihood.[47] Once the show closed down for the season, the Show Indians went hungry.

Business was so bad for the Sells-Floto Circus during the summer of 1928 that it sent its thirteen Show Indians home in the middle of the season. Surprisingly, Jermark took the side of the Indians in their claims against the show. To him, a contract was a contract. He defied Senators Arthur Robinson of Indiana and Charles Curtis of Kansas. Jermark told Curtis, the Republican candidate for vice president, that he felt it his solemn duty to protect the interests of the Indians. In the event of an unsatisfactory offer from the American Circus Corporation of Peru, Indiana, parent organization for Sells-Floto, then Jermark's only recourse "would be to put the bond to suit."[48] Assistant Commissioner Meritt sided with the monied interests; but Jermark put the matter before the commissioner who, immersed in other controversies, would rather have seen the matter dropped.[49] A "contract is of no avail," the superintendent reminded the commissioner, "if it may be abrogated at the pleasure of either party without the other's consent. The fact that the Show Company was not making the money they had anticipated is not sufficient reason for canceling its contracts."[50] When Jermark contacted the U.S. attorney in Sioux Falls, Sells-Floto decided to pay the Indians.[51] Jermark believed that it was useless to offer homilies to Indians about good citizenship unless the government were prepared to offer a refresher course in civics to exploitive businesses.

For his part, Frank Goings was glad to get his money. He was afraid the only thing he would have from his travels that summer was a tuxedo bought for him by a Boston philanthropist at a secondhand store. Nothing in the shop fit him except a stocking cap and the tuxedo. He wanted the cap; the philanthropist insisted on the evening dress. Goings feared that if the other members of the troupe saw him dressed in formal attire, "they would throw me in the Atlantic ocean" and be justified in doing so. He kept the tuxedo hidden from his companions.[52] He was glad to receive his back pay.

Joe Miller died accidently by carbon-monoxide poisoning in October 1927. His brother George took the show out the following season. George's death, in an automobile accident in February 1929, hastened the decline of the Miller Brothers' Wild West show.[53] To Zack Miller fell the neckerchief of leadership; but the organization was never the same. James Pulliam, an Oglala with the 101 Ranch show, spoke words that would have been echoed by countless Show Indians since the first tour of 1883. Writing to Jermark from Ogdensburg, New York, a few months after George Miller's death, he found life on the road exhilarating. "So far as I am concerned," he told the superintendent, "I like it fine here. If I had to pay for what I have seen so far, I would be broke the rest of my life."[54] Pulliam and his friends Howard and Alexander Bad Bear, Ralph Red Bear, and Charles Wounded had saved enough money to purchase a new Ford Model A in Pontiac, Michigan, and drive it home to the reservation.[55]

The Miller Brothers' organization ceased to serve as contracting agent for European circuses that wished to hire Indians, something that it had done intermittently since 1913. European circuses continued to hire Indians; but they sent their own agents among the tribes. The crash also buried the last great Wild West show. Try as he might, Zack Miller could not keep the organization from going into receivership in August 1931.[56]

Ray L. Wilbur, former president of Stanford University, a supporter of allotment, and a friend of Herbert Hoover, became secretary of the interior in March 1929.[57] About the time James Pulliam and his companions were off searching for America in their Ford sedan, the new secretary was busy composing a memorandum for release to the nation's newspapers. "Too much is being made of the Indian as showman cast in aboriginal roles," Wilbur mused. "Showmanship does not lead the Indian toward establishing himself on an even keel of self respecting indepen-

65 : *"Buffalo Hunt by Sioux Indians" from the Miller Brothers 101 Ranch Real Wild West, ca. 1929. (E. M. Botsford Papers, Southwest Collection, Texas Tech University, Lubbock)*

dence." Quite the reverse. The Show Indian created a "masquerade of a manner of life that no longer exists and can not exist in contact with the dominant civilization." The worst examples of such degradation occurred when the well-educated Indian Americans "bedeck themselves with paint and feather and engage in the dance of their grandfathers." Their dances benefited only those who used them to attract visitors. "Those individuals and communities may profit," Wilbur explained, "but the wholesome development of the Indian is interfered with and he is hurt." The secretary pledged that his department would do all it could "to discourage this showmanship as distinct from the natural celebrations of the Indians carried on among themselves."[58]

Some things had changed. Both the new secretary and commissioner continued to decry the exhibition of dancing tribes; but now, however, after years of heavy-handed attempts by Commissioner Burke and his subalterns to exorcize the dancing spirit from the Pueblos and the Great Plains, the Indian service would allow Indians presumably to be themselves, far from the paying crowds, and dancing to make their gods con-

66 : *Oglala Show Indians with the 101 Ranch show dancing during noon hour at the General Electric Plant in Chicago, ca. 1930. (E. M. Botsford Papers, Southwest Collection, Texas Tech University, Lubbock)*

tent. Likewise, Superintendent Jermark, with considerably less hostility than when he arrived at Pine Ridge, answered a request for Show Indians from Alice F. Fritcher, superintendent of public instruction in Chadron, Nebraska. Fritcher had wanted to bring a large group of Sioux to the Tri-State Fair at Crawford on September 6 and 7; and then to the county fair at Chadron on the following week. Jermark explained that, whereas it was true that part of his many duties as agent included the contracting of Show Indians, he now left it up to the professionals.[59] Older men such as Frank Goings and Peter Shangreau arranged the details for any interested party. Jermark's attitude had changed to such an extent that, when an advertising executive was looking to acquire "Indian relics" on the reservation, he could lament the loss of material culture. The executive was planning an advertising campaign for a bank that traded on the slogan "Since the Days of the Covered Wagon." Jermark advised that he should seek such treasure among the traders. "They're the only people with ceremonial garb and relics anymore."[60]

Jermark's tenure at Pine Ridge marked the transition from hostility to

67 : "Navajo Village" at the Pacific Southwest Exposition, Long Beach, 1928. The exposition lasted from July 27 to August 13. These same Show Indians sometimes donned the feathered headdress to appear in the Pueblo village. (National Archives)

grudging acceptance, and finally to open support for Show Indians. Even Commissioner Charles Rhoads, while voicing older sentiments about exhibitions retarding progress toward "normal" citizenship, nevertheless recognized that show business might individually "be to the interest of the Indian."[61] His idea of exploitation did not concern popular images, but rather "the peculiar danger of the Indians being taken advantage of by exhibit enterprises, such as circuses, rodeos, theatrical road shows, fairs, [and] motion picture concerns." He encouraged Indians to obtain contracts and thereby protect themselves from unscrupulous business practices.[62]

When the Fall River county Fair Board of Edgemont, South Dakota, informed the Sioux agents that Indians would no longer be welcome, B. G. Courtright, field agent in charge of Pine Ridge following Jermark's resignation, angrily replied. It was one thing to cease exhibitions of Show Indians; but it was quite another matter to bar Indians from attending. "Please be advised," Courtright wrote, "that the Pine Ridge Indians are all citizens of the United States and also of the State of South Dakota." As long as they behaved themselves, they could visit anywhere they chose.[63] Seven years before, Eugene Mossman and other agents among the Sioux had distributed a circular that discouraged fair associations from either employing Indians or inviting their attendance. Such an attitude was no longer fashionable, at least not officially. Back at Pine Ridge late in the season of 1931, Acting Agent Courtright could commiserate with an aspiring entrepreneur who had difficulty finding Indians to appear in his show. Colonel Lew Ruben of St. Louis wanted to stage Indian pageants under fraternal auspices on an average of one a week. He hoped to hire fourteen Sioux, eight men and six women. Courtright regretted that "all our real show Indians are now engaged for the next few months, the last troupe having just left for Germany." He advised the colonel to try the reservations closer to home.[64]

This change in attitude is even more apparent in the Indian Bureau preparations for the Century of Progress Exposition in Chicago in 1933. The purpose of the fair was to celebrate the one-hundredth anniversary of Chicago's incorporation. Planning for the fair among the members of the Indian service began slowly enough. James H. McGregor, the new superintendent at Pine Ridge, outlined a program of Sioux participation in which both the "folk dances" and "costumes" from the past would be displayed alongside newer themes, although, as ever, these tended to run toward "productive citizenship."[65] Philip Wells, the venerable scout and survivor of Wounded Knee, wrote McGregor that he hoped the Sioux would be prominently featured in Chicago. The superintendent agreed. What was more, McGregor insisted that the Sioux were preferable to other tribes. "I think that the Sioux are more dignified," he explained to Wells, "and are mentally superior to the Blackfeet Indians." He promised Wells that he would bring it to the attention of Senator Peter Norbeck of South Dakota, chairman of the banking and currency committee, in the hope that a little political pressure on the Interior Department and the Bureau and its fair committee might get them "to favor our people."[66] The Bureau, as it turned out, had other plans.

Commissioner Rhoads, in early August, learned that the Bureau's portion of the Interior-Department appropriation would be "insufficient for us to plan any large exhibit." The Bureau settled on an exhibit showing the current activities of the service "toward the welfare of our Indians." Its emphases would be on health and education. Cases holding arts and crafts of Native Americans would border the larger graphic display. Surrounding all would be murals in the main exhibit hall of the "Mayan Temple" painted by Southwestern Indian artists.[67] The government Indian displays, reminiscent of those at the Columbian Exposition, would be supplemental to the main anthropological exhibit.[68]

Professor Fay-Cooper Cole, of the Anthropology Department at the University of Chicago, directed the fair's division of social science. The managers had set aside twelve acres and approved a half-million-dollar budget for an exhibit of "native Indian cultures."[69] Since the 1893 fair, the plural had been added to "culture." The anthropology section planned an extensive exhibit of native life showing the ancient types of dwellings and the old Indian camp life. In 1893, Frederick Ward Putnam had hoped originally to create a village of Indians from throughout the United States, and include numerous representatives from Central and South America. A limited budget encouraged a less grandiose scheme. At the Century of Progress Exposition, by contrast, originally only five different tribes were to live in the Indian village (though it appears that four actually participated).[70]

"We are trying to portray life as it was before the whites disturbed it," Professor Cole explained, "but much of that same life still goes on."[71] A reporter for the Chicago *Daily News* observed that visitors to the village were learning that "an Indian isn't an Indian; that there is far more difference, for instance, between the modes of life pursued by Hopis and Sioux than between French and American."[72] Ceremonials presented several times daily at the village stadium proved to be popular. Not everyone, however, absorbed the newer ideas of cultural relativism.

Phyllis Crandall Connor worked as ceremonial director for the American Indian Villages and Ceremonials Company, sole contractor for the Indian village in the anthropological section of the fair. She explained to the *Daily News* reporter that these "are gigantic old Indians with painted faces who make white children feel creepy at first, but they soon learn they are friendly Indians." That had been the fear all along of Commissioner Rhoads and others in the service—the public might get the wrong idea. For all the time, effort, and money expended in Indian affairs since the Dawes Act, let alone the founding of Chicago, Indians still wore paint and feathers. However friendly they turned out to be, their appearance, or "presence," still menaced certain elements of Euroamerican society. This had been the world of thrills, of a vanishing America portrayed in Buffalo Bill's Wild West. First in his show and later in his epic film, Cody had demonstrated that those who were once enemies were now friends. Where there had been war—even with the terrible tragedy of Wounded Knee, which perhaps cried out to the Great Mystery for retribution—peace had been achieved. These images in degraded form became the sham battles of the Omaha exposition, the "Attack on the Deadwood Stage" raised to the level of sole contribution of American Indians to American history. At Chicago, in 1933, in the depths of another depression, certain people still felt "creepy" around Indians until they learned they were friendly. Others learned finally that there was no such thing as "The American Indian." Instead, there were Indians.

Stationery for the American Indian Villages and Ceremonials Company stated the theme of the exhibit: "*The Ceremonies of the Hopi, Navajo, Sioux and Winnebago* Survive *A Century of Progress.*" Irony imbued the phrase. Whether one hated or cherished the ceremonies of representative American Indians, one could agree with the pronouncement. Despite the relentless attacks on every aspect of their cultures, every element of their identities, either as members of individual tribes or collectively, Indians had survived. They had survived the "Winning of the West." They had also survived "centuries of progress." As John Collier and other intellectuals had discovered long before the despondency of the Great Depression, there were limits to one's faith in progress. Many people no longer spoke so cheerfully about the superiority of one culture over another.

When John Collier became commissioner in 1933, he continued the practice of encouraging contracts between Indians and circuses, rodeos, theatrical road shows, fairs, and motion pictures. When there was some discussion of staging a week-long American Indian Exposition as part of the Southeastern Fair at the Atlanta fairgrounds in September 1934, the commissioner enthused about the "decidedly promising and important" plan. To the president of the fair association, he wrote a long letter in which he summarized Indian removal and a "century of dishonor." In the one hundred years since removal, the United States had achieved a "barbaric record" of persecution of Indian cultures and denial of Indian religious liberty.[73] Now a New Deal for American Indians promised a reconstruction of family and community life, and the emancipation of native cultures. It would therefore be well for people throughout the South, and eventually the nation, to know the shameful record of government-Indian relations. Every child in school should learn that Indians, instead of vanishing, were to be a "permanent part of life."[74]

In letters to individual Indians and circulars to his superintendents, Collier explained that "we make no objection to [Indian] employment for show purposes."[75] The commissioner requested that each Bureau superintendent prepare a calendar that included religious ceremonies and large annual celebrations "such as pageants, rodeos, fairs, and May Day, Fourth of July and Christmas celebrations when they are of a widely tribal character." He hoped to encourage various motion-picture companies to film "some of the most interesting ones."[76] His enthusiasm, however, appears not to have been shared by the motion-picture companies. Rather than film documentaries on the reservations, they filmed their Westerns in the Hollywood hills, or east toward San Bernadino. Rare were the filmmakers these days who ventured onto the reservation and used real Indians to tell their stories—of attacks on the settler's cabin, of attacks on the Deadwood Stage, of harassing Pony-Express riders, and of the ever-present fights with the U.S. Cavalry.

Fifty years after the first performance in Omaha, the Bureau no longer objected to Indian employment in Wild West shows. By 1933, however, Show Indians had few opportunities to work full time. The heyday of Show Indians in the arena had passed. Thereafter, for well or ill, the images of American Indians would be shaped on motion-picture screens and, later still, on television screens. On rare occasions, Indians got to play themselves.

As much as anything else, Wild West shows had brought to the American people visions not only of the past, but also of the present, of Indian ceremonialism and Indian identity. For many years the Wild West show was the only place where other Americans could see American Indians. Buffalo Bill had invited the patrons of his show to tour the Indian encampment, to listen to what Indians had to say, and to see how they lived. In a way, he invited more intimate human contact, that welcome fire of hand touching hand. Friendship and understanding might result. Even someone as challenged as Phyllis Crandall Connor knew that however menacing the Indian seemed to appear on the surface, he or she might still be friendly.

Buffalo Bill's Wild West celebrated the courage, honor, and character of American Indians. Out of the Wild West show came the modern rodeo and powwow, where western skill and western artistry were displayed and rewarded. In the case of the powwow, it also became a means by which people could retain, restore, or, in certain instances, create through adaptation a modern Indian identity. The shows had provided an opportunity for Indians, not so much to play a role, but simply to be themselves. Indians shot from horseback, the dominant image of Western films, was hardly the only or indeed the most important contribution of the Wild West show to American culture. It was in the Wild West shows that people got to see firsthand Indians being Indians—cultural persistence across the generations. Before World War I, Buffalo Bill's Wild West show, and the imitators he spawned, helped to get Indians off the reservation, paid them a living

in London.
Dec. 1923.

Goes in Lodge. Louis Nethersole

68 : *Goes in Lodge, a Northern Arapaho, shaking hands with Louis Nethersole at Forest Park in London, December 1923, during an international convention of boy scouts. (Fremont County Pioneers' Museum, Lander, Wyoming)*

wage, kept them in the public eye, and freed some from the unremitting cultural repression of the Bureau of Indian Affairs and its Christian humanitarian friends.[77] Show Indians were not responsible for the Native American cultural renaissance that began in earnest in the 1930s; but they contributed to it by creating and sustaining powerful images of real Indians from real places in the American West. For many years, Show Indians had played to a full house.

EPILOGUE

On the afternoon of Wednesday, May 5, 1938, in a field not far from Union Station in Washington, D.C., Colonel Tim McCoy surveyed the folded canvas and scattered equipment of his Wild West show. It had been on the road for less than a month. The day before, a group of investors from Providence, Rhode Island, owed 17,500 dollars, had petitioned the show into receivership. McCoy seemed, a *Washington Times* reporter wrote, the "most tragic figure on the circus lot."[1] The Sioux and Northern Cheyenne performers headed for the office of Commissioner Collier to arrange their return to Pine Ridge. Some of the other employees, with saddles and suitcases loaded on their arms, thumbed rides out of town. The receivers hired a couple of wranglers off the lot to move the four hundred head of horses and other livestock to the old Bennings racetrack.

"I don't think folks have lost faith in the Wild West," McCoy mused aloud, "I guess we are folding because business generally is bad." As he turned away from the wreckage of his 300,000-dollar investment, representing most of his fortune made in Western films, cowgirls and cowboys surrounded him. The women hugged him as the men patted his shoulders. The colonel left for a friend's estate in rural Virginia.[2]

McCoy, though, had misjudged popular tastes. The public had indeed tired of the Wild West of the arena. Crowds no longer thrilled to scenes of other days, of the "Winning of the West," of Indians attacking the ubiquitous Deadwood stage, or of Colonel Tim talking in signs to the Cheyenne and Sioux performers. Like Cody's organization, McCoy's Wild West rejected a circus sideshow in favor of an Indian village open to the public. Like Catlin's gallery, experts, though non-Indians, lectured on Indian lives.[3] As one critic for *Time Magazine* observed, however, it all fell flat. The show needed more rodeo and less narration, many more examples of bulldogging and fewer historical reenactments such as the one commemorating the completion of the transcontinental railroad and the driving of the golden spike. The show lacked the excitement, the fun, and the unreality of the cinema. Amazed that the "pageantry stuff" failed as a crowd pleaser, McCoy nevertheless insisted that, like candles and Christmas, "it had to be there."[4] His show folded, an editor at *Time* observed, "a martyr to McCoy's belief that the Buffalo Bill tradition still has life in it."[5]

McCoy consoled himself in the belief, as he remarked in his memoirs, that the end of his Wild West show did not necessarily signal ringing down the curtain on the genre. After vacationing in Virginia with friends, he returned to Hollywood and began a series of eight pictures entitled *The Rough Riders*, with Buck Jones and Raymond Hatton.[6] Films indeed sustained and then vulgarized the images that the Wild West shows had created. Indians, however, only occasionally participated. Any number of white Hollywood actors, men and women, found work playing Indians. Colonel Cummins and Trader Barten had been right after all. Costumes created the identity, not persons and their histories.

In the years since Tim McCoy literally folded his tents, the ultimate absurdity of caricature may have been reached in the Disney feature-length cartoon version of *Peter Pan* (1952). Disney's porcine Show Indians speak in a language of severely challenged Carlisle dropouts while the lost boys ask the musical question, "What made the red man red?"[7] No mythologizing of history could make the Show Indians of Buffalo Bill's Wild West the animated residents of Never Land.

What films could not do, as in the Cody and McCoy shows, was to provide their audiences with an opportunity, once the lights went up in the theater, to visit the Indian encampment. The Indians on the screen had been the only reality. In the Indian village, other Americans could see and hear some of the first Americans, not as curiosities or "delegates from the Neolithic," but rather as people with vibrant cultures.[8]

The era of the Show Indians passed during the depression decade. By the 1990s, a few Indian actors maintained some of the traditions of the profession, of Indians playing Indians, and re-creating portions of their history and cultural heritage. The success of such films as *Dances With Wolves*, *Pow Wow Highway*, *Thunderheart*, *The Last of the Mohicans*, and *Geronimo* suggested renewed interest by the general public in sympathetic and largely positive portrayals of American Indians. The other tradition of Show Indians, of the pageantry of the dance—whether in the arena at Erastina, or the competition among dancers at Pine Ridge agency and Rushville, Nebraska, as they vied with one another for a contract—found expression in the modern powwow and the "Masking Indian" traditions of the African-American Mardi Gras in New Orleans.[9] The powwow especially, an institution of inter-tribal ceremonialism and celebration, became both an evocation of culture and a means of creating an adaptive culture for those Indian nations long separated from their landed heritage.

Attempts to re-create the Wild West show have met with modest success. In this regard, Tim McCoy may have been prescient. Even with the failure of his show, he believed that the public had not abandoned its affection for the Wild West show and the unique history it portrayed. In its

69 : *Charlie Bell and family, Northern Arapahos from Wind River, appeared as Show Indians in London, December 1923, during the international boy scout convention. (Fremont County Pioneers' Museum, Lander, Wyoming)*

1990s incarnation, however, the Wild West show production—as distinguished from the West of the theme park, the regional "frontier" cities or villages—commemorated the show itself. It represented a nostalgia for the show more than for the history presumably re-created in the show. On Memorial Day 1988, and for the next six years on that holiday, Pawnee Bill's Wild West Show, "The Amusement Triumph of the Age" according to its promotional literature, reappeared at Pawnee Bill State Park operated by the Oklahoma Historical Society just outside Pawnee.[10] Visitors went to experience the Wild West show, not the Wild West.

In the summer of 1994, Discoveryland!, Tulsa's producer of the Broadway show "Oklahoma!" for eighteen years, agreed to present the Pawnee Bill show at the historic Pawnee Bill Ranch for ten weekends between June and August. "The Wild West Show staged by Discoveryland! will be performed in the same spirit of the original show," explained the director. "It will contain many of the same 'wild west' acts depending on the availability of talent." It was the hope of the proprietors of Discoveryland! and the officers of the Oklahoma Historical Society that both the park and the show would become a "tourism destination."[11]

The Wild West Show, just as the American Civil War, had become a subject for reenactment. Reenactments, according to Greg Dening, "tend to hallucinate a past as merely the present in funny dress."[12] Yet in the very act of dressing up, the participants signal a kinship with a ritualized cultural memory. It is more than fantasizing the present in whimsical attire. Although no one in the re-creation of the Pawnee Bill Wild West had a memory of life when the West was supposedly wild, they nevertheless had a larger tradition upon which to draw. Left unanswered at the time was whether a younger generation of Show Indians might find summer employment as had their great grandparents.

Anne M. Butler suggests in *The Oxford History of the American West* that the Show Indians who raced into the arena alongside Buffalo Bill and other entrepreneurs demonstrated colorfully that twentieth-century forces of commercial capitalism marginalized native peoples. From the 1880s on, Indians found themselves in a fixed and ungenerous economic structure. They accepted one of the few jobs they could find, as entertainers. For much of the twentieth century economic opportunities for Indians rarely broadened and typically centered on their willingness to "play" Indians.[13] As just one among many native peoples, Indians may indeed have been marginalized by the American "economic structure." Yet they found in the Wild West shows a means to evoke and even to celebrate their cultures. "Playing" Indian could also be viewed as defiance.

Indian commissioners and humanitarian reformers certainly saw Indian participation in the shows as a stubborn refusal to abandon their cultures. Vine Deloria observes that Buffalo Bill and the first generation of Show Indians spent their declining years playacting the exploits of their youth. "Perhaps they realized in the deepest sense, that even a caricature of their youth was preferable to a complete surrender to the homogeni-

70 : *Buffalo Bill Cody at Ocean Beach, San Francisco, just south of the Cliff House, 1908. (Colorado Historical Society)*

zation that was overtaking American society."[14] For fifty years, the only place to be an Indian—and defiantly so—and still remain relatively free from the interference of missionaries, teachers, agents, humanitarians, and politicians was in the Wild West show.

Wild West shows, as Richard Slotkin reminds us, were not reality. They created "mythic" spaces that blended reality and legend, past and present. They ritualized history by acting out the myths that had been made of history.[15] For half a century, Indians participated in the creation of that newer history. Many of the negative stereotypes about Indians, on the other hand, were driven "deep into the collective American psyche,"[16] according to Deloria, by movies and the dime-novel literary tradition only after the Show Indians had been driven from the arena and off the silver screen by the economics of popular taste.

Ethnic identity need not be preserved through isolation; it may also be promoted through contact. Commissioner Morgan, Amy Leslie, and others had assumed that the Lakota—and by extension all Indians who sojourned with the shows—would be so awed by the world outside the reservation that they would abandon their cultures in favor of the one they had recently experienced. But contact strengthened rather than weakened culture. American Horse and Sitting Bull, to name just two Show Indians, found themselves drawn back to their own cultures by their travels with Buffalo Bill. At the same time, other Indians in the shows could discover and then nurture a common "Indian" identity (as they had done in the Ghost Dance) without weakening tribal ties. It would be wrong therefore to see the Show Indians as simply dupes, or pawns, or even victims. It would be better to approach them as persons who earned a fairly good living between the era of the Dawes Act and the Indian New Deal playing themselves, re-creating a very small portion of their histories, and enjoying it. As Joe Rockboy, an Ihanktonwan-Sicangu Sioux, explained about his job in Wild West shows during the early years of the twentieth century, "It gave me a chance to get back on a horse and act it out again." And at the end of the performance, to ride into the arena and to hear again the sounds of celebration and approval in the applause of the crowd.[17]

Acronyms and Abbreviations Used in the Notes

AAA	Assumption Abbey Archives
BBHC	Buffalo Bill Historical Center
CHS	State Historical Society of Colorado
CIA	Commissioner of Indian Affairs
Col.	Collection
Corres.	Correspondence
CUA	Consolidated Ute Agency
D	Denver
Div.	Division
DPL	Denver Public Library
FARC	Federal Archives and Records Center
IRA	Indian Rights Association
ISHD	Iowa State Historical Department
KC	Kansas City
LR	Letters Received
LS	Letters Sent
MDF	Main Decimal File
NA	National Archives and Records Service
n.d.	no date
n.p.	no page
NSHS	Nebraska State Historical Society
OHS	Oklahoma Historical Society
OSU	Oklahoma State University
OU	University of Oklahoma
PR	Pine Ridge reservation
RG	Record Group
SDSHS	South Dakota State Historical Society
SFA	Sac and Fox agency
WNIA	Women's National Indian Association

NOTES

INTRODUCTION

1 Reproductions of posters and other advertisements appear in various printed programs from the 1883 season found in William F. Cody Collection, Box 1, Western History Department, Denver Public Library, Denver, Colo. (cited hereafter as Cody Collection, DPL).

2 Hartford *Courant*, quoted in Henry Blackmen Sell and Victor Weybright, *Buffalo Bill and the Wild West* (Basin, Wyo.: Big Horn Books, 1979), 135–36.

3 Significant examinations of European and American images of Indians, including extensive notes to the literature, are Robert F. Berkhofer, Jr., *The White Man's Indian: Images of the American Indian from Columbus to the Present* (New York: Alfred A. Knopf, 1978), especially his discussion of "savagery," 10–22; and Brian W. Dippie, *The Vanishing American: White Attitudes and U.S. Indian Policy* (Middletown, Conn.: Wesleyan University Press, 1982).

4 Francis Paul Prucha, *The Great Father: The United States and the American Indians*, (Lincoln: University of Nebraska Press, 1984), 1: 8.

5 See Bernard W. Sheehan, *Savagism and Civility: Indians and Englishmen in Colonial Virginia* (Cambridge: Cambridge University Press, 1980); and, for a contrasting viewpoint, Karen Ordahl Kupperman, *Settling with the Indians: The Meeting of English and Indian Cultures in America, 1580-1640* (Totowa, N.J.: Rowman and Littlefield, 1980).

6 Prucha, *Great Father*, 1: 7–8.

7 See the chapter on "Paternalism" in Francis Paul Prucha, *The Indians in American Society: From the Revolutionary War to the Present* (Berkeley: University of California Press, 1985), 1–27.

8 The phrase, "a wild region inhabited by wild men," though used in a different context, belongs to Roy Harvey Pearce, *Savagism and Civilization: A Study of the Indian and the American Mind* (Baltimore: Johns Hopkins University Press, 1967), 3.

9 On December 21, 1866, Lt. Col. William J. Fetterman and eighty soldiers rode out from uncompleted Fort Phil Kearney to relieve a beleaguered wood train. The fort was being built along the Powder River road to protect travelers on their way to the gold fields of Montana. Oglala Lakota, probably under the leadership of Crazy Horse, wiped out Fetterman's command. The "Fetterman Massacre," as Euroamericans called it, was the greatest disaster to befall the army in the Far West up to that time. See James C. Olson, *Red Cloud and the Sioux Problem* (Lincoln: University of Nebraska Press, 1965), 50–51.

10 See Richard Slotkin, *Regeneration through Violence: The Mythology of*

the *American Frontier, 1600–1860* (Middletown, Conn.: Wesleyan University Press, 1973), 564–65.

11 Quoted in Ralph E. Friar and Natasha A. Friar, *The Only Good Indian . . . : The Hollywood Gospel* (New York: Drama Book Specialists/Publishers, 1972), p. 67. Chauncey Yellow Robe continued to denounce the shows. See his short commentary, "The Menace of the Wild West Show," *Quarterly Journal of the Society of American Indians*, 2 (1914):224–25. He is identified as a Brule in T. Emogene Paulson and Lloyd R. Moses, *Who's Who among the Sioux* (Vermillion, S.D.: Institute of Indian Studies, 1988), 274.

12 Friar and Friar, *The Only Good Indian*, 57.

13 Raymond William Stedman, *Shadows of the Indians: Stereotypes in American Culture* (Norman: University of Oklahoma Press, 1982), 79–80.

14 Ibid., 244.

15 Gretchen M. Bataille and Charles L. P. Silet, eds., *The Pretend Indians: Images of Native Americans in the Movies* (Ames: Iowa State University Press, 1980), xxii.

16 Donald L. Kaufmann, "The Indian as Media Hand-me-down," in Bataille and Silet, eds., *Pretend Indians*, 22.

17 Ibid., 26–27.

18 The phrase, if not the immediate context, is taken from Friar and Friar, *Only Good Indian*, 70.

19 Jon Tuska, *The American West in Film: Critical Approaches to the Western* (Westport, Conn.: Greenwood Press, 1985), 260.

20 Ibid., 237.

21 Aside from Sitting Bull, a Hunkpapa holy man, who traveled briefly with Buffalo Bill in 1885, two of the more famous showmen are Black Elk, an Oglala, and Luther Standing Bear, a Brule. See Raymond J. DeMallie, ed., *The Sixth Grandfather: Black Elk's Teachings Given to John G. Neihardt* (Lincoln: University of Nebraska Press, 1984), 7–11, 72, 245–51; and Luther Standing Bear, *My People the Sioux* (Lincoln: University of Nebraska Press, 1975), passim. See also Richard N. Ellis, "Luther Standing Bear," in L. G. Moses and Raymond Wilson, eds., *Indian Lives: Essays on Nineteenth- and Twentieth-Century Native American Leaders*, rev. ed. (Albuquerque: University of New Mexico Press, 1993), 139–57.

22 Information taken from Commissioner of Indian Affairs (hereafter cited as CIA) to Hugh Gallagher, agent, Pine Ridge Reservation, Aug. 6, 12, 1889, and Jan. 27, 1890, Records of Pine Ridge Reservation (hereafter, PR), General Records, Series 2, box 9, Records of the Bureau of Indian Affairs, Record Group Seventy-Five (hereafter, RG 75), Federal Archives and Records Center, Kansas City, Mo. (cited hereafter as FARC, KC). Other examples of yearly salaries among employees at Pine Ridge Reservation are: captain of Indian policy, 144 dollars; agency interpreter, 500 dollars; day-school teacher, 600 dollars; and agency physician, 1,200 dollars.

23 John Burke to CIA, n.d. (ca. 1886), Records of the CIA, Letters Received (hereafter cited as LR), No. 5564–1886, National Archives and Records Service (hereafter cited as NA), Washington, D.C.

CHAPTER ONE

1 Carolyn Thomas Foreman, *Indians Abroad, 1493–1928* (Norman: University of Oklahoma Press, 1943), xix.

2 Richard Slotkin, "The Wild West," in David H. Katzive et al., *Buffalo Bill and the Wild West* (New York: The Brooklyn Museum, 1981), 27.

3 See William Cronon, "Revisiting the Vanishing Frontier: The Legacy of Frederick Jackson Turner," *Western Historical Quarterly* 18 (April 1987):157–76, as one of the more recent critiques of the "Turner Thesis." It is also a highly readable introduction to the vast literature on the subject.

4 Frederick Jackson Turner, "The Significance of the Frontier in American History," in *Annual Report of the American Historical Association for the Year 1893* (Washington, D.C., 1894), 179.

5 Slotkin, "Wild West," 27.

6 Cronon, "Revisiting the Vanishing Frontier," 157.

7 Richard Slotkin, *Gunfighter Nation: The Myth of the Frontier in Twentieth-Century America* (New York: Harper Perennial, 1992), 81.

8 Berkhofer, *White Man's Indian*, 86–87.

9 Ibid., 80.

10 Quoted in A. Irving Hallowell, "The Beginnings of Anthropology in America," in Frederica DeLaguna, ed., *Selected Papers from the American Anthropologist, 1888–1920* (Evanston, Ill.: Row and Peterson, 1960), 25.

11 Ibid., 18.

12 For an extended discussion of the expedition's collection of ethnographic information, see James P. Ronda, *Lewis and Clark among the Indians* (Lincoln: University of Nebraska Press, 1984).

13 Paul L. Reddin, "Wild West Shows: A Study in the Development of Western Romanticism" (Ph.D. diss., University of Missouri, 1970), 8.

14 Ibid., 9.

15 Quoted in Berkhofer, *White Man's Indian*, 89.

16 Quoted in Reddin, "Wild West Shows," 20.

17 Ibid., 20.

18 Prucha, *Great Father*, 1: 89–114, 179–214.

19 Peter H. Hassrick, "The Artists," in Katzive, *Buffalo Bill and the Wild West*, 18.

20 Reddin, "Wild West Shows," 38–39; and Hassrick, "Artists," 19.

21 New York *Morning Herald*, Oct. 4, 1837, quoted in Hassrick, "Artists," 20.

22 Reddin, "Wild West Shows," 39.

23 Michael M. Mooney, ed., *George Catlin: Letters and Notes on the North American Indians* (New York: Clarkson N. Potter, 1975), 6. See also Hassrick, "Artists," 20. Paul Reddin writes at the close of his introduction: "Catlin's ideas themselves would have been less important if he had not undertaken a campaign to sell his Indian artifacts and paintings to the American government. In the process of publicizing his collection, he created the first Wild West show." Reddin, "Wild West Shows," 30.

24 Mooney, *George Catlin*, 61; and Marjorie Catlin Roehm, *The Letters of George Catlin and His Family: A Chronicle of the American West* (Berkeley: University of California Press, 1966), 146–47.

25 Reddin, "Wild West Shows," 49.

26 Loyd Haberly, *Pursuit of the Horizon: A Life of George Catlin, Painter and recorder of the American Indian* (New York: Macmillan Co., 1948), 135.

27 Reddin, "Wild West Shows," 50; Mooney, *George Catlin*, 63–64; and Foreman, *Indians Abroad*, 166–67.

28 Mooney, *George Catlin*, 66–67.

29 Reddin, "Wild West Shows," 20, 60, 66.

30 L. G. Moses, "Wild West Shows, Reformers, and the Image of the American Indian, 1887–1914," *South Dakota History* 14 (Fall 1984):195.

31 Paul Fees, "The Flamboyant Fraternity," *The Gilcrease Magazine of American History and Art* 6 (January 1984):1, 5.

32 Slotkin, "Wild West," 31.

33 As an example, Indians performed in Hartford, Connecticut, with "A. Mann and Company" on June 3 and 4, 1840. According to the advertisement, the group included Comanches, Sacs, "Esquimaux," and Winnebagos. Whether the troupe displayed such a diverse tribal group is unknown. The advertisement nevertheless stressed the unique aspects of the exhibition. For twenty-five cents, the customer could listen to war songs and watch dances of the performers, all of whom wore their native costumes. In 1870, "Washburn's Sensation" played at Robert's Opera House. A small band of unidentified Indians danced and demonstrated arrow shooting. In 1878, Buffalo Bill appeared in "The Red Right Hand; or Buffalo Bill's First Scalp for Custer"—a melodrama based upon his killing of a Cheyenne, Yellow Hand (or Hair), at War Bonnet Creek during the summer of 1876. An Indian, probably a Pawnee, played the part of Yellow Hand. The information is taken from a clipping of the *Hartford Courier*, July 19, 1927, in the Gordon W. Lillie Papers, 1911–1943, box 11, Western History Collections, University of Oklahoma Library, Norman (hereafter cited as Lillie Papers, OU). For an explanation of Cody's encounter with Yellow Hand, see Don Russell, *The Lives and Legends of Buffalo Bill* (Norman: University of Oklahoma Press, 1960), 214–30.

34 Arrell M. Gibson, "Medicine Show," *The American West* 4 (February 1967): 36, 76.

35 Philip Borden, "Found Cumbering the Soil: Manifest Destiny and the Indian in

the Nineteenth Century," in Gary B. Nash and Richard Weiss, eds., *The Great Fear: Race in the Mind of America* (New York: Holt, Rinehart and Winston, 1970), 72.

36 John C. Ewers, "The Emergence of the Plains Indian as the Symbol of the North American Indian," in Roger L. Nichols, ed., *The American Indian: Past and Present*, 2d ed. (New York: John Wiley and Sons, 1981), 10.

37 Ibid.

38 According to Richard White, Buffalo Bill literally brought images to life. Whereas books, or art, or ever other shows offered only words, pictures, or white actors, Cody presented real Indians, who now inhabited their own representations. This, White suggests, was the most complex reproduction: "Indians were imitating imitations of themselves. They reenacted white versions of events in which some of them had actually participated." In this way, Cody's Wild West as history prefigured the historical images in motions pictures. For countless Americans—and eventually Europeans—his representation of the West became the reality. "The genius of Buffalo Bill," White concludes, "was to recognize the power of the mimetic, of the imitation, in the modern world." Richard White, "Frederick Jackson Turner and Buffalo Bill," in James R. Grossman, ed., *The Frontier in American Culture: An Exhibition at the Newberry Library, August 26, 1994-January 7, 1995 / Essays by Richard White and Patricia Nelson Limerick* (Berkeley: University of California Press, 1994), 35.

CHAPTER TWO

1 In addition to those Indians who performed in melodramas, medicine shows, and circuses, a few traveled with shows that could best be described as exposition companies. As an example of the latter, Edward T. Basye toured the country in the early 1880s with his "Great Extra Attractions," which could be secured for large picnics, barbecues, and according to the handbill, "general public Celebration[s]." Basye would rent a fairground or park and charge ten cents admission to customers who would bring along their picnic baskets. Inside the park, the revelers would be entertained with demonstrations of trick shooting, roping, and knife throwing. Indians would perform a game of lacrosse that would last "from thirty minutes to three hours—as the occasion may require. These indians [*sic*] (40 in all including Squaws and Papooses) are genuine Western Indians in charge of a Government Indian agent." "Description of My New Show," ca. 1882, found in Ed. T. Basye to U.S. Indian Agent, Quapaw Agency, Feb. 14, 1882, Quapaw Agency Fair Files, microfilm, roll 17, Indian Archives Division, Oklahoma Historical Society (hereafter, OHS), Oklahoma City.

2 Richard J. Walsh, in collaboration with Milton S. Salsbury, *The Making of Buffalo Bill: A Study in Heroics* (Indianapolis, Ind.: The Bobbs-Merrill Co., 1928), 217.

3 For the development of the modern rodeo, see Kristine Fredriksson, *American Rodeo: From Buffalo Bill to Big Business* (College Station, Tex.: Texas A&M Press, 1985), 7–20.

4 Walsh, *Making of Buffalo Bill*, 218.

5 Sarah J. Blackstone, *Buckskins, Bullets, and Business: A History of Buffalo Bill's Wild West* (Westport, Conn.: Greenwood Press, 1986), 13.

6 Carver to Thorp, Feb. 16, 1927, in William Frank Carver Papers, folder 1, Nebraska State Historical Society (hereafter cited as NSHS), Lincoln, Nebraska.

7 Reddin, "Wild West Shows," 82.

8 1883 Program, Cody Collection, DPL. See also Blackstone, *Buckskins, Bullets, and Business*, 14.

9 Quoted in L. O. Leonard, "Buffalo Bill's First Wild West Rehearsal," *The Union Pacific Magazine* (August 1922):26–27; and Nellie Snyder Yost, *Buffalo Bill: His Family, Friends, Fame, Failures, and Fortunes* (Chicago: Swallow Press, 1979), 133.

10 Walsh, *Making of Buffalo Bill*, 229–31.

11 Russell, *Lives and Legends of Buffalo Bill*, 292. The fifty circuses that toured in 1885 represented the greatest number ever in the United States.

12 Yost, *Buffalo Bill*, 143.

13 Ibid. Yost identifies the eyewitness as "Death Valley Scotty."

14 When the Great Sioux Reservation was established by treaty in 1868, Standing Rock and Cheyenne River agencies were located on the Missouri River. Red Cloud and Spotted Tail agencies were located farther west, and were actually placed in Nebraska, south of the reservation boundary. Following the Sioux "War" of 1876, the Indian Office transferred Red Cloud agency to Pine Ridge, and Spotted Tail became Rosebud agency, both within the reservation itself. At the time of the breakup of the Great Sioux Reservation in 1889, the agencies, such as Pine Ridge and Rosebud, became the names of the reservations. The six "western" Sioux reservations were Pine Ridge, Rosebud, Crow Creek, Lower Brule, Standing Rock, and Cheyenne River reservations. For an explanation of changing boundaries of the Great Sioux Reservation, see Robert M. Utley, *The Last Days of the Sioux Nation* (New Haven, Conn.: Yale University Press, 1963), 42, 63.

15 Ewers, "Emergence of the Plains Indian," 9–10.

16 Louis Pfaller, "'Enemies in '76, Friends in '85'—Sitting Bull and Buffalo Bill," *Prologue* 1 (Fall 1969):17.

17 Ibid., 20–21.

18 Telegram: Cody to Secretary of the Interior, Apr. 29, 1885, Records of the CIA, LR, No. 9429–1885, RG 75, NA.

19 CIA to Cody, May 2, 1885, quoted in Pfaller, "'Enemies in '76, Friends in '85'" 21. See also Cody to Lamar, May 2, 1885, Records of the CIA, LR, No. 10488–1885, RG 75, NA.

20 Cody to CIA, May [14], 1885, Records of the CIA, LR, No. 11212–1885, RG 75, NA.

21 Pfaller, " 'Enemies in '76, Friends in '85,' " 21.

22 Joseph G. Rosa and Robin May, *Buffalo Bill and His Wild West: A Pictorial Biography* (Lawrence: University Press of Kansas, 1989), 89.

23 Walsh, *Making of Buffalo Bill*, 255.

24 Stanley Vestal, *Sitting Bull, Champion of the Sioux: A Biography* (Norman: University of Oklahoma Press, 1957), 250; and Pfaller, " 'Enemies in '76, Friends in '85,' " 23. Sitting Bull had insisted in his contract, negotiated by "Arizona John" Burke, that he have the exclusive right to sell his photograph. See also Robert M. Utley, *The Lance and the Shield: The Life and Times of Sitting Bull* (New York: Henry Holt and Co., 1993), 265.

25 Vestal, *Sitting Bull*, 251.

26 Walsh, *Making of Buffalo Bill*, 256.

27 Salsbury to Herbert Welsh, May 18, 1891, The Mary C. Collins Family Papers, folder 48: "Wild West Shows," South Dakota State Historical Society, Pierre, S.D. (cited hereafter as Collins Papers, SDSHS).

28 Quoted in Walsh, *Making of Buffalo Bill*, 256.

29 Quoted in Vestall, *Sitting Bull*, 250. See also Russell, *Lives and Legends of Buffalo Bill*, 316–17.

30 Pfaller, " 'Enemies in '76, Friends in '85,' " 26.

31 Vestal, *Sitting Bull*, 251.

32 Announcement: "Buffalo Bill's Wild West," Buffalo Bill Cody Scrapbook, William Frederick Cody Papers, 1887–1919, The State Historical Society of Colorado (cited hereafter as CHS, an abbreviation for "Colorado Historical Society"), Denver, Colo. Although identified as the Cody Scrapbook, the book was actually kept by Robert "Pony Bob" Haslam, a longtime member of Cody's Wild West. When acquired by the CHS, it was placed in the Cody Papers.

33 Ibid.

34 Yost, *Buffalo Bill*, 156.

35 Blackstone, *Buckskins, Bullets, and Business*, 16.

36 Ibid., 19.

37 McLaughlin to Burke, April 16, 1886, Maj. James McLaughlin Papers, Correspondence and Miscellaneous Papers, 1855–1937, microfilm edition, roll 20, frames 479–80, Assumption Abbey Archives (AAA), Richardton, North Dakota (cited hereafter as McLaughlin Papers, AAA). Microfilm edition courtesy of the SDSHS.

38 Ibid.

39 Contract: Cody and Salsbury, April 21, 1886, sent to Washington in McGillycuddy to CIA, May 1, 1886, Records of the CIA, LR, No. 13400–1886, RG 75, NA.

40 Ibid.

41 Ibid.

42 Cody to Lamar, Oct. 11, 1889, Records of the CIA, LR, No. 27648–1886, RG 75, NA.

43 Assistant Secretary of the Interior to CIA, Oct. 26, 1886, Records of the CIA, LR, No. 14044–1886, RG 75, NA.

44 Sell and Weybright, *Buffalo Bill and the Wild West*, 148–51; Rosa and May, *Buffalo Bill and His Wild West*, 92; Yost, *Buffalo Bill*, 171; Russell, *Lives and Legends of Buffalo Bill*, 318; and Shirley A. Leckie, *Elizabeth Bacon Custer and the Making of a Myth* (Norman: University of Oklahoma Press, 1993), 246–47.

45 Quoted in Walsh, *Making of Buffalo Bill*, 257.

46 Ibid.

47 Contracts: Dec. 17, 1886, and Jan. 17, 1887, Records of the CIA, LR, No. 9855–1887, RG 75, NA. In January, the Sioux Red Shirt, Yellow Horse, Kills Plenty, American Bear, and Wounds One Another joined the show at twenty-five dollars per month. A missionary, paid sixty dollars a month, accompanied the showmen to Madison Square Garden.

48 Reddin, "Wild West Shows," 99; and Blackstone, *Buckskins, Bullets, and Business*, 18.

49 Walsh, *Making of Buffalo Bill*, 262.

50 Blackstone, *Buckskin, Bullets, and Business*, 19; and Rosa and May, *Buffalo Bill and His Wild West*, 92.

51 Blackstone, *Buckskin, Bullets, and Business*, 19.

52 Ibid.

53 Ibid., 20.

54 Walsh, *Making of Buffalo Bill*, 262.

55 Blackstone, *Buckskin, Bullets, and Business*, 20. Richard Slotkin aptly observes that "Custer's Last Fight" became the center of a reorganized program. Unlike the other fights with Indians, Custer's last battle referred to a struggle that was as yet incomplete. Bands of Chiricahua Apaches still inhabited mountain strongholds in the Sierra Madre, and many of the victors of the Little Bighorn lived "uneasily on the reservation." Cody's role in the tableau was, according to Slotkin, both "self-abnegating and self-aggrandizing." His suggestion that he might have saved Custer was clearly pretense; but, more important, Cody assumed the role of elegiac commentator, no longer acting the role of stage avenger holding aloft the bloody first scalp for Custer (though later, the misnamed Battle of War Bonnet Creek would be added to both Cody's Wild West and Cody's epic film). Custer's Last Stand was not only the last act of the Wild West show, but symbolically an elegy for the *entire* period of American pioneering. See Slotkin, *Gunfighter Nation*, 76, 79.

Richard White suggests that Cody showed a certain genius at using frontier iconography. He exploited the American talent for mass-producing imitations of an original. Buffalo Bill turned such icons of the western frontier as the six-shooter, stagecoach, settler's log cabin (adapted from the wooded East and somewhat out of place in the treeless prairies), and menacing Indians, into so many stage props. He re-created himself "as a walking icon, at once real and make believe." In Custer's defeat, Buffalo Bill helped to create the greatest icon of all, that of the conquering victim. Custer the victimizer became instead the victim; and Cody his chief avenger. The nation, led by such heros as Buffalo Bill, retaliated against the perpetrators of the slaughter. The Indians afterward surrendered their lands and roving ways. The story Cody retold countless times in the Wild West gained credence as Indians endorsed it with their participation. Cody, presumably, had lived that history; and Indians who had fought Custer at the Greasy Grass also attacked him, twice a day, in the arena. White, "Frederick Jackson Turner and Buffalo Bill," 11, 29, 32.

56 G. H. Bates to CIA, Dec. 31, 1886, Records of the CIA, LR, No. 34611–1886, RG 75, NA.

57 Unidentified newspaper clipping: n.d., in G. H. Bates to CIA, Jan. 13, 1887, Records of the CIA, LR, No. 1296–1887, RG 75, NA. A few of Cody's Indians may also have appeared in a theatrical production before the opening of "The Drama of Civilization." Sioux and Pawnees performed at the People's Theatre for one week, beginning January 3, in John Stone's five-act play *Metamora*, staring Edmund Collier as the Wampanoag sachem. Cody's Indians, who spoke no lines and only had to look the part, appeared as Metamora's followers. Unidentified newspaper clipping: n.d., in the William Frederick Cody Collection, box 2, folder 6, Buffalo Bill Historical Center (BBHC), Cody, Wyoming (cited hereafter as Cody Collection, BBHC).

58 Newspaper clipping: "After Buffalo Bill's Scalp," *The World* (N.Y.), n.d., in G. H. Bates to Secretary of the Interior, Jan. 11, 1887, Records of the CIA, LR, No. 1124–1887, RG 75, NA.

59 Ibid.

60 Unidentified newspaper clipping: n.d., in Capt. Alex S. Williams, New York Municipal Police, to Secretary of the Interior, Jan. 14, 1887, Records of the CIA, LR, No. 1881–1887, RG 75, NA. "No scandal, quarrells, arrests or viciousness has been developed," Captain Williams informed the secretary. "As to the Indians I can testify to the guardianship held over their conduct and also to the admirable manner in which they have conducted themselves."

61 Ibid.

62 Ibid.

63 Ibid.

64 Acting Secretary of the Interior to G. W. Lillie, April 21, 1887, Records of the CIA, Letters Sent (hereafter cited as LS), No. 2141–1887, RG 75, NA.

65 Quoted in Yost, *Buffalo Bill*, 173.

66 Quoted in Russell, *Lives and Legends of Buffalo Bill*, 323.

67 Sell and Weybright, *Buffalo Bill and the Wild West*, 159.

68 See Rita G. Napier, "Across the Big Water: American Indians' Perceptions of Europe and Europeans, 1887–1906," in Christian F. Feest, ed., *Indians and*

Europe: An Interdisciplinary Collection of Essays (Aachen, the Netherlands: Rader Verlag, 1987), 398.

CHAPTER THREE

1 Don Russell, *The Wild West: A History of the Wild West Shows* (Fort Worth, Tex.: Amon Carter Museum of Western Art, 1970), 26; and Yost, *Buffalo Bill*, 185.

2 Sell and Weybright, *Buffalo Bill and the Wild West*, 159. Paulson and Moses, in *Who's Who among the Sioux*, 193, identify Red Shirt as "a full-blooded Brule Sioux." He and his band, however, in the 1880s and 1890s lived just south of the Pine Ridge agency, among the Oglalas. A number of Brules had joined the Oglalas in the 1850s. For an explanation of Brules living among the Oglalas, see Utley, *Last Days of the Sioux Nation*, 78–79, 137, 272–73.

3 Newspaper clipping: London *Daily News*, April 16, 1887, in Johnny Baker Scrapbook, 1887, Cody Collection, DPL. See also Russell, *Lives and Legends of Buffalo Bill*, 327. Most sources, usually citing the autobiography of Buffalo Bill, state that one horse died during the voyage to England. Black Elk, an Oglala visionary in the Indian party, remarked that some of the buffalo and elk died and had to be thrown overboard. The dead buffalo especially saddened Black Elk, who commented that he felt as if he and the other Sioux were throwing part of the Indians' power overboard. See DeMallie, *Sixth Grandfather*, 248.

4 Reddin, "Wild West Shows," 106; and William Frederick Cody, *The Story of the Wild West and Campfire Chats* (Philadelphia: Historical Publications Co., 1888), 710.

5 Blackstone, *Buckskins, Bullets, and Business*, 22.

6 *The Sheffield Leader*, May 5, 1887, quoted in Napier, "Across the Big Water," 383.

7 Quoted in Walsh, *Making of Buffalo Bill*, 264–65.

8 See DeMallie, *Sixth Grandfather*, 248.

9 Napier, "Across the Big Water," 385. Black Elk's words appear in John G. Neihardt, *Black Elk Speaks: Being the Life Story of a Holy Man of the Oglala Sioux* (Lincoln: University of Nebraska Press, 1961), 221.

10 DeMallie, *Sixth Grandfather*, 246.

11 Napier, "Across the Big Water," 386.

12 Newspaper clipping: *Newcastle Daily Chronicle*, May 4 (?), 1887, quoted in ibid.

13 Newspaper clipping: *Pall Mall Gazette*, April 26, 1887, in Baker Scrapbook, 1887, Cody Collection, DPL.

14 Napier, "Across the Big Water," 386.

15 Newspaper clipping: *Era*, April 23, 1887, in Baker Scrapbook, 1887, Cody Collection, DPL. See also Rosa and May, *Buffalo Bill and His Wild West*, 105–6.

16 *The Times* (London), April 21, 1887.

17 Ibid. See also Napier, "Across the Big Water," 391.

18 Ibid.

19 Newspaper clipping: *Daily Post*, May 8, 1887, Baker Scrapbook, 1887, Cody Collection, DPL; and Napier, "Across the Big Water," 399–400.

20 Newspaper clipping: London *Daily Telegraph*, April 29, 1887, Baker Scrapbook, 1887, Cody Collection, DPL.

21 Quoted in Sell and Weybright, *Buffalo Bill and the Wild West*, 165.

22 *The Times* (London), April 29, 1887. See also Napier, "Across the Big Water," 395.

23 Russell, *Lives and Legends of Buffalo Bill*, 329; and Rosa and May, *Buffalo Bill and His Wild West*, 108–9.

24 Cody, *Story of the Wild West*, 728.

25 Newspaper clipping: London *Morning Post*, May 5, 1887, Baker Scrapbook, 1887, Cody Collection, DPL.

26 Quoted in Sell and Weybright, *Buffalo Bill and the Wild West*, 166.

27 Ibid., 168.

28 In truth, for months past the queen had been attending concerts, laying foundation stones, and opening exhibitions. Walsh, *Making of Buffalo Bill*, 267. Victoria had "commanded" Cody and his show to attend her at Windsor Castle. Cody politely pointed out that the show was too big to take there. To everyone's surprise, the queen agreed to journey to the West End. She stipulated, however, that the show was to last only one hour. Rosa and May, *Buffalo Bill and His Wild West*, 116.

29 Napier, "Across the Big Water," 387; and Neihardt, *Black Elk Speaks*, 224.

30 DeMallie, *Sixth Grandfather*, 249–50. See also Neihardt, *Black Elk Speaks*, 225, for a variation of the speech given by the queen. Napier, in "Across the Big Water," 387, quotes from the Neihardt-edited text of the speech.

31 Cody Scrapbook, 1887–1890, 1, Cody Collection, DPL; unidentified newspaper clipping, May 12, 1887, Cody Collection, box 2, folder 11, BBHC; and newspaper clipping: *The Graphic* (London), May 7 and misc. dates, 1887, Peter H. Davidson Collection, box 1, BBHC.

32 Napier, "Across the Big Water," 389.

33 Neihardt, *Black Elk Speaks*, 227.

34 Queen Victoria's Journal, May 11, 1887, The Royal Archives, Windsor Castle, quoted in Rosa and May, *Buffalo Bill and His Wild West*, 120–21.

35 Bates to Secretary of the Interior, Sept. 12, 1907, Central Correspondence Files, file 74676/07, box 178, RG 75, NA.

36 Unidentified newspaper clippings: n.d., Cody Collection, box 2, folder 11, BBHC.

37 See Sell and Weybright, *Buffalo Bill and the Wild West*, 157–76; Walsh, *Making of Buffalo Bill*, 264–75; Russell, *Lives and Legends of Buffalo Bill*, 324–41; Yost, *Buffalo Bill*, 188–203; Rosa and May, *Buffalo Bill and His Wild West*,

102–35; Blackstone, *Buckskin, Bullets, and Business,* 22–23; and Reddin, "Wild West Shows," 113–16, 121–22.

38 Reddin, "Wild West Shows," 123–24.

39 Unidentified newspaper clippings: n.d., Cody Scrapbook 1887–1890, 1, Cody Collection, DPL.

40 Yost, *Buffalo Bill,* 466n.

41 Unidentified newspaper clipping: n.d., Cody Scrapbook 1887–1890, 1, Cody Collection, DPL; and Yost, *Buffalo Bill,* 203.

42 Ibid. John Burke proclaimed that Red Shirt was the first American Indian to visit Parliament, though the record indicates that four Mohawk leaders attended a session in 1710, and three Cherokees visited in 1762.

43 "The Wild, Wild West of London," words by George Horncastle, music by A. E. Durandeau, Peter H. Davison Collection, box 1, BBHC. Another song poked fun at the Wild West show's success. In "Buffalo Bill or the Wild West," words and music by Harry Starr of London, the songwriter proclaimed, "Oh, we chase the Buffalo, oh we chase the Buffalo! Through the 'Wild West' we wandered, capturing the foe, But now we kill the ladies, charge a shilling for the show, In the 'Wild West' of Kensington we chase the Buffalo." Ibid.

44 Newspaper clipping: Manchester *Examiner and Times,* Dec. 19, 1887, in Cody Scrapbook, 77, CHS.

45 Rosa and May, *Buffalo Bill and His Wild West,* 135.

CHAPTER FOUR

1 Extract from the *Annual Report of the Commissioner of Indian Affairs,* Oct. 24, 1881, in Francis Paul Prucha, ed., *Documents of United States Indian Policy* (Lincoln: University of Nebraska Press, 1975), 155–57.

2 Ibid.

3 Francis Paul Prucha, ed., *Americanizing the American Indians: Writings by the "Friends of the Indian," 1880–1900* (Lincoln: University of Nebraska Press, 1978), 3–5.

4 L. G. Moses, *The Indian Man: A Biography of James Mooney* (Urbana: University of Illinois Press, 1984), 147–48.

5 Prucha, *Americanizing of the American Indians,* 5.

6 Ibid., 6.

7 In 1879, a federal judge acknowledged on behalf of the Ponca leader, Standing Bear, the right of a "peaceful Indian to come and go as he wishes with the same freedom accorded to a white man." This ruling, however, was often ignored. See Arrell M. Gibson, *The American Indian: Prehistory to the Present* (Lexington, Mass.: D. C. Heath and Co., 1980), 465; Francis Paul Prucha, *American Indian Policy in Crisis: Christian Reformers and the Indian, 1865–1900* (Norman: University of Oklahoma Press, 1976), 321; and Thomas Henry Tibbles,

The Ponca Chiefs: An Account of the Trial of Standing Bear, ed. Kay Graber (Lincoln: University of Nebraska Press, 1972), 118–24.

8 Contract, April 21, 1886, in Records of the CIA, LR, No. 13400–1886, RG 75, NA.

9 There were essentially two types of bonds. The first represented money, often cash, supplied by the entrepreneur and held by the Department of the Interior for faithful execution of the provisions of the contract. Early on, these sums were significant. Later, however, the shows secured a bond from a surety company. Should the show go bankrupt, or should the Indians find themselves stranded far from home, then this money could be used to pay salaries and repatriate the Show Indians. This type of bond frequently assisted stranded entertainers, especially after 1900.

10 Quoted in Sell and Weybright, *Buffalo Bill and the Wild West*, 166.

11 Cody to Lamar, Oct. 16, 1886, Records of the CIA, LR, No. 27648–1886, RG 75, NA.

12 Robinson to Cody, Oct. 2, 1886, in ibid.

13 CIA to Hugh D. Gallagher, March 26, 1887, PR, LR, box 11, RG 75, FARC, KC.

14 What appeared as abandonment to Gallagher may have been the desire of the showmen to remain in Europe. R. C. Dawe of Berlin, owner of a traveling ethnological exhibit, had taken his show to Budapest in May and June 1886, and then on to Vienna. Fifteen Lakota men and women appeared in the show that featured a display of breaking camp and taking to the road; a parade of mounted warriors; bareback riding; demonstration of skill with the bow and arrow; and a presentation of how Indians attack and scalp a family of white settlers caught while sitting around an evening campfire. Most of the troupe probably returned to the United States at the end of the season in the fall of 1886. With his remaining two or three Indians and museum displays, including paintings and drawings by the artist Rudolf Cronau, who had spent the years 1880–1883 in the United States, Dawe attached himself to other circuses. This reconstruction is based upon information taken from CIA to Gallagher, Feb. 19, 1889, Records of the CIA, LS, RG 75, NA; Secretary of State to CIA, Jan. 7, 1889, Records of the CIA, LR, Law and Lands, No. 698–1889, ibid.; and Miklós Létay, "'Redskins at the Zoo': Sioux Indians in Budapest, 1886," in Feest, *Indians and Europe*, 375–81.

15 The sequence of events is summarized in CIA to Gallagher, Nov. 14 and 19, and Dec. 21, 1888, PR, General Records, box 9, RG 75, FARC, KC.

16 Belt to Gallagher, April 24, 1889, and CIA to Gallagher, Nov. 1, 1889, ibid.

17 Southard P. Warner to John R. Carter, Secretary of the American Embassy, London, Aug. 17, 1909, Records of the CIA, Classified Files 1907–1939, file 47363–09–PR–047, RG 75, NA.

18 Anonymous to CIA, Sept. 8, 1888, Records of the CIA, LR, No. 30392–1888, RG 75, NA. He further reported that Indians were selling their "clothing, blankets &c. that have been issued by the Government" to William A. Coffield,

who ran a small store on Wounded Knee Creek. Coffield then sold the goods to farmers in Nebraska. "There is hardly a farmhouse in northern Nebraska," he continued, "but what has a liberal supply of these goods."

19 Gallagher to CIA, Dec. 4, 1888, Records of the CIA, LR, No. 30463–1888, RG 75, NA.

20 Oberly to Secretary of the Interior, March 30, 1889, Records of the CIA, LS, RG 75, NA. Also quoted in Prucha, *American Indian Policy in Crisis*, 320.

21 Floyd A. O'Neil, "John H. Oberly (1888–89)," in Robert M. Kvasnicka and Herman J. Viola, eds., *The Commissioners of Indian Affairs, 1824–1977* (Lincoln: University of Nebraska Press, 1979), 190.

22 Vilas to Oberly, Feb. 18, 1889, PR, General Records, LR, Miscellaneous Correspondence, Feb. 13, 1889-Dec. 20, 1890, box 27, RG 75, FARC, KC.

23 CIA to Gallagher, Feb. 23, 1889, PR, General Records, ibid., box 9.

24 R. V. Belt, Acting CIA, to Carver, May 10, 1889, and John H. Oberly to Gallagher, March 21, 1889, PR, General Records, ibid., box 9; and John Noble to CIA, March 22, 1889, Sac, Fox, and Shawnee Agency Files, "Show and Exhibitions," Indian Archives Div., OHS.

25 Belt to Carver, May 10, 1889, PR, General Records, LR, Miscellaneous Corres., Feb. 13, 1889-Dec. 20, 1890, box 9, RG 75, FARC, KC.

26 Oberly to CIA, March 22, 1889, Sac, Fox, and Shawnee Agency Files, "Shows and Exhibitions," Indian Archives Div., OHS.

27 Belt to Carver, May 10, 1889, PR, General Files, box 9, RG 75, FARC, KC.

28 Noble to CIA, May 9, 1889, Records of the CIA, LR, No. 19902–1889, RG 75, NA.

29 Gibson, "Medicine Show," 76.

30 Belt to Gallagher, May 6, 1889, PR, General Records, box 9, RG 75, FARC, KC.

31 Ibid.

32 Gallagher to CIA, Dec. 6, 1889, Records of the CIA, LR, No. 35666–1889, RG 75, NA.

33 Ibid.

34 CIA to Dawes, April 15, 1889, Henry L. Dawes Papers, Library of Congress Manuscripts Division, Washington, D.C.

35 Prucha, *American Indian Policy in Crisis*, 321.

36 The "Crook Commission" negotiated acceptance of the Sioux Bill of 1889, a complex series of agreements passed by Congress. The commission negotiated land cessions preliminary to allotment and the breakup of the Great Sioux Reservation into six smaller reserves. See Utley, *Last Days of the Sioux Nation*, 48–59; and Olson, *Red Cloud and the Sioux Problem*, 312–19.

37 Newspaper clipping: New York *Herald*, Aug. 6, 1889, in Buffalo Bill Scrapbook, 1889, BBHC.

38 Ibid.

39 Morgan to Secretary of the Interior, Oct. 1, 1889, reproduced in *Fifty-eighth*

Annual Report of the Commissioner of Indian Affairs to the Secretary of the Interior, 1889 (Washington: Government Printing Office, 1889), 3.

40 One copy of the circular can be found as Morgan to Gallagher, Nov. 1, 1889, PR, General Records, LR, Miscellaneous Corres., Feb. 13, 1889-Dec. 20, 1890, box 9, RG 75, FARC, KC.

41 Scobey to CIA, Nov. 13, 1889, Records of the CIA, LR, No. 33121–1889, RG 75, NA.

42 Barthalomew to CIA, Nov. 14, 1889, Records of the CIA, LR, No. 33341–1889, ibid.

43 McKusick to CIA, Nov. 15, 1889, Records of the CIA, LR, No. 33340–1889, ibid.

44 Sears to CIA, Nov. 15, 1889, Records of the CIA, LR, No. 33677–1889, ibid.

45 Ashley to CIA, Jan. 9, 1890, Records of the CIA, LR, No. 1239–1890, ibid.

46 C. E. Vandever, Navajo Agency, New Mexico Territory, to CIA, Nov. 19, 1889, Records of the CIA, LR, No. 33740–1889, ibid.

47 Wood to CIA, Jan. 7, 1890, Records of the CIA, LR, No. 1171–1890, ibid.

48 George to CIA, Nov. 25, 1889, Records of the CIA, LR, No. 34973–1889, ibid.

49 Gallagher to CIA, Dec. 6, 1889, Records of the CIA, LR, No. 35666–1889, ibid.

50 Bullis to CIA, Nov. 20, 1889, Records of the CIA, LR, No. 34530–1889, ibid.

51 Noble to CIA, Jan. 30, 1890, Records of the CIA, LR, No. 3013–1890, ibid.

52 Noble to CIA, Feb. 12, 1890, PR, General Records, LR, Miscellaneous Corres., Feb. 13, 1889-Dec. 20, 1890, box 9, RG 75, FARC, KC.

53 Copy of circular, CIA to U.S. Indian Agents, March 8, 1890, found in Sac, Fox, and Shawnee Agency Files, "Shows and Exhibitions," Indian Archives Div., OHS.

54 Morgan to U.S. Indian Agents and School Superintendents, Jan. 30, 1890, in Records of the Consolidated Ute Agency (CUA), Main Decimal Files (MDF), box 161, 005/910 "Deserving Indians," RG 75, FARC, Denver (D).

CHAPTER FIVE

1 Yost, *Buffalo Bill,* 210.

2 Russell, *Lives and Legends of Buffalo Bill,* 349–50; Yost, *Buffalo Bill,* 211; and Rosa and May, *Buffalo Bill and His Wild West,* 140.

3 Yost, *Buffalo Bill,* 211.

4 Newspaper clippings: New York *Herald, Sun,* and *Times,* April 28, 1889, in Buffalo Bill Scrapbook, 1889, BBHC. The reporter for the *Herald* was particularly flippant. He wrote: "Mr. Red Shirt, the pampered favorite of European sovereigns, sought the seclusion of a squaw's cabin. . . . Besides him there were on board 102 more or less untutored sons of the forest, four squaws and five papooses. . . . They are all Sioux and mostly from the Ogallala and Redbud [sic] agencies. Burke says they are better than the lot taken last year—the aristoc-

racy as it were. Their names, as entered on the ship's passenger list, are more striking than euphonious, Medicine Horse, No Neck, Raw Meat, Sick Antelope, Dog's Ghost, and other members of the Indian Four Hundred. . . . The Indians are quartered in the steerage of the Monarch. Just below them on two decks, are the 190 Indian ponies, as ugly as sin."

5 Quoted in Walsh, *Making of Buffalo Bill*, 276.

6 Yost, *Buffalo Bill*, 221.

7 Rosa and May, *Buffalo Bill and His Wild West*, 141; Buffalo Bill is quoted in Walsh, *Making of Buffalo Bill*, 276; and Sell and Weybright, *Buffalo Bill and the Wild West*, 178.

8 Newspaper clipping: New York *Home Journal*, July 12, 1889, Buffalo Bill Scrapbook, 1889, BBHC.

9 Newspaper clipping: New York *Herald*, Aug. 10, 1889, in ibid.

10 Newspaper clipping: London *Daily Telegraph*, Aug. 14, 1889, in ibid.

11 *Le Petit Journal*, Oct. 7, 1889, quoted in Napier, "Across the Big Water," 396.

12 Napier, "Across the Big Water," 396–97. See also Royal B. Hassrick, *The Sioux: Life and Customs of a Warrior Society* (Norman: University of Oklahoma Press, 1964), 32–61, 296–339; and James R. Walker, *Lakota Society*, ed. Raymond J. DeMallie (Lincoln: University of Nebraska Press, 1982), 28–71.

13 Telegram: Burke to Lamar, July 12, 1887, Records of the CIA, LR, No. 18450–1887, RG 75, NA. See also *Baltimore American*, July 29, 1887, 3. For the most thorough account of Black Elk's adventures, see DeMallie, *Sixth Grandfather*, 7–8, 251–54. In this instance, we are dependent on Black Elk for the story that four members of Cody's troupe missed the train. There is no evidence within the records thus surveyed that either verifies or refutes Black Elk's numbers.

14 Foreman, *Indians Abroad*, 201; and DeMallie, *Sixth Grandfather*, 8.

15 Newspaper clipping: New York *Herald*, Sept. 29, 1889, in Buffalo Bill Scrapbook, 1889, BBHC.

16 Burke to CIA, n.d. [ca. February 1886], Records of the CIA, LR, No. 5564–1886, RG 75, NA.

17 For contracts and rates of pay for women, see George P. Comer, Pine Ridge agency clerk, to Cody and Salsbury, April 19, 1893, PR, General Files, box 15, RG 75, FARC, KC; and Agent Charles G. Penny, Pine Ridge, to CIA, March 28, 1891, PR, LS, press copy book, Vol. 10, 1890, box 3, RG 75, FARC, KC.

18 From *Buffalo Bill's Wild West, Historical Sketches & Programme*, quoted in Walsh, *Making of Buffalo Bill*, 277–78. See also Foreman, *Indians Abroad*, 202–3; and Russell, *Lives and Legends of Buffalo Bill*, 351–52.

19 Sell and Weybright, *Buffalo Bill and the Wild West*, 181.

20 Seven Indians contracted to Cody did die in accidents or from illness during the 1889–90 European tour. The source of the confusion seems to be Richard J. Walsh, in *Making of Buffalo Bill* (278), who implies that the seven died in Spain. Don Russell, in *Lives and Legends of Buffalo Bill* (352), writes that four Indians died in Spain. Nellie Snyder Yost, in *Buffalo Bill* (223), mentions that

"several Indians died" in Barcelona. None cite sources for their tallies. Joseph Rosa and Robin May, citing Yost in their *Buffalo Bill and His Wild West* (144), repeat the comment that several Indians died while in Spain. The mortality of Indians on tour with Cody is taken up later in this chapter; but for a convenient summary, see Robert V. Belt, Acting Commissioner, to Agent Daniel F. Royer, Pine Ridge, Nov. 24, 1890, and "List of Indians, Pine Ridge, with Cody," n.d., in PR, General Records, box 9, RG 75, FARC, KC.

21 Rosa and May, *Buffalo Bill and His Wild West*, 144; and Russell, *Lives and Legends of Buffalo Bill*, 352.

22 Russell, *Lives and Legends of Buffalo Bill*, 352; and Sell and Weybright, *Buffalo Bill and the Wild West*, 181.

23 Newspaper clippings: *The Rome Herald*, March 1, 1890; and *New York Herald* [Paris ed.], March 3, 1890, in Buffalo Bill Scrapbook, Rome, 1890, BBHC.

24 Newspaper clipping: *New York Herald* [London ed.], March 4, 1890, ibid.

25 Quoted in Naila Clerici, "Native Americans in Columbus's Home Land: A Show within the Show," in Feest, *Indians and Europe*, 422.

26 Ibid.

27 Nate Salsbury, "At the Vatican," *The Colorado Magazine* 33 (July 1955):212.

28 Newspaper clipping: *New York Herald* [London ed.], March 4, 1890, Buffalo Bill Scrapbook, Rome, 1890, BBHC.

29 John Burke, *Buffalo Bill from Prairie to Palace* (Chicago: Rand McNally, 1893), 244. This book became part of the promotional literature during the show's run at the Columbian Exposition.

30 Walsh, *Making of Buffalo Bill*, 279.

31 Napier, "Across the Big Water," 397.

32 Ibid, 398.

33 Augustus O. Bourn, Rome, to William F. Wharton, Assistant Secretary of State, March 12, 1890, PR, General Records, box 9, RG 75, FARC, KC. The body was interred at the chief cemetery in Rome, known as "Campo Verano," where it was to remain for ten years. Then the bones would be dug up and placed in the ossuary of the same cemetery. Bourn explained that a lot for a permanent grave and tablet would cost from 120 dollars to 130 dollars. "I found upon inquiry, that 'Little Ring's' habits had been good, and that he was considered one of the best Indians attached to the Company. He left no personal effects but his clothing, which was taken in charge by his brothers 'Piece of Iron' and 'Yellow Horse.' He usually sent his pay monthly to his family at home. His wages were $25.00 per month and would have been due March 23rd instant, the last payment having been made February 23rd."

34 Salsbury, "At the Vatican," 213.

35 Ibid.

36 Napier, "Across the Big Water," 399.

37 Newspaper clipping: *New York Herald* [Paris ed.], March 16, 1890, Buffalo Bill Scrapbook, Rome, 1890, BBHC.

38 Ibid.

39 Clerici, "Native Americans in Columbus's Home Land," 422–23.

40 Sell and Weybright, *Buffalo Bill and the Wild West*, 182.

41 Quoted in Yost, *Buffalo Bill*, 224. See also Rosa and May, *Buffalo Bill and His Wild West*, 145.

42 Yost, *Buffalo Bill*, 224.

43 Rosa and May, *Buffalo Bill and His Wild West*, 145. The authors point out that the photograph of the gondola shows the Indians all trying to hold still for the photographer, as was necessary in those days of extremely slow lenses, and even more so in a boat. It is hardly proof, as has been claimed in Time-Life Books, *The End of the Myth* (New York: Time-Life, 1979), 75, that the Indians were posing grudgingly. By that token, write Rosa and May, all Victorians were an unhappy lot! See also newspaper clipping: *The Galignani Messenger*, April 15, 1890, Cody Scrapbook, 1887–1890, Cody Collection, DPL.

44 Sell and Weybright, *Buffalo Bill and the Wild West*, 182; and Burke, *Buffalo Bill from Prairie to Palace*, 60.

45 Newspaper clipping: *Munchener Neueste Nachrichten*, April 19, 1890, Cody Scrapbook, 1887–1890, Cody Collection, DPL; and Russell, *Lives and Legends of Buffalo Bill*, 353.

46 See Rudolf Conrad, "Mutual Fascination: Indians in Dresden and Leipzig," in Feest, *Indians and Europe*, 457–58, 461. May actually began his career as a novelist in 1876. His interest in Indians seems to have been piqued by the victory of the Sioux at the Battle of the Little Bighorn.

47 Rosa and May, *Buffalo Bill and His Wild West*, 147. See also "Sie Ritten Da'lang, Podner," *Time*, June 18, 1979, 51. Such groups as the twenty-five-hundred-member Western Bund or the equally large Gemeinschaft Norddeutscher Indianerfreunde (North German Society of Indian Friends) help to perpetuate western images first introduced by Cody and reinforced in the writings of Karl May.

48 See, for example, newspaper clipping: *Berliner Tageblatt*, Aug. 1, 1890, Buffalo Bill Scrapbook, Dresden, June 7-October, 1890, BBHC.

49 Noble to CIA, Aug. 4, 1890, Records of the CIA, LR, No. 23943–1890, RG 75, NA.

50 Sequence of events summarized in Wharton to John Noble, Aug. 27, 1890, Records of the CIA, LR, No. 26491–1890; and Nate Salsbury, Cologne, to W. H. Edwards, Consul General, Berlin, Sept. 18, 1890, Records of the CIA, LR, No. 33697–1890, RG 75, NA.

51 Rosa and May, *Buffalo Bill and His Wild West*, 147.

52 Charles B. Trail, U.S. Consul, Marseilles, to Wharton, Jan. 27, 1890, PR, General Files, box 9, RG 75, FARC, KC.

53 CIA to U.S. Indian Agents, March 8, 1890, copy in Sac, Fox, and Shawnee Agency Files, microfilm, roll 36–6, Indian Archives Div., OHS.

54 On Pawnee Bill's Wild West show, see Russell, *Wild West*, 31–33; and Glenn

Shirley, *Pawnee Bill: A Biography of Major Gordon W. Lillie* (Lincoln: University of Nebraska Press, 1965), 133–47.

55 CIA to Gallagher, April 1, 1890, PR, General Records, box 9, RG 75, FARC, KC.

56 Edward Camphausen, Consul, Naples, Italy to Wharton, Feb. 19, 1890, Records of the CIA, LR, No. 7465–1890, RG 75, NA; and Augustus O. Bourn, Consul General, Rome, to Wharton, March 12, 1890, and also Robert V. Belt, Acting CIA, to Gallagher, April 15, 1890, PR, General Files, box 9, RG 75, FARC, KC.

57 F. C. Langley, Moscow, to CIA, June 3, 1890, Records of the CIA, LR, No. 20543–1890, RG 75, NA.

58 George C. Crager to Secretary of the Interior, June 21, 1890, Records of the CIA, LR, No. 19021–1890, ibid.

59 O'Beirne to Gallagher, July 4, 1890, PR, General Records, Miscellaneous Correspondence Received, box 27, RG 75, FARC, KC.

60 Ibid.

61 *New York Times*, July 20, 1890, 9. Fred Matthews is identified as "Richard" Matthews in the newspaper article. For background on Fred Matthews, see Russell, *Lives and Legends of Buffalo Bill*, 294, 308. See also Yost, *Buffalo Bill*, 463n.

62 Rosa and May, *Buffalo Bill and His Wild West*, 149; for Cody's first contracting Sioux for his combination, see Russell, *Lives and Legends of Buffalo Bill*, 258; and O'Beirne to Gallagher, July 4, 1890, PR, General Records, Miscellaneous Correspondence Received, box 27, RG 75, FARC, KC.

63 Quoted in Walsh, *Making of Buffalo Bill*, 280.

64 Gallagher to CIA, July 28, 1890, PR, LS, press copy book, Vol. 9, 1889–1890, box 3, RG 75, FARC, KC.

65 O'Beirne to CIA, Aug. 3, 1890, Records of the CIA, LR, No. 23831–1890, RG 75, NA.

66 Noble to CIA, Aug. 4, 1890, Records of the CIA, LR, No. 23943–1890, ibid.

67 CIA to Gallagher, Aug. 13 and Sept. 2, 1890, PR, General Records, box 9, RG 75, FARC, KC.

68 Gallagher to CIA, Aug. 13, 1890, ibid.

69 Tonner to CIA, Aug. 14, 1890, Records of the CIA, LR, No. 25163–1890, RG 75, NA.

70 Salsbury to W. H. Edwards, Consul General, Berlin, Sept. 18, 1890, Records of the CIA, LR, No. 33697–1890, RG 75, NA.

71 Quoted in Russell, *Lives and Legends of Buffalo Bill*, 351. See also Sell and Weybright, *Buffalo Bill and the Wild West*, 186,

72 Hugo M. Starkloff, U.S. Consul, Bremen, to Wharten, Sept. 26, 1890, Records of the CIA, LR, No. 33015–1890, ibid.

73 Rosa and May, *Buffalo Bill and His Wild West*, 149.

74 Quoted in Walsh, *Making of Buffalo Bill*, 280.

75 Quoted in Russell, *Lives and Legends of Buffalo Bill*, 351.

76 Cablegram: Burke to Morgan, Oct. 26, 1890, Records of the CIA, LR, No. 33009–1890, RG 75, NA.

77 L. G. Moses, "Jack Wilson and the Indian Service: The Response of the BIA to the Ghost Dance Prophet," *American Indian Quarterly* 5 (November 1979): 303.

78 Belt to U.S. Indian Agents, Oct. 1, 1890, Sac, Fox, and Shawnee Agency Files, microfilm roll, 36–6, Indian Archives Div., OHS.

79 Herbert Welsh to George Chandler, Acting Secretary of the Interior, Nov. 13, 1890, Records of the CIA, LR, No. 35081–1890, RG 75, NA. See also William T. Hagan, *The Indian Rights Association: The Herbert Welsh Years, 1882–1904* (Tucson: University of Arizona Press, 1985), 144. Welsh did not care much for Father Craft. He had once referred to him as "a very unreliable and mischevious [*sic*] person." Quoted in ibid., 107.

80 Telegram: Welsh to Chandler, Nov. 13, 1890, Records of the CIA, LR, No. 35080–1890, RG 75, NA; Welsh to Chandler, Nov. 13, 1890, Records of the CIA, LR, No. 35081–1890, ibid; and telegram: Burke to Morgan, Oct. 26, 1890, Records of the CIA, LR, No. 33009–1890, ibid.

81 "Examination of the Indians Traveling with Cody and Salsbury's Wild West Show by the Acting Commissioner of Indian Affairs," contained in Belt to Secretary of the Interior, Nov. 18, 1890, Records of the CIA, Correspondence Land Division, LS, Vol. 104, Nov. 11–Dec. 20, 1890, Letter Book 207, 191–204, RG 75, NA.

82 Ibid., 196.

83 Ibid., 197.

84 Ibid., 198–99.

85 Ibid., 200–1.

86 Ibid., 202.

87 Ibid.

88 Ibid., 204.

89 O'Beirne to Belt, Nov. 17, 1890, Records of the CIA, LR, No. 35577–1890, RG 75, NA.

90 Belt to Royer, Nov. 24, 1890, PR, General Records, box 9, RG 75, FARC, KC.

91 Utley, *Last Days of the Sioux Nation*, 102, 103.

92 Telegram: Royer to Belt, Nov. 15, 1890, Records of the Bureau of Indian Affairs, Special Case 188, Ghost Dance, 1890–1898, RG 75, NA (hereafter cited as SC 188).

93 Belt to Secretary of the Interior, Dec. 1, 1890, Records of the CIA, Correspondence Land Division, LS, Vol. 104, Nov. 11–Dec. 20, 1890, Letter Book 207, 484–85, RG 75, NA.

CHAPTER SIX

1 James Mooney, "The Ghost Dance Religion and the Sioux Outbreak of 1890," *Fourteenth Annual Report of the Bureau of Ethnology*, Part 2 (Washington, D.C.: Government Printing Office, 1896), 928; Utley, *Last Days of the Sioux Nation*, 113–15; and Raymond J. DeMallie, "The Lakota Ghost Dance: An Ethnohistorical Account," *Pacific Historical Review* 51 (1982):385–405.

2 L. G. Moses, " 'The Father Tells Me So!' Wovoka: The Ghost Dance Prophet," in Clifford E. Trafzer, ed., *American Indian Prophets: Religious Leaders and Revitalization Movements* (Newcastle, Calif.: Sierra Oaks Publishing Co., 1986), 97; Michael Hittman, "The 1870 Ghost Dance at Walker River Reservation: A Reconstruction," *Ethnohistory* 20 (1973):247–78. Hittman argues persuasively that Wovoka never preached the destruction of non-Indians. See also Cora DuBois, "The 1870 Ghost Dance," *University of California Anthropological Records* 3 (Berkeley: University of California Press, 1939), 3–7.

3 Mooney, "Ghost Dance Religion," 746–802.

4 In the historiography of the religion, James Mooney's classic is unrivaled. For an appreciation of the literature on the subject, see Michael Hittman, *Wovoka and the Ghost Dance: A Sourcebook* (Carson City, Nev.: The Grace Dangberg Foundation, 1990).

5 L. G. Moses, "Jack Wilson and the Indian Service," 306–7. See also Robert Wooster, *Nelson A. Miles and the Twilight of the Frontier Army* (Lincoln: University of Nebraska Press, 1993), 176–78.

6 Morgan to Secretary of the Interior, Jan. 2, 1891, SC 188.

7 See Agent D. F. Royer, Pine Ridge, to Morgan, Jan. 10, 1891, Records of the CIA, LR, Land, No. 1891–3186, RG 75, NA. On the dismissal of Agent Royer, see Utley, *Last Days of the Sioux Nation*, 279–80.

8 Miles to Adjutant General, Jan. 26, 1890, File 5412-PRD-1890, Records of the Adjutant General's Office (AGO), 1780s-1917, Record Group 94, National Archives Microfilm Publication M983, *Reports and Correspondence Relating to the Army Investigations of the Battle of Wounded Knee and to the Sioux Campaign of 1890–1891* (hereafter cited as M983, RG 94, NA).

9 Cody to CIA, Feb. 26, 1891, Records of the CIA, LR. No. 7678–1891, RG 75, NA.

10 C. F. Manderson et al. to CIA, Feb. 26, 1891, Records of the CIA, LR, No. 7676–1891, ibid. Other signatories were: Rep. Gilbert L. Laws, Sen. Algernon S. Paddock, and Rep. George W. E. Dorsey.

11 Miles to Adjutant General, March 14, 1891, M983, RG 94, NA.

12 Unidentified newspaper clipping, n.d., Cody Scrapbook, 13, CHS.

13 Cody to L. A. Grant, Acting Secretary of War, May 26, 1891, M983, RG 94, NA. Morgan's attitude and response are explained in Morgan to James McLaughlin, March 9, 1891, Records of Standing Rock Reservation, General Records, Miscellaneous Corres., 1891, box 517204, RG 75, FARC, KC; handwritten

routebook, Cody Collection, box 6, folder 7, BBHC; and Russell, *Wild West*, 39. Some of the prisoners were judged too ill to travel and therefore remained behind. Four of them were sent home shortly after Cody's visit.

14 See the editor's introduction in Richmond L. Clow, ed., "Autobiography of Mary C. Collins, Missionary to the Western Sioux," *South Dakota Historical Collections* 41 (1982):12.

15 Agent James McLaughlin's opinion about Sitting Bull as well as his attitude toward Wild West shows were well known to Collins. He described Sitting Bull's tour with Cody in 1885 as "detrimental." "Being made so much of and lionized by the public," McLaughlin once wrote to Herbert Welsh, Sitting Bull "was greatly inflated upon his return and gave me considerable trouble for several months afterwards from his increased insolence and the exaggerated reports that he made to the Indians of the importance that the 'Great Father' (he having called upon President Cleveland) and the public generally attached to him as not only the 'Head Chief' of the Sioux Nation but King of all the Indians of the United States." See McLaughlin to Welsh, April 9, 1891, McLaughlin Papers, roll 22, AAA.

16 "Statement of Mary Collins," 2–3, ca. April 1891, Collins Papers, SDSHS.

17 Ibid., 3. General Miles reported to the adjutant general that some worthy people were trying to stop the Cody deal. An unnamed woman had recently visited the prisoners and had been "causing mischief." Miles recommended that nothing should interfere with Cody taking the prisoners to Europe. Miles to Adjutant General, March 17 and 19, 1891, M983, RG 94, NA.

18 *The Christian Register*, March 26, 1891, in Collins Papers, SDSHS. Isabel C. Barrows of Boston, wife of the editor of the *Register*, sent copies of the editorial to Commissioner Morgan. Barrows to CIA, March 31, 1891, Records of the CIA, LR, No. 12090–1891, RG 75, NA.

19 Cutter to Redfield Proctor, March 25, 1891, M983, RG 94, NA.

20 *The Independent* (Gordon, Nebr.), ca. March 1891, Collins Papers, SDSHS.

21 "Statement of Mary Collins," 4, ibid.

22 The secretary of the interior explains his position in Noble to CIA, April 20, 1891, SC 188.

23 Welsh to CIA, April 3, 1891, ibid. Welsh wrote: "Please inform me what is the present status of Buffalo Bill's application to the Government for possession of the Indian prisoners at Camp Sheridan for exhibition purposes. I am preparing a statement for [the] public on this point, based upon the very interesting detailed information with which I have just been supplied by Miss Collins. . . . I wish to know whether the Government has definitely and positively granted Mr. Cody authority to take the Indians, and whether he already has possession of them." The Fort Sheridan prisoners had been turned over to Cody's representatives on the morning of March 30 and immediately left for Philadelphia. See Col. R. E. A. Crofton, commanding Fort Sheridan to Adjutant General, March 31, 1891, M983, RG 95, NA.

24 Salsbury to Penny, May 8, 1891, PR, General Records, LR, MDF, 047 Buffalo Bill's Wild West Show Contracts (1891, 1895), box 162, RG 75, FARC, KC.

25 Ibid.

26 Welsh to Collins, April 17, 1891, Collins Papers, SDSHS.

27 Mary C. Collins, "To the Members of the Congregational Club of Chicago," April 7, 1891, ibid.

28 New York *Evening Post*, April 27, 1891, in ibid.

29 Salsbury to Welsh, May 18, 1891, ibid.

30 Welsh to Gen. Samuel C. Armstrong, June 3, 1891, ibid.

31 McLaughlin to Welsh, June 12, 1891, McLaughlin Papers, roll 22, AAA.

32 Welsh to Collins, June 26, 1891, Collins Papers, SDSHS.

33 Hazel W. Hertzberg, *The Search for an American Indian Identity: Modern Pan-Indian Movements* (Syracuse, N.Y.: Syracuse University Press, 1971), 25.

34 See H. A. Taylor to Secretary of the Interior, Sept. 8, 1891, Records of the Interior Department, Correspondence, World's Columbian Exposition, 1891–94, box 1, RG 48, NA (cited hereafter as Columbian Exposition, RG 48, NA).

35 Cody to Lewis A. Grant, Acting Secretary of War, May 26, 1891, M983, RG 94, NA.

36 Russell, *Wild West*, 40; Walsh, *Making of Buffalo Bill*, 293; and Rosa and May, *Buffalo Bill and His Wild West*, 154. According to Don Russell, "rough rider" enjoyed considerable usage in the West. Where Cody got the inspiration for it is unclear. The cowboy who was given the fewest broken horses was said to be "riding the rough string." An Illinois cavalry regiment during the Civil War called itself the *rough riders*. Russell, *Lives and Legends of Buffalo Bill*, 370. Theodore Roosevelt used the term "roughrider" [*sic*] in correspondence twelve years before he charged up Cuba's San Juan Hill. See Walsh, *Making of Buffalo Bill*, 293.

37 Quoted in Walsh, *Making of Buffalo Bill*, 293–94.

38 Russell, *Wild West*, 40.

39 Russell, *Lives and Legends of Buffalo Bill*, 373.

40 On Cody's need for a vacation, see Rosa and May, *Buffalo Bill and His Wild West*, 155.

41 Unidentified Chicago newspaper clipping, ca. March 1892, Cody Scrapbook, 73, CHS.

42 Nate Salsbury to Secretary of War, Feb. 19, 1892, AGO, file 27 PRD 1891 filed with 5412 PRD 1890, RG 94, NA; and Marion Maus, aide-de-camp, Chicago, to Gen. Nelson A. Miles, Shoreham Hotel, Washington, D.C., March 11, 1892, AGO, Series VII, file 27617 PRD 1892 filed with 5412 PRD 1890, ibid.

43 Salsbury to Miles, Feb. 29, 1892, M983, RG 94, NA.

44 Scofield to Secretary of War, March 2, 1892, AGO, Series VI, file 27240 PRD 1891 filed with 5412 PRD 1890, RG 94, NA.

45 Miles to Adjutant General, March 14, 1892, Records of the Adjutant General's Office, Series VII, file 27617 PRD 1892 filed with ibid.

46 Kelton to Howard, March 14, 1892, ibid.

47 Croger to Secretary of War, March 12, 1892, ibid.

48 Unidentified Chicago newspaper clipping, ca. March 1892, Cody Scrapbook, 73, CHS.

49 See the series of correspondence, letters, and affidavits in Cody to Capt. Charles G. Penny, Acting Agent, Pine Ridge, May 29, 1891, PR, General Records, box 12, RG 75, FARC, KC; Cody to Secretary of War, June 6, 1891, AGO, Series V, file 10112 PRD 1891 filed with 5412 PRD 1890, RG 94, NA; Cody to Secretary of War, July 17, 1891, Records of the CIA, LR, No. 28591–1891, RG 75, NA; and Cody to Secretary of War, Aug. 19, 1891, Records of the CIA, LR, No. 32171–1891, RG 75, NA.

50 Unidentified Chicago newspaper clipping, ca. March 1892, Cody Scrapbook, 73, CHS. Eagle Star's death is also reported in John Shangreau, interpreter, to U.S. Agent, Sept. 12, 1891, Records of Rosebud Reservation, Incoming Correspondence Index, July 1889-June 1891, Book 202, 76, RG 75, FARC, KC.

51 Noble to Secretary of War, March 29, 1892, AGO, Series IX, file 29022 PRD filed with 5412 PRD 1890, RG 94, NA.

52 John Noble to Agent George LeRoy Brown, April 14, 1892, Records of the CIA, LR, No. 13917–1892, RG 75, NA; and Acting Commissioner R. V. Belt to James McLaughlin, April 18, 1892, Records of Standing Rock Reservation, General Records, Commissioner's Corres. 1892, box 517204, RG 75, FARC, KC.

53 Morgan to Noble, April 29, 1892, AGO, Series X, file 30329 PRD 1892 filed with 5412 PRD 1890, RG 94, NA.

54 Ibid.

55 Noble to Elkins, May 4, 1892, ibid.

56 Brown to CIA, Oct. 15, 1890, Records of the CIA, LR, No. 38098–1892, RG 75, NA. When the remainder of the original Fort Sheridan prisoners returned with Cody to the United States in October, they too were allowed to return to the Dakotas. See Adjutant General to Cody, Dec. 3, 1892, AGO, Series XI, file 39592 PRD 1892 filed with 5412 PRD 1890, RG 94, NA.

57 Miles to Adjutant General, June 7, 1892, ibid.

58 For an explanation of the events leading to the Carver ban, see Brown to CIA, June 14 and 16, 1892; Brown to Carver, June 20, 1892; and Sworn Affidavit of Fast Thunder, June 16, 1892, PR, Miscellaneous LS, box 6, RG 75, FARC, KC.

59 Morgan to Brown, June 14, 1892, Records of the CIA, LS, No. 21230–1892, RG 75, NA.

60 *Oakland Tribune*, Aug. 30, 1962, in Carver Papers, folder 1, NSHS. The story quotes extensively from contemporary newspaper articles.

61 Ibid.

62 See Cody to Secretary of War, Aug. 19, 1891, Records of the CIA, LR, No. 32171–1891, RG 75, NA. Standing Bear suffered from "lung problems," probably pneumonia, caused, as Cody believed, by "exposure during last win-

ter's troubles." Although a Brule, he resided at Pine Ridge rather than Rosebud reservation.

63 *Oakland Tribune*, Aug. 30, 1962, Carver Papers, folder 1, NSHS.

64 See copy of the circular, Morgan to Brown, June 14, 1892, Records of the CIA,
LS, No. 21230–1892, RG 75, NA.

65 Kapus to Brown, April 23, 1893, PR, LR and General Files, Series 1, box 14,
RG 75, FARC, KC.

66 Morgan to Brown, quoted in Prucha, *American Indian Policy in Crisis*, 323;
and Moses, "Wild West Shows," 212–13.

67 *Chicago Tribune*, June 16, 1893, Buffalo Bill Scrapbook, Chicago Season, 1893,
BBHC.

68 Moses, "Wild West Shows," 214.

69 *Oakland Tribune*, Aug. 30, 1962, Carver Papers, folder 1, NSHS.

70 Pratt to Collins, March 31, 1891, Collins Papers, SDSHS.

71 Buffalo Bill Scrapbook, 1892, BBHC.

72 Newspaper clipping: *The Oracle*, May 28, 1892, found in ibid.

73 Rosa and May, *Buffalo Bill and His Wild West*, 155.

74 Yost, *Buffalo Bill*, 236.

75 Rosa and May, *Buffalo Bill and His Wild West*, 156.

76 Walsh, *Making of Buffalo Bill*, 298.

77 *The Echo* (London), June 14, 1892, in Buffalo Bill Scrapbook, 1892, BBHC.

78 *Morning* (London), Aug. 18, 1892, ibid.

79 Russell, *Wild West*, 42; and Rosa and May, *Buffalo Bill and His Wild West*, 157.

80 Pine Ridge Register, 208–9, PR, RG 75, FARC, KC.

81 Little Wolf, an Oglala of Pine Ridge reservation, should not be confused with
Little Wolf of the Northern Cheyenne, the more famous veteran of the Chey-
enne flight from Indian Territory. See Gary L. Roberts, "In Search of Little
Wolf . . . A Tangled Photographic Record," *Montana, the Magazine of Western
History* 28 (1978):48–61.

CHAPTER SEVEN

1 Much of the introduction to this chapter is derived from the narrative in Moses,
Indian Man, 74–76.

2 David F. Burg, *Chicago's White City of 1893* (Lexington: University Press of
Kentucky, 1976), 109.

3 Ibid., 110.

4 Ibid.

5 Daniel B. Shepp and James W. Shepp, *Shepp's World's Fair Photographed* (Chicago: Global Bible Publishing Co., 1893), 306.

6 Ralph W. Dexter, "Putnam's Problems in Popularizing Anthropology," *American Anthropologist* 54 (1966):315–16.

7 Ibid., 320, 323–24.

8 See *Ninth Annual Report of the Indian Rights Association for the Year Ending December 15, 1890* (Philadelphia: Office of the Indian Rights Association, 1891), 41.

9 The Smithsonian Institution sponsored ethnological museum exhibits at the centennial exposition in Philadelphia. Until Congress thwarted their plans by failing to appropriate the necessary money, both the Smithsonian and the BIA proposed a living display of Indians under their joint supervision. See Robert W. Rydell, *All the World's a Fair: Visions of Empire at American International Expositions, 1876–1916* (Chicago: University of Chicago Press, 1984), 26.

10 See Curtis M. Hinsley, Jr., *Savages and Scientists: The Smithsonian Institution and the Development of American Anthropology, 1846–1910* (Washington, D.C.: Smithsonian Institution Press, 1981), 130–39; and Moses, *Indian Man*, 30–31.

11 For descriptions and analyses of ethnological displays at American World's Fairs, see Rydell, *All the World's a Fair*, passim; Hinsley, *Savages and Scientists*, 110–12, 219, 231; and Frederick E. Hoxie, *A Final Promise: The Campaign to Assimilate the Indians, 1880–1920* (Lincoln: University of Nebraska Press, 1984), 85–92. Hinsley argues persuasively that, in some ways, the anthropologist-adventurer of the 1880s and 1890s replaced the trappers, pathfinders, hunters, and soldiers—buckskinned Buffalo Bills—as heroes. This is especially evident in the career and writings of Frank Hamilton Cushing. His adventures at Zuni he celebrated in *Century Illustrated Monthly Magazine* in 1882–83. See Hinsley, *Savages and Scientists*, 190–92.

12 George Brown Goode, "First Draft of a System of Classification for the World's Columbian Exposition," Exposition Records of the Smithsonian Institution and the United States National Museum, 1875–1916, box 37, Record Unit 70, Smithsonian Institution Archives, Washington, D.C. See also Rydell, *All the World's a Fair*, 43–44; and Hinsley, *Savages and Scientists*, 111–12.

13 Morgan's comments can be found in F. W. Clarke, Department of the Interior, to Secretary of the Interior, Nov. 8, 1893, Columbian Exposition, box 1, RG 48, NA.

14 "Indian Office Exhibit at the World's Columbian Exposition" (report of conversation held in Office of Commissioner of Indian Affairs), Feb. 1, 1892, ibid. Frederick E. Hoxie gives a different account of the split. He suggests that both the groups represented by Putnam and Morgan intended to present their own work rather than adhere to a common theme. Dividing the Indian exhibit between Putnam's and Morgan's jurisdiction was more than a bureaucratic convenience, for the themes of the two displays were strikingly different. The

Indian village "conveyed the idea that Indians were members of an exotic race with little connection to modern America." The model Indian school, by concentrating on Indian progress, "pointed to the possibility of Indian assimilation," Hoxie notes. "What is more, there seemed to be a good deal of uncertainty — among the organizers of the fair as well as the public — over which focus was more appropriate" (Hoxie, *Final Promise*, 88–89). Hoxie may be right about the ambivalence of both patrons *and* commissioner, but Morgan had intended to undertake the Indian encampment. "As stated in my annual report," he wrote to Interior Secretary John W. Noble, "this exhibit of Indians in civilized conditions ought to have for its back-ground a setting forth of the Indian in primitive conditions. It was my intention to have the Indian Office undertake this work; but the lack of expert services for the making of such an exhibit, and more especially the complete lack of funds required to make it a success, have made the Office very glad to accept the suggestion of Professor Putnam." Morgan to Noble, Feb. 10, 1892, Columbian Exposition, box 1, RG 48, NA.

15 "Indian Office Exhibit at the World's Columbian Exposition," Jan. 30, 1892, ibid.

16 Ibid. Daniel M. Browning, Morgan's successor as commissioner, reported enthusiastically about the success of the exhibit, which attracted over one hundred thousand people each week. The secretary of the Board of Indian Commissioners, on the other hand, described the school as "a little, mean-looking building in the midst of those grand and imposing structures" (quoted in Prucha, *American Indian Policy in Crisis*, 325–26). Under orders from the secretary of the interior, Josephus Daniels, chief of the department's appointment division, spent ten days at the fair examining government exhibits. He later criticized the school. Daniels preferred Morgan's original plan of contrasting the primitive Indians with those approaching civilization as he supposed. "I regard it as a mistake," he wrote, "not to have carried out the original plan and give a picturesque and impressive comparison by presenting here the primitive Indian . . . as he was before he had ever felt the helpful — or hurtful — hand of civilization." Daniels to Secretary of the Interior, July 24, 1893, Columbian Exposition, box 1, RG 48, NA.

17 Delos Avery, "Buffalo Bill," *Chicago Sunday Tribune*, March 26, 1944, graphic section, 5, folder 4, Cody Papers, NSHS; Blackstone, *Buckskins, Bullets, and Business*, 26; Cody and Salsbury Contract, April 15, 1893, in George LeRoy Brown to Cody, April 19, 1893, PR, LR, Series 1, box 15, RG 75, FARC, KC; *Chicago Record*, April 14, 1893, Buffalo Bill Scrapbook, Chicago Season, 1893, BBHC. On another occasion, when the superintendent of the fair outraged public opinion by refusing free admission to the homeless and poor children of Chicago, Cody made them his guests at the Wild West, an act that won him a great amount of goodwill, not to mention favorable publicity. See Reddin, "Wild West Shows," 137.

18 "Amy Leslie at the Fair," undated newspaper clipping in Buffalo Bill Scrapbook, Chicago Season, 1893, BBHC. See also Amy Leslie, *Amy Leslie at the Fair* (Chicago: W. B. Conkey Co., 1893), 13.

19 *Chicago Herald,* May 2, 1893, and *Chicago Record,* June 14, 1893, in Buffalo Bill Scrapbook, Chicago Season, 1893, BBHC.

20 Rydell, *All the World's a Fair,* 62.

21 Ibid., 41.

22 Ibid., 63.

23 See, for example, the evocative description by Amy Leslie of her visit behind the scenes at the Wild West show with Buffalo Bill. All the Show Indians, wanting to meet her, "seized my hand in a friendly way, smile[d] large oleaginous smiles at me and looked straight into my eyes in rather an informal but reassuring manner." The Indians danced for her, and she rhapsodized about the glories of the American landscape when compared to any other place, of how the delicate musculature of the Indians represented "perfection in outline." These are hardly words of ridicule. *Chicago News,* n.d., 5, Cody Scrapbook, CHS.

24 Russell, *Lives and Legends of Buffalo Bill,* 375; Blackstone, *Buckskins, Bullets, and Business,* 27; and Prucha, *American Indian Policy in Crisis,* 324. Some sources claim that as many as six million people saw the show. This seems excessive. The show would have had to fill the grandstands three times a day for one hundred days to reach the inflated figure.

25 Undated newspaper clipping, 5, Cody Scrapbook, CHS.

26 Quoted in Yost, *Buffalo Bill,* 237.

27 *Chicago Reform Advocate,* May 19, 1893, in Buffalo Bill Scrapbook, Chicago Season, 1893, BBHC.

28 The Cody contracts appear in various locations. See, for example, earlier contracts such as T. J. Morgan to James McLaughlin, March 9, 1891, Records of Standing Rock Reservation, General Records, Miscellaneous Corres., 1891, box 517204, and Acting Agent Charles G. Penny, PR, to CIA, March 28, 1891, PR, LS, Press Copy Book 10, box 3, both RG 75, FARC, KC. On this occasion, Commissioner Morgan informed Agent McLaughlin that Cody had recently signed one contract and provided surety bond for "seventy-five Indians of agencies in North and South Dakota, sixty of whom are adult males and fifteen are women and children." Captain Penny forwarded the original contract to the BIA. Cody's 1893 contract appears in George LeRoy Brown to Cody and Salsbury, April 19, 1893, PR, LR and General Files, Series A, box 15, RG 75, FARC, KC. The individual 1894 contracts are reported in C. D. Marwell, Attorney, to Penny, Feb. 14, 1894, PR, General Records, June 12, 1891-Dec. 14, 1895, box 23, RG 75, FARC, KC.

29 *The Independent,* ca. March 1891, Collins Papers, folder 48, SDSHS. See above, 115.

30 Richard Walsh has written that Buffalo Bill displayed the bullet-riddled cabin of Sitting Bull on the grounds of the Wild West. If this is so, it was after the

Chicago fair. See Walsh, *Making of Buffalo Bill*, 299. See the explanation in Utley, *Lance and the Shield*, 312.

31 Henry De Ford should not be confused with Edward Jonathan Hoyt, another, more famous "Buckskin Joe," of Buckskin Joe's Wild West. Edward Hoyt had organized the cowboy band in Pawnee Bill's Wild West. Later, he toured on his own. See Russell, *Wild West*, 33, 65.

32 Russell, *Wild West*, 65; Prucha, *Great Father*, 2, 712–15; and Hagan, *Indian Rights Association*, 121, 144–45.

33 Russell, *Lives and Legends of Buffalo Bill*, 375.

34 George LeRoy Brown to Cody, April 26, 1893, PR, Miscellaneous LS, Press Copy Book 23, 1893, 31, RG 75, FARC, KC.

35 Quoted in Yost, *Buffalo Bill*, 240.

36 Rosa and May, *Buffalo Bill and His Wild West*, 160.

37 Francis Paul Prucha, "Thomas Jefferson Morgan (1889–93)," in Kvasnicka and Viola, *Commissioners of Indian Affairs*, 202. See also William T. Hagan, "Daniel M. Browning (1893–97)," in ibid., 205.

38 Hagan, "Daniel M. Browning," 205–6.

39 *Annual Report of the Commissioner of Indian Affairs, 1891* (Washington, D.C.: Government Printing Office, 1891), 79 (cited hereafter as CIA, *Annual Report*, 1891).

40 CIA to George LeRoy Brown, July 14, 1893, PR, General Records, March 11, 1893-Dec. 27, 1893, box 21, RG 75, FARC, KC.

41 *Eighteenth Annual Report of the Executive Committee of the Indian Rights Association* (Philadelphia: Office of the Indian Rights Association, 1901), 18–19 (hereafter cited as IRA, *Eighteenth Annual Report*). See also W. David Baird, "William A. Jones (1897–1904)," in Kvasnicka and Viola, *Commissioners of Indian Affairs*, 215.

42 CIA, *Annual Report*, 1891, 79.

43 Ibid.

44 Rydell, *All the World's a Fair*, 96–97. According to Rydell, a leading attraction at Atlanta was the Indian Village organized by C. P. Jordan, formerly employed at the Rosebud reservation. It included survivors of the slaughter at Wounded Knee. Ibid., 95.

45 Russell, *Wild West*, 26, 33, 40, 60–61.

46 Blackstone, *Buckskins, Bullets, and Business*, 27.

47 Walsh, *Making of Buffalo Bill*, 312.

48 "History of the Indian," *Omaha Daily Bee*, Aug. 16, 1897, quoted in Rydell, *All the World's a Fair*, 111.

49 Robert Bigart and Clarence Woodcock, "The Trans-Mississippi Exposition: The Flathead Delegation," *Montana, the Magazine of Western History* 29 (Autumn 1979):19–20.

50 CIA to U.S. Indian Agents, March 22, 1898, PR, General Records, box 22, RG 75, FARC, KC; and Rydell, *All the World's a Fair*, 113–17.

51 Quoted in Moses, *Indian Man*, 119.

52 CIA to William H. Clapp, Acting Agent, Pine Ridge, July 12 and 13, 1899; CIA to Sioux Indian Agents, Nov. 28, 1900; and Rev. William J. Cleveland to CIA, Nov. 8, 1900, all in PR, General Records, Jan. 8, 1898-Dec. 21, 1899, box 22, RG 75, FARC, KC. See also CIA to Mary C. Collins, Jan. 15, 1900, Collins Papers, folder 48, Wild West Shows, SDSHS; and IRA, *Eighteenth Annual Report*, 18-20.

53 Rydell, *All the World's a Fair*, 125.

54 Quoted in ibid., 136-37.

55 Ibid.

56 See CIA to John R. Brennan, Dec. 14, 1901, PR, General Records, Jan. 4, 1901-Dec. 14, 1901, box 22, RG 75, FARC, KC; and the document file, "Indian Congress, Pan-American Exposition, Frederick T. Cummins, Concessionaire & Gen's Manager," in AGO, Document File, 1890-1917, No. 445841, Old Military Branch, RG 94, NA. See also Rydell, *All the World's a Fair*, 143, 146, 149.

57 "Effects of Indian Exhibitions," ca. June 1901, Collins Papers, folder 48, Wild West Shows, SDSHS.

58 Ibid.

59 Walsh, *Making of Buffalo Bill*, 313-21; show program reproduced in Rosa and May, *Buffalo Bill and His Wild West*, 158. The program shows "Attack on a Settler's Cabin" overprinted with "Battle of the Little Big Horn, or Custer's Last Charge."

60 See the fascinating discussion of the change of context in Slotkin, *Gunfighter Nation*, 83-84. Slotkin argues that the substitution of an imperial theme, as in the charge at San Juan Hill, for "Custer's Last Stand," completed the evolution of the Wild West from a memorialization of the past to a celebration of the imperial future.

61 George LeRoy Brown to Cody, April 26, 1893, PR, Miscellaneous LS, Press Copy Book 23, 1893, RG 75, FARC, KC.

CHAPTER EIGHT

1 Quoted in John Wesley Hanson, *The Official History of the Fair, St. Louis, 1904* (St. Louis: Printed by the author, 1904), 53.

2 Rydell, *All the World's a Fair*, 157.

3 Moses, *Indian Man*, 155-56.

4 Rydell, *All the World's a Fair*, 155.

5 Memorandum, Samuel M. McCowan, "The Government's Indian Exhibit at the Louisiana Purchase Exposition," ca. July 1904, Chilocco Fair Files, 1905, Indian Archives Div., OHS (cited hereafter as McCowan Memorandum, OHS).

6 See *Indian School Journal*, May 15, 1904, 19, OHS. The journal replaced the *Chilocco Farmer and Stock Grower*, the newspaper of the Indian agricultural

training school. The *Indian School Journal* inaugurated its publication at the fair. In the same issue, the director continued: "Many a white man and woman can say with an old colored mammy who visited the Indian school: 'Law, honey, I ain't never had no chance as these people have.'"

7 CIA to U.S. Indian Agents, May 6, 1903, CUA, 22MDF, .897, Educational Exhibits, 1892–1935, box 161, RG 75, FARC, D. For details of the Interior Department's participation in St. Louis, see Sundry Civil Act of June 28, 1902, 32 Stats., 445.

8 McCowan to Charles M. Harvey, St. Louis *Globe-Democrat*, May 27, 1904, Chilocco Fair File, Indian Archives Div., OHS (cited hereafter as Chilocco Fair File, OHS). See also Robert A. Trennert, Jr., *The Phoenix Indian School: Forced Assimilation in Arizona, 1891–1935* (Norman: University of Oklahoma Press, 1988), 57–66. For additional biographical information, see Larry L. Bradfield, "A History of Chilocco Indian School" (Master's thesis, University of Oklahoma, 1963), 68, 72.

9 William John McGee signed his initials without using periods. The editor has amended his wishes.

10 McCowan Memorandum, OHS.

11 CIA to Indian Superintendents, May 6, 1903, PR, General Records, Jan. 7, 1903-Dec. 30, 1904, box 23, RG 75, FARC, KC.

12 McCowan's circular is quoted in O. A. Mitscher, U.S. Indian Agent, Osage Indian Agency, Pawhuska, Oklahoma Territory, to McCowan, June 24, 1903, Chilocco Fair file, OHS.

13 Seger to McCowan, June 22, 1903, ibid. Seger, in the early days of the Cheyenne and Arapaho reservation in Indian Territory, had taken a group of children to establish Colony. Seger could read and spell after a fashion, and served the early years at the colony as both agent and teacher. His secretaries usually cleaned up his correspondence with members of the Indian Office. Some of his unedited, handwritten letters may be found in the Hamlin Garland Collection, University of Southern California Library, Los Angeles. See also his heavily edited memoir, John H. Seger, *Early Days among the Cheyenne and Arapahoe Indians* (Norman: University of Oklahoma Press, 1934).

14 CIA to Joseph O. Smith, Agent, Southern Ute Agency, July 24, 1903, CUA, MDF, .897 Educational Exhibits, 1892–1935, box 161, RG 75, FARC, D.

15 CIA to Secretary of the Interior, Oct. 22, 1903, Chilocco Fair file, OHS.

16 McCowan to Theodore C. Lemmon, superintendent, Grand Junction School, Colo., Nov. 27, 1903, ibid. Superintendent Lemmon had written to McCowan on the twenty-fourth, offering to employ Jake Morgan, one of the Chilocco carpenters, for 750 dollars a year. McCowan kept the offer a secret because, as he told Lemmon, he needed Morgan, one of the leading cornets, in the World's Fair band. "I am paying him at the rate of $600.00 a year here. If he learn [*sic*] of this offer, of course he is liable to be discontented and leave, and I am doing my best to secure the finest band material in the country for the Fair."

17 Quoted in McCowan Memorandum, OHS.

18 Ibid.

19 Ibid; and *Indian School Journal*, May 15, 1904, 19, Indian Archives Div., OHS.

20 McCowan to Skiff, Oct. 26, 1903, Chilocco Fair file, OHS.

21 Ibid.

22 Ibid.

23 Handbill, "A Marvelous Reproduction of the Cliff Ruins in the Mancos Cañon," ibid.

24 Tobin to McCowan, Jan. 22, 1904, ibid. Tobin advertised his cliff-dweller ruins as a theme made famous by a number of noted lecturers, including Walter Hough of the National Museum. By inference, obviously, the gentlemen of science presumably endorsed Tobin's enterprise. Another of Tobin's handbills proclaimed that the Cliff Dwellers at the World's Fair was "an educational, historical, dramatic and sensational exhibition" and "unparalleled in history." It promised intense realism, "showing, in a manner never heretofore attempted, the ancient Arts, Crafts, Sciences, History, Ethnology and Progress of the Inhabitants of Yesterday." Ibid.

25 Anonymous, opening remarks and "Program of Original Indian Field Sports," Chilocco Fair file, OHS. McCowan certainly reviewed the remarks.

26 McCowan to Bush, Dec. 28, 1903, ibid.

27 See Chief Blue Horse to McCowan, Jan. 28, 1904; and McCowan to Chief Blue Horse, Feb. 1, 1904, Chilocco Fair file, OHS. The "Laramie Loafers" were Indians who had settled near the trading post and had become largely dependent on Euroamerican trade items. Later, Blue Horse was identified as among the "progressive" chiefs of the Oglalas by the government. See Olson, *Red Cloud and the Sioux Problem*, 20, 35; and Utley, *Last Days of the Sioux Nation*, 104, 135. Blue Horse had been one of Cummins's Show Indians at the Pan-American Exposition, and had also toured on occasion with Buffalo Bill.

28 McCowan to W. M. Peterson, Superintendent, Fort Lewis School, Colo., Dec. 12, 1903; and McCowan to McGee, Dec. 7, 1903, Chilocco Fair file, OHS.

29 McCowan to Chief Joseph, Spokane, Wash., Dec. 16, 1903, ibid.

30 McCowan to Earle T. McCarthur, Dec. 16, 1903, ibid.

31 Lieutenant General Samuel B. M. Young, Chief of Staff, to McCowan, Jan. 6, 1904, ibid.

32 Sayre to McCowan, March 27, 1904, ibid.

33 McCowan to J. W. Haddon, Superintendent, U.S. Indian School, Lawton, Okla., June 7, 1904, ibid.

34 Benjamin Levering, Chicago, to McCowan, July 30, 1904, ibid. Geronimo sold his signature for ten cents; he also sold signed photographs at fifty cents for a small one, two dollars for a larger one. See McCowan to Dr. G. F. Follansbee, Cleveland, Ohio, Oct. 4, 1904, ibid. See also Angie Debo, *Geronimo: The Man, His Time, His Place* (Norman: University of Oklahoma Press, 1976), 409–17.

35 McCowan to Follansbee, Oct. 4, 1904, Chilocco Fair file, OHS.

36 McCowan to Davis, Feb. 9, 1904, ibid.

37 Moya to McCowan, June 28, 1903, ibid.

38 The correspondence between McCowan and his former students and employ-
ees is extensive. Among the more revealing and, in some instances, poignant
examples are Jerdie Faber, Yuma Indian School, Ariz., to McCowan, Dec. 7,
1903, and March 21, 1904; Stella Hall, Sacaton, Ariz., to McCowan, Jan. 4, 1904;
Stacy Matlack, Uintah and Ouray Agency, Whiterocks, Utah, to McCowan,
Nov. 30 and Dec. 20, 1903; Frederick Freeman, Tacoma, Wash., to McCowan,
Dec. 24, 1904; and Theodore G. Lemmon, Superintendent, Grand Junction
Indian School, Colo., to McCowan, Dec. 9, 1903. Lemmon sent one of his former
students who was currently working in Grand Junction as a carpenter's assistant for thirty-five cents an hour to work for McCowan for transportation
costs, room, and board.

  Stacy Matlack, a Pawnee, after leaving Chilocco had completed voice training in Italy under the sponsorship of a Dr. Cutter of Boston. After a few performances in Oklahoma Territory, and little prospect of earning a living as an
opera singer, he returned to the Indian service. He became an issue clerk at
the Uintah and Ouray agency. He joined the chorus as a temporary employee
in the model Indian-school dining room.

39 McCowan Memorandum, OHS.

40 Ibid. To carry out his scheme of displaying the "Old Indian," McCowan "col-
lected" fifteen Apaches; nine Chiricahau Apache prisoners of war at Fort
Sill; forty-five Arapahos; thirty-five Cheyennes; twenty Chippewas; nineteen
Cocopas; five Comanches; five Maricopas; twenty-one Navajos; twenty Osages;
forty Pawnees; seven Pimas; thirty "Pueblo" Indians from San Juan, New
Mexico; two Pomos; thirty-six Sioux; and thirty Wichitas. In addition, five
Klackwaht and two Kwagiutl from Vancouver, British Columbia joined the
Indian encampment and occasionally performed in the school building.

41 McCowan to Emma McCowan, Feb. 16, 1904, Chilocco Fair file, OHS. The band
and chorus performed both secular and religious music. See McCowan to J. W.
Jenkins' Sons Music Co., Kansas City, Mo., Jan. 11, 1904, ibid.

42 McCowan to Charles E. McChesney, Rosebud, S.D., June 13, 1904, ibid.

43 McCowan to P. Staufer, May 23, 1904, ibid. McCowan elsewhere refers to the
Hopi or Moki. Hoopa is obviously a mistake by his typist, which was not caught
when the superintendent signed the document.

44 Staufer to McCowan, June 20, 1904, ibid.

45 McCowan to Staufer, June 27, 1904, ibid.

46 Sayre to McCowan, May 30, 1904, ibid.

47 Ibid.

48 McCowan Memorandum, OHS.

49 Ida Little Pifer, "World's Fair U.S. Indian Exhibit," *Indian School Journal*,
May 15, 1904, 15, Indian Archives Div., OHS.

50 Ibid. On the west wall of the building and in the chapel were displayed class-

room and industrial exhibits from the following government schools: Canton-
ment, Okla.; Riverside, Okla.; Pryor Creek, Mont.; Rosebud Reservation Day
Schools, S.D.; Santa Fe, N.M.; Rigg's Institute, Flandreau, S.D.; Chemawa,
Oreg.; Seneca School, Wyandotte, Indian Territory; St. Francis Mission, Rose-
bud, S.D.; Cheyenne School, Okla.; Zuni Training School, Zuni, N.M.; Rapid
City, S.D.; Genoa, Nebr.; Pima Reservation Day Schools, Ariz.; Ft. Shaw,
Mont.; Southern Ute, Ignacio, Colo.; Chilocco, Okla.; Grand Junction School,
Colo.; Crow Creek, S.D.; Grande Ronde, Oreg.; Osage, Okla.; Puyallup, Wash.;
Pine Ridge Day Schools, S.D.; Seger Training School, Okla.; Fort Apache,
Ariz.; Tomah, Wis.; Mt. Pleasant, Mich.; Western Shoshone, Nev.; Ponca School,
Okla.; Yankton, S.D.; Chamberlain, S.D.; and Hayward Training School, Wis.

51 Ibid., 16.

52 Ibid.

53 Ibid.

54 McCowan Memorandum, OHS.

55 Ibid.

56 Ibid.

57 McCowan to Emma Johnson, Sacaton, Ariz., Dec. 28, 1903, Chilocco Fair file,
OHS.

58 Alice M. Robertson, School Supervisor for the Creek Nation, Muskogee, Indian
Territory, to McCowan, Oct. 1, 1904, ibid. Apparently, the number of recent
deaths at Carlisle contributed to the willingness of the Indian service to force
the irascible Pratt from his tenure, dating from 1879, as superintendent. As
the agent at Wind River reservation explained to McCowan, out of the last fifteen Shoshonis who went to Carlise, only two remained alive; and of the five
Arapaho children, only one was alive. U.S. Agent, Shoshoni Agency, Wyo., to
McCowan, May 17, 1904, ibid.

59 Prucha, *Great Father*, 2:697–98; John S. Steckbeck, *Fabulous Redmen:
The Carlisle Indians and Their Famous Football Teams* (Harrisburg, Pa.:
J. Horace McFarland Co., 1951), 5, 8, 13, 17, 31; and Trennert, *Phoenix Indian
School*, 81–82.

60 Pelham to McCowan, Feb. 11, 1904, Chilocco Fair file, OHS.

61 In a variation on Pelham's desire for the band members to appear as "real," or
Show Indians, McCowan himself purged a few members of his band who looked
"too white" for other performers from the Sherman Institute, Riverside, Calif.,
who more closely resembled the part they were to play. See McCowan to
Robert M. Pringle, Riverside [*sic*] Indian School, Riverside, Calif., Jan. 26,
1904, ibid.

62 Handbill, "1904 season 1905, Special Announcement," Chilocco Fair file, OHS;
and McCowan to the Pastor of St. Paul's Methodist Church, Wichita, Kans.,
March 22, 1904, ibid.

63 William Cypher to C. H. Asbury, Oct. 18, 1904, ibid.

64 McCowan to Asbury, Nov. 10, 1904, ibid.

65 Rydell, *All the World's a Fair*, 182.

66 See Hoxie, *Final Promise*, 91.

67 *Indian School Journal*, Oct. 4, 1904, Indian Archives Div., OHS.

CHAPTER NINE

1 Russell, *Wild West*, 68.

2 See, for example, the correspondence in the Miller Brothers 101 Ranch Collection, box 100, Western History Collections, University of Oklahoma Library, Norman, Okla. (hereafter cited as 101 Ranch Col., OU).

3 Russell, *Wild West*, 68.

4 Ibid, 68, 70, 72, 76, 80, 85; the various circus files, "Show Correspondence: U.S. and Foreign," PR, General Records, MDF, boxes 163 and 166, RG 75, FARC, KC; and the W. H. Barten Papers, 1904-1924, MS 406, series 1, correspondence, folder 2, NSHS. Although only a partial list, some of the larger and more successful organizations included: Colonel Frederick T. Cummins' Wild West and Indian Congress, 1898-1911; the Wallace and Hagenbeck Circus; the Gabriel Brothers Champion Long Distance Riders Wild West (which gave way to the Scout Gabriel's Wild West and Indian Shows, 1908); the Great Forepaugh Wild West (Fish-Luella Forepaugh Wild West), 1903- ; Broncho John, Famous Western Horseman, and His Corps of Expert Horsemen, 1906; Bud Atkinson's Circus and Wild West, "The Largest and Best in the Eastern Hemisphere," 1912-1913; R. C. Carlisle's Wild West, ca. 1909; Cherokee Ed's Wild West, 1909; Dickey's Circle D Ranch Wild West and Frontier Day Fetes (Will A. Dickey, manager), 1909 and again in 1914 with the Cooper Brothers Famous Shows; Diamond Bar Ranch Wild West, 1909; Indian Bill's Wild West, 1903, became Indian Bill's Wild West and Cole and Rogers Circus Combined, 1906, which later still became Jones Brothers Buffalo Ranch Wild West, 1910, and Kit Carson's Buffalo Ranch Wild West, 1911-1914 (Thomas F. Wiedemann, proprietor); Lone Star May's Wild West, 1909; Captain Ed Seneschal's Wild West, 1904; McCaddon's International Shows and Wild West; Miller Brothers 101 Ranch Real Wild West, 1907-1916; Pawnee Bill's Historic Wild West, 1889-1908, and then combined the next year with Buffalo Bill; Snyder Brothers Wild West, 1909; Texas Bill's Wild West, ca. 1904, became Yankee Robinson Three-Ring Circus and Texas Bill's Wild West, 1911-1912; Texas Bud's Wild West, 1909; Texas Jack's Wild West, 1903; Tiger Bill's Wild West, 1909-1913; Tompkins Wild West and Frontier Exhibition, 1911, which combined with Cooper and Witby's European Circus in 1913; and Young Buffalo Wild West, 1909-1911, which combined with Colonel Fred Cummins' Far East, 1912.

5 Rosa and May, *Buffalo Bill and His Wild West*, 161, 174; Yost, *Buffalo Bill*, 340-41; and Russell, *Lives and Legends of Buffalo Bill*, 440-42.

6 Aberdeen, Scotland, *Daily Journal*, Aug. 27, 1904. A copy of the newspaper,

in the author's possession, was sent from the University of Aberdeen by Ferenc M. Szasz while on sabbatical, July 8, 1992.

7 Standing Bear, *My People the Sioux*, 252.

8 London *Daily Graphic*, Oct. 10, 1905, in the Peter H. Davidson Collection, box 1, BBHC.

9 Newspaper clipping: *The West Briton*, June 2, 1904, Cody Collection, box 2, folder 11, BBHC; and *Aberdeen Daily Journal*, Aug. 27, 1904, in author's possession.

10 See Standing Bear, *My People the Sioux*, 248.

11 George LeRoy Brown, Pine Ridge, to CIA, June 13, 16, 17, and 18, 1892, PR, General Records, Miscellaneous LS, vol. 19, box 6, RG 75, FARC, KC; George LeRoy Brown to CIA, Oct. 15, 1892, Records of the CIA, LR, Land Division, No. 38098–1892, RG 75, NA; and Newspaper clipping: *Chicago Times*, April 30, 1893, in Buffalo Bill Scrapbook, Chicago Season, 1893, BBHC.

12 Manuscript record, Barten Papers, 1904–1924, MS 406, NSHS.

13 Cummins to Brennan, Feb. 5, 1913, PR, General Records, MDF, "Show Correspondence: U.S. & Foreign," box 166, RG 75, FARC, KC.

14 See the contracts signed on Nov. 6, 1906, April 29, 1907, and April 10, 1908, in Barten Papers, Series 2, folder 2, contracts, NSHS.

15 Ibid. The clause reads, "the party of the second part [by his signature or mark] hereby acknowledges that the amount of said debt is correct, true, and for full value received and not subject to dispute after date and signing hereof."

16 Joe Paints Yellow to Barten, April 20, 1908, Barten Papers, Series 1, folder 2, NSHS.

17 Miller to Barten, May 1, 1908, ibid.

18 Pine Bird to Barten, June 7, 1910, ibid.

19 Barten to Bear in the Woods, May 16, 1910, ibid.

20 Barten to J. C. Miller, March 12, 1909, ibid.

21 Barten to Seaver, Feb. 25, 1914, ibid.

22 On one occasion, when Indians left the 101 Ranch Real Wild West and returned to Pine Ridge reservation via Gordon, Nebraska, they expressed their unhappiness with the Miller Brothers to trader Barten. When Joe Miller learned of this, he was outraged. "I never treated a bunch better and am sure they never had better quarters or food with any show," he wrote to Barten. "They were chronic kickers from the start. Nearly all claiming you had them sign the statement before you filled in the amts. and then made it more." See J. C. Miller to Barten, July 11, 1908, ibid. On another occasion, Barten proposed a solution to the problem of Indians leaving the show before the end of the season. "It seems that perhaps you may find some scheme by which they can be prevented from thus running away," he wrote to J. C. Miller. "[A]s soon as you get to a town to give exhibitions go to the railroad ticket agents and tell them not to sell tickets to any of your Indians except with your permission, that the Indians are under contract with you to stay the full season and that you are

their guardian for the season. The R.R. Agts. will no doubt thus help and favor you." Barten to J. C. Miller, June 11, 1908, ibid.

23 For the story of the Miller Brothers, see Fred Gipson, *Fabulous Empire: Colonel Zack Miller's Story* (Boston: Houghton Mifflin Co., 1946); and the courier, Miller Brothers, *101 Ranch Real Wild West and Great Far East* (Ponca City, Okla., n.d. [1927])—both items are in the Angie Debo Collection, Special Collections and University Archives, Oklahoma State University Library, Stillwater, Okla. (hereafter cited as OSU). See also Michael Wallis, "The Miller Brothers and the 101 Ranch," *Gilcrease Journal* 1 (Spring 1993):6—29.

24 Russell, *Lives and Legends of Buffalo Bill*, 384; Russell, *Wild West*, 78; and Wallis, "Miller Brothers," 21-22. When doing her research for her book on Geronimo, Angie Debo bought a copy of Fred Gipson's *Fabulous Empire*. On p. 230, she crossed out with a black fountain pen the following sentence that described Geronimo and the last buffalo hunt: "Twenty years before, it would have been no stunt at all for the old Apache to have killed a white man at twice the distance, hanging to the off-side of a running horse and shooting from under the animal's neck." In the left margin, she wrote "ignorant."

25 Russell, *Wild West*, 80–82.

26 Miller to Barten, May 9, 1907, Barten Papers, Series 1, folder 2, NSHS.

27 Barten to Miller, May 11, 1907, ibid.

28 Battice to W. C. Kohlenberg, April 30, 1907, Sac and Fox Agency files (SFA), folder 36, Indian Archives Div., OHS.

29 Battice to Kohlenberg, June 4, 1907, ibid.

30 Battice to Kohlenberg, Aug. 1, 1907, ibid.

31 Battice to Kohlenberg, Aug. 7, 1907, ibid.

32 Frank Shot Eyes to Joe Miller, Sept. 7, 1910, 101 Ranch Col., box 11, OU.

33 High Chief to Joe Miller, Dec. 28, 1910, ibid.

34 Miller to High Chief, Jan. 3, 1911, ibid.

35 Lucas to Miller, Dec. 22, 1910, ibid. American Indian "cowboys" and the development of Indian rodeo are examined in Peter Iverson, *When Indians Became Cowboys: Native Peoples and Cattle Ranching in the American West* (Norman: University of Oklahoma Press, 1994), 74–76, 190–91.

36 Pratt to Montezuma, April 27, 1911, Richard Henry Pratt Papers, box 14, folder 355, The Beinecke Rare Book and Manuscript Library, Yale University, New Haven, Conn. For Davis's work for the Bureau of American Ethnology, see Moses, *Indian Man*, 129-54.

37 Davis to Miller, Jan. 6, 1911, 101 Ranch Col., box 100, OU.

38 Miller to Davis, Jan. 7, 1911, ibid.

39 Battice to Kohlenberg, Sept. 14, 1911, SFA files, folder 36, Indian Archives Div., OHS. Battice added facetiously, "Big saying for a small person, is it not?"

40 For the Miller Brothers program, see Gipson, *Fabulous Empire*, 253; and the courier, *Miller Brothers 101 Ranch Real Wild West*, Special Collections, OSU.

41 Gipson, *Fabulous Empire*, 187.

42 The quotation is taken from printed letterhead paper of the Sarrasani Circus in Hans Stosch-Sarrasani to John Brennan, Pine Ridge, June 6, 1914, PR, General Records, MDF, box 165, Sarrasani Circus, 1900–1927, RG 75, FARC, KC.

43 Ibid.

44 Moore, Washington, D.C., to Miller, New York, July 2, 1913, Records of the CIA, Classified Files, 1907–1939, file 71231–13 PR 047, RG 75, NA.

45 Beasley to Miller, July 22, 1913, 101 Ranch Col., box 102, OU.

46 Beasley to Miller, July 22, 24, and Aug. 15, 1913; and Miller to Beasley, Sept. 5, 1913, in ibid.

47 Ibid., 336.

48 Miller to Brennan, Nov. 2 and Dec. 10, 1913, PR, General Records, MDF, 047, "Miller Bros. 101 Ranch Real Wild West Show, 1913–15," box 165, folder 1, RG 75, FARC, KC.

49 Gipson, *Fabulous Empire*, 345, 347, 350; and Russell, *Wild West*, 83.

50 Ibid.

51 J. C. Miller to E. B. Linnann, Chief Inspector, BIA, Aug. 13, 1914, Records of the CIA, Central Corres. Files, file 88704–14, box 180, RG 75, NA.

52 J. K. Jones, Esq., of the law firm engaged by the Miller Bros., to CIA, Aug. 14, 1914; and CIA to J. C. Miller, Aug. 15, 1914, ibid.

53 Gipson, *Fabulous Empire*, 350, 352.

54 H. H. Morgan, New York City, to Bill Arthur, Washington, D.C., Dec. 21, 1918, William Arthur Collection, Wyoming State Archives, Museum and Historical Department, Cheyenne, Wyoming.

55 Brennan to CIA, Oct. 21, 1914, PR, General Records, MDF, box 163, RG 75, FARC, KC; and Gipson, *Fabulous Empire*, 352. E. H. Gohl, a white missionary and teacher, reported other Show Indians stranded in Europe. Another German circus based in Berlin hired a group of sixteen Onondagas (twelve men, three women, and an infant). When war broke out, half the group was performing in Trieste on the Adriatic and the other group with the show in Essen. The performers reunited in Hamburg where, apparently, they too were mobbed by angry Germans and also thrown into jail as Russian and Serbian spies. Through the good offices of Congressman J. R. Clancy of Syracuse, some of the group got out through Stockholm, whereas the other group eventually made its dash across the Atlantic, starting from Cristiana, Norway, on October 16. Gohl's remarks may be found in "The Effect of Wild Westing," *The Quarterly Journal of the Society of American Indians* 2 (July–September 1914):226–28.

56 Miller to Brennan, Oct. 13, 1914, PR, General Records, MDF, box 160, RG 75, FARC, KC.

57 *New York Times*, Sept. 22, 1914, 4. Herbert Hoover, the London-based chairman of the American Relief Commission, estimated that since August 6, 87,000 Americans had fled Europe, of whom 8,637 received assistance. See *New York Times*, Oct. 1, 1914, 3.

58 John Brennan to J. C. Miller, Oct. 2, 1914; E. B. Meritt, Assistant CIA, to

Brennan, Oct. 26, 1914; and Miller to Meritt, Oct. 29, 1914, 101 Ranch Col., box 164, OU.

59 Miller to Brennan, Oct. 13, 1914, ibid.

60 Russell, *Wild West*, 88, 90.

61 Cody to R. Farington Elwell, Hopkington, Mass., Oct. 1, 1906, Cody Collection, box 1, folder 18, BBHC; and Commissioner Francis Leupp to G. W. Woodruff, Assistant Attorney General, Feb. 17, 1908, Records of the CIA, Classified Files, 1907–1939, file 11192–1908 PR 047, RG 75, NA. The Justice Department brought suit against McCaddon and the American Bonding Company of Baltimore, Md., for the purpose of recovering the unpaid salaries and the costs of transportation due the Indians. The suit was eventually settled, in July 1908, in favor of the six Lakotas employed by McCaddon. See John Brennan to Acting CIA, July 10, 1908, PR, General Records, MDF, box 163, RG 75, FARC, KC. Interestingly enough, Don Russell reports the McCaddon circus going bankrupt; but two pages later, he writes about Joseph T. McCaddon, brother-in-law to James A. Bailey, and apparently a partner in circuses. Russell, *Lives and Legends of Buffalo Bill*, 443, 445.

62 Cody to Michael R. Russell, Aug. 15, 1906, Raymond A. Burnside Papers, box 1, file 5, Iowa State Historical Department, Division of Historical Museum and Archives, Des Moines, Iowa (hereafter cited as Burnside Papers, ISHD).

63 Newspaper clipping: *The Dresden Daily*, Aug. 19, 1906, Cody Collection, box 2, folder 11, BBHC.

64 Cody to Russell, Aug. 15, 1906, Burnside Papers, box 1, file 5, ISHD.

65 Russell, *Lives and Legends of Buffalo Bill*, 443; Yost, *Buffalo Bill*, 341; and Rosa and May, *Buffalo Bill and His Wild West*, 179.

66 Russell, *Lives and Legends of Buffalo Bill*, 444–45.

67 Unidentified newspaper clipping, ca. April 1907, in Brennan Papers, box 1, SDSHS.

68 Ibid.

69 Russell, *Wild West*, 50–54, 75.

70 Courier, 1909 season, Buffalo Bill's Wild West and Pawnee Bill's Far East Combined, BBHC.

71 Rosa and May, *Buffalo Bill and His Wild West*, 204, 206.

72 Russell, *Lives and Legends of Buffalo Bill*, 452–56.

73 Ibid., 456. Among the buyers were the Miller Brothers' 101 Ranch Real Wild West, the Bison motion-picture company, and other circus organizations.

74 Yost, *Buffalo Bill*, 392, 395. Edward Arlington, a veteran of the Barnum and Bailey staff, was active with the Pawnee Bill Wild West show in 1907. The next year he joined the Miller Brothers organization, and later still owned the Oklahoma Ranch Wild West with a partner, Fred Beckman. After 1910, the Miller Brothers show became the Miller Bros. and Arlington show. Arlington's talents seem to have been those of an advance man, general agent, and railroad contractor. See Russell, *Wild West*, 57, 76, 82.

75 Russell, *Lives and Legends of Buffalo Bill*, 471–72.

76 The Barnum and Bailey Circus, however, apparently stayed on the road. On July 4, 1917, in Sioux Falls, South Dakota, their brochure proclaimed that "a circus ticket is an investment in democracy, in the glorious spirit of democracy which includes also that of sanity and humanity." Program, 1917, Cody Collection, box 8, folder 5, BBHC.

77 *New York Times*, Jan. 11, 1917, 14.

78 *The Outlook*, Jan. 24, 1917, in Burnside Papers, file 5, box 1, ISHD.

79 Newspaper clipping: *New York Times*, Jan. 17, 1917, in ibid.

CHAPTER TEN

1 Gohl, "Effect of Wild Westing," 227.

2 Ibid.

3 The phrase is taken from Chauncey Yellow Robe, "Menace of the Wild West Show," 224. The availability of alcohol most concerned Yellow Robe.

4 I borrow William T. Hagan's identification of Indians as "freedom fighters" from "How the West Was Lost," in Frederick E. Hoxie, ed., *Indians in American History* (Arlington Heights, Ill.: Harlan Davidson, 1988), 179–202.

5 Donald L. Parman, "Francis Ellington Leupp (1905–09)," in Kvasnicka and Viola, *Commissioners of Indian Affairs*, 224.

6 Ibid., 225–26; and Prucha, *Great Father*, 2:875–77.

7 Leupp to G. W. Woodruff, Assistant Attorney General, Feb. 17, 1908, Records of the CIA, Classified Files, 1907–1939, file 11192–1908 PR .047, RG 75, NA; Frank M. Conser, chief clerk, BIA, to John Brennan, Feb. 1, 1907, PR, General Records, box 23, RG 75, FARC, KC; and Larrabee to Brennan, July 10, 1908, PR, General Records, MDF, box 163, ibid.

8 Reid to Leupp, Oct. 13, 1908, PR, General Records, MDF, box 165, RG 75, FARC, KC.

9 Wynne to Leupp, Jan. 18, 1909, ibid.

10 Leupp to Gandy, Feb. 9, 1909, ibid.

11 Leupp to Brennan, Feb. 9, 1909, ibid.

12 Leupp to Brennan, Feb. 10, 1909, ibid.

13 Ibid.

14 Parman, "Francis Ellington Leupp," 230.

15 Prucha, *Great Father*, 2:767n.

16 Francis Leupp, *The Indian and His Problem* (New York: Charles Scribner's Sons, 1910), 324–35.

17 Ibid.

18 Gandy to Brennan, March 4, 1909, PR, General Records, MDF, .047 The Red Man's Syndicate (Earl B. Gandy), box 164, RG 75, FARC, KC.

19 Gandy to Brennan, May 5, 1908, PR, General Records, MDF, Box 165, RG 75,

FARC, KC. Goings, at various times, served as both agency interpreter and chief of agency police at Pine Ridge.

20 Gandy to Brennan, May 26, 1909, ibid.

21 Goings to Brennan, Aug. 11, 1909, ibid.

22 Earl Gandy to CIA, Aug. 26 and 30, 1909, ibid.

23 Brennan to CIA, Oct. 18, 1909, ibid.

24 Gandy to CIA, Aug. 30, 1909, ibid.

25 Gandy to CIA, June 2, 1910, PR, General Records, MDF, "Show Corres.: U.S. & Foreign," box 166, RG 75, FARC, KC.

26 Goings to Brennan, June 3, 1910, ibid.

27 Goings to Brennan, June 13, 1910, ibid.

28 Goings to Brennan, June 24, 1910, ibid.

29 Goings to Earle B. Gandy, July 9, 1910, ibid.

30 Goings to CIA, July 11, 1910, Records of the CIA, Classified Files, 1907–1939, file 58540–09, PR, transfer box 267, RG 75, NA.

31 R. Hardy, White Star Line, to Brennan, July 6, 1910, PR, General Records, MDF, box 164, RG 75, FARC, KC. Goings tried to remain cordial with Earle Gandy in London. He told him about the condition of the troupe and of the recent death of Kills Enemy's little girl, who died of "brain fever." All the troubles made Goings nervous and "nearly crazy." Unfortunately, no copies of letters written by Gandy to Goings survived. Goings to Gandy, July 9, 1910, ibid.

32 Hardy to Brennan, July 27, 1910, ibid.

33 Gandy to Brennan, July 29, 1910, ibid.

34 Telegram: White Star Line to Brennan, Aug. 3, 1910, and J. H. Dorch to Brennan, Sept. 13, 1910, ibid.

35 Contracts: Fernand Akoun and Co., April 5, 1911, PR, General Records, MDF, box 163, RG 75, FARC, KC. Akoun paid his employees below-the-average salary for Show Indians. He offered only $2.50 per week for all of the Indian employees.

36 "Report from the Office of the Mayor by the Poor Tax Committee," Records of the CIA, Central Corres. Files, General Corres. .047, file 97118–10, box 179, RG 75, NA.

37 Alvey A. Adee, Acting Secretary of State to Secretary of the Interior, Oct. 6, 1911, ibid.

38 Brennan to CIA, March 19, 1912, ibid.

39 Valentine to Congressman William A. Ashbrook, Johnstown, Ohio, Sept. 10, 1910, Records of the CIA, Central Corres. Files, General Service, 047 1910, file 69925–10, box 178, RG 75, NA.

40 See Diane T. Putney, "Robert Grosvenor Valentine (1909–12)," in Kvasnicka and Viola, *Commissioners of Indian Affairs*, 240–41.

41 Contract: Thomas Brown Eyes with John P. Tiffen, April 22, 1911. PR, General Records, MDF, box 160, RG 75, FARC, KC.

42 Bud Atkinson to Brennan, Oct. 20, 1912, PR, MDF, Show Correspondence:

U.S. and Foreign, box 166, RG 75, FARC, KC. Atkinson touted the salubrious climate, explaining also that the "death rate in Australia is the lowest of any country in the world. I mention this fact as some people are afraid of their health when they cross the Equator." Bud Atkinson had never crossed a reservation boundary.

43 Thomas Brown Eyes to Brennan, Nov. 15, 1912, PR, MDF, .047 Bud Atkinson, box 161, RG 75, FARC, KC. Four of the Indians joined Atkinson in Chicago and apparently were not under contract, and therefore were not covered by the bond that the show left with Brennan. Two were Brule from Rosebud, George Sky Eagle and wife; and two were Anishinaabeg from White Earth, Minnesota, Sherman Charging Hawk and Emmet Eagle Bear. Information taken from Brennan to CIA, June 20, 1913, Records of the CIA, Classified Files, 1907–1939, PR .047, file 108031–12, RG 75, NA.

44 Brown Eyes to Brennan, Dec. 27, 1912, PR, MDF, .047 Bud Atkinson, box 161, FARC, KC.

45 Smith to Brennan, Jan. 7, 1913, ibid.

46 Brown Eyes to Brennan, Jan. 30, 1913, ibid. He had other bad news to report as well. The infant of John Eagle Horse died on January 28 after a three-day illness described as "summer complaint and bowel trouble."

47 Janis to Brennan, Jan. 31, 1913, ibid.

48 Smith, "on board the 'Ventura,'" to Brennan, April 22, 1913, ibid.

49 Telegram: Bryan to Brennan, March 31, 1913, ibid.

50 Brown Eyes to Brennan, June 9, 1913, ibid.

51 Brennan to CIA, June 20, 1913, ibid.

52 Brown Eyes to Brennan, June 9, 1913, ibid.

53 Brennan to Mensch, July 24, 1913, ibid.

54 F. M. Conser, Chief Clerk of the BIA, to Superintendent H. H. Johnson, Puyallup Indian School, Dec. 18, 1908, Records of the CIA, Central Corres. Files, General Service, .047 Correspondence relative to Indian Office Exhibit at the Alaska-Yukon-Pacific Exposition at Seattle, 1909, file 56460–08, box 178, RG 75, NA.

55 Sells to Superintendents in Charge of Indians, April 4, 1914, Chilocco Fair file, OHS. The featured "academic" subjects included composition, penmanship, geography (papier-mâché models of the school plants and relief maps of the reservation), hygiene and physiology, nature study (mounted wildflowers), and drawing.

56 Paul Wilson to Charles E. McConnell, May 26, 1905, CUA, MDF, .047, box 1, RG 75, FARC, D.

57 Explained in C. F. Larrabee to Custer, July 21, 1905, ibid.

58 Custer to Larrabee, May 21, 1906, ibid.

59 Telegram: Larrabee to Custer, July 5, 1906, ibid. The committee was established in Philadelphia during the spring of 1879, first as an Indian committee of the Women's Home Mission Society of the First Baptist church. In June 1881,

the organization changed its name to the Indian Treaty-Keeping and Protective Association, and finally, in October 1883, as the Women's National Indian Association (WNIA). By 1886 there were eighty-three branches of the organization. In 1888, the group began to publish a monthly paper called *The Indian's Friend*. With the rise of the IRA by the late 1880s, the WNIA involved itself mainly in missionary work and in improving the domestic economy of Indian homes. In 1901, the organization's title reverted to simply the National Indian Association. See Prucha, *Great Father*, 2:612–13.

60 Bertha P. Dutton, *American Indians of the Southwest* (Albuquerque: University of New Mexico Press, 1975), 153–54.

61 Larrabee to Custer, July 5, 1905, CUA, MDF, .047, box 1, RG 75, FARC, D.

62 Records of the Southern Ute fairs are taken from Southern Ute Agency files, box 161, RG 75, FARC, D.

63 United States Indian Service Bulletin, No. 1, "Indian Fairs," Dec. 31, 1909, 1, in Chilocco Fair file, OHS.

64 Ibid.

65 Ibid., 2.

66 Ibid.

67 Ibid.

68 Ibid., 3.

69 Ibid., 2.

70 Ibid., 4–5.

71 Ibid., 5.

72 Ibid.

73 Ibid., 6.

74 Souvenir Program, Third Annual Fair, Lower Brule, South Dakota, Sept. 10–13, 1912, Chilocco Fair file, OHS.

75 Ibid.

76 Summary was compiled from Records of the CIA, Central Corres. Files, General Service, General Corres. .047, file 85991–14, box 180, RG 75, NA.

77 Lawrence C. Kelly, "Cato Sells (1913–21)," in Kvasnicka and Viola, *Commissioners of Indian Affairs*, 244–46.

78 So great was the demand for Show Indians that, on occasion, a superintendent had to advise prospective employers that none were available. As John Brennan wrote to one showman interested in hiring twenty Oglalas from Pine Ridge in a Wild West show that would perform at London's Crystal Palace, he regretted "to say that our supply of show Indians is about exhausted. Buffalo Bill, 101 Wiedemann or Young Buffalo and other shows have secured about all available show Indians from Pine Ridge for this season. The 101 people have taken 25 Pine Ridge Indians to Germany; another bunch [Atkinson] of them is in Australia. I believe it would be a waste of time for you to come here." Brennan to James R. Quirk, Wheatland, Wyo., April 2, 1913, PR, General Records, MDF, box 160, RG 75, FARC, KC. Brennan could also have listed Indians with

Sells-Floto Circus; Oklahoma Bill's Wild West Show; Thomas Wiedemann, who was actually managing the Kit Carson's Buffalo Ranch Wild West Show; the Patterson Carnival Company of Shreveport, La.; the New York Hippodrome (which, in addition to the Pine Ridge Sioux, also employed twenty residents of the Rio Grande Pueblos); the Hagenbeck Circus in Germany; Indian Pete's Wild West Show and Congress of Rough Riders; and Lucky Tull and Yoder's Combined Wild West and Dog Shows, of Daw Burew, Arkansas. Contracts appear in PR, Central Corres. Files, General Service, General Corres. .047, box 179, RG 75, FARC, KC.

79 Sells to Seldomridge, July 19, 1913, CUA, MDF, .047 Fairs & Exhibitions, box 1, RG 75, FARC, D. The phrase "promiscuous employment of Indians" first appeared in Commissioner Valentine's letter to the Rev. John Eastman, Mdewakanton Sioux and brother to Dr. Charles A. Eastman. The Presbyterian minister had written to the commissioner after the annual meeting of the Conference of Presbyterian and Congregational Churches of South Dakota. The conference found Wild West shows "antagonistic to advancement in either civilization or christianization." See R. G. Valentine to John P. Williamson and John Eastman, Greenwood, S.D., April 14, 1911, Records of the CIA, Central Corres. Files, General Service, General Corres. .047, file 15677–11, box 179, RG 75, NA. The phrase was repeated in Assistant Commissioner Abbot's admonition to Jack Red Cloud not to encourage employment in the shows and then went on to stress that the "office . . . is endeavoring in every way to induce them to settle on their allotments and become industrious, self-respecting citizens." Had both Valentine and Abbot stopped there, Bureau policies would have pleased Sells; but they did not. "There are, of course, some reputable exhibition companies in whose employment Indians who are not actively engaged in some profitable industrial pursuit on the reservation may desire advantages." See Abbot to Red Cloud et al., Jan. 10, 1912, PR, General Records, MDF, box 162, RG 75, FARC, KC.

80 Sells to Hayden, Oct. 8, 1913, Records of the CIA, Central Corres. Files, General Corres. .047, file 109311–13, box 179, RG 75, NA.

81 For an explanation of the factionalism and events at Hopi, see Frederick J. Dockstader, "Hopi History, 1850–1940," in Alfonso Ortiz, ed., *Handbook of North American Indians, Southwest*, vol. 9 (Washington: Smithsonian Institution, 1979), 528–29; and Parman, "Francis Ellington Leupp," 226.

82 E. B. Meritt to Walter Runke, n.d. [ca. Nov.-Dec. 1914], Central Corres. Files, General Corres. 047, file 91249–14, RG 75, NA. Along the Joy Zone, the Santa Fe Railroad operated a concession, a three-dimensional rendering of the Grand Canyon, which also included a model pueblo staffed by Hopi potters and Navajo weavers and managed by Fred Harvey, the famous restaurateur and hotelier. Rydell, *All the World's a Fair*, 228,

83 Telegram: Sells to Brennan, Jan. 29, 1914, PR, MDF, .047 Miller Bros. 101 Ranch Real Wild West Show, 1913-15, box 164, FARC, KC. The following year,

when the Miller Brothers again applied for permission to hire forty Indians for their road show, Brennan wired the commissioner that "the better plan . . . would be for the Office not to sanction or approve employment of Indians for show purposes, [I] believe very few Indians would join shows if the Government refused to protect their contracts." But as Sells had observed the previous year, Indians were bound to join the shows. Yes, one could discourage participation in the shows; but to protect the Indian Office from unwarranted expenses, surety bonds or cash deposits were the best means. See telegram: Brennan to CIA, Jan. 25, 1915, ibid.

84 Cato Sells to L. H. Connolly, Secretary of the Missouri Slope Agriculture and Fair Association, Mandan, N.D., Aug. 24, 1914, Records of the CIA, Classified Files, 1907–1939, file 82541–14 Standing Rock 047, RG 75, NA; and newspaper clipping: n.d., in Records of the CIA, Central Corres. Files, General Service, file 99510–14, box 180, RG 75, NA. See also Prucha, *Great Father*, 2:879–880.

85 Circular: CIA to Superintendents in charge of Indians, March 28, 1913, Records of the CIA, Central Corres. Files, General Service, file 37954–14, box 180, RG 75, NA.

86 Albert H. Kneale to CIA, Sept. 29, 1914, Records of the CIA, Classified Files, 1907–1939, Standing Rock, file 137441–14 Standing Rock 047, RG 75, NA.

87 For an explanation of the Interior Department suggestions, see Andrieus A. Jones, First Assistant Secretary of the Interior, to Edward Everett Young, President of the San Juan, New Mexico, Civic League, Oct. 7, 1915, Records of the CIA, Central Corres. Files, General Service, General Corres. 047, file 106579–15, box 182, RG 75, NA. Jones wrote: "As the Indians are ultimately to be absorbed into the body of American citizenship, their destiny is bound up with that of the whites, and for this reason it is better for the Indians to exhibit their products at county fairs in direct competition with those of white farmers wherever they may be sufficiently advanced to do this with profit to themselves, thus making them feel that they are an integral part of the community on the same basis of the whites." Young answered that it might be pretty to think so in theory, but the "Navajos are poor and scattered and are herders anyway." Young to Jones, Oct. 14, 1915, ibid.

88 Covey to CIA, Sept. 1, 1916, Records of the CIA, Classified Files, 1907–1939, file 67506–1916, Standing Rock 047, RG 75, NA.

89 Telegram: CIA to Covey, Sept. 16, 1916, ibid.

90 Sells to Brennan, May 5, 1916, PR, MDF, box 160, RG 75, FARC, KC.

91 Meritt to Cochrane, Aug. 4, 1916, ibid.

92 Percival S. Ridsdale to Indian Superintendents, Aug. 14, 1917, CUA, MDF, .897 Southern Ute Fair, 1907–1939, box 161, RG 75, FARC, D.

93 See E. J. Ayers, Acting Assistant Secretary of the Interior to CIA, Aug. 10, 1917, and E. B. Meritt to Ayers, Aug. 21, 1917, Records of the CIA, Central Corres. Files, General Service, General Corres. 047, file 76094–17, box 183, RG 75, NA.

CHAPTER ELEVEN

1 Steven Mintz and Randy Roberts, *Hollywood's America: United States History through Its Films* (St. James, N.Y.: Brandywine Press, 1993), 10. Indians, perhaps some of them from Buffalo Bill's Wild West, had already appeared in 1894 in vignettes filmed by the Edison company for the penny-arcade peep shows. Although at first considered a novelty, film historians Ralph and Natasha Friar have explained that the Kinetoscope and its competitor, the Mutoscope, became popular. Screen projections began two years later. See Friar and Friar, *Only Good Indian*, 69–70.

2 Mintz and Roberts, *Hollywood's America*, 10.

3 Ibid., 7, 10.

4 Ibid., 12.

5 William K. Everson, *The Hollywood Western* (New York: Citadel Press, 1992), 12.

6 Ibid., 23; and Berkhofer, *White Man's Indian*, 100.

7 Friar and Friar, *Only Good Indian*, 78.

8 Everson, *Hollywood Western*, 23.

9 Ibid., 23–34.

10 Ibid., 25, 26.

11 Michael Welsh, "Origins of Western Film Companies, 1887–1920," in Richard W. Etulain, ed., *Western Films: A Brief History* (Manhattan, Kans.: Sunflower University Press, 1983), 5–8; and Everson, *Hollywood Western*, 28, 29.

12 Everson, *Hollywood Western*, 29.

13 Ibid., 33; Kevin Brownlow, *The War, the West, and the Wilderness* (New York: Alfred A. Knopf, 1979), 256; and Jon Tuska, *The Filming of the West* (Garden City, N.Y.: Doubleday and Company, 1976), 25.

14 Everson, *Hollywood Western*, 35. Tuska, on the other hand, remarks that "Ince didn't care two pins about 'starring' Westerns in the Broncho Billy vein"; he gave William Eagleshirt a major role, but it was not necessarily a starring role. Tuska, *Filming the West*, 25.

15 Everson, *Hollywood Western*, 35.

16 Tuska, *Filming the West*, 24.

17 Everson, *Hollywood Western*, 37.

18 Tuska lists *The Battle of Elderbush Gulch* as a Biograph release in 1914, whereas both Everson and Brownlow write that it appeared in 1913 and therefore *before* Cody's work. See Tuska, *Filming the West*, 25; Everson, *Hollywood Western*, 37; and Brownlow, *War, the West, and the Wilderness*, 330.

19 Russell, *Lives and Legends of Buffalo Bill*, 456; and Rosa and May, *Buffalo Bill and His Wild West*, 204. Evidence exists, however, to suggest that Cody had been considering making a film such as *The Indian Wars* for some time. In the summer of 1910, Cody's sometime friend, Captain Jack Crawford, "The Poet Scout," learned about Cody's plans to make historical films. Crawford

approached the Miller Brothers, who were themselves making movies, and suggested that they go into partnership. Crawford would go to Pine Ridge, hire Indians, and reenact the "Custer Massacre." "The pictures," he explained to Joe Miller, "would be worth a barrel of money. In fact I could myself take the pictures and lecture, telling the story and reciting my poems at the same time." Crawford to Miller, July 21, 1910, 101 Ranch Col., box 100, OU.

20 Cody eventually paid the fifty-three veterans of the Two Bills show their lost wages with $1,313.48 out of his own pocket. By doing so, he also generated goodwill on the reservation, which probably benefited the production of *The Indian Wars*. Cody explained to his former employees, "I want all you boys to be satisfied. I don't want one of you to suffer—and I'm not going to allow it. You need the money and you are going to have it. You have been my friends and I am going to be yours—to the limit." Quoted in Ryley Cooper to Denver *Post*, Oct. 28, 1913, in Brennan Papers, Scrapbook 1, SDSHS.

21 Bob Lee, "Cody Assembles 'Greats' for 'Indian Wars' Film," *Rapid City Journal*, June 22, 1969, in Brennan Papers, Scrapbook 1, SDSHS. Lee wrote a series of articles that appeared every Sunday between June 15 and August 3, 1969 (hereafter cited as Lee, "Indian Wars").

22 Nancy M. Peterson, "Buffalo Bill, the Movie Maker," *Empire Magazine*, Feb. 27, 1977, p. 66, and notes in Victor Weybright Corporate Papers, 1920–1974, University of Wyoming Library, Division of Rare Books and Special Collections, Laramie, Wyo. See also Ryley Cooper to Denver *Post*, October 10, 1913, in Brennan Papers, Scrapbook 1, SDSHS. Cooper had been sent by Tammen to report on the events surrounding the filming. He filed by "day press rate collect" his daily column for both the Denver *Post* and the Kansas City *Post*. Apparently, Agent John Brennan kept the typescript of Cooper's dispatches.

23 Newspaper clipping: Denver *Post*, n.d., Buffalo Bill Scrapbook, 1914, BBHC.

24 Garrison to Brennan, Aug. 28, 1913, in Brennan Papers, Scrapbook 1, SDSHS.

25 Lee, "Indian Wars."

26 Telegram: Cody to Brennan, Aug. 26, 1913, Brennan Papers, Scrapbook 1, SDSHS.

27 Telegram: Sells to Lane, Aug. 27, 1913, Records of the CIA, Classified Files, 1907–1939, file 104090–13 PR 047, RG 75, NA.

28 Telegram: Brennan to Sells, Aug. 29, 1913, Brennan Papers, folder 25, SDSHS.

29 Sells to Brennan, Oct. 3, 1913, Records of the CIA, Classified Files, 1907–1939, file 104090–13 PR 047, RG 75, NA.

30 In Cooper to Denver *Post*, Oct. 9, 1913, in Brennan Papers, Scrapbook 1, SDSHS. From promotion brochures, one may also reconstruct the descriptions of each reel. Cody divided the film into two sections. Section 1 contained two reels. The first opened with shots of Generals Miles, Frank Baldwin, Marion Maus, and Charles King; Colonel H. C. Sickels, commander of the Seventh Cavalry; Scout Phillip Wells; Jack Red Cloud; Short Bull; and Cody; and finished with the Battle of Summit Springs. Reel 2 depicted the Battle of Warbonnet

Creek, the fight with Yellow Hand, and "The First Scalp for Custer." Section 2 represented the original theme of "The Last Indian War." Reel 1 portrayed the origins of the Ghost Dance, Cody's abortive mission to Sitting Bull's camp, and the death of Sitting Bull. Reel 2 represented the Sioux flight to the badlands, Big Foot's surrender at Porcupine Butte, and going into camp at Wounded Knee creek. Reel 3 depicted the slaughter at Wounded Knee. Reel 4 encompassed the Drexel Mission fight and the Indians' council with General Miles. Reel 5 showed the surrender of the Indians and the grand review of troops. Reel 6 concluded the feature with "School Days and Now—1914," filmed at the market holiday at Pine Ridge, purportedly showing the transition of "the Red Man from the warpath to peace pursuits, under the American Flag—the Star Spangled Banner." The program, n.d., is for a performance at the Tabor Grand Opera House in Denver, with daily matinees at 2:15 and reserved seating at twenty-five cents. At evening performances, reserved seating went for twenty-five cents and fifty cents. Printed program is taken from Cody Collection, folder 1, box 2, BBHC.

31 Cooper to Denver *Post*, Oct. 11, 1913, in Brennan Papers, Scrapbook 1, SDSHS.

32 Miles to Brennan, Oct. 12, 1913, ibid. Cody explained to a reporter that "no amount of money would tempt Gen. Miles to view the reproduction of this battle." Newspaper clipping: Gordon (Nebr.) *Independent*, Oct. 24, 1913, in ibid.

33 Reconstructed from several dispatches by Ryley Cooper, which appear in ibid.

34 Louisa Frederici Cody and Courtney Ryley Cooper, *Memories of Buffalo Bill* (New York: Appleton, 1919), 306.

35 Cody, *The Moving Picture World*, March 14, 1914, quoted in Lee, "Indian Wars."

36 Ibid.

37 Newspaper clipping: The Chadron *Chronicle*, Oct. 16, 1913, in Brennan Papers, Scrapbook 1, SDSHS.

38 Newspaper clipping: The Martin (Nebr.) *Messenger*, Oct. 18, 1913, ibid.

39 Unidentified newspaper clipping: Chadron, Sheridan County, Nebr., Oct. 24, 1913, ibid.

40 Walsh, *Making of Buffalo Bill*, 345—46.

41 Newspaper clipping: Martin (Nebr.) *Messenger*, Oct. 18, 1913, in Brennan Papers, Scrapbook 1, SDSHS.

42 Cooper to Tammen, Oct. 15, 1913, in ibid.

43 See Utley, *Last Days of the Sioux Nation*, 231—38.

44 Newspaper clipping: Denver *Post*, Oct. 18, 1913, in Brennan Papers, Scrapbook 1, SDSHS.

45 Ibid.

46 Cooper to Tammen, Oct. 16, 1913, Brennan Papers, Scrapbook 1, SDSHS.

47 Cooper to Denver *Post*, Oct. 21, 1913, in ibid.

48 Cooper to Denver *Post*, Oct. 23, 24, and 27, 1913, in ibid.

49 Cooper to Denver *Post*, Oct. 28, 1913, in ibid.

50 *Rapid City Journal*, Oct. 21, 1913, quoted in Lee, "Indian Wars."

51 New York *World*, Nov. 30, 1913, 1. Gilmore was quoted in an earlier newspaper account dated Nov. 4. In it, he claimed that the Indians were given all the blame for the massacre when, in fact, the soldiers were the ones to blame. The way the motion picture company re-created the massacre was "a disgrace to the government under whose sanction it was taken." *Iowa City Journal*, Nov. 4, 1913, 1.

52 Ibid. The exact number of dead from Big Foot's band of Minneconjous may never be known. The burial detail that went out from Pine Ridge five days after the battle interred 146 bodies gathered from the battlefield. There were 51 wounded Indians who reached Pine Ridge agency, and of these, at least 7 later died. Robert M. Utley suggests that another 20 to 30 who had escaped the killing ground died from wounds and exposure and were buried by family or friends. Utley, *Last Days of the Sioux Nation*, 270, 227–30. Survivors and their friends may also have removed some of the dead and dying before the burial party arrived from Pine Ridge. Joseph Horn Cloud, an Oglala, later listed the names of 186 dead. Former agent and later Indian Inspector James McLaughlin conducted his own interviews and suggested that Horn Cloud did not account for all casualties. Some sources suggest total deaths probably exceed 250. See Richard E. Jensen, R. Eli Paul, and John E. Carter, *Eyewitness at Wounded Knee* (Lincoln: University of Nebraska Press, 1991), 20.

53 *Iowa City Journal*, Nov. 4, 1913, 1.

54 Brennan to Miles, Dec. 6, 1913, Brennan Papers, Scrapbook 1, SDSHS.

55 Brennan to Moorehead, Jan. 19, 1914, in ibid.

56 Baldwin to Brennan, Dec. 6, 1913, in ibid. Baldwin, acting assistant inspector general at the time of the Ghost Dance troubles at Pine Ridge, was appointed by Miles to head a court of inquiry into the Wounded Knee massacre. See Utley, *Last Days of the Sioux Nation*, 245.

57 Baldwin to Brennan, Dec. 6, 1913, Brennan papers, Scrapbook 1, SDSHS.

58 Day to Brennan, Dec. 8, 1913, PR, General Records, MDF, Buffalo Bill Wild West Show Bankruptcy, 1913, box 162, RG 75, FARC, KC.

59 Philip Wells to Editor, Jan. 10, 1914, in the *Daily Journal* (Rapid City, S.D.), n.d., in Brennan Papers, Scrapbook 1, SDSHS.

60 Jack Red Cloud, Good Lance, Fire Lightning, Thunder Bear, Short Horn, Chief Knife, White Tail, Long Cat, Afraid of Bull, Good Dog, Bird Necklace, Iron Crow, Short Dog, Eagle Pipe, Red Tomahawk, and Two Bull, President, Edward Brown, Secretary, to William Howard Taft, Dec. 23, 1913, PR, General Records, MDF, Buffalo Bill Wild West Show Bankruptcy, box 162, RG 75, FARC, KC.

61 The assertion that the government delayed the release of the film by six months is made in Wooster, *Nelson A. Miles and the Twilight of the Frontier Army*, 259.

62 Lee, "Indian Wars."

63 Brownlow, *War, the West, and the Wilderness*, 228. Brownlow cites William

S. E. Coleman, a Cody researcher who wrote for *Player* magazine, as the source for the Black Elk quotation. No other source exists that lists the Oglala holy man as a participant in the re-creation of Wounded Knee.

64 Brownlow also writes that Miles's most "tactless action" was to reenact the Battle of Wounded Knee "precisely where the massacre had occurred, over the graves of the victims. This led to an outcry from the Indians." Ibid., 232–33.

65 Cody to Elwell, Dec. 13, 1913, Cody Collection, box 1, folder 25, BBHC. Biographical information on Elwell comes from Russell, *Lives and Legends of Buffalo Bill*, 267.

66 Unidentified newspaper clipping, Dec. 25, 1913, in Cody Collection, box 1 folder 25, BBHC.

67 Newspaper clipping: *Daily News* (Lawton, Okla.), Jan. 11, 1914, in ibid.

68 Yost, *Buffalo Bill*, 481n.

69 Lee, "Indian Wars."

70 Hauke to E. J. Ayers, Chief Clerk for Department of the Interior, Jan. 14, 1920, Records of the CIA, Central Corres. Files, General Service, General Corres. 047, file 10697–19, box 184, RG 75, NA.

71 Newspaper clipping: *Chicago Examiner*, Jan. 22, 1914, in ibid.

72 Quoted in Lee, "Indian Wars." President Wilson, Cato and Mrs. Sells, and E. B. Meritt, assistant commissioner, and his wife saw the film at another special screening sometime in April at the Home Club. Unidentified newspaper clipping, ca. April, 1914, in Cody Collection, Buffalo Bill Scrapbook, 1914, BBHC.

73 Brochure, "First Public Presentation," Cody Collection, box 2, folder 1, BBHC.

74 Newspaper clipping: Washington *Herald*, Feb. 28, 1914, Cody Collection, Buffalo Bill Scrapbook, 1914, BBHC.

75 Newspaper clipping: *Washington Post*, n.d., in ibid.

76 Newspaper clipping: Omaha *World Herald*, March 18, 1914, in ibid.

77 John F. Murray to CIA, March 9, 1913, Records of the CIA, Central Corres. Files, General Service, General Corres. 047, file 27458–14, box 180, RG 75, NA.

78 Newspaper clipping: Denver *Post*, March 7, 1914, Cody Papers, CHS; and Peterson, "Buffalo Bill, the Movie Maker," 66, in Victor Weybright Corporate Papers, 1920–1974, American Heritage Center, University of Wyoming, Laramie.

79 Newspaper clipping: Denver *Post*, n.d., in Cody Collection, Buffalo Bill Scrapbook, 1914, BBHC.

80 Quoted in Lee, "Indian Wars."

81 Ibid.

82 See advertisement in Yost, *Buffalo Bill*, 391. These distributors included: F. W. Redfield of Atlanta, who had exclusive rights to Georgia, Tennessee, Florida, Alabama, North Carolina, and South Carolina; John F. Connolly of Salt Lake City for Montana, Utah, Wyoming, New Mexico, Colorado, and Nevada; Robert A Brackett of Los Angeles for California and Arizona; W. T. Norton of Portland for Oregon, Washington, and Idaho; and E. H. Painter of Cleveland for Ohio.

83 Garlow to Cody, April 5, 1914, Cody Collection, box 4, folder 4, BBHC.

84 Peterson, "Buffalo Bill, the Movie Maker," 66.

85 Circular: Fred Garlow to Theatre Managers, April 6, 1914, Cody Collection, box 4, folder 4, BBHC.

86 E. B. Meritt to William Jim Gabriel, May 22, 1914, PR, General Records, MDF, 048, box 166, RG 75, FARC, KC.

87 CIA to L. C. Wheeler, the Selig Polyscope Co., Chicago, Jan. 4, 1918, Records of the CIA, Central Corres. Files, General Service, General Corres. 047, file 629-18, box 183, RG 75, NA. Companies that offered film as an educational tool proved most successful in their dealings with the Bureau. A few even offered to sell, at reasonable prices, moving-picture projectors to the government, which could then use them in reservation schools. See C. L. Chester to Brennan, May 9, 1917, PR, General Corres., MDF, 047 1917, box 160, RG 75, FARC, KC; and CIA to O. B. Wood, Lea-Bel Co., Chicago, Feb. 27, 1917, Records of the CIA, Central Corres. Files, General Service, General Corres. 047, file 16163-17, box 183, RG 75, NA.

88 Yellow to Brooks, Aug. 17, 1916, Records of the CIA, Classified Files 1907-1939, file 128345-15 PR 047, RG 75, NA.

89 Rosa and May, *Buffalo Bill and His Wild West*, 209.

90 Ibid; and Russell, *Lives and Legends of Buffalo Bill*, 458, 463, 469.

91 Yost, *Buffalo Bill*, 405-6.

92 Tim McCoy, with Ronald McCoy, *Tim McCoy Remembers the West: An Autobiography* (Garden City, N.Y.: Doubleday and Co., 1977), 161-86; and Bodie Thoene and Rona Stuck, "Navajo Nation Meets Hollywood," *American West* 20 (1983):38-44.

93 Commissioner Sells, for example, insisted on occasion that Indians appearing in films should be dressed in "civilized dress"—which obviously defeated the purpose of hiring the Show Indians in the first place. See Sells to O. B. Wood, Lea-Bel Co., Chicago, Feb. 27, 1917, Central Corres. Files, General Service, file 16163-17, box 183, RG 75, NA.

CHAPTER TWELVE

1 Russell, *Wild West*, 85. 106, 112. See also Fredriksson, *American Rodeo*, 21.

2 Joe C. Miller to W. H. Barten, Nov. 5, 1924, Barten Papers, Series 1, F6 1920-1924, NSHS.

3 See Ellsworth Collings and Alma Miller England, *The 101 Ranch*, with a foreword by Glen Shirley (Norman: University of Oklahoma Press, 1971), 187-214.

4 Jermark to Colonel Frederick Cummins, Los Angeles, June 29, 1925, PR, MDF, 047, 1925-1928, box 161, RG 75, FARC, KC. It had been some time since Colonel Cummins employed Show Indians. Jermark had no idea who he was. The superintendent told the colonel that, were he familiar with Indians and

their actual living conditions, he would realize "that it is a demoralizing influence, and that the day should be hastened when the Indian will cease to make a spectacle of himself."

5 See Prucha, *Great Father*, 2:800–804; and Lawrence C. Kelly, *The Assault on Assimilation: John Collier and the Origins of Indian Policy Reform* (Albuquerque: University of New Mexico Press, 1983), 257, 323. As Prucha points out, Burke's order did not aim to end Indian dancing per se, but was far more concerned with the waste of time that Indian dancing represented. Prucha probably draws too fine a distinction, however, between the assimilationists who obsessed over wasting time, and those who saw *all* Indian dances as immoral.

6 John Harshfield, The Old Range Roundup, Sutherland, Nebr., to E. W. Jermark, Aug. 5, 1925, PR, General Records, MDF, 047 Celebrations 1924, box 161, RG 75, FARC, KC.

7 Prucha, *Great Father*, 2:763.

8 Meritt to Hazzard, Sept. 2, 1920, Records of the CIA, Central Corres. Files, General Service, file 69591–20, box 184, RG 75, NA.

9 Hazzard to Meritt, Aug. 3, 1920, ibid. Ironically, years later, Assistant Commissioner Meritt joined in a scheme with Vice President Charles Curtis (Kaw) to establish a "reservation" for Indians outside Washington, where they could market their arts and crafts. The establishment would charge an entrance fee, and take a percentage of the Indians' receipts. The plan finally came to fruition after Meritt's death. The Indian Stomp Grounds, "Where Indians Live as they did in the days gone by," opened in the summer of 1935. It was located at Mt. Vernon Blvd. at River Bend in Alexandria, Virginia. The "Director General" was one Edna Acker, who styled herself as "Indian Claim Agent." Commissioner John Collier, who had clashed with Meritt frequently and probably took some satisfaction in knowing that Meritt had not succeeded Charles Rhoads as commissioner, denounced the seemingly official-sounding title of Miss Acker. He forbade the service to accept contracts of Indians with representatives of the Indian Stomp Grounds after a group of Oglala from Pine Ridge, in September 1935, left the compound in disgust and began hitchhiking back to South Dakota. They complained of meager pay and poor living conditions. See the series of letters in PR, General Records, MDF, 047, 1933–1935, box 161, RG 75, FARC, KC.

10 Charles Cole, Chicago, to Henry M. Tidwell, Pine Ridge, March 16, 1921, PR, MDF, 047, 1918–1921, RG 75, FARC, KC; and Raymond W. "Colorado Cotton" Smith, Denver, to Tidwell, Feb. 4, 1922, PR, MDF, 047 Sells-Floto Circus, 1922, box 165, RG 75, FARC, KC.

11 Tidwell to Cole, March 26, 1921, PR, MDF, 047, 1918–1921, box 160, RG 75, FARC, KC.

12 Tidwell to Smith, Feb. 13, 1922, PR, MDF, 047 Sells-Floto, 1922, box 165, RG 75, FARC, KC.

13 Burke to Tidwell, March 15, 1922, in ibid.

14 For a biography of Burke, see Lawrence C. Kelly, "Charles Henry Burke (1921-29)," in Kvasnicka and Viola, *Commissioners of Indian Affairs*, 251-61.

15 Office Memorandum, May 24, 1921, Records of the CIA, Central Corres. Files, General Service, General Corres. 047, file 34070-21, box 184, RG 75, NA. Agents also added their own variations. Henry Tidwell and his successor at Pine Ridge, E. W. Jermark, required the employer to come to the reservation himself—or his representative with power of attorney—to execute the contracts and to post the appropriate bond. See correspondence in ibid.

16 Philip Poor Boy to Tidwell, June 23, 1922, and Bat Shangreau to Tidwell, June 28, 1922, PR, MDF, 047 Sells-Floto, 1922, box 165, RG 75, FARC, KC.

17 Tidwell to Patterson's Trained Animal Circus, Paola, Kans., Dec. 11, 1922, PR, MDF, 047, 1922-1928, box 160, RG 75, FARC, KC.

18 Although it would be some time until the configurations of the modern pow-wows were set, fair associations and chambers of commerce were already negotiating with the Sioux and other groups to put on the celebration that featured demonstrations (rather than competitions) of dancing that would attract large crowds. In July 1923, for example, the assistant cashier of the First National Bank of Midland, South Dakota, and Post Adjutant of the Midland American Legion, wrote to Agent Tidwell at Pine Ridge asking how much the Sioux might charge "for putting on a powwow dressed in their regalia." Ivan S. Welch to Tidwell, July 18, 1923, PR, MDF, 047, 1922-1928, box 160, RG 75, FARC, KC.

19 Tidwell describes salaries in Tidwell to Patterson's Trained Animal Circus, Dec. 19, 1922, in ibid.

20 Bataille and Silets, *Pretend Indians*, xxii.

21 Goings to Tidwell, July 8, 1923, PR, MDF, 047, 1922-1928, box 160, RG 75, FARC, KC.

22 Newspaper clipping: Denver *Post*, July 8, 1923, in PR, General Records, MDF, .049, box 166, RG 75, FARC, KC.

23 Goings to Tidwell, July 9, 1923, PR, MDF, Frontier Days Cheyenne, box 163, RG 75, FARC, KC.

24 Goings to Tidwell, July 27, 1923, ibid. The Knights of Columbus Rodeo toured the eastern United States in 1924, but it went bankrupt during its Brooklyn engagement. The Pine Ridge Lakota, however, were given their full pay and sent home in the last week of June 1924. See the series of newspaper clippings from *The Brooklyn Daily Times* and the *Daily Mirror* in PR, General Records, MDF, U.S. Championship Cowboy Rodeo and 047 Young Buffalo Bill Show, box 166, RG 75, FARC, KC.

25 Burke's letter to the Home Missions Council, New York, is quoted at length in E. B. Meritt to Tidwell, March 17, 1924, PR, MDF, Celebrations 1924, box 161, RG 75, FARC, KC. Meritt's letter was in response to Tidwell's request about "Indian Day," May 10, 1924. Flying Hawk had heard that festivities were to

take place "down mouth of Wounded Knee Creek. but I think there are not right. and I think only one the Manderson District Farmer Office . . . for the any kind doing of the Celebrations." Neither Manderson nor Wounded Knee were scenes of the celebration that year after Tidwell wrote to the commissioner and received, instead, a chilly letter from the assistant commissioner. Flying Hawk to Tidwell, March 4, 1924, ibid.

26 CIA to Marshall, June 18, 1924, PR, MDF, 047, 1925–1928, box 161, RG 75, FARC, KC.

27 Ibid.

28 Ibid.

29 See his circular to agency employees, Jan. 30, 1922, in Albert L. Hurtado and Peter Iverson, eds., *Major Problems in American Indian History* (Lexington, Mass.: D. C. Heath and Co., 1994), 379–80.

30 Jermark to CIA, Aug. 7, 1924, PR, MDF, 047 1925–1928, box 161, RG 75, FARC, KC. Bureau appropriations had actually been reduced with various economizing efforts and retrenchment during the Burke regime. See Prucha, *Great Father*, 2:791–93.

31 Jermark to CIA, Aug. 7, 1924, PR, MDF, 047 1925–1928, box 161, RG 75, FARC, KC.

32 CIA to Jermark, Aug. 23, 1924, ibid.

33 This program is outlined in Circular No. 5–1142, of Eugene D. Mossman, superintendent, Standing Rock Indian School, in Records of CIA, Classified Files, 1907–1939, file 88044–1924 Standing Rock 047, RG 75, NA (hereafter cited as Mossman circular). Prucha explains that the Five-Year Program for economic and agricultural development originated on the Blackfeet reservation in 1921. With certain successes, the program spread to other reservations. By 1927 Five-Year programs operated at fifty-five reservations. Progress, however, was not universal. See Prucha, *Great Father*, 2:887.

34 Mossman circular.

35 Mossman to Jermark, Jan. 8, 1925, PR, MDF, 1925–1928, box 161, RG 75, FARC, KC. The circular was signed by R. C. Craige, superintendent of Cheyenne River reservation; E. W. Jermark; P. H. Moller, superintendent of Fort Peck Reservation, Poplar, Mont.; C. M. Ziebach, superintendent of Crow Creek reservation; W. R. Beyer, superintendent of Fort Totten reservation, N.D.; J. H. McGregor, superintendent of Rosebud reservation; Stephen Janus, superintendent at Fort Berthold reservation, N.D.; and Mossman.

36 Mossman circular.

37 Jermark's note is scrawled across the bottom of the page in Mossman to Jermark, Jan. 8, 1925, PR, MDF, 047, 1925–1928, box 161, RG 75, FARC, KC.

38 Brown to Jermark, June 11, 1925, ibid.

39 Telegram: Penny to Jermark, July 15, 1925, ibid.

40 See Jermark to A. L. Taylor, Trenton, Nebr., July 15, 1925, ibid.

41 See the extensive correspondence between Jermark and members of the

National Custer Memorial Association in, PR, MDF, 047 Custer Memorial, box 163, RG 75, FARC, KC.

42 Jermark to Shoemaker, June 29, 1926, ibid.

43 See Burke to Roger S. Brown, secretary, the Cosmopolitan Club, Sioux Falls, S.D., July 30, 1926; and Burke to Mrs. Lillie McCoy, Philadelphia, Sept. 18, 1926, in Records of the CIA, Central Corres. Files, General Service, 047 file 36595–1926, box 188, RG 75, NA.

44 Frank Goings makes mention of the differences in the amount of work that he and his companions had to perform with the Sells-Floto Circus, and the work done by their friends with other shows, especially the Miller Brothers. See Goings to Jermark, June 7, 1927, PR, MDF, 047 Sells-Floto 1927, box 165, RG 75, FARC, KC.

45 See Jermark to John Robinson, July 15, 1927, PR, MDF, 047 John Robinson Circus, box 163, RG 75, FARC, KC.

46 Goings to Jermark, Sept. 3, 1927, PR, MDF, 047 Sells-Floto 1927, box 165, RG 75, FARC, KC.

47 Jermark to John Benson, Nashua, N.H., March 8, 1927, PR, MDF, 047, 1925–1928, box 161, RG 75, FARC, KC.

48 Jermark to Curtis, Sept. 19, 1928, PR, MDF, 047 Sells-Floto 1928, box 166, RG 75, FARC, KC; and Jermark to Robinson, Sept. 12, 1928, ibid.

49 Meritt to Robinson, Sept. 12, 1928, ibid.

50 Jermark to CIA, Sept. 1, 1928, ibid.

51 Jermark to Olaf Eidem, Sept. 26, 1928, ibid.

52 Goings to Jermark, May 9, June 4, and June 13, 1928, ibid.

53 Collings and England, *101 Ranch*, 186, 192.

54 Pulliam to Jermark, June 14, 1929, PR, MDF, 047-D Miller Bros. 101 Ranch, 1929, box 164, RG 75, FARC, KC.

55 Ed Botsford to Jermark, July 6, 1929, ibid.

56 Collings and England, *101 Ranch*, 197. The following year, Zack Miller, with his own show bankrupt, wanted to employ about sixty Indians at a camp near Rochester, New York, for the entire summer. He saw the exposition as an opportunity for Show Indians "to spend a summer where the living conditions would be ideal and at the same time [they would] be self-supporting." See Miller to U.S. Indian Agent, April 15, 1932, PR, General Records, MDF, 047 Miller Brothers 101 Ranch, 1931–1933, box 164, RG 75, FARC, KC. In endorsing Miller's proposal to Commissioner Rhoads, Agent McGregor at Pine Ridge observed that it was just as profitable, "or more so," to let Indians somewhat past middle age go to such shows rather than have them remain on the reservation. More timidly, he reassured the commissioner that "we should [not] encourage this, nor even approve of young or middle age Indians going; but . . . I am inclined to believe it is a good way for them to earn a living." McGregor to CIA, April 21, 1932, Records of the CIA, Classified Files, 1907–1939, file 22336–32 PR 047, RG 75, NA.

57 Prucha, *Great Father*, 2:922–23.

58 Memorandum of Aug. 1, 1929, in PR, MDF, 047 Show Indians 1929, box 161, RG 75, FARC, KC. Wilbur wrote the memorandum in response to a petition sent by the Episcopal Convocation of the Sioux Indians at Pine Ridge. The convocation protested the exploitation by cities, towns, fair associations, rodeos, booster clubs, or any organization, for that matter, which thought it could attract a crowd by hiring Indians in paint and feathers.

59 Jermark to Fritcher, July 30, 1929, ibid.

60 Jermark to C. L. Stephens, Rapid City, S.D., Nov. 12, 1929, PR, General Records, MDF, 042 Relics, box 159, RG 75, FARC, KC.

61 CIA to James McGregor, May 18, 1932, PR, General Records, MDF, 047 Show Indians, 1930–1932, box 161, RG 75, FARC, KC.

62 Rhoads to Charles Eggers, superintendent, Shawnee Indian Agency, Okla., March 1, 1933, PR, General Records, MDF, 047 Miller Bros. 101 Ranch, 1931–1933, box 164, RG 75, FARC, KC.

63 Courtright to C. F. Clark, secretary, Fall River Country Fair Board, June 18, 1931, ibid. The following year, the association cooperated fully with the Pine Ridge agent. The fair sponsored Indian races and dances. On this occasion, the new secretary of the association praised both the Indians and their agent. M. H. Prelieu to James H. McGregor, Sept. 7, 1932, ibid.

64 Courtright to Ruben, Sept. 15, 1931, ibid.

65 McGregor to Senator Williamson, March 2, 1932, PR, General Records, MDF, 047-W World's Fair, Chicago, box 166, RG 75, FARC, KC.

66 McGregor to Wells, Sept. 14, 1932, PR, General Records, MDF, 047 Show Indians, 1930–1932, box 161, RG 75, FARC, KC.

67 Rhoads to Prof. J. F. Lenger, Niobrara, Nebr., Aug. 5, 1932; and Rhoads to J. B. Michener, Sanford, Tex., March 3, 1933, Records of the CIA, Central Corres. Files, General Service, file 50754–1929, Chicago World's Fair, 1933, part 1, box 189, RG 75, NA.

68 See also Robert W. Rydell, *World of Fairs: The Century-of-Progress Expositions* (Chicago: University of Chicago Press, 1993), 82–84.

69 Joseph M. Dixon, Acting Secretary of the Interior, to Hon. Harry S. New, Commissioner to the Century of Progress, Department of State, July 25, 1932, Records of the CIA, Central Corres. Files, General Service, file 50754–1929, Chicago World's Fair, 1933, part 1, box 189, RG 75, NA.

70 Ibid. Dixon, more than the commissioner, was concerned about the "erroneous conception of Indian life as it is today" from a visit to the anthropological exhibit.

71 Newspaper clipping: Chicago *Daily News*, July 6, 1933, in Vertical Files, Century of Progress, Chicago Historical Society.

72 Ibid.

73 Collier to Mike Benton, president, Southeastern Fair Assoc., Atlanta, June 12,

1934, Records of the CIA, Central Corres. Files, General Service, file 19125–1934, box 190, RG 75, NA.

74 Ibid. Collier recommended that the fair association expand the Indian Exposition significantly to include "the remarkable Pueblo Tribes." Robert Rydell sees the hallmark of Collier's support for Indian arts and crafts at the San Francisco Golden Gate International Exposition of 1939, which emphasized the ability of "the colonized to pay for themselves, thereby giving them a measure of autonomy." It is a persuasive argument; but it needs to be seen largely within a larger context of change — the basic transformation of attitudes from hostility toward anything Indian to a view supportive of Indian cultures — and not just for economic reasons. See Rydell, *World of Fairs*, 89–90.

75 See Collier to Thomas S. Horses, Pine Ridge Agency, July 29, 1935, PR, General Records, MDF, 047, 1933–1935, box 161, RG 75, FARC. KC.

76 Circular, CIA to All Superintendents, Oct. 15, 1935, ibid. Emil A. O. Hawk prepared a two-page summary of the annual religious ceremonies of the Sioux. See Hawk to McGregor, Nov. 6, 1935, ibid.

77 Cultural terrorism died hard. Reformers of the Dawes-Act era still had considerable influence within certain governmental circles well into the era of the Indian New Deal. For example, Elaine Goodale Eastman, as a young woman in the fall of 1883, joined the teaching staff at Hampton Institute in Virginia. She taught English to Indians. She later taught on the Great Sioux Reservation. Following Wounded Knee, she married *Ohiyesa*, or Charles Eastman. She espoused Indian assimilation throughout her life. She eventually left Indian country and returned to her native New England. She also separated from Dr. Eastman. In 1937, she found some sympathy from M. W. Stirling, chief of the Bureau of American Ethnology, especially his beliefs about American Indian religions. To Stirling she wrote: "I wish you could convince Commissioner Collier that Indian religions are non-ethical and are based on fear and the propitiation of supposed malicious spirits or deities!" Eastman to Stirling, March 6, 1937, Vertical File, Eastman, Elaine G., Smithsonian Institution, National Anthropological Archives, Washington, D.C. See also Raymond Wilson, *Ohiyesa: Charles Eastman, Santee Sioux* (Urbana: University of Illinois Press, 1983), 47, 49.

EPILOGUE

1 *Washington Times*, May 6, 1938, quoted in Fred D. Pfening, Jr., *Col. Tim McCoy's Real Wild West and Rough Riders of the World: Complete History and Official Route Book* (Columbus, Ohio: Pfening and Snyder, 1955), 49.

2 Pfening, *Col. Tim McCoy's Real Wild West*, 49. Sources consulted by Pfening put McCoy's investment at 100,000 dollars. Pfening estimated that it represented an initial outlay of 200,000 dollars; whereas McCoy himself put his

losses, when adjudicated at closer to 300,000 dollars. McCoy, *Tim McCoy Remembers the West*, 251.

3 Ibid., 39.

4 "The Real McCoy," *Time Magazine* 31 (April 25, 1938):42; and Program: Col. Tim McCoy's Real Wild West and Rough Riders of the World, Magazine and Daily Review, in the author's possession.

5 "Last Roundup," *Time Magazine* 31 (May 16, 1938):53.

6 McCoy, *Tim McCoy Remembers the West*, 251.

7 More than forty years later, the Disney Studios could create a more positive character, the environmentally correct Pocahontas, who in song tweaks the blond and beardless Captain John Smith by wondering what sort of people thinks that whatever land they see belongs to them?

8 I borrow the phrase from Richard White, who used it in a conversation as we drove to the Will Rogers International Airport in Oklahoma City in March 1992.

9 Not too long after a visit by Buffalo Bill's Wild West to New Orleans in 1885, V. K. Batiste founded the first African-American "tribe" of Indians, the Creole Wild West, who hit the streets during Mardi Grass dressed in buckskin and turkey feathers. Over the years more than a dozen rival "gangs" were organized. Competitions were restricted to the Big Chiefs. Gang members spent months designing and then sewing the elaborate costumes. On the first day of Mardi Gras the Big Chiefs would dress up in their costumes and head uptown to Shakespeare Park. There the Big Chiefs would strut and dance and, from the applause of the crowd, determine which Indian was the most beautiful. As Batiste's great nephew remarked in 1988, when he put on the costume he became an Indian. See "Masking Indians," Trent Harris producer, a segment of "National Geographic Explorer" that appeared on the NBC network, May 5, 1988. The author viewed a videotaped recording of the program in the McCracken Library, BBHC.

10 *NewsPress* (Stillwater, Okla.), March 14, 1994, 5.

11 Ibid.

12 Greg Dening, *Mr Bligh's Bad Language: Passion, Power and Theatre on the Bounty* (Cambridge: Cambridge University Press, 1992), 4.

13 Anne M. Butler, "Selling the Popular Myth," in Clyde A. Milner II, Carol A. O'Connor, and Martha A. Sandweiss, eds., *The Oxford History of the American West* (New York: Oxford University Press, 1994), 780.

14 Deloria, "The Indians," 56.

15 Slotkin, "The Wild West," 34.

16 Deloria, "The Indians," 56.

17 Leonard Bruguier to author, April 21, 1994.

BIBLIOGRAPHY

ARCHIVAL MATERIALS

Government Depositories

Denver, Colo. Federal Archives and Records Center. Record Group 75, Records
   of the Bureau of Indian Affairs: Consolidated Ute Agency.
Kansas City, Mo. Federal Archives and Records Center.
   Record Group 75, Records of the Bureau of Indian Affairs:
       Pine Ridge Agency,
       Rosebud Agency, and
       Standing Rock Agency.
Washington, D.C. National Archives.
   Record Group 48, Records of the Department of the Interior:
   World's Columbian Exposition.
   Record Group 75, Records of the Bureau of Indian Affairs:
       Letters Received;
       Letters Sent;
       Central Files;
       Classified Files; and
       Special Case 188, The Ghost Dance, 1890–1898.
   Record Group 94, Records of the Adjutant General's Office, 1780–1917:
       Letters Received,
       Letters Sent, and
       Old Military Branch.
   ———. National Museum of Natural History, Smithsonian Institution.
   Smithsonian Institution National Anthropological Archives:
       Elaine Goodale Eastman Vertical File and
       Records of the Bureau of American Ethnology.
   ———. Smithsonian Institution Archives.
   Record Unit 70:
       Exposition Records of the Smithsonian Institution and the U.S. National
       Museum.

Other Depositories

Berkeley, Calif. University of California, Bancroft Library.
   Wyoming Collection, 1858–1903.
Canyon, Tex. Panhandle Plains Historical Society.
   Susan Janney Allen Papers, 1904–1945.

Cheyenne, Wyo. Wyoming State Archives Museums and Historical Department.
William Frederick Cody Vertical File and
William Arthur Collection.

Chicago, Ill. Chicago Historical Society.
Century of Progress Exposition Vertical File.

Cody, Wyo. The Harold McCracken Research Library, Buffalo Bill Historical
Center.
William F. Cody (Buffalo Bill) Collection,
Peter H. Davidson Collection and
F. M. Sandburg Collection.

Denver, Colo. Western History Department, Denver Public Library.
John Wallace Crawford Papers, 1877–1917, and
William F. Cody Collection.
———. The State Historical Society of Colorado.
William Frederick Cody Papers, 1887–1919.

Des Moines, Iowa. Iowa State Historical Department.
Raymond A. Burnside Papers, 1892–1957.

Golden, Colo. Buffalo Bill Memorial Museum.
Miscellaneous Collections.

Lander, Wyo. Freemont County Pioneer Museum.
E. J. Farlow Collection.

Laramie, Wyo. Division of Rare Books and Special Collections, University of
Wyoming Library.
Victor Weybright Corporate Papers, 1920–1974.

Lincoln, Nebr. Nebraska State Historical Society.
Aspinwal Family Papers, 1808–1960;
Richard Jerome Tanner Papers, 1866–1955;
Judge Eli S. Ricker Collection;
Clarence Reckmeyer Papers, 1910–1939;
W. H. Barten Papers, 1904–1924; and
William Frederick Cody Collection, 1878–1955.

Los Angeles, Calif. University of Southern California Library.
Hamlin Garland Collection.

Lubbock, Tex. Western History Collections, Texas Tech University.
E. M. Botsford Papers, 1893–1952.

Norman, Okla. Western History Collections, University of Oklahoma Library.
Doris Duke Oral History Collection;
Indian Pioneer Papers;
Miller Brothers 101 Ranch Collection; and
Gordon William Lillie Papers, 1911–1943.

Oklahoma City, Okla. Indian Archives Division, Oklahoma Historical Society.
Chilocco School Records and Agency Files—Cheyenne and Arapaho, Kiowa
and Comanche, Sac and Fox, and Quapaw.

Pierre, S.D. South Dakota State Historical Society.
John R. Brennan Family Papers, 1882–1972, and Mary Clementine Collins
Family Papers.
Richardton, N.D. Assumption Abbey Archives.
Maj. James McLaughlin Papers, 1855–1937.
Stillwater, Okla. Special Collections and University Archives, Oklahoma State
University Library.
Angie Debo Collection.
Tucson, Ariz. Special Collections, University of Arizona Library.
William Frederick Cody Papers, 1911–1932.
Tulsa, Okla. Thomas Gilcrease Museum.
Gilcrease Miscellaneous Collections and Emil Lenders Collection.
Vermillion, S.D. University of South Dakota.
Institute of American Indian Studies Archives.

PUBLISHED AND UNPUBLISHED MATERIAL

Printed Government Sources

Biographical Director of the American Congress, 1774–1971. Washington, D.C.:
Government Printing Office, 1971.
U.S. Commissioner of Indian Affairs. *Annual Reports.* Washington, D.C.:
Government Printing Office, 1880–1934.

Organization's Journals and Proceedings

The American Indian Magazine (Society of American Indians), 1916–1920.
Annual Reports of the Executive Committee of the Indian Rights Association,
1885–1901.
*Proceedings of the Annual Meetings of the Lake Mohonk Conference of Friends
of the Indian,* 1888–1894.
The Quarterly Journal of the Society of American Indians, 1913–1915.

Newspapers

Baltimore American
Daily Journal (Aberdeen, Scotland)
Iowa City Journal
NewsPress (Stillwater, Okla.)
New York Times
New York World
The Times (London)

Books, Monographs, and Articles

Anderson, Lindsay. *About John Ford*. New York: McGraw-Hill Co., 1981.

Bataille, Gretchen M., and Charles L. P. Silet, eds. *The Pretend Indians: Images of Native Americans in the Movies*. Ames: Iowa State University Press, 1980.

Berkhofer, Robert F., Jr. *The White Man's Indian: Images of the American Indian from Columbus to the Present*. New York: Alfred A. Knopf, 1978.

Bigart, Robert, and Clarence Woodcock. "The Trans-Mississippi Exposition: The Flathead Delegation." *Montana, the Magazine of Western History* 29 (Autumn 1979).

Blackstone, Sarah J. *Buckskins, Bullets, and Business: A History of Buffalo Bill's Wild West*. Westport, Conn.: Greenwood Press, 1986.

Blanchard, David. "Entertainment, Dance and Northern Mohawk Showmanship." *American Indian Quarterly* 7 (1983).

Bradfield, Larry L. "A History of Chilocco Indian School." Master's thesis, University of Oklahoma, 1963.

Brownlow, Kevin. *The War, the West, and the Wilderness*. New York: Alfred A. Knopf, 1979.

Burg, David F. *Chicago's White City of 1893*. Lexington: University Press of Kentucky, 1976.

Burke, John. *Buffalo Bill from Prairie to Palace*. Chicago: Rand McNally, 1893.

Clow, Richmond L., ed. "Autobiography of Mary C. Collins, Missionary to the Western Sioux." *South Dakota Historical Collections* 41 (1982).

Cody, Louisa Frederici, and Courtney Ryley Cooper. *Memories of Buffalo Bill*. New York: Appleton, 1919.

Cody, William Frederick. *The Story of the Wild West and Campfire Chats*. Philadelphia: Historical Publications Co., 1888.

Collings, Ellsworth, and Alma Miller England. *The 101 Ranch*. With a foreword by Glen Shirley. Norman: University of Oklahoma Press, 1971.

Cronon, William. "Revisiting the Vanishing Frontier: The Legacy of Frederick Jackson Turner." *Western Historical Quarterly* 18 (April 1987).

Debo, Angie. *Geronimo: The Man, His Time, His Place*. Norman: University of Oklahoma Press, 1976.

DeLaguna, Frederica, ed. *Selected Papers from the American Anthropologist, 1888-1920*. Evanston, Ill.: Row and Peterson, 1960.

DeMallie, Raymond J. "The Lakota Ghost Dance: An Ethnohistorical Account." *Pacific Historical Review* 51 (1982).

————. *The Sixth Grandfather: Black Elk's Teachings Given to John G. Neihardt*. Lincoln: University of Nebraska Press, 1984.

Dening, Greg. *Mr Bligh's Bad Language: Passion, Power and Theatre on the Bounty*. Cambridge: Cambridge University Press, 1992.

Dexter, Ralph W. "Putnam's Problems in Popularizing Anthropology." *American Anthropologist* 54 (1966).

Dippie, Brian W. *The Vanishing American: White Attitudes and U.S. Indian Policy*. Middletown, Conn.: Wesleyan University Press, 1982.

DuBois, Cora. "The 1870 Ghost Dance." *University of California Anthropological Records* 3 (1939).

Dutton, Bertha P. *American Indians of the Southwest*. Albuquerque: University of New Mexico Press, 1975.

Etulain, Richard W. *Western Films: A Brief History*. Manhattan, Kans.: Sunflower University Press, 1983.

Everson, William K. *The Hollywood Western*. New York: Citadel Press, 1992.

Feaver, Eric. "Indian Soldiers, 1891–95: An Experiment in the Closing Frontier." *Prologue* 7 (Summer 1975).

Fees, Paul. "The Flamboyant Fraternity." *The Gilcrease Magazine of American History and Art* 6 (January 1984).

Feest, Christian F., ed. *Indians and Europe: An Interdisciplinary Collection of Essays*. Aachen, the Netherlands: Rader Verlag, 1987.

Foreman, Carolyn Thomas. *Indians Abroad, 1493–1928*. Norman: University of Oklahoma Press, 1943.

Fowler, Don D., Robert C. Euler, and Catherine S. Fowler. *John Wesley Powell and the Anthropology of the Grand Canyon*. Washington, D.C.: Government Printing Office, 1969.

Fredriksson, Kristine. *American Rodeo: From Buffalo Bill to Big Business*. College Station, Tex.: Texas A&M Press, 1985.

Friar, Ralph E., and Natasha A. Friar. *The Only Good Indian . . . The Hollywood Gospel*. New York: Drama Book Specialists Publishers, 1972.

Gibson, Arrell M. *The American Indian: Prehistory to the Present*. Lexington, Mass.: D. C. Heath and Co., 1980.

———. "Medicine Show." *The American West* 4 (February 1967).

Gipson, Fred. *Fabulous Empire: Colonel Zack Miller's Story*. Boston: Houghton Mifflin Co., 1946.

Gohl, E. H. "The Effect of Wild Westing." *The Quarterly Journal of the Society of American Indians* 2 (July-September 1914).

Grossman, James R., ed. *The Frontier in American Culture: An Exhibition at the Newberry Library, August 26, 1994-January 7, 1995 / Essays by Richard White and Patricia Nelson Limerick*. Berkeley: University of California Press, 1994.

Haberly, Loyd. *Pursuit of the Horizon: A Life of George Catlin, Painter and Recorder of the American Indian*. New York: Macmillan Co., 1948.

Hagan, William T. *The Indian Rights Association: The Herbert Welsh Years, 1882-1904*. Tucson: University of Arizona Press, 1985.

Hanson, John Wesley. *The Official History of the Fair, St. Louis, 1904*. St. Louis: Printed by the author, 1904.

Hassrick, Royal B. *The Sioux: Life and Customs of a Warrior Society*. Norman: University of Oklahoma Press, 1964.

Hertzberg, Hazel W. *The Search for an American Indian Identity: Modern Pan-Indian Movements*. Syracuse, N.Y.: Syracuse University Press, 1971.

Hinsley, Curtis M., Jr. *Savages and Scientists: The Smithsonian Institution and the Development of American Anthropology, 1846-1910*. Washington, D.C.: Smithsonian Institution Press, 1981.

Hittman, Michael. "The 1870 Ghost Dance at Walker River Reservation: A Reconstruction." *Ethnohistory* 20 (1973).

———. *Wovoka and the Ghost Dance: A Sourcebook*. Carson City, Nev.: The Grace Dangberg Foundation, 1990.

Hoxie, Frederick E. *A Final Promise: The Campaign to Assimilate the Indians, 1880-1920*. Lincoln: University of Nebraska Press, 1984.

———, ed. *Indians in American History*. Arlington Heights, Ill.: Harlan Davidson, 1988.

Hurtado, Albert L., and Peter Iverson, eds. *Major Problems in American Indian History*. Lexington, Mass.: D. C. Heath and Co., 1994.

Iverson, Peter. *When Indians Became Cowboys: Native Peoples and Cattle Ranching in the American West*. Norman: University of Oklahoma Press, 1994.

Jennings, Francis. *The Invasion of America: Indians, Colonialism, and the Cant of Conquest*. Chapel Hill: University of North Carolina Press, 1975.

Jensen, Richard E., R. Eli Paul, and John E. Carter. *Eyewitness at Wounded Knee*. Lincoln: University of Nebraska Press, 1991.

Katzive, David H., et al. *Buffalo Bill and the Wild West*. New York: The Brooklyn Museum, 1981.

Kelly, Lawrence C. *The Assault on Assimilation: John Collier and the Origins of Indian Policy Reform*. Albuquerque: University of New Mexico Press, 1983.

Kupperman, Karen Ordahl. *Settling with the Indians: The Meeting of English and Indian Cultures in America, 1580-1640*. Totowa, N.J.: Rowman and Littlefield, 1980.

Kvasnicka, Robert M., and Herman J. Viola, eds. *The Commissioners of Indian Affairs, 1824-1977*. Lincoln: University of Nebraska Press, 1979.

"Last Roundup." *Time Magazine* 31 (May 16, 1938).

Leckie, Shirley A. *Elizabeth Bacon Custer and the Making of a Myth*. Norman: University of Oklahoma Press, 1993.

Leonard, L. O. "Buffalo Bill's First Wild West Rehearsal." *The Union Pacific Magazine* (August 1922).

Leslie, Amy. *Amy Leslie at the Fair*. Chicago: W. B. Conkey Co., 1893.

Leupp, Francis. *The Indian and His Problem*. New York: Charles Scribner's Sons, 1910.

McCoy, Tim, with Ronald McCoy. *Tim McCoy Remembers the West*. Garden City, N.Y.: Doubleday and Co., 1977.

McNamara, Brooks. *Step Right Up*. Garden City, N.Y.: Doubleday and Co., 1976.

———. "The Indian Medicine Show." *Educational Theatre Journal* 23 (1971).

Miller, Darlis A. *Captain Jack Crawford: Buckskin Poet, Scout, and Showman.* Albuquerque: University of New Mexico Press, 1993.

Milner II, Clyde A., Carol A. O'Connor, and Martha A. Sandweiss, eds. *The Oxford History of the American West.* New York: Oxford University Press, 1994.

Mintz, Steven, and Randy Roberts. *Hollywood's America: United States History through Its Films.* St. James, N.Y.: Brandywine Press, 1993.

Mooney, James. "The Ghost Dance Religion and the Sioux Outbreak of 1890." *Fourteenth Annual Report of the Bureau of Ethnology*, Part 2. Washington, D.C.: Government Printing Office, 1896.

Mooney, Michael MacDonald. *George Catlin: Letters and Notes on the North American Indians.* New York: Clarkson N. Potter, 1975.

Moses, L. G. *The Indian Man: A Biography of James Mooney.* Urbana: University of Illinois Press, 1984.

———. "Jack Wilson and the Indian Service: The Response of the BIA to the Ghost Dance Prophet." *American Indian Quarterly* 5 (November 1979).

———. "Indians on the Midway: Wild West Shows and the Indian Bureau at World's Fairs, 1893–1904." *South Dakota History* 21 (1991).

———. "Wild West Shows, Reformers, and the Image of the American Indian, 1887–1914." *South Dakota History* 14 (1984).

Moses, L. G., and Raymond Wilson, eds. *Indian Lives: Essays on Nineteenth- and Twentieth-Century Native American Leaders.* Rev. ed. Albuquerque: University of New Mexico Press, 1993.

Nash, Gary B., and Richard Weiss, eds. *The Great Fear: Race in the Mind of America.* New York: Holt, Rinehart and Winston, 1970.

Neihardt, John G. *Black Elk Speaks: Being the Life Story of a Holy Man of the Oglala Sioux.* Lincoln: University of Nebraska Press, 1961.

Nichols, Roger L., ed. *The American Indian: Past and Present.* 2d ed. New York: John Wiley and Sons, 1981.

Olson, James C. *Red Cloud and the Sioux Problem.* Lincoln: University of Nebraska Press, 1965.

Ortiz, Alfonso, ed. *Handbook of North American Indians, Southwest.* Vol. 9. Washington, D.C.: Smithsonian Institution Press, 1979.

Pearce, Roy Harvey. *Savagism and Civilization: A Study of the Indian and the American Mind.* Baltimore, Md.: Johns Hopkins University Press, 1963.

Pfaller, Louis. "'Enemies in '76, Friends in '85'—Sitting Bull and Buffalo Bill." *Prologue* 1 (Fall 1969).

Pfening, Fred D., Jr. *Col. Tim McCoy's Real Wild West and Rough Riders of the World: Complete History and Official Route Book.* Columbus, Ohio: Pfening and Snyder, 1955.

Prucha, Francis Paul. *American Indian Policy in Crisis: Christian Reformers and the Indian, 1865–1900.* Norman: University of Oklahoma Press, 1976.

———, ed. *Americanizing the American Indians: Writings by the "Friends of the Indian," 1880–1900.* Lincoln: University of Nebraska Press, 1978.

———. *A Bibliographic Guide to the History of Indian-White Relations in the United States.* Chicago: University of Chicago Press, 1977.

———, ed. *Documents of United States Indian Policy.* Lincoln: University of Nebraska Press, 1975.

———. *The Great Father: The United States and the American Indians.* 2 vols. Lincoln: University of Nebraska Press, 1984.

———. *The Indians in American Society: From the Revolutionary War to the Present.* Berkeley: University of California Press, 1985.

"The Real McCoy." *Time Magazine* 31 (April 25, 1938).

Reddin, Paul L. "Wild West Shows: A Study in the Development of Western Romanticism." Ph. D. diss., University of Missouri, 1970.

Renno, Edward L. "The Wild and Wonderful Magic of the 101 Ranch." *Persimmon Hill* 12 (1982).

Roberts, Gary L. "In Search of Little Wolf . . . A Tangled Photographic Record." *Montana, the Magazine of Western History* 28 (1978).

Roehm, Marjorie Catlin. *The Letters of George Catlin and His Family: A Chronicle of the American West.* Berkeley: University of California Press, 1966.

Ronda, James P. *Lewis and Clark among the Indians.* Lincoln: University of Nebraska Press, 1984.

Rosa, Joseph G., and Robin May. *Buffalo Bill and His Wild West: A Pictorial Biography.* Lawrence: University Press of Kansas, 1989.

Russell, Don. "Cody, Kings, and Coronets." *The American West* 7 (1970).

———. *The Lives and Legends of Buffalo Bill.* Norman: University of Oklahoma Press, 1960.

———. *The Wild West: A History of the Wild West Shows.* Fort Worth, Tex.: Amon Carter Museum of Western Art, 1970.

Rydell, Robert W. *All the World's a Fair: Visions of Empire at American International Expositions, 1876–1916.* Chicago: University of Chicago Press, 1984.

———. *World of Fairs: The Century-of-Progress Expositions.* Chicago: University of Chicago Press, 1993.

Salsbury, Nate. "At the Vatican." *The Colorado Magazine* 33 (July 1955).

Sarf, Wayne Michael. *God Bless You, Buffalo Bill: A Layman's Guide to History and the Western Film.* East Brunswick, N.J.: Associated University Presses, 1983.

Seger, John H. *Early Days among the Cheyenne and Arapahoe Indians.* Norman: University of Oklahoma Press, 1934.

Sell, Henry Blackmen, and Victor Weybright. *Buffalo Bill and the Wild West.* Basin, Wyo.: Big Horn Books, 1979.

Sheehan, Bernard W. *Savagism and Civility: Indians and Englishmen in Colonial Virginia.* Cambridge: Cambridge University Press, 1980.

Shepp, Daniel B., and James W. Shepp. *Shepp's World's Fair Photographed.* Chicago: Global Bible Publishing Co., 1893.

Shirley, Glenn. *Pawnee Bill: A Biography of Major Gordon W. Lillie.* Lincoln: University of Nebraska Press, 1965.

Slotkin, Richard. *The Fatal Environment: The Myth of the Frontier in the Age of Industrialization, 1800–1890.* New York: Atheneum, 1985.

———. *Gunfighter Nation: The Myth of the Frontier in Twentieth-Century America.* New York: Harper Perennial, 1992.

———. *Regeneration Through Violence: The Mythology of the American Frontier, 1600–1860.* Middletown, Conn.: Wesleyan University Press, 1973.

Smith, Jane F., and Robert M. Kvasnicka. *Indian-White Relations: A Persistent Paradox.* Washington, D.C.: Howard University Press, 1976.

Standing Bear, Luther. *Land of the Spotted Eagle.* Lincoln: University of Nebraska Press, 1975.

———. *My People the Sioux.* Lincoln: University of Nebraska Press, 1975.

Stedman, Raymond William. *Shadows of the Indians: Stereotypes in American Culture.* Norman: University of Oklahoma Press, 1982.

Steckbeck, John S. *Fabulous Redmen: The Carlisle Indians and Their Famous Football Teams.* Harrisburg, Pa.: J. Horace McFarland Co., 1951.

Taylor, Graham D. "Anthropologists, Reformers, and the Indian New Deal." *Prologue* 7 (1975).

Tibbles, Thomas Henry. *The Ponca Chiefs: An Account of the Trial of Standing Bear.* Edited, with an introduction by, Kay Graber. Lincoln: University of Nebraska Press, 1972.

Thoene, Bodie, and Rona Stuck. "Navajo Nation Meets Hollywood." *The American West* 20 (1983).

Time-Life Books. *The End of the Myth.* New York: Time-Life, 1979.

Trafzer, Clifford E., ed. *American Indian Prophets: Religious Leaders and Revitalization Movements.* Newcastle, Calif.: Sierra Oaks Publishing Co., 1986.

Trennert, Robert A., Jr. *The Phoenix Indian School: Forced Assimilation in Arizona, 1891–1935.* Norman: University of Oklahoma Press, 1988.

Turner, Frederick Jackson. "The Significance of the Frontier in American History." *Annual Report of the American Historical Association for the Year 1893.* Washington, D.C., 1894.

Tuska, Jon. *The American West in Film: Critical Approaches to the Western.* Westport, Conn.: Greenwood Press, 1985.

———. *The Filming of the West.* Garden City, N.Y.: Doubleday and Co., 1976.

Utley, Robert M. *The Lance and the Shield: The Life and Times of Sitting Bull.* New York: Henry Holt and Co., 1993.

————. *The Last Days of the Sioux Nation*. New Haven, Conn.: Yale University Press, 1963.

Vestal, Stanley. *Sitting Bull, Champion of the Sioux: A Biography*. Norman: University of Oklahoma Press, 1957.

Viola, Herman J. *Diplomats in Buckskins: A History of Indian Delegations in Washington City*. Washington, D.C.: Smithsonian Institution Press, 1981.

Walker, James R. *Lakota Society*. Edited by Raymond J. DeMallie. Lincoln: University of Nebraska Press, 1982.

Wallis, Michael. "The Miller Brothers and the 101 Ranch." *Gilcrease Journal* 1 (Spring 1993).

Walsh, Richard J., in collaboration with Milton S. Salsbury. *The Making of Buffalo Bill: A Study in Heroics*. Indianapolis, Ind.: The Bobbs-Merrill Co., 1928.

Wooster, Robert. *Nelson A. Miles and the Twilight of the Frontier Army*. Lincoln: University of Nebraska Press, 1993.

Yellow Robe, Chauncey. "The Menace of the Wild West Show." *Quarterly Journal of the Society of American Indians* 2 (1914).

Yost, Nellie Snyder. *Buffalo Bill: His Family, Friends, Fame, Failures, and Fortunes*. Chicago: Swallow Press, 1979.

Index

References to photographs are printed in italic type

Adventures of Buffalo Bill, 250
Agricultural fairs, 142–43
Akoun, Fernand, 202
Alaska-Yukon-Pacific Exposition, 106
Albert Edward, Prince of Wales
 as greatest fan of Wild West shows,
  43
Alexandra, Princess of Wales
 visits Wild West show, 50
Al Fresco Amusement Company, 175
Allen, Alvaren
 of "Sitting Bull Combination," 25
American Bear
 stranded in Australia, 125–26
American Bonding Company, 197
American Circus Corporation, 264
American Horse, 279
 on travel with Wild West shows, 33
American Horse, Ben, 242
American Indian Village Company, 270
 at Columbian Exposition, 139
American Wild West Show Company,
 200
Anderson, Gilbert M. ("Broncho
 Billy")
 as "star" of Westerns, 226
Anglo-American Exposition, 185
Anishinaabeg
 artisans at St. Louis fair, 159
 employed by Catlin, 17
 at Minnesota State fair, 254–55
Apaches, 4
 with Carver's Wild America, 125
 Chiricahua prisoners, 144, 157
Arlington, Edward
 joins Miller Brothers, 249
Arthur, Bill, *187*
 escapes Germany, 187–88
Asay, James F.
 as contracting agent, 124, 171

Ashley, Robert A.
 Omaha and Winnebago agent, 75
Assimilation, 3
Atkins, John D. C. (CIA)
 opposition to Cody, 27
 violates spirit of Standing Bear
  decision, 66
Attsose Bitcilly, 209
Australian Aborigines
 at Louisiana Purchase Exposition,
  156

Babbitt brothers, 215
Bad Bear, Alexander, 265
Bailey, James A.
 death of, 189
 manages Cody's Wild West, 144, 169
Baker, Johnny, 257
Baldwin, Brig. General Frank
 on filming *Indian Wars*, 242
Barnum, P. T.
 endorses Cody's Wild West, 75
 first visit to Wild West show, 33
Barnum and Bailey Circus, 144, 169
Barten, Angelique (Cordier), 173
Barten, W. H.
 contracts Show Indians, 174–75
 exploitation of Show Indians, 318
  n 22
 as Indian trader, 173
 as Wild West show outfitter, 227
Barthalomew, Charles A.
 Southern Ute agent, 75
Bastille
 commemoration of fall, 82
Bates, G. H., *36*
 chaperons Show Indians, 37–38
 on Show Indian demeanor, 55
Battice, Walter, 179, *181*
 at Hampton Institute, *189*

Battice, Walter (*continued*)
  partnership with Richard Davis,
    182
Battle of Elderbush Gulch, 228
Battle of Little Bighorn, 4, 169
  fiftieth anniversary, 261
Battle of Summit Springs
  added to Cody's Wild West, 190
  film recreation, 213
Battle of Warbonnet Creek, 231
Battle of Wounded Knee
  casualties, 331 n 52
  film recreation, 232
Bear Dance
  outlawed, 206
Bear Lies Down, 122
Bear Runs In the Woods
  quits 101 Ranch Show, 174
Beecher, Henry Ward, 37
Belasco, David, 91
Belgenland, 100
Bell, Charlie, *276*
Belt, Robert V. (Acting CIA)
  investigates Show Indians, 100,
    103–4, 107–8
"Big Water," 43
Bigelow, Texas Charlie, 71
Bill Penny Circus, 261
Bison Moving Picture Company, 228,
    248
Black Elk, 44, 284 n 21
  on Queen Victoria's visit, 51–52
  stranded in England, 84–85
Black Elk, Ben, 243
Black Elk Speaks, 44
Black Heart, 82, *102*
  defends Cody, 103
Black Owl
  death in Moscow, 94
Blackstone, Sarah J.
  circus practices, 144
  on Cody's success, 31
Bliss (Marland), Okla., 179
Blue Bird, Jammie, 182
Blue Bird, Minnie, 182

Blue Horse
  snubbed by CIA, 157
  "Laramie Loafer," 314 n 27
Board of Indian Commissioners, 62
Boas, Franz
  organization of museum exhibits,
    130–31
Bonfils, Frederick G.
  bankrolls Cody's film, 228
Bonheur, Rosa
  with Buffalo Bill, *83*
  paints Show Indians, 82
Both Sides White, 122
Brave, 122
Brennan, John, 188
  with Cody, *232*
Brings the White, 122, 124
Broncho Billy and the Baby, 226
Brooks, W. A., 248
Brown, Edward, 261
Brown Eyes, Thomas, 200
Browning, Daniel M. (CIA), 126
  tolerates Wild West shows, 141–42
Brownlow, Kevin
  on suppression of *Indian Wars*,
    243–44
Bud Atkinson Show
  tours Australia, 203
Buffalo Bill
  See Cody, William F.
Buffalo Bill Historical Picture
  Company
  marketing *Indian Wars*, 246–48
Buffalo Bill Memorial Museum
  dedication of, 257
Buffalo Bill's Wild West
  adds Rough Rider segment, 147
  at Columbian Exposition, 134–35,
    138
  and Deadwood stage, *148*
  earliest film images, 223
  at Erastina, 33–34
  European tours, *52*, 91–92, 119, *86*,
    170
  most successful season, 137–40
  performances, 1, *24*, *90*, 190

Bullis, John L.
  agent at San Carlos, Arizona, 76
Bureau of American Ethnology, 182
  display at Tennessee Centennial
    Exposition, *143*
  evolutionary anthropology, 132
Bureau of Catholic Indian Missions, 25
Bureau of Indian Affairs
  assimilation program, 3
  display at Columbian Exposition,
    131, 133–34
  opposition to Wild West shows, 40,
    255
  regulation of Show Indians, 8,
    63–64, 137–38, 176
  storage of films, 245
  on stranded Show Indians, 203
Burke, Charles (CIA)
  "dance order," 253
  on limited authority, 255, 259
Burke, John ("Arizona John")
  on anthropological congresses, 144
  authenticity of Wild West show, 171
  on benefits to Show Indians, 8
  as Cody's business manager, 22
  organizes visit to Vatican, 87–88
  at premier of *Indian Wars*, 246
  press agentry, 43, 82
Burke Act, 197
Bush, Charles S., 157
Butler, Anne M., 277

Campbell, Timothy, 39
Carlisle Indian School, 182
  band, 158, 165
  football team, 165
Carnot, Sadi, 82
Carver, Dr. William F.
  BIA sanctions against, 70, 124
  partnership with Cody, 1
Carver's Wild America, 70, 171
  opposition to, 124
  tours Russia, 94
Catlin, George
  attitude toward Indians, 14–15
  employs Iowas, 17

  Indian gallery, 15, 16
  as showman, 17
  Tableaux vivants, 16, 34
Central Lyceum Bureau, 166
Century of Progress Exposition
  BIA display at, 269
Charging Alone, Scott, 160
Charging Thunder, 122
Cheyenne and Arapaho Reservation,
  182
Cheyenne Frontier Days Wild West,
  205, 257, 261
Cheyennes, 125, 179
  with Buffalo Bill, 34
  with 101 Ranch Wild West, 180
  at Louisiana Purchase Exposition,
    159
Chicago Coliseum, 178
Chief Joseph
  at Louisiana Purchase Exposition,
    157
Chilocco Indian School, 151
Chippewas
  See Anishinaabegs
Christian humanitarian reformers
  benevolent associations, 62
  civilization programs, 78
  complaints against Indian fairs, 212
  oppose Wild west shows, 3, 5
  restrictions on Indian employment,
    32
Circus Krembser, 67
Clahetosoue, 209
Cleveland, Grover
  meets Show Indians, 81
  opens Columbian Exposition, 130
Cliff Dwellers Exhibit Company, 156
Cody, William F., *278*
  on anthropological displays, 132
  appears in melodramas, 18
  attitudes toward assimilation, 64
  cuts short European tour, 98
  death of, 193, 249
  on employment of Indians, 8, 26–27,
    44
  farewell tours, 189, 191

Cody, William F. (*continued*)
  finances, 189–91, 248
  generosity of, 122, 173
  hero of two continents, 58, 80
  Historical Pictures Company, 224
  leading Show Indians, *2*
  on making *Indian Wars*, 229, *230*,
    244
  memorial, 257
  as *Pahaska*, 257
  partnership with Doc Carver, 1, 22
  permits visits to Indian
    encampment, 46
  recreates Custer's Last Stand, 35
  with Sells-Floto circus, 228, 248
  and "Sioux Outbreak," *110*
  welfare of Show Indians, 94–95,
    122, 176
Cole, Fay-Cooper, 270
Collier, John (CIA)
  opposes "dance order," 253
  supports Show Indians, 271
Collins, Mary C., *114*
  protests release of ghost dancers,
    111–15
  visits Cummins's Indian Village,
    148–49
  visits Herbert Welsh, 116–17
Colorado College, 151
Colorado Springs fair, 213
Colorado State Fair and Exposition,
  206
Columbian Exposition, 118, 165
  opening ceremonies, 129–30
Columbus, Christopher, 10
  Show Indians visit statue, 85–86
Comanches, 179
Congregational Club, 115
Congress of Rough Riders
  and novelty acts, 119
  See also Buffalo Bill's Wild West
Continental Amusement Company, 201
Cooks Tours
  arranges travel for Show Indians,
    200

Cooper, James Fenimore
  film adaptation of novels, 225
  Indian images, 13, 18
Cooper, Ryley
  on filming *Indian Wars*, 238
  on filming Wounded Knee, 237
Cotton States and International
  Exposition, 143
Council of National Defense, 221
Covey, Claude
  superintendent at Standing Rock
    school, 218
Cox, Samuel S., 39
Craft, Father Francis M., 100
Cripple Creek Bar Room
  as first Western, 225
Croger, George
  as interpreter, 119
  turns over Sioux prisoners, 121
Crook, General George, 26
Crow fair, 207–9
Crows, 207
Cummins, Col. Frederick T.
  complaints against Indian traders,
    173
  manages Greater American
    Exposition, 145
  manages Indian Congress, 146
  stranded in Europe, 186–87
Curtis, Charles, 264
Custer, Burton B., 206
Custer, Elizabeth
  endorses Wild West show, 33
Custer, Lieut. Colonel George A.
  admiration for plains Indians, 19–20
  death of, 4, 27, 28
Custer Memorial Association
  hires Show Indians, 261
Custers Last Stand, 228
Custer's Last Stand, 189, 290 n 55
  performed at Pan-American
    Exposition, 147–48
Cypher, William, 166

Dance order, 253
Dances with Wolves, 275

Davis, Richard, 158, 183
Dawes, Senator Henry L., 73
Dawes Act, 66, 185, 213
Day, Vernon M
    produces *Indian Wars*, 229
Deadwood Stagecoach, 34, 169
De Ford, Henry ("Buckskin Joe"), 139
Deloria, Vine, 277
DeMallie, Raymond, 46
Denver Post, 192
Drexel Mission
    See Holy Rosary Catholic Mission

Eagle Bird, 122
Eagle Elk
    stranded in Australia, 125–26
Eagle Horn, *96*
Eagleshirt, William
    first Indian film actor, 227
Earl's Court, 185
Edison, Thomas
    development of motion pictures,
        223–24
Eiffel tower, 82
Elkins, Stephen (Sec. of War)
    on Ghost Dance, 124
Elks Club, 206
Elwell, R. Farrington, 244
Erastina, 33, 189
Essanay Film Company
    origins, 226
    provides equipment for Cody,
        228–29
Ethnological exhibits
    at Columbian Exposition, 130–31
    Wild West shows as part of, 137
Everson, William, 227
Evolutionary anthropology, 146
Ewers, John C.
    images of Indians, 19
Exposition Universale, 81

Farm Bureau, 260
Featherman
    contracts smallpox in Marseilles, 94
    at Eiffel Tower, 82

Fetterman Fight, 4, 283 n 9
Fifth Field Artillery
    participate in motion picture, 244
Film
    See motion pictures
Fly Above, 57
Flying Hawk, 257
Forepaugh agreement, 70, 196
Forepaugh circus, 34
Fort Sheridan prisoners, 109
    allowed to join Wild West, 109
    return from Europe, 122
Franz Ferdinand, 186
Frederick, Crown Prince of Denmark,
    50
Friar, Natasha,
    cultural genocide, 7
    Indians in westerns, 225
Friar, Ralph, 7, 225
Fritcher, Alice F., 267

Gallagher, Hugh
    calls council at Pine Ridge, 71
    on destitute Show Indians, 97
    on mistreatment of Show Indians,
        66–67
    numbers of Show Indians, 75–76
Gallup Inter-Tribal Ceremonial, 258
Gandy, Earl B.
    manages Red Man's Syndicate, 197
    pays high wages, 199–200
Gandy, Franklin, 200
Garlow, Fred, 246
Garrison, Lindley, M. (Sec. of War)
    assists *Indian Wars*, 229
General Allotment Act
    See Dawes Act
Genoa Training School, 159
Georgia State Fair, 179
Geronimo, 157
    last buffalo hunt, 177
    as last Indian warrior, 167
    at Trans-Mississippi Exposition,
        144
Ghost Dance
    and Cody's Show Indians, *108*

Ghost Dance (*continued*)
    on film, 228
    impedes Show Indian investigation,
        104
    origins, 106–7
    ringleaders imprisoned, 109, *112*
Ghost Dog, 128
Gilmore, Melvin R., 241
Girl of the Golden West, 91
Gladstone, William
    visits Show Indians, 49
Goes Flying
    dies in Naples, 94
Goes in Lodge, *273*
Goings, Frank
    as contracting agent, 201, 267
    gift from philanthropist, 265
    as interpreter, 200, 257
    with Sells-Floto circus, 264
Good Elk, 128
Good Lance, 242
Grand Army of the Republic, 37
Grass, Jim, 242
Great Bear, Billy, 142
Greater American Exposition, 145
Great Sioux Reservation, 288 n 14
The Great Train Robbery, 225–26
Griffith, D. W., 226
    influence on westerns, 227–28

Hagenbeck Brothers Circus, 264
Hampton Institute, 179
Harris, Carey Allen (CIA), 14
Harrison, Benjamin
    invites Show Indians to White
        House, 101
Harvard University, 130
Haskell Institute, 159
Has No Horses, 122, *123*
Hauke, C. F., 245
Hayden, Carl, 213
Hazard, George P. 254
Her Blanket, 122
Hertzberg, Hazel, 118
Hickok, Wild Bill, 18
High Chief, 180

High Eagle, 122
Historians
    attitudes toward Show Indians, 7
    critical of Wild West shows, 6
Holy Bird, 122
Holy Rosary Catholic Mission
    filming fight at, 237
Home Club, 245
Hopis
    at Louisiana Purchase Exposition,
        156, 160
    at Panama-Pacific Exposition, 213
    problems with missionaries, 161
Horn Cloud, Joe, 242
Hotchkiss guns
    at Wounded Knee, 234
Howard, General Oliver O., 111
Hoxie, Frederick
    on Louisiana Purchase Exposition,
        167
101 ("Hundred and One") Ranch Real
    Wild West, 173, *178*
    European tour, 177, 183–84
    immigrant act, *65*
    Indians employed by, 179
    and motion pictures, 227
    property losses, 183, 186, 188

Improved Order of Red Men
    sham battles with Show Indians,
        145
Ince, Thomas, 226
Inceville, 227
Indian and His Problem, 199
Indian Congress and Village Company,
    146
Indian fairs, 218
    origins, 207
    and World War I, 221
Indian images, xii, 279
    at Columbian Exposition, 131
    identity, 279
    noble savage, 3
    reformers and, 63
    savagery and civilization, 147
    stereotypes, 6, 41

vanishing American, 4, 136, 170
winning of the West, 271
Indian policy
  citizenship, 206
  civilization programs, 61–62
  removal, 15
Indian removal, 15
Indian Rights Association, 5, 176
  criticizes Leupp, 199
  established, 62
  members visit Sitting Bull, 28
Indians
  terminology, xiv
Indian Sagwa
  patent medicine, 71
Indian School Journal, 164
  at Louisiana Purchase Exposition, 159
Indian Wars, 224
  premier in Washington, D.C., 245
  reel list, 329 n 30
  scene list, 231–32
Ingraham, Prentiss, 18
Iowas, 17
Iron Tail, 188
Iroquois, 71
Irwin, Col. C. B., 261
Irwin Brothers, 205

James, Darwin Rush, 38
Jamestown Tercentenary Exposition, 178
Janis, Henry
  arrested in Australia, 203
Jardine Acclimation, 202
Jefferson, Thomas, 13
Jermark, Ernest W., 258–59
John Robinson Circus, 264
Joliet Prison
  visited by ghost dancers, 124
Jones, William A. (CIA)
  hostility toward Wild West shows, 142
  opposition to Show Indians, 142, 145, 191
  plans BIA display, 151

J. T. McCaddon Company, 189, 197
Judson, Edward Z. C. ("Ned Buntline"), 18

Kapus, William
  reports on stranded Show Indians, 125–26
Kaufman, Donald, 6
Keams Canyon Indian School, 160
Kelton, J. C., 121
Kickapoo Medicine Company, 75, 142, 171
  employment of Indians, 19, 71
Kicking Bear, *113*, *122*
  at Columbian Exposition, 135
  praises Cody, 111
  recites brave deeds, 119
  released from Fort Sheridan, 124
  returns from Europe, 122
Kills Crow, 122
Kills Plenty (*Otakte*), 82
  death in New York City, 95
Kingfisher, Okla., 182
Kiowa-Comanche fair, *211*
Kiowas, 179
Knights of Columbus rodeo, 257
Knows His Voice, 122
Koster and Bial's Music Hall, 224

Lake Mohonk Conference, 62
Lakota Sioux
  terminology, xii
  religious beliefs and power, 88–89
Lamar, Lucius Q. C. (Sec. of Interior)
  opposes Sitting Bull's employment, 26
Lane, Franklin, 245
"Laramie Loafers," 157, 314 n 27
Larrabee, Charles F. (Asst. CIA)
  bans Indian dances, 207
  contracting Show Indians, 197
Last of the Mohicans (film), 275
Last of the Mohicans (novel), 13
Lee, Bob, 243
Leo XIII, Pope
  blesses Show Indians, 87

Leslie, Amy
  reports on Columbian Exposition, 135, 310 n 23
Leupp, Francis (CIA) 206
  dismisses complains against Wild West shows, 199
  investigates Red Man's Syndicate, 197–98
  as IRA agent, 196
  remarks about Show Indians, 198
  resumes contracts, 173
Lillie, Gordon ("Pawnee Bill")
  joins Cody's Wild West, 40
  "Two Bills" show, 190
Little Bighorn River (Greasy Grass), 28
Little Bull, 57
Little Iron, 128
Little Ring (*Depostas*)
  death of, 89, 299 n 33
Little Wolf, 200
London International Horticultural Exhibition, 127
Lone Bear
  portrays Big Foot, 242
Lone Bear, Samuel, *73*
Long Bull, 122
Long Wolf
  death in London, 127
Lorne, Marquis of, 50
Louisiana Purchase Exposition, 149, 160
  Cliff Dwellers exhibit, 160
  model Indian school, 154–55, *155*, 161
  Old Indian exhibit, 155–56, 159, 162–63
Lower Brule fair, 212
Lucas, Harry, 182
Lucca, Prince
  returns to Russia, 186

McCowan, Samuel M., *153*
  manages BIA exhibit, 149, 151, 157
McCoy, Tim, *249*
  bankruptcy of show, 274

McGee, W. J.
  heads anthropology department, 152
McGregor, James H.
  Sioux at Century of Progress, 269
Macheradse, Prince Ivan Rostomov
  leads cossacks, 127
Mackaye, Steele
  produces "Drama of Civilization," 34, 44
McKussick, William, 75
McLaughlin, James
  defends Cody, 118
  opposition to Wild West shows, 25
Madison Square Garden, 31, 180, 219–20
Manderson, Charles F.
  supports Show Indians, 109
Maricopas
  potters at Louisiana Purchase Exposition, 159
Mark Twain, 33
Marland, Okla.
  See Bliss, Okla.
Mash the Kettle, xi
Matthews, Fred, 95
May, Karl
  popular novels, 92
Medicine Horse, 122
Mercer, Capt. William A.
  supervises Indian congress, 144
Meritt, Edgar B. (Asst. CIA)
  ban on dancing, 215
  wants to hire Show Indians, 334 n 9
Merriman, Truman, 39
Midway Heights (Atlanta), 143
Midway Plaisance
  at Columbian Exposition, 134
Miles, General Nelson A.
  filming Wounded Knee, 241–42
  on Ghost Dance, xi, 107
Miller, George
  death, 265
Miller, J. C. (Joe), 176
  death, 265
  on hiring Indians, 179

Miller, Zach, 176, 265
  bankruptcy, 337 n 56
  leadership of 101 Ranch, 265
  outbreak of World War I, 186
Miller and Arlington Wild West Show
  preparedness pageant, 192
Miller Brothers, 169, *177*
  exploitation of Show Indians, 175
  Wild West show revival, 252–53
Miller Brothers 101 Ranch Real Wild
  West
  See 101 ("Hundred and One")
    Ranch Real Wild West under *H*
Minnesota Territorial Pioneers, 254
Mintz, Steven, 224
Montezuma, Dr. Carlos, 182
Moorehead, Warren King, 242
Moqui Snake Dance, 245
Morgan, Lewis Henry
  evolutionary theories, 132
Morgan, Matt, 34
Morgan, Thomas Jefferson (CIA)
  assimilation, 74–75
  blames Miles for Wounded Knee, 107
  encourages agricultural fairs,
    142–43
  investigates treatment, 93–94
  opposition to shows, 73, 77–78, 94,
    125
  plans for Columbian Exposition,
    133–34, 152, 309 n 16
  praises Show Indians, 109
  tours reservation schools, 101
Mossman, Eugene, 269
  circular against Show Indians, 260
Motion pictures
  create Indian imagery, xi, 272
  early techniques, 226
  at 101 Ranch, 183
  and social classes, 224
  the western, 224–25
"Mountain Meadows Massacre," 183
Moya, Andres, 159
Mulhall, Lucille
  as first cowgirl, 177
Mulhall, Zach, 180

Naiche, 158
Napier, Rita
  on Black Elk, 44, 53
  Indians as tourists, 48
  Lakota political life, 84
National Editorial Association, 177
National Indian Association, 207
National Press Club, 245
Navajo fair, 209
Navajos
  artisans at Louisiana Purchase
    Exposition, 156, 159
Nebraska State Historical Society, 241
Nebraska State militia, 42
Neihardt, John G., 54
Nelson, John Y.
  family portrait, *51*
Nelson, Rose (*Wakachasha*), *56*
New York Hippodrome, 173
Nez Perce, 157
Noble, John (Sec. of Interior)
  bans permits, 93
  favors Show Indian employment,
    76–77
  on Sioux prisoners, 124
Noble Savage
  See Indian images
No Neck, *99*
  on Show Indian deaths, 97
  appears in *Indian Wars*, 232
North, Major Frank
  commands Pawnee Scouts, 23
North Platte, Neb.
  "Old Glory Blowout," 22
Notes on the State of Virginia, 13

Oakley, Annie
  befriends Sitting Bull, 27
  illness in Spain, 87
  on Prussian general staff, 119
  as Show Indian, *120*
O'Beirne, James R.
  on poor treatment of Indians, 95,
    100–101
Oberly, John (CIA)
  opposition to Wild West shows, 69

Ochiltree, Tom, 39
Ogilasa
    See Red Shirt
Oglalas
    join Red Man's Syndicate, 197
    memories of Wounded Knee, 230
    recreate Wounded Knee, 235
Ojibwas
    See Anishinaabeg
"Oklahoma!" 277
Oklahoma Historical Exhibition
    Company, 70
Oklahoma Historical Society, 277
Old Glory Blowout, 176
Oliver, Dr. N. T. ("Nevada Ned"), 19
One Star, 122
Oxford History of the American West,
    277

Pacific Southwest Exposition, *268*
Paints Yellow, Joe, 174, 248
Palatine Guards, 88
Pan-American Exposition, 145
    "Rainbow City," 146
Paris, Comtesse de, 50
Parman, Donald
    cultural disparity theory, 196
"Pat Hennessy Massacre," 183
Pawnee Bill's Historic Wild West, 190
    revival of, 276
Pawnee Bill State Park, 276
Pawnees, 40, 71
    as first Show Indians, 23
Peabody Museum, 130
Pené, Xavier
    manages Darkest Africa village, 146
Penny, Capt. Charles G., 116
    replaces Royer at Pine Ridge, 115
Persian Monarch, 59
Peter Pan, 275
Pifer, Ida Little
    on Old Indian exhibit, 162
Pimas
    basket makers at Louisiana
        Purchase Exposition, 159
Pine Bird, 174

Pine Ridge reservation, 134
    as Show Indian center, 25
Poinsette, Joel R., 14
Poncas
    relations with Miller brothers,
        177–78
Poor Boy, Philip
    complains of poor treatment, 256
Popular images
    anxieties about actors, 32
Porter, Edwin S., 225
Powwow, 272, 275
Plenty Blanket, 122
Plenty Coups, 210
Pratt, Richard Henry, 126
    criticizes Wild West shows, 182
    retirement, 164
Price, Hiram (CIA)
    on assimilation, 61–62
Prucha, Francis Paul, 73
Prussian high command, 119
Puccini, Giacomo
    visits Wild West, 91
Pulliam, James, 265
Pulls Him Out, 122
Putnam, Frederick Ward
    on anthropology at Columbian
        Exposition, 130
    manages Indian village, 133

Quanah Parker, 157

Red Bear, Ralph, 265
Red Cloud, Jack, 135
Red Fish, Frank, 180
Red Shirt (*Ogilasa*), *44, 214*
    on crossing Atlantic, 43
    experiences visions, 48–49
    joins Red Man's Syndicate, 200
    in London, *47,* 57
    in Paris, 82
    as spokesman, 44, 49, 51, 64
Reformers
    See Christian humanitarian
        reformers
Reid, Whitelaw, 198

Revenge, 122
Reynolds, Samuel G.
    organizes Crow fair, 207–8
Rhoads, Charles (CIA), 269
Roberts, Randy, 224
Robinson, Arthur, 264
Robinson, Rev. J.
    missionary at Pine Ridge, 65–66
Rockboy, Joe, 279
Rocky Bear
    at Columbian Exposition, 135, 140
    defends Show Indians, 101–2
    in Europe, 83–84, 90–91
    on papal visit, 88–89
    speaks with Zulus, 119
rodeo
    origins, 22
Roosevelt, Theodore
    opens Louisiana Purchase
        Exposition, 150–51
    depicted in Wild West shows, 148
Rosebud reservation, 135, 160
Rosewater, Edward
    proposes Omaha World's Fair, 144
"Rough rider"
    definition, 305 n 36
Royer, Daniel F.
    investigates Show Indians, 103, 108
Runke, Walter, 215
Running Bear, Alfred, 200
Rydell, Robert
    on aesthetics and anthropology, 145
    American imperialism, 166–67
    anthropology at Columbian
        Exposition, 136
    racial landscape, 151

Sac and Foxes, 179
St. Louis Fair
    See Louisiana Purchase Exposition
St. Paul, 186
St. Paul's Cathedral (London), 127
Salsbury, Nate
    creates Congress of Rough Riders,
        118–19
    declining health and death, 169, 171

organizes trip to England, 40
origins of Wild West show, 22
relations with Kicking Bear, 121
relations with Mary Collins, 117–18
on Show Indians' finances, 115–16
visit to Vatican, 88
visit to Washington, D.C., 103
San Juan School, 209
Sarrasani Circus, 186, 264
Schauss, Lewis, 178
Schofield, General John M., 121
Scobey, C. R. A., 75
Scott, Maj. Gen. Hugh Lenox
    on preparedness pageant, 248
Sears, S. S., 75
Seaver, Vernon C., 175
Seger, John H.
    on Indian expositions, 154
Seger School, 154
Seldomridge, H. H., 213
Sells, Cato (CIA)
    approves *Indian Wars*, 229–30
    on assimilation, 205, 212
    bans dancing, 218
    plans for Panama-Pacific
        Exposition, 206
    supports historical reenactments,
        221
Sells Brothers Circus, 40
Sells-Floto Circus, 192, 264
Seventh Cavalry
    at Wounded Knee, 234
Shangreau, Bat, 256
Shangreau, John, 140
Shangreau, Peter, 267
Sheridan, General Philip, 26
Shoemaker, J. A., 261
Shongopavi, 160
Shooting Star, 122
Short Bull, 121, *122*
    appears in *Indian Wars*, 232,
        234–35
    at Columbian Exposition, 135
    ghost dance leader, xi, 237
    released from prison, 124
    return from Europe, 122

Short Horn, 97
Short Man, 122
Shot Eyes, Frank, 180
Show Indians, *262–63*
  bans on employment, 77–78
  at Columbian Exposition, 135, *136*
  contracts, 31
  costumes, 173
  death and disease, 92–93, 127
  declining opportunities, 256, 264,
    272
  definitions, xiii, 128, 138–39
  at fairs and pageants, 196, 210–11,
    218–19, 257
  government versions, 139–40,
    161–65, 221
  methods of payment, 199
  mistreatment of, 77, 175–76
  in motion pictures, 227, 250–51
  performances, *35*, 38
  perils of travel, 94, 184–85, 186–88,
    320 n 55
Shubert Anderson Company, 173
Sioux
  artisans at Louisiana Purchase
    Exposition, 159
  with Carver's Wild America, 125
  civic virtues among, 84
  with Kickapoo Medicine Company,
    71
  See also Lakota Sioux, and
    individual tribes
"Sioux Outbreak," 108
Sitting Bull
  altruism, 31
  blamed for Ghost Dance, 111, 117
  death of, 107, 157
  reception in Canada, 28
  as Show Indian, 23–24, 27, *29*, 304
    n 15
"Sitting Bull's Cabin"
  at Columbian Exposition, 139
Skiff, Frederick J. V., 156
Slocum, William F., 151
Slotkin, Richard, 12
  frontier myth, 11

  on "mythic" spaces, 278
Smith, "Colorado Cotton," 255
Smith, M. C., 203–4
Society of American Indians, 6
  supports "Indian Day," 257
Spoor, George
  origins of Essanay Film Company,
    226
Spotted Bear, 135
Spotted Tail
  gives nickname to Carver, 22
Spotted Weasel, 200, 257
Standing Bear, Luther, 122, *172*, 182
  as interpreter, 170, 284 n 21
Standing Bear v. Crook, 63, 76, 176,
  294 n 7
Standing Rock reservation, 111, 135
Stanley, Henry M., 119
Star, 128
State of Nebraska, 42
Stedman, Raymond, 6
Stephan, Father Joseph A., 25
Stosch-Sarrasani, Hans
  partnership with Miller brothers,
    184
Swift Hawk, 94
Swiss Guards, 88

Tabor Grand Opera House, 246
Taft, William Howard, 243
Tammen, Harry H.
  wrecks "Two Bills" show, 191–92,
    228
Tatanka Iyotake
  See Sitting Bull
Taylor, Buck
  "King of Cowboys," 35
Tennessee Centennial Exposition, 143
Terrell, Zach
  manages Sells-Floto Circus, 256
Terry, General Alfred, 26
Texicole-Charley's Wild West, 255
Thaw, Harry K., 180
Tiften, John P.
  takes show to Australia, 203
Tobin, W. Maurice, 156

Tonner, Dr. Joseph A., 98
Trade fairs, 141, 142
Trans-Mississippi and International
    Exposition (Omaha), 144
Tri-State fair, 267
Turner, Frederick Jackson, 11
Tuska, Jon, 7, 227
Twelfth Cavalry
    on filming *Indian Wars*, 229
"Two Bills" Show, 190
Two Elks, 127

Uses the Sword, 98
Utes, 206

Valentine, Robert (CIA), 203
    support for Indian fairs, 210
Vanity Fair, 143
Vestal, Stanley, 27
Victoria, Queen
    fascination with cossacks, 127
    Golden jubilee, 40
    thoughts about Indians, 54–55
    visits Earl's Court, 52
Vilas, William F.
    procedures for contracting Indians,
        70

Walsh, Richard J., 235
War on the Plains, 228
Washos
    with Carver's Wild America, 125
Watson, James E., 255
Wells, Philip
    survives Wounded Knee, 242
Welsh, Herbert, 118
    condemns Wild West shows, 131
    investigates conditions, 100–101
    protests release of prisoners, 115
Western Navajo School, 215
Western Slope Fair, 206
Wet Moccasin (*Hampa Naspa*), 66–68
Wharton, Theodore
    directs *Indian Wars*, 229
White, Richard
    on Cody's genius, 287 n 38
White, Stanford, 180

White Calf, Dick, 185
White Eyes, 67
White Eyes, Jacob, 242
White Horse, 97
White House, 122
Whitney, Fred C.
    teams with Carver, 124
Whitley, John Robinson, 40
Wichasha yatapika, 84
Wild West shows
    congressional opposition to, 38–39
    enduring images, 1
    with ethnological exhibitions, 144
    heyday of, 168
    list of, 317 n 4
    reformers' opposition to, 63, 118
Wilson, Woodrow, 243
Windsor Castle, 127
    command performance at, 53
Woman's Dress, 232
Women's National Indian Association,
    62
Wood, D. J. M., 75
World War I, 186
Wounded, Charles, 265
Wounded Knee, 107, 270
Wounds One Another, 97
Wounds With Arrows, 122
Wovoka, 107, *247*
    depicted in *Indian Wars*, *238*, *239*
Wynne, Robert J., 198

Yankton Sioux, 182
Yellow Bird, 236
Yellow Blanket (aka Eagle Horse)
    death in Poland, 67
Yellow Hair, 160
Yellow Robe, Chauncey, *240*
    criticizes Wild West shows, 6, 196
    protests *Indian Wars*, 239–41
    translates for BIA, 101
Yellow Wolf, Charley, 200
Yost, Nellie Snyder, 244
Young Buffalo Wild West, 173
Young Man Afraid of His Horses
    at Columbian Exposition, 135

Zulus, 119
Zunis
    at Louisiana Purchase Exposition,
        156
    at Panama-California Exposition,
        217